Prinzip Held*

Gefördert durch die Deutsche Forschungsgemeinschaft (DFG)
Projektnummer 181750155 – SFB 948

PRINZIP HELD*

Von Heroisierungen und Heroismen
Of Heroizations and Heroisms

Herausgegeben von | Edited by
Ralf von den Hoff und Gorch Pieken

im Auftrag des Zentrums für Militärgeschichte
und Sozialwissenschaften der Bundeswehr und
des Sonderforschungsbereichs 948 der Universität Freiburg

Wallstein Verlag

INHALT

Vorwort __ 8

Ralf von den Hoff
PRINZIP HELD*. Bausteine von Heroisierungen oder:
Was geschieht, wenn es um das Heroische geht? __ 12

Anne Hemkendreis
HELD:INNEN UND IHR PUBLIKUM. Zur Wahrnehmung
und Bildwerdung wirkmächtiger Figuren __ 26

Vera Marstaller
MEDIALISIERUNG __ 46

Johanna Pink
POLARISIERUNG __ 64

Stefan Tilg
KAMPF __ 80

Tobias Schlechtriemen
GRENZÜBERSCHREITUNG __ 96

Dorna Safaian
HANDLUNGSMACHT __ 114

Olmo Gölz
EINSATZ __ 128

CONTENTS

Preface __ 9

Ralf von den Hoff
PRINZIP HELD*. Components of Heroizations or:
What Happens When the Heroic is Concerned? __ 13

Anne Hemkendreis
HEROES AND THEIR AUDIENCE. On Perception
and Iconisation of Powerful Figures __ 27

Vera Marstaller
MEDIALISATION __ 47

Johanna Pink
POLARISATION __ 65

Stefan Tilg
FIGHTING __ 81

Tobias Schlechtriemen
CROSSING BOUNDARIES __ 97

Dorna Safaian
AGENCY __ 115

Olmo Gölz
COMMITMENT __ 129

Georg Eckert
VORBILD __ 144

Joachim Grage
MASKULINITÄT __ 168

Frank Reichherzer
MIT DEM FUßBALL DURCHS NIEMANDSLAND.
Suchfelder des Heroischen in der
Sinnlosigkeit des Massenkrieges.
Ereignis: »The best kicked goal in history« __ 188

PRINZIP HELD*. Eine Ausstellung __ 208

Literatur __ 240

Abbildungsnachweise __ 247

Impressum __ 258

Georg Eckert
ROLE MODELS __ 145

Joachim Grage
MASCULINITY __ 169

Frank Reichherzer
WITH A FOOTBALL THROUGH NO MAN'S LAND.
Searching for the Heroic in the Senselessness of Mass Warfare.
Event: "The Best-Kicked Goal in History" __ 189

PRINZIP HELD*. An Exhibition __ 208

Works Cited __ 240

Image Credits __ 247

Imprint __ 258

VORWORT

Der Sonderforschungsbereich (SFB) 948 »Helden – Heroisierungen – Heroismen. Transformationen und Konjunkturen von der Antike bis zu Moderne« beendet 2024 seine langjährige Forschung. Das an der Albert-Ludwigs-Universität Freiburg angesiedelte Projekt wurde seit 2012 von der Deutschen Forschungsgemeinschaft (DFG) gefördert. Als 2019 die letzte Arbeitsphase in die Planung ging, hat das Zentrum für Militärgeschichte und Sozialwissenschaften der Bundeswehr (ZMSBw) in Potsdam – damals mit Michael Epkenhans als Leitendem Wissenschaftler – sehr gerne den Vorschlag aufgenommen, eine Ausstellung als abschließendes Kooperationsprojekt zu realisieren, um wichtige Forschungsergebnisse einem größeren Publikum zugänglich zu machen. Das Ergebnis ist die Ausstellung *Prinzip Held**, die vom 21. Juni bis zum 3. November 2024 im Militärhistorischen Museum der Bundeswehr (MHMBw) Flugplatz Berlin-Gatow gezeigt wird. Das vorliegende Begleitbuch greift die Inhalte der Ausstellung auf und fasst wichtige Ergebnisse der Forschungen zum Heroischen, zu Heroisierungen und Heroismen zusammen.

Die Zusammenarbeit zwischen SFB, ZMSBw und MHMBw war auf vielen Ebenen fruchtbar. Vor allem der wechselseitige, unterschiedliche Blick der Beteiligten auf das Thema hat die Ausstellung geprägt und neue Erkenntnisse hervorgebracht: die Perspektiven eines interdisziplinären Forschungsverbundes an einer Universität, diejenigen eines militärhistorischen und sozialwissenschaftlichen Ressortforschungsinstituts und diejenigen kuratorischer, pädagogischer und gestalterischer Expertinnen und Experten. Das Ziel, das Heroische als ein bleibend wichtiges kulturelles und soziales Phänomen wissenschaftlich fundiert besser verständlich zu machen, konnten wir in einem solchen Verbund auf neue Weise erreichen.

Das innovative Konzept der Ausstellung, Bausteine und Wirkungen, die im Spiel sind, wenn es um Heldinnen und Helden geht, zu erklären und zugleich erfahrbar zu machen, haben wir im Laufe der Kooperation entwickelt. Daran waren viele beteiligt. Mit Gorch Pieken stellte das ZMSBw einen erfahrenen, kreativen leitenden Kurator, dem Katja Widmann (SFB) und Andreas Geißler (MHMBw Flugplatz Berlin-Gatow) im Teilprojekt T des SFB zur Seite standen. Ihre Arbeit legte die Grundlage für das gemeinsame Projekt. In Potsdam hat allen voran Heiner Bröckermann als Leiter des Bereiches Grundlagen Historische Bildung am ZMSBw das Vorhaben gefördert; für das MHMBw Dresden nennen wir stellvertretend seinen Direktor, Rudolf J. Schlaffer. Ohne die Unterstützung und Offenheit am MHMBw Flugplatz Berlin-Gatow durch Ralf-Gunter Leonhardt und Doris Müller-Toovey mit ihren Teams wäre die Ausstellung nicht möglich gewesen. Dass wir das renommierte Theater-Label *Rimi-*

PREFACE

In 2024, the Sonderforschungsbereich (SFB, or Collaborative Research Centre) 948 "Heroes – Heroizations – Heroisms. Transformations and Conjunctures from Antiquity to the Modern Age" concludes its long-term research activities. This project, which is under the auspices of the Albert Ludwig University of Freiburg, has been funded by the German Research Foundation (Deutsche Forschungsgemeinschaft, DFG) since 2012. As planning began in 2019 for the last working phase, the Bundeswehr Centre of Military History and Social Sciences (Zentrum für Militärgeschichte und Sozialwissenschaften der Bundeswehr, ZMSBw) in Potsdam – with Michael Epkenhans as leading researcher at the time – welcomed the proposal to develop an exhibition as a final cooperation project so that important research findings could be made available to a larger public. This resulted in the exhibition *Prinzip Held** ("The Hero Principle"), which will be held at the Gatow Airfield branch of the Bundeswehr Museum of Military History (Militärhistorisches Museum der Bundeswehr, MHMBw) from the 21st of June until the 3rd of November 2024. This collection of essays picks up on the subject matter of the exhibition and outlines important results of our research on heroizations and herosims.

Cooperation between SFB, ZMSBw and MHMBw has been fruitful on many levels. The collaborative and contrasting views of the participants as regards the subject matter, in particular, have had a significant influence on the shape of the exhibition and provided fresh insight: the perspectives of an interdisciplinary university research team, those of a research institute that focuses on military history and social science, and those of curatorial, pedagogical, and creative experts. This cooperation allowed us to find new ways of achieving our goal of using science to make the heroic more accessible as a cultural and social phenomenon of lasting importance.

In the course of our collaboration, we developed an innovative exhibition concept to explain and also make tangible the components and effects that influence heroines and heroes. Many people were involved in the project. With Gorch Pieken, ZMSBw provided an experienced, creative lead curator, assisted by Katja Widman (SFB) and Andreas Geißler (MHMBw Berlin-Gatow Airfield) in the SFB's subproject T. Their work laid the foundation for this joint project. In Potsdam, Heiner Bröckermann, head of the Basic History Education Division at ZMSBw, led the way in promoting this endeavour. In the case of MHMBw Dresden, we would like to thank director Rudolf J. Schlaffer and colleagues. The exhibition would not have been possible without the support and open-mindedness of Ralf-Gunter Leonhardt, Doris Müller-Toovey and their teams at the MHMBw Gatow Airfield branch. *Rimini Protokoll*, the renowned Ger-

ni Protokoll für die Gestaltung gewinnen konnten, hat die Ausstellung geprägt. Und es brachte neue, experimentelle Impulse für die Erforschung des Heroischen, die ohne das gemeinsame Vorhaben nicht möglich gewesen wären. Vor allem Helgard Haug und Daniel Wetzel sowie Dominik Steinmann sind hier zu nennen. Mit dem Wallstein Verlag stand uns erneut, wie über viele Jahre im SFB 948, ein bewährter Partner für die Publikation dieses Begleitbandes zur Seite.

Schließlich war es eine großartige Erfahrung, dass und wie die Mitglieder des SFB 948 Ausstellung und Begleitband erst ermöglicht haben. Nennen möchten wir hier Sebastian Meurer, Ulrike Zimmermann und Philipp Multhaupt mit ihren Teams in der zentralen Administration und der Redaktion im SFB, die vom Bundessprachenamt unterstützt wurde. Getragen wurden die Inhalte der Ausstellung von den mehr als vierzig Forschenden des SFB, die an der Vorbereitung beteiligt waren – von Promovierenden bis zu pensionierten Professoren. Sie haben zum Vorhaben ideell, durch ihre Diskussionen und durch ein Mehr an eigener und kooperativer Tätigkeit entscheidend beigetragen: zur Konzeption des Ganzen, zu den Fallstudien, die in der Ausstellung gezeigt werden, und zu den Essays, die, erweitert durch einen Beitrag von Frank Reichherzer vom ZMSBw, diesen Begleitband bilden.

Als Sprecher des SFB 948 und als Kommandeur des ZMSBw danken wir allen Beteiligten sehr – auch den hier nicht namentlich genannten. Wir wünschen der Ausstellung und dem Begleitband ein Publikum, das nicht einfach Helden und Heldinnen sucht, sondern offen ist für Neues zu heroischen Figuren und nach Besuch und Lektüre reicher an Kenntnis, aber auch an neuen eigenen Fragen zum Heroischen und an Perspektiven auf das, was das Heroische ausmacht.

Freiburg im Breisgau und Potsdam im Januar 2024

Prof. Dr. Ralf von den Hoff *Oberst Dr. Sven Lange*
Sprecher des SFB 948 *Kommandeur des ZMSBw*

man theatre label and artists' collective, played an essential role in designing the exhibition and provided new, experimental ideas for researching the heroic, which would not have arisen without our joint endeavour. Helgard Haug, Daniel Wetzel and Dominik Steinmann deserve a special mention. As it has done for many years, the publishing house Wallstein Verlag once again lent its reliable support to the SFB 948 as a tried-and-trusted partner to publish this exhibition guide.

Finally, it was wonderful to experience how the SFB 948 members made creating and designing the exhibition and this publication possible in the first place. We would also like to mention Sebastian Meurer, Ulrike Zimmermann and Philipp Multhaupt along with their teams in central coordination and editing in the SFB, who were supported by the German Federal Office of Languages. More than forty researchers of the SFB provided the contents of the exhibition – from doctoral candidates to retired professors. Their contributions were decisive for this project, in terms of ideas, debating concepts, going above and beyond in their individual and collaborative efforts: for the conceptual whole, the exhibition's case studies and the essays contained in this book, which also features a contribution by Frank Reichherzer (ZMSBw).

As the spokesperson of SFB 948 and as the commander of ZMSBw, we would like to thank all participants – including those not mentioned by name. We hope that the exhibition and this accompanying book reach an audience that is not only looking for heroes and heroines, but is also open to new insights into heroic figures and that gains fresh perspectives from the exhibition and this publication, at the same time asking its own, new questions regarding the heroic and what makes a hero or a heroine.

Freiburg im Breisgau and Potsdam in January 2024

Prof Dr Ralf von den Hoff
SFB 948, Spokesperson

Colonel Dr Sven Lange
ZMSBw, Commander

© 2024 Ralf von den Hoff / Sven Lange, Publikation: Wallstein Verlag; DOI https://doi.org/10.46500/83535581-001 | CC BY-NC-ND 4.0

Ralf von den Hoff

PRINZIP HELD*
Bausteine von Heroisierungen oder: Was geschieht, wenn es um das Heroische geht?

Wer ist die größte Heldin oder der größte Held der Menschheit? Die Umfrage »Greatest Heroes of Mankind« beim Medienportal *Ranker* führt 2023 Jeanne d'Arc an, gefolgt von Alexander dem Großen und George Washington.[1] Zwanzig Jahre vorher ermittelte *Focus* als größte Helden der Deutschen die Feuerwehrleute des 11. September 2001 – das damals aktuelle Ereignis hatte neue Helden hervorgebracht. Es folgten Mutter Teresa, Oskar Schindler, Hans und Sophie Scholl, Claus Schenk Graf von Stauffenberg und der Reformator Martin Luther – vor Jesus Christus.[2] 2015 lag Mahatma Gandhi vorne, gefolgt von den Eltern der Befragten und Jesus Christus, so ermittelte *YouGov*. Nur zwölf Prozent der Deutschen, viel weniger als in den USA und Großbritannien, gaben an, überhaupt eine:n Held:in »zu haben«.[3]

Einigkeit bei den ›größten Held:innen‹ gibt es augenscheinlich nicht. Vor allem liegt das daran, dass eine einheitliche Definition dessen fehlt, was eine heroische Figur tut oder auszeichnet: Geht es um Taten oder um ›Größe‹, um Erfolg oder gute Absicht, um den Dienst an der Allgemeinheit oder das Bestehen eines Abenteuers? Und verstehen überhaupt alle dasselbe unter denselben Begriffen? Bei der *Focus*-Umfrage nannten 61 Prozent Mut und 51 Prozent Selbstlosigkeit als wichtigste heroische Eigenschaft. Das *Digitale Wörterbuch der deutschen Sprache* definiert Held als jemanden, »der Hervorragendes leistet«, und zwar in erster Linie »aufgrund seines Mutes, besonders im Kampf«.[4] Auf heroisierte Eltern trifft dies nur in einer sehr übertragenen Bedeutung zu. Im Sinne dieser Definition aber sahen Sympathisierende des islamistischen Netzwerks al-Qaida die Attentäter des 11. September 2001 als Helden an; für andere, die die New Yorker Feuerwehrleute heroisierten, waren die Attentäter terroristische Schurken. Was von den einen als heroisch betrachtet wird, muss nicht für alle als heroisch gelten.

Um zum Verständnis dieser widersprüchlichen Situation zu kommen, stellt sich jedoch die ganz andere Frage, was eigentlich geschieht, was im Spiel ist, wenn ein Mensch als heroisch bezeichnet wird. Was zeichnet die Jahrtausende alte Praxis aus, Menschen zu Heroen oder Held:innen zu machen und von ›Heldentaten‹ zu erzählen, und wie leben wir in dieser Tradition? Gibt es trotz aller Deutungsunterschiede und Bewertungsvielfalt Gemeinsamkeiten, die sich über Zeiten und Kulturen hinweg bei Heroisierungen und in Heroismen erkennen lassen?

Diesen Fragen ist, gefördert von der Deutschen Forschungsgemeinschaft, von 2012 bis 2024 der Sonderforschungsbereich 948 an der Universität Freiburg im Breisgau

Ralf von den Hoff

PRINZIP HELD*
Components of Heroizations or: What Happens When the Heroic is Concerned?

Who is the greatest hero of mankind? In the "Greatest Heroes of Mankind" survey featured in the media portal *Ranker* in 2023, Joan of Arc ranks top, followed by Alexander the Great and George Washington.[1] Twenty years earlier, *Focus* magazine revealed the 9/11 firefighters as the Germans' greatest heroes – recent events had produced new heroes. They were followed by Mother Teresa, Oskar Schindler, Hans and Sophie Scholl, Claus Schenk Graf von Stauffenberg and reformer Martin Luther – all ahead of Jesus Christ.[2] In 2015, Mahatma Gandhi was in the lead, followed by the respondents' own parents and Jesus Christ, according to *YouGov*. Only twelve percent of Germans, far fewer than in the USA and Great Britain, claimed they had "no hero" at all.[3]

There seems to be no consensus on the 'greatest heroes'. This is mainly due to the lack of a unified definition of what a heroic figure does or represents: Is it about deeds or 'greatness', about success or good intentions, about serving the common good or about going on an adventure? And do the same terms mean the same to everyone? In the *Focus* survey, 61 percent cited courage, and 51 percent cited selflessness as the most important heroic qualities. The *Digital Dictionary of the German Language* defines a hero as someone "who achieves something outstanding", primarily "because of his courage, especially in battle".[4] When it comes to heroized parents, this only applies in a very metaphorical sense. According to this definition, however, the 9/11 terrorists were heroes for sympathisers of the Islamist al Qaeda network, while others who heroized the New York firefighters viewed the attackers as terrorist villains. What is considered heroic by some may not be seen as heroic by all.

However, in order to understand this contradictory situation, a different question arises as to what actually happens, what factors are at play when a person is referred to as heroic. What characterises the millennia-old practice of creating heroes and talking about 'heroic deeds', and how do we live in this tradition? Despite the differences in interpretation and evaluation, are there commonalities that can be recognised across times and cultures in these acts of heroization and heroisms?

From 2012 to 2024, the Collaborative Research Centre SFB 948 at the University of Freiburg in Breisgau, funded by the German Research Foundation, pursued these very questions:[5] from ancient times to the present day; in politics, media, historiography, literature, film, art, and music; from fictitious to historical figures. Due to the researchers and disciplines involved, the research focused on examples

nachgegangen:[5] von der Antike bis heute, in Politik, Presse, Geschichtsschreibung, Literatur, Film, Kunst und Musik, zu fiktiven Figuren wie zu historischen. Die Forschungen waren an Beispielen orientiert, die sich aufgrund der Forschenden und Disziplinen, die beteiligt waren, auf Europa, Nordamerika, den Mittleren Osten und China bezogen. Es bleibt also noch viel mehr vergleichend zu erforschen, vor allem zu nicht-westlichen Weltregionen und Kulturen. Die Ergebnisse haben gleichwohl unseren Blick auf Held:innen schon jetzt entscheidend verändert.

Das liegt auch daran, dass bereits der Ausgangspunkt der Forschungen ein Perspektivwechsel war: Zur Heldin oder zum Helden kann man nicht alleine werden. Man kann behaupten, ›heroisch‹ zu sein, oder etwas ›Heldenhaftes‹ tun. Aber andere müssen es auch so sehen und publik machen. Held:innen brauchen ein Publikum, dann bringen Bewunderung und Verehrung eine heroische Figur hervor und halten sie am Leben. Heldentum ist also Zuschreibung. Wir nennen das Heroisierung.[6] Wer aus welchen Gründen heroisiert wird, wie man sich in Heroismen heroische Verhaltensmuster aneignet, sagt ebenso viel über das Publikum aus wie über die heroisierte Figur: Sage mir, welche Held:innen du hast, und ich sage dir, wer du bist!

    Wenn Heroisierung aber nur geschehen kann, indem eine heroische Figur präsentiert und und indem an das erinnert wird, was man ihr als heroisch zuschreibt, dann ist Heroisierung Kommunikation. Ohne Kommunikation keine Held:innen. Damit lässt sich die Frage »Was ist im Spiel, wenn es um Held:innen geht?« ergänzen und präzisieren: Was geschieht beim kommunikativen Akt einer Heroisierung, welche Bestandteile sind dafür typisch? Wenn man dies besser versteht, kann auch klarer werden, wozu Menschen eigentlich so beständig Held:innen brauchen – oder was es bedeuten würde, auf sie zu verzichten.

In Ergänzung zur der Ausstellung »Prinzip Held*«, die in einem weiteren Teil dieses Buches vorgestellt wird, sollen die folgenden Essays Annäherungen an Antworten auf diese Frage bieten. Sie behandeln parallel zur Ausstellung typische Bausteine des Heroischen.[7] Mit diesen Bausteinen sind Bestandteile gemeint, die im Spiel sind, wenn ein Mensch heroisiert wird. Sie sind aber in unterschiedlichen Heroisierungen unterschiedlich wichtig und stark: Mal überwiegt die Bedeutung des einen Bausteins, mal die eines anderen. Durch dieses unterschiedliche Gewicht können sie zugleich als Such- oder Fragefelder dienen, um Vielfalt und Ähnlichkeiten von Heroisierungen besser zu verstehen. Jede Heroisierung lässt sich befragen nach Inhalten und Gewicht jedes Bausteins. In einem solchen System kann besser als in statischen Definitionen erkennbar werden, welche Konstanten und Unterschiede Heroisierungen haben, aber auch, was in welchen Bereichen unseres Denkens und Handelns geschieht, was erreicht, was verloren, was behauptet wird, wenn man heroisiert – und wie vergleichbar, aber auch kontrovers dies ist.

related to Europe, North America, the Middle East and China. There is still much more comparative research to be done, especially regarding non-Western regions and cultures. Nevertheless, the results have already significantly changed our perspective on heroes.

This is, in part, due to the fact that the starting point of the research was already a change of perspective: Becoming a hero or heroine does not occur in a vacuum. One can claim to be heroic or to have done something 'heroic'. But others must share this view and make it public. Heroes need an audience: admiration and reverence are what produce a heroic figure and keep it alive. Heroism is attribution. We call this heroization.[6] Who is heroized and for what reasons, and how heroism is practiced, says just as much about the audience as it does about the heroized figure: Tell me who your heroes are, and I will tell you who you are!

However, if heroization can only occur by presenting a heroic figure and reminding us of how what is attributed to them is heroic, then heroization is communication. Without communication, there are no heroes. Thus, we can extend the question "What elements are at play when it comes to heroes?" with the more specific question: "What happens in the communication act of heroization, and what typical components are involved?" If we could understand that better, it could help clarify why people constantly need heroes – or what it would mean to live without them.

Serving as supplements to the exhibition *Prinzip Held**, which is presented in another part of this book, the following essays aim to provide various approaches to this question. They deal with typical components of the heroic, as does the exhibition.[7] These components play a role when a person is heroized. However, they are of varying importance and weight in different contexts of heroization: Sometimes, one component is more significant, at other times, another takes precedence. Due to this variation in significance, they can also serve as fields of inquiry or questioning to help us better understand the diversity and similarities of different heroizations. Every heroization can be investigated with regards to the content and weight of each component. In such a system, it becomes more apparent than in static definitions what constants and differences exist in heroizations, and what happens in different areas of our thinking and actions, what is achieved, what is lost, what is claimed when we heroize – and how comparable but also controversial heroization processes are. These aspects are explained in more detail in the essays. How do their findings fit together?

Let us start with *the audience*: A heroic figure is created and sustained when individuals emerge from an audience who admire or worship them,[8] who are excited, overwhelmed or even submissive. They may be looking for closeness or rather main-

In den Beiträgen werden diese Aspekte genauer erläutert. Wie hängen ihre Ergebnisse zusammen?

Wir beginnen mit dem *Publikum*: Eine heroische Figur entsteht und wird am Leben gehalten, wenn aus einem Publikum diejenigen hervorgehen, die sie bewundern oder verehren,[8] die begeistert, überwältigt oder sogar unterwürfig sind. Sie suchen Nähe oder wahren ehrfurchtsvolle Distanz. Sie vollziehen bestimmte Rituale, seien es Jubel oder Gebet, ein Opfer, eine Buchlektüre oder der Aufruf eines Videos; ja, sie können sich heroisches Verhalten zum Vorbild nehmen. Heroisierung bewegt, und die Bewunderer bewegen wiederum andere, das heißt, sie ist emotional und affektiv.[9] Es sind außerdem, sieht man von privaten Held:innen ab, immer Gruppen und Gemeinschaften, die heroisieren. Heroisierungen formieren aus einem Publikum eine affektive, also stark emotional verbundene Gemeinschaft, seien es eine Nation, eine Religion, ein Verein oder eine Berufsgruppe bis zu Fans. Sie halten die Gemeinschaft zusammen und schließen gleichzeitig diejenigen aus, die ihr nicht angehören oder angehören sollen. Insofern sind Heroisierungen und Heroismen in Situationen besonders wichtig, in denen Gemeinschaftsbildung gebraucht wird. Trotz ›großer Taten‹ kann das Publikum aber auch unbeteiligt bleiben, und dann bleibt eine Heroisierung aus oder folgt erst viel später.

Da Heroisierung also Kommunikation mit einem Publikum ist, ist sie immer auch *Medialisierung*.[10] Dies ist unser zweiter Baustein. Unter Medialisierung verstehen wir jede Art des Weitertragens einer Geschichte oder Erinnerung. Sie erreicht unterschiedliches Publikum an unterschiedlichen Orten auf unterschiedliche Weise und spricht unterschiedliche Sinne an: im Theater anders als bei der Lektüre einer Zeitung, am Smartphone anders als auf dem ›Heldenplatz‹, im religiösen Ritual oder beim spontanen, begeisterten Erzählen über eine heroische Tat. Über Jahrhunderte war das Epos eines der wirksamsten Mittel der Heroisierung – von Homers Achilleus in der *Ilias* bis zu Anne Webers eher ironischem *Annette, ein Heldinnenepos*, das 2020 den Deutschen Buchpreis erhielt. Statuen von Held:innen, die nicht mehr als heroisch angesehen werden, können auf hoch emotionale Weise gestürzt werden: geradezu rituelle Deheroisierungen. Helden, von denen niemand mehr erzählt, geraten in Vergessenheit. Natürlich haben Medialisierungen mit den Medien zu tun, in denen Helden dargestellt werden. Man kann vor diesem Hintergrund danach fragen, wie Medien eine Heroisierung möglicherweise auch gelöst vom heroenhaften Inhalt prägen. Es scheint, als habe schon das Wort ›Held‹ eine attraktive Wirkung im medialen Einsatz: Warum wirbt man sonst heute für ›Helden‹, wenn man Profis braucht, wie in einer Armee,[11] oder für einen Apfel als ›Bio-Held‹? So lässt sich vor diesem Hintergrund auch analysieren, auf welche Weise zum Beispiel die Werbung, Social Media oder Politikberatung Heroisierungs-Bausteine für Erzählungen nutzen und verbreiten, um ihr Zielpublikum zu begeistern,

tain a reverential distance. They perform certain rituals, whether it is exultation, prayer, sacrifice, reading a book or watching a video, or they model their own behaviour after a heroic role model. Heroization evokes emotions in the admirer, and the admirers, in turn, evoke emotions in others – it is an emotional and affective process.[9] Aside from private heroes, it is always groups and communities that engage in heroization. Heroizations shape an affective, strongly emotionally connected community within an audience, be it a nation, a religion, a club, a profession or fans. They hold the community together, simultaneously excluding those who do not belong or are not welcome. Heroizations and heroisms are therefore particularly important in situations where community formation is required. However, even in the face of great 'deeds', the audience can remain uninvolved, and there may be no heroization at all or it may only follow much later.

Since heroization is communication with an audience, it is always *medialisation* as well.[10] This is our second component. By medialisation, we mean any way in which a story or memory is conveyed. It reaches different audiences in different places in different ways and appeals to different senses: a hero conveyed in the theatre is different from reading about one in a newspaper; seeing a hero on a smartphone is different from seeing one on 'Heldenplatz' (Heroes Square); learning of a heroic deed via a religious ritual is a different experience to hearing of it through spontaneous, enthusiastic storytelling. For centuries, epics were the most effective means of heroization – from Homer's Achilles in the *Iliad* to Anne Weber's somewhat ironic *Annette, ein Heldinnenepos* (Annette: An Epic Heroine) who received the German Book Award in 2020. Statues of heroes who are no longer considered heroic can be toppled in highly emotional ways: almost ritual deheroizations. Heroes that no one talks about anymore are forgotten. Medialisations are, of course, connected to the type of media in which heroes are depicted. Against this background, one inquires into how media may shape heroization independently of the heroic content. It seems that even the word 'hero' has an attractive effect when used by the media: why else would you advertise for 'heroes' today when professionals are needed, as in an army,[11] or advertise an apple as an 'organic hero'? Against this background, we can also analyse how advertising, social media or political consultancy use and disseminate the components of heroization for stories in order to inspire, persuade and perhaps even manipulate their target audience – without any need for heroic content at all. Anyone who knows how heroizations work can understand their strategies.

These questions lead us to the typical characteristics of heroization. One has already been mentioned: One person's hero is another person's villain. Heroization means *polarisation*. It creates communities and, in doing so, divides the world into supporters and adversaries. It makes a huge difference whether an attacker is celebrated as a hero or convicted as a criminal. When we are aware of heroized figures,

zu überzeugen und vielleicht gar zu manipulieren – ohne dass es dazu überhaupt noch heroenhafte Inhalte braucht. Wer weiß, wie Heroisierungen funktionieren, kann ihre Strategien durchschauen.

Diese Fragen führen zu typischen Eigenschaften von Heroisierungen. Eine wurde bereits genannt: Des einen Held ist des anderen Schurke. Heroisierung ist *Polarisierung*. Sie schafft Gemeinschaften und teilt dabei die Welt in Anhänger und Gegner auf. Es macht einen gewaltigen Unterschied, ob ein Attentäter als Held gefeiert oder als Verbrecher verurteilt wird. Sofern man von ihnen Kenntnis hat, muss man sich gegenüber heroisierten Figuren verhalten: zustimmend oder ablehnend. Ein Dazwischen gibt es nicht, außer man vergisst oder ignoriert sie. Deshalb zielen Heroisierungen nicht auf Kompromisse ab, sondern auf Konfrontation und Entscheidung. Wer heroisiert, schärft Konfliktlinien, weil provoziert wird, dass andere die Heroisierung ablehnen.

Eng mit Polarisierungen verbunden ist es, dass bei Heroisierungen immer Kampf und Grenzüberschreitung im Spiel sind. Von Heroen zu erzählen bedeutet, vom *Kampf* zu erzählen – sei es vom konkreten, physischen Kampf, vom Wettkampf oder inneren Kampf, vom Widerstand, Dagegenhalten oder Durchhalten. Die Agonalität, das Sich-Bewähren in der Auseinandersetzung, gehört in Europa seit Homer zum Heroischen, anfangs vor allem als Kampf im Krieg. Aber es gilt auch: »Was immer Helden tun […], es gerät ihnen zum Kampf« (Ulrich Bröckling).[12] Heroisierung erklärt Handeln zum Kampf. Macht man etwa Greta Thunberg zur Heldin, wird ihr Handeln zum Kampf gegen eine globale Politik, die aus dem Klimawandel keine Konsequenzen zieht. Es geht dann um mehr als bloße Krisenbewältigung.

In solchen Kämpfen leisten Held:innen, so erzählen es heroische Geschichten, mehr als durchschnittliche Menschen und mehr, als geboten und erwartbar ist. Sie verkörpern *Grenzüberschreitungen*.[13] Sie stehen jenseits von Alltag und Normen: außeralltäglich, außerordentlich, transgressiv. Indem sie Grenzen überschreiten, ziehen sie diese neu, können aber auch andere bestätigen. Antigone negiert die dominante Ordnung der Geschlechter und verweigert die Befolgung kriegerischer Normen; sie untermauert aber die Bedeutung göttlicher Gesetze und der Bruderliebe und ist bereit, dafür die existenzielle Grenze des Todes zu überschreiten. Insofern können wir Heroisierungen als ›Arbeit an Grenzen‹ (*boundary work*) verstehen.[14] Immer, wenn heroisiert wird, geht es um Grenzen. Was als heroische Tat bezeichnet wird, das zeigt, welche Grenzen und Normen gerade wichtig oder fraglich sind. Es sind krisenhafte Grenzsituationen, die besonders oft Held:innen hervorbringen: etwa in Revolutionen, wenn sich Erfahrungswelten grundsätzlich verändern, Identität neu bestimmt werden muss, wenn soziale Strukturen aufbrechen.[15] Haben Sie Ihre Heldenfiguren schon daraufhin befragt, um welche Grenzen es geht und welche Krise sie zu bewältigen helfen durch ihre Geschichten und für die, die sie verehren?

we must take a stance towards them: either approving or disapproving. There is no in between unless we forget or ignore them. This is why heroizations do not try to find compromises but rather aim for confrontation and decision-making. Those who heroize sharpen lines of conflict because they provoke others to reject the heroization.

Closely related to polarisation is the fact that heroizations always involve struggle and crossing boundaries. Talking about heroes means talking about *fighting* – be the fight a concrete, physical conflict, be it competition or inner struggle, resistance, opposition or endurance. In Europe, agonality, proving oneself in a conflict, has been part of the understanding of heroism since Homer, initially mainly as combat in war. But the following also applies: "Whatever heroes do […], it turns into a fight" (Ulrich Bröckling).[12] Heroization turns actions into battles. If, for example, we make Greta Thunberg a heroine, her actions become a battle against a global policy that does not address the consequences of climate change. It goes beyond mere crisis management.

In such struggles, heroes, according to heroic stories, achieve more than average people and more than is required or expected. They represent transgressiveness.[13] They exist beyond everyday life and norms: unusual, extraordinary, exceptional, transgressive. By *crossing boundaries*, they redefine them, but they can also reinforce others. Antigone negates the dominant gender order and refuses to comply with military norms; however, she reinforces the importance of divine laws and brotherly love and is prepared to cross the existential boundary of death for it. In this sense, we can understand heroizations as *boundary work*.[14] Whenever heroization occurs, it is about boundaries. What is considered a heroic act shows which boundaries and norms are currently important or questionable. It is crisis-ridden boundary situations that often produce heroes: in revolutions, for example, when experiences change fundamentally, when identity must be redefined, when social structures fall apart.[15] Have you ever asked yourself which boundaries your heroic figures address and which crisis they help to navigate, according to those who admire them?

When people are heroized by being linked to boundary crossing and struggle, another component comes to bear: Special *agency* is typical of heroes.[16] This includes two aspects: they are credited with a 'heroic deed' or with a strong inner attitude; and the story is told as if they were acting autonomously without help: Alexander the Great 'opened up the world', Joan of Arc 'saved' France, Louis Pasteur saved humanity by discovering the principle of vaccination – although, of course, they never acted on their own. This once again shows the great extent to which heroizations are attributions and only selectively represent reality, not always accurately. The nature of heroization can be better understood when looking at how and in what way specific agency and autonomous performance are demonstrated or attributed. In some periods, situations and cultures, for example, the – almost always male –

Wenn Menschen heroisiert werden, indem man sie mit Grenzüberschreitungen und Kampf zusammenbringt, dann kommt ein weiterer Baustein zum Tragen: Besondere *Handlungsmacht* (englisch: *agency*) ist typisch für Held:innen.[16] Das beinhaltet zweierlei: Ihnen wird eine ›Heldentat‹ – oder auch eine starke innere Haltung – zugeschrieben. Und es wird davon erzählt, als würden sie ohne Hilfe autonom handeln: Alexander der Große ›öffnete die Welt‹, Jeanne d'Arc ›rettete‹ Frankreich, Louis Pasteur die Menschheit durch die Entdeckung des Prinzips der Schutzimpfung – obgleich sie natürlich faktisch nie alleine agierten. Hier wird nochmals deutlich, wie stark Heroisierungen Zuschreibungen sind und Wirklichkeit nur selektiv abbilden, nicht immer faktentreu. Das Wesen von Heroisierung lässt sich besser verstehen, wenn man darauf schaut, auf welche Weise welche Handlungsmacht und autonome Leistung demonstriert oder zugeschrieben wird. In manchen Epochen, Situationen und Kulturen gelten beispielsweise der – fast immer männliche – Körper und seine Kraft als entscheidend,[17] in anderen eher geistige Qualitäten, technische Fertigkeiten oder eine widerständige Haltung.

Das bringt uns zum nächsten Baustein: Im Handeln von Held:innen steht immer etwas auf dem Spiel. Ihr besonderer *Einsatz* zeichnet sie aus: das Einsetzen oder die Aufgabe von *etwas* in einer Auseinandersetzung zugunsten eines höheren Ziels, wie Besitz, Ideen, Status oder Macht, oder das physische Einsetzen ihrer *selbst* in der Bereitschaft, den eigenen Körper, ja das Leben zu opfern. Heroischer Einsatz geschieht dabei zum Nutzen für andere(s), sei es für höhere Werte, sei es für andere Menschen – wenigstens erheben diejenigen, die jemanden heroisieren, solche Behauptungen. Welcher Einsatz als heldenhaft gilt, das lässt sich je nach Situation, aber auch nach bestimmten Epochen oder kulturellen Prägungen unterscheiden. Es fragt sich dann, unter welchen Bedingungen eigentlich das Erdulden von körperlichem Leid und die Opferrolle bis zum Sterben »für jemanden oder etwas« zur heldenhaften Qualität werden kann.[18] Und das macht deutlich, dass es bei Heroisierungen auch darum gehen kann, dem Tod Sinn zu geben, seine Endgültigkeit nicht zu akzeptieren: Schon Achilleus sollte in Homers *Ilias* als Heros durch seinen Nachruhm ›überleben‹, der aber des vorherigen Todes bedurfte.

In dem, was sie einsetzen und tun, können Held:innen *Vorbilder* sein. Auch dies ist ein wichtiges Feld ihrer Bewertung. Vielfach werden, so auch in den zu Beginn genannten Umfragen, Vorbild und Held:in gleichgesetzt, aber ist beides dasselbe? Held:innen setzen sich für Werte ein, deren Gültigkeit den Verehrer:innen wichtig ist – und gegen andere. Sie können dazu motivieren, appellieren oder mobilisieren. Sie können Leitbilder sein für die Selbstfindung und Erziehung,[19] sie können Heroismen begründen. Leisten sie als heroisierte Figuren aber viel mehr, als durchschnittliche Menschen zu leisten in der Lage sind, können sie kaum wirklich imitiert werden. Wenn alle handeln könnten wie Held:innen – übermenschlich, autonom und Grenzen überschreitend –, wäre nichts mehr heldenhaft und alle Grenzen und

body and its strength are considered decisive,[17] in others it is rather mental qualities, technical skills or a resistant attitude that count.

This brings us to the next component: There is always something at stake in the actions of heroes. Their special *commitment* distinguishes them: the use or sacrifice of *something* in a confrontation for the benefit of a higher objective, such as possession, ideas, status or power, or the physical commitment of *themselves*, the willingness to sacrifice their own bodies, even their own lives. Heroic commitment is for the advantage of others, be it for higher values, or for other people – at least, those who heroize someone make such claims. What is considered heroic commitment may differ depending on the situation, but also on specific eras or cultural influences. The question then arises under what conditions physical suffering and the victim's role until death "for someone or something" can actually become heroic qualities.[18] This makes it clear that heroizations can also be about giving meaning to death, not accepting its finality: In Homer's *Iliad*, Achilles was meant to 'survive' as a hero through his posthumous fame, however that required prior death.

Heroes can *be role models* in what they commit and what they do. This, too, is an important aspect of their evaluation. Often, as in the surveys mentioned at the beginning, role models and heroes are equated, but are they the same? Heroes advocate values that are important to their admirers – and against others. They can motivate, appeal to or mobilise. They can be role models for self-discovery and education,[19] they can initiate heroisms. However, as heroized figures they achieve much more than average people are able to do and can hardly be imitated. If everyone could act like heroes – superhuman, autonomous and boundary-crossing – nothing would be heroic any more, and all boundaries and rules would be at risk. Do we thus use heroization to transfer what should actually be collective responsibility to those who can do it and who are heroized by us? Are heroes, as it were, symbolic substitutes, 'scapegoats' in a positive sense?[20] Or do heroizations always demand more from everyone than is possible, as in an unfulfillable, perpetual agonal task? As role models, heroized figures are very ambivalent.

Finally, the last component of the heroic: *masculinity*.[21] Since ancient times, heroism has predominantly been associated with men. There have always also been women who were heroized, but they either excelled in areas that are typically associated with men (as in the case of the combative Joan of Arc) or possessed qualities associated with femininity such as caregiving (an example of this would be Mother Teresa). In both cases, the admiration of heroines reinforces a polar gender order. Thus, heroism is a concept rooted in masculinity, and this cannot easily be broken by declaring women or people who do not fit into the binary gender system as heroes. When analysing heroizations in this sense, one can see that they strengthen certain gender roles but also challenge gender concepts. Hence, heroizations perpetuate masculinity, but can they also be subversive?

Regeln kämen in Gefahr. Schieben wir damit durch Heroisierung das, was eigentlich für alle geboten wäre, auf diejenigen ab, die es können und die wir heroisieren? Sind Held:innen gleichsam symbolischer Ersatz, ›Sündenböcke‹ im positiven Sinn?[20] Oder fordern wir durch Heroisierungen immer von allen mehr, als möglich ist, wie in einer unerfüllbaren agonalen Daueraufgabe? Als Vorbilder sind heroisierte Figuren sehr ambivalent.

Schließlich der letzte Baustein des Heroischen: *Maskulinität*.[21] Heldentum ist seit der Antike überwiegend mit Männern verbunden worden. Es gab immer auch Frauen, die heroisiert wurden, doch zeichnen sie entweder Leistungen aus, die sonst eher Männern zugeschrieben wurden (wie bei der kämpferischen Jeanne d'Arc) oder Eigenschaften wie etwa Fürsorglichkeit, die mit Feminität verbunden wurde (ein Beispiel dafür wäre Mutter Teresa). In beiden Fällen bestätigt die Verehrung von Heldinnen eine polare Geschlechterordnung. Heldentum ist insofern ein maskulin gedachtes Phänomen, und das lässt sich nicht einfach aufbrechen, indem man Frauen oder Menschen, die sich nicht in das binäre Geschlechtssystem einordnen, zu Held:innen erklärt. Analysiert man Heroisierungen in diesem Sinne, dann sieht man, dass sie bestimmte Geschlechterrollen stärken, aber auch Geschlechtervorstellungen in Gefahr bringen. Heroisierungen schreiben also Maskulinität fort, aber können sie auch subversiv sein?

Unsere Erkenntnisse zu Bausteinen des Heroischen – und auch die darauf aufbauende Ausstellung – zeigen, was typisch und in vieler Hinsicht charakteristisch für Heroisierungen und Heroismen ist. Die hier versammelten Essays lassen sicherlich viele Held:innen unerwähnt. Doch man wird sie weniger vermissen, wenn man sich darauf einlässt, dass es nicht um einzelne heroische Figuren geht, sondern um wiedererkennbare Prinzipien von Heroisierungen und deren typischen Bausteine – eben das »Prinzip Held*«. Mit diesen als Rüstzeug lässt sich jede heroisierte Figur untersuchen und einordnen. Insofern geben unsere Beiträge auch Fragen an die Hand, die es ermöglichen, unterschiedliche Heroisierungen als kulturelle und kommunikative Handlungen vergleichbar zu machen und so besser zu verstehen, was geschieht, wenn Menschen jemanden heroisieren – auch einzelne ganz persönlich. So lassen sich ›Heldentum‹ und der menschliche Bedarf an Held:innen zwar nicht abschließend erklären. Aber man nähert sich dem in einer Beschreibung an, die gegenüber gängigen Vorstellungen irritierend ist und kritische Fragen aufwirft. Das ist heute umso mehr geboten, weil Heroisierungen Nutzen mit Gefahren verbinden: Sie werden politisch instrumentalisiert, schaffen aber auch Gemeinschaft, mobilisieren für das Gemeinwohl – dies indes nicht, ohne andere auszuschließen, Hierarchien zu stärken und zu polarisieren, aber auch nicht, ohne dass Attentate mit tausenden Opfern zu Heldentaten erhoben werden. Bedrohte Demokratien und die Klimakrise könnten neue Held:innen brauchen, manche rekrutie-

Our findings on the components of the heroic, which our exhibition also builds upon, show what is typical and in many respects characteristic of heroizations and heroisms. The essays gathered here may leave many heroes unmentioned. However, they will be missed less if we accept that it is not about individual heroic figures but about recognisable principles of heroizations and their typical components, i.e. the 'hero principle' (*Prinzip Held**). With these tools, any heroized figure can be examined and categorised. Thus, our contributions also raise questions that allow different heroizations to be compared as cultural and communicative actions and thus enable us to better understand what happens when people heroize someone – even individuals personally. This does not of course fully explain 'heroism' and the human need for heroes. But we can approach it with a description that is unsettling in comparison with common ideas, and which raises critical questions. This is all the more necessary today because heroizations combine benefits with dangers: they are politically instrumentalised, yet they also create community, mobilise for the common good. At the same time, they can exclude others, strengthen and polarise hierarchies, or even elevate acts of violence with thousands of victims into acts of heroism. Endangered democracies and the climate crisis might need new heroes, but others recruit fighters for wars as heroes – and at the same time, heroes shape the entertainment culture as masculine superheroes, *Wonder Woman* or adventurers. The exploration of *Prinzip Held** in the following essays and in the exhibition is intended to help you navigate this field with better information, but also to challenge you, encouraging critical re-evaluation. The question is reframed: What does it say about us and what do we do, individually and collectively, when we produce, have, or need heroes?

ren als Held:innen aber auch Kämpfer für Kriege – und zugleich prägen Held:innen die Unterhaltungskultur als maskuline Superhelden, *Wonder Woman* oder Abenteurer. Die Auseinandersetzung mit dem Prinzip Held* – in den folgenden Essays und in der gleichnamigen Ausstellung – soll dazu beitragen, sich in diesem Feld besser informiert zurechtzufinden, sich aber auch irritieren zu lassen, um es kritisch zu überdenken. So stellt sich die Frage neu: Was sagt es jeweils über uns und was tun wir, wenn wir Held:innen hervorbringen, haben oder brauchen?

Anmerkungen

1 www.ranker.com/list/greatest-heroes-of-mankind/polar-bear (24. Juni 2023).
2 www.focus.de/magazin/archiv/jahrgang_2002/ausgabe_9 (24. Juni 2023).
3 yougov.de/topics/politics/articles-reports/2015/03/25/nur-jeder-achte-deutsche-hat-einen-helden (25. Juni 2023).
4 www.dwds.de/wb/Held (23. Juni 2023).
5 heroicum.net; vgl. zu Grundkonzepten des Forschungsvorhabens jetzt: Feitscher 2023.
6 Sonderforschungsbereich 948 2022a.
7 Vgl. Bröckling 2020, 19–75.
8 Asch und Butter 2016a; Sonderforschungsbereich 948 2022b.
9 Siehe Aurnhammer u. a. 2024.
10 Sonderforschungsbereich 948 2019b.
11 Siehe www.bundeswehr.de/de/organisation/cyber-und-informationsraum/aktuelles/cir-soldaten-ausgezeichnet-5213698 (25. Juni 2023); www.presseportal.de/pm/116137/3444210 (25. Juni 2023); vgl. Koch 2018.
12 Bröckling 2020, 32.
13 Schlechtriemen 2021; vgl. Bröckling 2020, 23–32.
14 Schlechtriemen 2018.
15 Eckert u. a. 2024.
16 Schlechtriemen 2016; Schlechtriemen 2019.
17 Feitscher 2019.
18 Giesen 2004.
19 Siehe Safaian u. a. 2024.
20 Vgl. Schlechtriemen 2016, 18.
21 Siehe Plackinger u. a. 2024.

Notes

1. www.ranker.com/list/greatest-heroes-of-mankind/polar-bear (24 June 2023).
2. www.focus.de/magazin/archiv/jahrgang_2002/ausgabe_9 (24 June 2023).
3. yougov.de/topics/politics/articles-reports/2015/03/25/nur-jeder-achte-deutsche-hat-einen-helden (25 June 2023).
4. www.dwds.de/wb/Held (23 June 2023).
5. heroicum.net; cf. on basic concepts of the research project: Feitscher 2023.
6. Sonderforschungsbereich 948 2022a.
7. Cf. Bröckling 2020, 19–75.
8. Asch and Butter 2016a; Sonderforschungsbereich 948 2022b.
9. See Aurnhammer et al. 2024.
10. Sonderforschungsbereich 948 2019b.
11. See www.bundeswehr.de/de/organisation/cyber-und-informationsraum/aktuelles/cir-soldaten-ausgezeichnet-5213698 (25 June 2023); www.presseportal.de/pm/116137/3444210 (25 June 2023); cf. Koch 2018.
12. Bröckling 2020, 32.
13. Schlechtriemen 2021; cf. Bröckling 2020, 23–32.
14. Schlechtriemen 2018.
15. Eckert et al. 2024.
16. Schlechtriemen 2016; Schlechtriemen 2019.
17. Feitscher 2019.
18. Giesen 2004.
19. See Safaian et al. 2024.
20. Cf. Schlechtriemen 2016, 18.
21. See Plackinger et al. 2024.

© 2024 Ralf von den Hoff, Publikation: Wallstein Verlag; DOI https://doi.org/10.46500/83535581-002 | CC BY-NC-ND 4.0

Anne Hemkendreis

HELD:INNEN UND IHR PUBLIKUM
Zur Wahrnehmung und Bildwerdung wirkmächtiger Figuren

Von Held:innen wird angenommen, dass sie eine besonders intensive emotionale Regung in einem Publikum hervorrufen. Kalt lassen sie angeblich niemanden.[1] Dass dies jedoch nicht unweigerlich für die bildnerische Darstellung heroischer Figuren epochenübergreifend gilt, thematisiert der Fotograf Thomas Struth im Museumskontext (Abb. 1).

Abb. 1: Wer Thomas Struths Fotografie von 2004 betrachtet, sieht ein Museumspublikum beim Betrachten. Doch das Ziel der Wahrnehmung, die berühmte Figur des David von Michelangelo, zeigt der Fotograf nicht. Indem Struth die Perspektive wechselt, macht er unterschiedliche Grade emotionaler Ergriffenheit im Anblick von heldischen Figuren deutlich. Der Künstler thematisiert zudem die Rolle des Museums als Ort heroischer Inszenierungen.
Fig. 1: In Thomas Struth's 2004 photograph, we can see museum visitors gazing at a piece of artwork. However, the photo does not show what, exactly, they are observing: Michelangelo's famous statue of David. By changing the viewers' perspective, Struth reveals different degrees of emotion that museum visitors experience when looking at heroic figures. The photographer also addresses the role a museum plays when displaying heroic pieces of art.

Anne Hemkendreis

HEROES AND THEIR AUDIENCE
On Perception and Iconisation of Powerful Figures

It is assumed that heroes cause a particularly intense emotional response in an audience: They leave no one cold.[1] That this does not necessarily hold true for the way heroic figures are portrayed in pictures across the epochs is an issue the photographer Thomas Struth addresses in the context of museum exhibitions (Fig. 1).

Struth's 2004 series of large-sized photographs, entitled "Audiences", shows various visitors of the Galleria dell'Accademia in Florence upon seeing the monumental David sculpture by Michelangelo. However, as Struth had positioned his tripod camera next to the camera base, the sculpture itself is not visible. David, allegedly the "definition of militant and masculine heroism in the early modern tradition of the Western world",[2] is thus only indirectly present in the picture, becoming the vanishing point for the attention of individual museum visitors. Struth expects those who look at his photographs to perform an act of reconstruction: the visitors have to mentally add the hero in order to complete and understand the situation of reception.

Struth thus resorts to a method of separation already used by Michelangelo. The sculpture shows David as a youthful hero ready to fight the giant Goliath. Earlier David sculptures – for

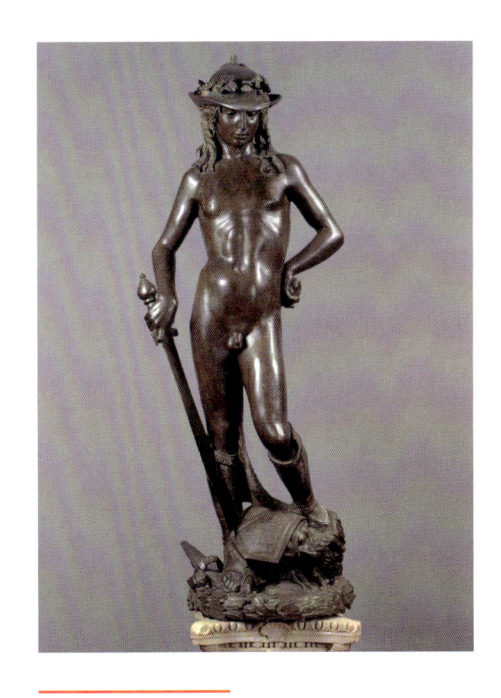

Abb. 2: Siegreich präsentiert sich Donatellos David (1430/50) nach dem Kampf gegen Goliath. Michelangelos David steht der Kampf gegen den Riesen dagegen noch bevor. Seine kontemplative Haltung antizipiert bereits das bevorstehende Heldentum und erweckt in den Betrachter:innen eine gespannte Erwartungshaltung. Dadurch erfahren sich die Rezipient:innen als aktive Instanzen innerhalb von Heroisierungsprozessen.

Fig. 2: Donatello's David (1430/50) stands victorious after his battle against Goliath. Michelangelo's David, on the other hand, has yet to fight the giant. His contemplative posture already foreshadows immanent glory and evokes a sense of tense expectation from viewers. As a result, these viewers perceive themselves to be active agents in David's heroization process.

Struths großformatige Foto-Serie *Audiences* von 2004 zeigt verschiedene Besucher:innen der Galleria dell'Accademia in Florenz bei ihrer Begegnung mit der Monumentalskulptur des David von Michelangelo. Da Struth seine Stativkamera neben dem Sockel positioniert hatte, ist die Skulptur selbst aber nicht zu sehen. David, angeblicher »Inbegriff des militanten und männlichen Heldentums in der frühneuzeitlichen Tradition des Abendlandes«[2], ist nur indirekt im Bild zugegen, nämlich als Fluchtpunkt der Aufmerksamkeit einzelner Museumsbesucher:innen. Von den Betrachter:innen der Fotografien erwartet Struth eine Konstruktionsleistung: Sie müssen den Heros gedanklich ergänzen, um die Rezeptionssituation zu vervollständigen und nachzuvollziehen.

Struth greift damit auf eine Methode der Vereinzelung zurück, die bereits Michelangelo anwandte. Die Skulptur zeigt David als jugendlichen Helden, der zum Kampf gegen den Giganten Goliath bereit ist. Frühere David-Skulpturen – wie von Donatello oder Verrocchio – präsentieren David als triumphierenden Sieger mit dem abgeschlagenen Kopf des Riesen (Abb. 2). Bei Michelangelos David müssen die Rezipient:innen die Komplementärfigur Goliath dagegen aus Davids Blickrichtung erschließen. Struth verwendet mit seinen Fotografien eben dieses Gestaltungsprinzip, indem er die David-Skulptur als das Gegenüber der Museumsbesucher:innen ausspart. Damit rücken für die Betrachter:innen der Fotografien die emotionalen Austausch- und Zuschreibungsprozesse in den Vordergrund, die das Publikum mit der heldischen Figur verbinden.

In den Fotografien werden die unterschiedlichen Intensitätsgrade deutlich, mit der die Skulptur in ihrer heroischen Wirkung wahrgenommen wird.[3] So zeigt die Aufnahme »Audience 7, Florence 2004« Besucher:innen, die den Kopf in den Nacken gelegt haben und offenbar überwältigt sind von der Wirkmacht der überlebensgroßen Darstellung. Dieser Effekt des Heroischen lässt sich jedoch nicht für alle Anwesenden gleichermaßen behaupten. Ein Beispiel für eine offensichtlich ausbleibende oder zumindest unterbrochene Wirkung des Heroischen ist – neben dem Jungen links, der aus dem Bild herausblickt – der Mann mit Hut, der prominent breitbeinig in der Bildmitte steht und lieber den Fotografen beobachtet, als dem Heros seine Aufmerksamkeit zu schenken. Bei genauem Hinsehen entdecken die Betrachter:innen der Fotografie die David-Skulptur als Spiegelbild in der Sonnenbrille des Mannes (Abb. 3), wodurch sich die gedanklich vervollständigte Rezeptionssituation vereindeutigt. Die Miniaturisierung des Helden als Spiegelbild auf einem Brillenglas – ein wohl zunächst zufälliger, vom Künstler in seiner Bildauswahl jedoch absichtlich beibehaltener Effekt – wirkt wie eine ironische Brechung des Heroischen, eine »Infragestellung des Heroischen als solchem«[4] womöglich.

Indem Struth nur das Publikum selbst zeigt, macht er es als heterogene Gemeinschaft erkennbar. Ihre Mitglieder zeigen individuelle Grade von Ergriffenheit und Überwältigung, sie kommen und gehen oder bleiben für eine Weile, sind ganz auf

example by Donatello or Verrocchio – portray David as a triumphant victor with the severed head of the giant (Fig. 2). Regarding Michelangelo's David, however, the recipients themselves have to add, from David's perspective, the complementary figure of Goliath. In this way, Struth exploits the same design principle in his photographs by not showing the David sculpture as the one facing the audience. For those looking at the photographs, the emotional exchange and attribution processes which occur between audience and heroic figure are thus brought to the fore.

Struth's photographs highlight the varying degrees of intensity with which the sculpture and its heroic effects are perceived.[3] The photograph "Audience 7, Florence 2004", for example, shows visitors who have tilted their heads back and appear to be overcome by the power of this larger-than-life display, though this effect of the heroic does not take hold of everyone to the same degree. In addition to the boy on the left who looks out of the picture, another example of an apparently absent or at least interrupted effect of the heroic is the man with a hat who stands, legs apart, prominently in the middle of the picture and prefers to watch the photographer rather than pay attention to the hero. If you look closely, it is possible to see the sculpture of David reflected in the man's sunglasses. This again brings the way that we, as viewers, mentally complete the photograph into focus. The miniaturisation of the hero into a reflection on the lens of a pair of sunglasses (Fig. 3) – an initially unintended effect that was later deliberately kept by the artist in his selection of frame – seems like an ironic comment on the heroic; a "questioning of the heroic as such"[4], perhaps.

By solely portraying the hero's recipients in his photographs, Struth shows the museum's visitors as a heterogeneous community whose members embody varying degrees of overwhelm. A hero's audience is characterised as a community whose members come and go or stay for a while, who may fully concentrate on the heroic figure or get distracted. The strong emotional response heroes attract from those who – mentally or physically – gather around them is thus a possible, yet not inevitable, effect.[5] This observation appears to be

Abb. 3: Das Spiegelbild in der Sonnenbrille verklart und verunklart gleichermaßen. Es vermittelt den Betrachter:innen der Fotografie, wen die Museumsbesucher:innen bestaunen, während es den monumentalen Helden zu einem winzigen Abbild miniaturisiert.

Fig. 3: The reflection in this man's sunglasses both clarifies and obscures. It conveys to the viewer of the photograph who the museum visitors are admiring, while miniaturizing the monumental hero into a tiny image.

die heroische Figur konzentriert oder lassen sich ablenken. Die starke emotional-verehrende Wirkung von Held:innen auf diejenigen, die sich – ideell oder physisch – um sie versammeln, erweist sich damit als ein möglicher, jedoch nicht verallgemeinerbarer Effekt.[5] Diese Beobachtung scheint für die Beschäftigung mit dem Verhältnis von heldischen Figuren und ihren Rezipient:innen zentral. Schließlich bezeugt das Publikum in Struths Fotografie sowohl eine andauernde Präsenz heroischer Darstellungen in kulturellen Kontexten (wie Museen) als auch den dortigen Bedeutungsverlust des Heroischen.

Natürlich spielt im Fall heroischer Darstellungen auch die Berühmtheit des Künstlers bzw. der Künstlerin eine Rolle, denn auch diese können in der gesellschaftlichen Wahrnehmung einen heroischen Status erhalten. Michelangelos künstlerische Kühnheit in der Erschaffung einer Kolossalstatue nach antikem Vorbild wurde beispielsweise schon von Zeitgenossen als eine heroische Gesinnung bezeichnet.[6] Die Frage, ob das Publikum in »Audience 7, Florence 2004« sich aufgrund der Bekanntheit der Skulptur, der Berühmtheit ihres Schöpfers oder der Bedeutung des biblischen Helden um das Kunstwerk versammelt hat, lässt sich nicht zweifelsfrei beantworten.

Held:innen werden gemacht / Held:innen konstituieren ihr Publikum

Indem Struth sich der Affizierungskraft von Held:innen widmet, verhandelt er modellhaft die wechselseitige Bezogenheit von Held:innen und ihrem Publikum. Heroisierungsprozesse erweisen sich als ein relationales Gefüge, das sich nur dann etabliert, wenn eine heroisierte Person den gestalthaften Fokus einer Verehrergemeinschaft zu bilden vermag. Medialisierungen haben jedoch auch den Anspruch, epochenübergreifend zu wirken. Damit steigt das Risiko eines Misslingens des heroischen Effekts.

Ein Beispiel hierfür ist der Kult um den Dichter Stefan George (1868–1933) und dessen Rezeption. Georges Gedichte übten vor allem auf junge, sinnsuchende Erwachsene eine große Faszination aus, der Dichter umgab sich mit einem sorgsam ausgewählten Kreis junger, intellektueller männlicher Verehrer. George war Initiator und Angehöriger eines Kultes um den früh verstorbenen Gymnasiasten Maximilian Kronberger, gleichzeitig aber auch dessen sinnstiftende Orientierungsfigur und das eigentliche Ziel der Verehrung. Nach Georges Tod wirkten die Erinnerung an den Dichter und an seinen Kult inspirierend für politische Akteure wie die Geschwister Scholl oder die Brüder Stauffenberg in ihrem Widerstand gegen das nationalsozialistische Unrechtssystem. In Rainer Werner Fassbinders Film *Satansbraten* von 1976, einer filmischen Rezeption des Georgekultes, scheitert der Dichter Walter Kranz in seiner Darstellung als Dichterfürst in der Manier Georges jedoch: Seine Referenz auf das Vorbild misslingt. Im Selbstentwurf als Heros vermag

central for discussing the relationship between heroic figures and their recipients. After all, the audience in Struth's photographs testifies to the continued presence of heroic displays in cultural contexts (e.g. museums), but at the same time to the possible loss of the fascination of the heroic.

Of course, the popularity of the artist also plays a role in heroic contexts as they, too, can obtain the status of heroes. Michelangelo's artistic boldness in creating a colossal statue modelled on classical role models was, for example, considered a heroic attitude even among his contemporaries.[6] The question of whether the viewers in "Audience 7, Florence 2004" have gathered around this piece of art because of the fame of the sculpture, the fame of its creator or the relevance of the biblical hero cannot be answered with certainty.

Heroes are made

By focusing on the hero's power to affect, Struth negotiates the mutual relations between heroes and their audiences. Heroization processes prove to be relational structures that establish themselves only if a heroized person is able to become a figure that a community of admirers can focus on. Medialisation practices also have an effect on heroization processes across epochs, which is why a risk of failure of the heroic effect is always possible and increasing over time.

This is exemplified by the cult around the poet Stefan George (1868–1933) and his reception. George's poems fascinated in particular young adults searching for meaning as the poet surrounded himself with a carefully chosen circle of young, intellectual male admirers during his lifetime. George was not only the initiator and a member of a cult around the student Maximilian Kronberger, who died young, but also the figure that provided meaning and orientation to it, and consequently the actual subject of admiration. After George's death, the memory of the poet and his cult had an inspiring effect on Hans and Sophie Scholl as well as the Stauffenberg brothers in their resistance against the National Socialist system of injustice. In the 1976 film *Satansbraten* by Rainer Werner Fassbinder – a cinematic take on the cult around George – the poet Walter Kranz fails in his portrayal of the famous poet in that his reference to his particular role model remains unsuccessful. A self-styled hero, the protagonist is unable to establish a community of admirers; instead, he exposes himself to ridicule (Fig. 4). This example shows how different audiences at different times set their own standards for what is considered worthy of admiration.

The central status of heroized individuals within groups of admirers generally shows that communities of interpretation are themselves powerful.[7] Ronald G. Asch and Michael Butter state that heroes do not exist without an audience, as at-

Abb. 4: Heroisierungsprozesse bilden ein relationales Gefüge, das stimmig sein muss. Wo das heroische Vorbild übermächtig ist, wirkt die misslungene Anverwandlung lächerlich: Kurt Raab in der Rolle des Dichters Walter Kranz, der seinem heroischen Vorbild Stefan George nicht gewachsen ist.
Fig. 4: Heroization processes make up a relational structure that must be coherent. When the heroic role model is overpowering, the unsuccessful adaption appears ridiculous: This is the case with fictional poet Walter Kranz (played by Kurt Raab), who fails to live up to his heroic role model Stefan George.

es der Protagonist nicht, eine Verehrergemeinschaft zu bilden; stattdessen gibt er sich selbst der Lächerlichkeit preis. Dies ist ein Beispiel dafür, dass zu unterschiedlichen Zeiten verschiedene Publika eigene Maßstäbe dafür setzen, was als verehrungswürdig gilt (Abb. 4).

Allgemein zeigt der zentrale Stellenwert von heroisierten Personen innerhalb von Adorationsgruppen, dass Heldenverehrung die Bildung von Interpretationsgemeinschaften bedeutet, die selbst wirkmächtig sind.[7] Ronald G. Asch und Michael Butter stellen fest, dass Held:innen ohne ein Publikum nicht existieren, da ohne eine externe Wahrnehmung Versuche der Fremd- und Selbstinszenierung ins Leere laufen. Held:innen sind demnach auf ein Publikum hin orientiert und auf dieses angewiesen. Das Publikum fungiert nicht nur als Ziel, sondern auch als Ausgangspunkt von Heroisierungsprozessen, was vor allem in Darstellungen des Heroischen deutlich wird. Die heroische Figur erzeugt durch ihre Interaktion mit einem Kollektiv Reaktionen, die auf sie selbst zurückwirken. Anhaltende Erinnerungen an heroische Figuren durch diejenigen, die sie verehren, sind ein »rekonstruktiver Akt, der den Gegenwartsbezug von Heroisierungen immer wieder neu herstellt«.[8]

Michelangelos David gibt in Struths Fotografie eine bestimmte Betrachter:innenperspektive (von unten) vor und ist damit im Bild implizit präsent. Das partielle Hälserecken und die Andacht, mit der die Museumsbesucher:innen den David betrachten, macht sie zu essentiellen Bestandteilen von Heroisierungsprozessen, auch außerhalb des Bildes. Schließlich zeigen sich die Museumsbesucher:innen ergriffen und fordern in ihrer Haltung auch die Rezipient:innen der Fotografie zu einer Teilhabe an der staunenden Betrachtung auf (hier an der heroischen Kontemplation vor dem Kampf). Auf sozialer Ebene bildet das bildinterne Publikum eine Verehrergemeinschaft. Sie konstituiert die Darstellung des David als eine heroische. Solange sich die Museumsbesucher:innen unbeobachtet wähnen, vermitteln sie den

tempts to style oneself or others in a heroic fashion come to nothing without external perception. Accordingly, heroes are oriented towards and dependent on an audience. The audience is not only a target but also a starting point for heroization processes, as becomes evident primarily in displays of the heroic. Through interaction with a collective, the heroic figure triggers reactions that reflect back on themselves. Continued remembrance of heroic figures by those who worship them constitutes "an act of reconstruction, which recreates the contemporary relevance of heroizations over and over again".[8]

In Struth's photograph, the size of Michelangelo's David prescribes a specific viewer's perspective (from below), which makes the sculpture itself implicitly present in the picture. The craning of the necks and the devotion with which some of the museum's visitors reflect on David show that an overwhelming sensation is an essential part of heroization processes, even affecting the viewers outside the picture. In fact, most of the museum's visitors appear to be emotionally moved and their poses invite the viewers of the photographs to participate in their state of innercontemplation (in this case, the heroic time of reflection before the fight). On a social level, the audience depicted in the photograph forms a community of admirers. It is this community that makes the presentation of David a heroic one. When not being observed, the visitors give the recipients of the photograph the impression that they can partake in the overwhelming feelings the museum audience seems to be experiencing.[9] However, as some viewers appear to be unimpressed and look out of the picture rather than at the hero, the opportunity for emotional participation via the perception of the visitors remains ambivalent. Struth shows moments where the hero is present but the heroic effect may fail to materialise and does not always constitute the focus of interest. In these cases, it is the viewers of the photographs themselves who seem to become the focus of attention for those visitors of the museum who are looking at the camera. This shift in focus can invite the recipients of the photograph to question their own stance towards heroism. The coexistence of undivided and divided attention within the audience therefore invites and at the same time excludes the recipients of the photograph.

The heroic stubbornly persists in the idolatry of popular culture and sports. The way star cults are presented in the media is typically characterised by a front shot of an emotionalised audience in tense expectation or jubilant ecstasy (Fig. 5). The great power of the heroic in popular culture is imparted through pictures in horizontal formats, made in the style of history paintings, which suggest that the audience is participating in a special, possibly historic event. Struth plays with these effects when he photographs famous history paintings or copies the format of history paintings, as he did in his Louvre series (1989) (Fig. 6). His large-sized photographs address the heroic at the threshold between art, culture and the popular. They reflect the presence of the heroic in specific contexts of perception and pres-

Abb. 5: Die Fotografie zeigt ein Publikum in euphorischem Warten auf die Teilnehmenden einer Tour de France der 1930er Jahre. Die Wirkmacht der Sporthelden ist schon vor ihrer Ankunft anhand der aufgeregten Haltung des Publikums spürbar.

Fig. 5: This photograph shows spectators excitedly awaiting the participants of a Tour de France race in the 1930s. The power exerted by the athletes – another type of hero – can be felt from the spectators' excitement before they even arrive.

Eindruck einer ungestörten Teilhabemöglichkeit an ihren überwältigenden Empfindungen.[9] Da jedoch einzelne Betrachter:innen unbeeindruckt scheinen und lieber aus dem Bild herausblicken, als dem Heros ihre Aufmerksamkeit zu schenken, bleibt die emotionale Teilhabemöglichkeit an dem Museumspublikum für die eigentlichen Rezipient:innen der Fotografie ambivalent. Struth zeigt Augenblicke, in denen der Heros präsent ist, die heroische Wirkung jedoch ausbleiben kann und nicht immer den Fokus des Interesses bildet. Für die Betrachter:innen der Fotografie, die scheinbar selbst zum Aufmerksamkeitsfokus der widerständigen, vom Heroischen unbeeindruckten Museumsbesucher:innen werden, stellt sich die Frage der eigenen Haltung zum Heldentum. Die Ko-Existenz geteilter und ungeteilter Aufmerksamkeit im Publikum lädt die Betrachter:innen der Fotografie ein und schließt zugleich aus.

Bis heute hält sich das Heroische hartnäckig in der Idolatrie der Popkultur und dem Sport. Die mediale Inszenierung von Starkulten zeichnet sich typischerweise durch die Frontalaufnahme eines emotionalisierten Publikums in gespannter Erwartung oder jubelnder Ekstase aus (Abb. 5). Die starke Wirkmacht des Heroischen in der Popkultur wird durch Bilder in horizontalen Formaten vermittelt, die an die Gattung des Historienbildes angelehnt sind und die Partizipation an einem besonderen, möglicherweise geschichtsträchtigen Moment suggerieren. Struth spielt mit diesen Effekten, wenn er – wie in seiner Serie zum Museumspublikum im Louvre (1989) – berühmte Historiengemälde abfotografiert oder das Format von Historienbildern für seine Fotografien übernimmt (Abb. 6). Damit thematisieren seine großformatigen Fotografien das Heroische an der Grenze zwischen Kunst, Kultur und Populärem. Reflektiert wird die andauernde Präsenz des Heroischen in bestimmten Wahrnehmungs- und Präsentationskontexten, in denen die nationale, kulturelle und soziale Bedeutung von Held:innen konstruiert oder verhandelt wird. Struths Fotografien befassen sich entsprechend auch mit der »Frage nach der gesellschaftlichen Funktion [der] Kommunikations-

Abb. 6: Monumentalität in der bildenden Kunst kann heroische Bedeutung zum Tragen bringen, sie aber auch lediglich suggerieren. Thomas Struths großformatige Fotografien, die in Galerien alter Meister auf den ersten Blick selbst wirken wie Historiengemälde, können für die Betrachter:innen ein Anlass sein, über die Wirkmacht und Überzeugungskraft heroischer Wirklichkeitskonstruktionen zu reflektieren.

Fig. 6: In visual arts, monumentality can emphasise heroic significance, but it can also merely suggest it. Thomas Struth's large-format photographs, which, at first glance, appear to be historical paintings in old master galleries, can provide viewers with an opportunity to reflect on the power and persuasiveness of heroic constructions of reality.

entation in which the national, cultural, and social relevance of heroes is constructed or negotiated. Struth's photographs thus focus on "the question of the societal function of communication processes about the heroic" as well as the role of various media and institutions as a means of heroization and reality construction.[10] Traditional heroes and their historiographic significance, especially their relevance for the present, are put up for debate.

As early as 1840, Thomas Carlyle considered the worship of heroes in any society as an anthropological constant, although today this theory is rightly considered eurocentric.[11] Still, Carlyle's thoughts are helpful for understanding expectations that take for granted the significance of the heroic in specific contexts, such as large museums and media presentations. Even if the sight of a hero does not cause any great emotions, "some of the [heroic] energy potential remains palpable in the ironic breaking with, or rejection of, the appeal".[12] Ulrich Bröckling notes

prozesse über das Heroische« sowie mit der Rolle unterschiedlicher Medien und Institutionen als Mittel der Heroisierung und Wirklichkeitskonstruktion.[10] Überlieferte Held:innen werden in ihrem historiographischen Stellenwert und insbesondere ihrer Bedeutung für die Gegenwart zur Diskussion gestellt.

Thomas Carlyle bezeichnete bereits 1840 die Verehrung von Helden als Fundament einer jeden Gesellschaft und damit als anthropologische Konstante, wobei diese These heute zu Recht als eurozentrisch gilt.[11] Dennoch ist Carlyles Überlegung für das Verständnis einer Erwartungshaltung hilfreich, die die Bedeutung des Heroischen in bestimmten Kontexten, wie großen Museen oder auch spezifischen medialen Darstellungsformen voraussetzt. Selbst wenn der Anblick eines Heros keine großen Emotionen auslöst, »bleibt noch in der ironischen Brechung oder Zurückweisung des Appells etwas von [dem heroischen] Energiepotenzial spürbar«.[12] Ulrich Bröckling bemerkt hierzu, dass heroische Kontexte in der Regel »Kraftfelder« erzeugen, die »alle, die in ihre Reichweite gelangen, auf den Heldenpol auszurichten versuchen«.[13]

Struth thematisiert die Rolle bestimmter Darstellungsweisen hinsichtlich ihrer heroischen Wirkmacht, indem er auch das Ausbleiben heroischer Attraktionskraft zeigt. Damit wird deutlich, dass Museen und Historienbilder heute nicht allein der Konstruktion und Bestätigung von Held:innen dienen, sondern auch ihrer Verhandlung. Der Ausgang dieses Prozesses ist nicht vorherbestimmt, sondern hängt vom jeweiligen Publikum und der Epoche ab.

Medien und Institutionen als Held:innenmacher

Struths Museumsfotografien entstanden in einer Zeit, als Museumsbauten im großen Stil neu geplant wurden und sich als ein populäres Ziel des internationalen Tourismus etablierten.[14] Die hochrangigen Museen, in denen Struth fotografierte – der Prado in Madrid, der Pariser Louvre, die Galleria dell'Accademia in Florenz und das Pergamonmuseum in Berlin – waren vor allem zur Zeit der Nationalstaatengründungen Orte der kulturellen Verständigung und der nationalen Selbstvergewisserung sowie des Prestiges gewesen. Struth hatte seine Museumsfotografien zunächst als eine Art »Erinnerungskampagne« geplant, in der die Fähigkeit von Kunst reflektiert werden sollte, den Besucher:innen eine lebhafte Einbeziehung in die Geschichte und ihre Protagonist:innen zu gewähren (Abb. 7).[15]

Inspiriert von Restaurierungsarbeiten an Gemälden, denen der Künstler beiwohnen durfte, interessierte er sich zunehmend für die verschiedenen Zeitschichten von Bildern, die er nicht allein auf materieller Ebene, sondern auch hinsichtlich der sich wandelnden Rezeptionskontexte reflektierte. Die Fotografie nutzt Struth ähnlich wie einen »Zeitraffer«, der die unterschiedlichen historischen Wirkweisen eines Kunst-

that heroic contexts usually generate "energy fields" that "try to align with the heroic pole all those who are within their range".[13]

Struth addresses the role of specific forms of presentation with regard to their heroic power, also by showing the absence of the heroic force of attraction. It becomes obvious that museums and history pictures today do not only play a part in constructing and confirming someone's status as a hero but also its negotiation. The outcome of this process is not predetermined but depends on the respective audience and the epoch.

Media and institutions as hero-makers

Struth's photographs were taken at a time when new museum buildings were being planned on a large scale and established themselves as popular destinations of international tourism.[14] The world-class museums where Struth took his pictures – the Museo del Prado in Madrid, the Louvre in Paris, the Galleria dell'Accademia in Florence and the Pergamon Museum in Berlin – have all been places of cultural communication, national self-assurance and prestige, especially at the time the national states were founded. Struth initially conceived his museum photographs as a sort of "remembrance campaign" that was intended to reflect art's capability to permit the audience vivid involvement in history and its protagonists (Fig. 7).[15]

Inspired by restoration work on paintings, he became increasingly interested in the different time layers of images, which he reflected upon not only on a material level but also with regard to the changing contexts of reception. Struth uses photography as a sort of "time-lapse", which makes the

Abb. 7: Struths Museumsfotografien vermitteln, dass sich »Zeitschichten« nicht nur im wörtlichen Sinne auf die ausgestellten Objekte selbst legen. Im übertragenen Sinne können sie sich mit zunehmendem Zeitverlauf auch zwischen Objekten und ihrem Publikum bilden und die Rezeption erschweren, weil sich Verstehens- und Rezeptionskontexte wandeln.

Fig. 7: Struth's museum photographs suggest that "layers of time" are not only applied to the exhibited objects themselves in a literal sense. In a figurative sense, such layers can also develop between objects and their audience as time passes, making reception more difficult because the contexts of understanding and perception change.

Abb. 8: Jean-Léon Gérôme malte 1868 den Leichnam des Marshall Ney, der während der Unruhen der Französischen Revolution mehrfach die Seiten gewechselt hatte. Thema des Historienbildes ist nicht die Exekution der einst heldischen Figur, sondern der achtlos zurückgelassene Leichnam. In diesem Wandel kündigt sich eine Kritik am Heroischen im Medium Bild an bzw. ein Zweifel an der allgemeinen und überzeitlichen Wirkmacht von Held:innen. Ihr heroischer Status beruht auf Dynamiken der Zuschreibung und ist dementsprechend veränderlich.

Fig. 8: Jean-Léon Gérôme's 1868 painting of Marshall Michel Ney's dead body. This French Commander had changed sides several times during the turmoil surrounding the French Revolution and was subsequently shot for committing treason. The theme of this historical painting is not the brutal execution of a once heroic figure, but rather the careless abandonment of his body. This artistic shift suggests a critique of heroism in the painting's visual medium, as well as doubts about the universal and timeless power of heroes. Their heroic status is based on the dynamics of attribution and is accordingly volatile.

werks in verdichteter Form zugänglich macht.[16] Als ein »psychologischer Seismograph« schreiben sich die großformatigen Fotografien in die Geschichte der Historienmalerei ein, die von unterschiedlichen Phasen der Erschütterung heroischer Darstellungskonventionen geprägt wurde.[17]

Struth wählte für seine Fotografien ungewöhnlich große Formate, die ihnen den Titel »Historienfotografien« einbrachten. Das Historienbild ist in der Kunstgeschichte die Gattung heroischer Darstellung; es erzählt von Held:innen und ihren geschichtsschreibenden Taten. Seit dem 19. Jahrhundert wird in dieser Gattung jedoch auch die Krise des Heroischen verhandelt, die u. a. auf die Französische Revolution zurückgeht, in der das aufbegehrende Volk an die Stelle eines einzelnen Heros trat.[18] Die künstlerische Abarbeitung am Heroischen findet sich bei Malern wie Francisco de Goya, Jean Léon Gerôme (Abb. 8) oder Édouard Manet im Motiv des gewaltsamen Heldentodes und zeichnet sich durch Dezentrierung des Helden oder seine Darstellung als zunächst achtlos liegengelassener Leichnam aus. Wolfgang Kemp bezeichnet die Verschiebung eines Interesses der Kunst von der heroischen Figur auf ihre (ausbleibende) Wirkmacht als eine Trivialisierung des Heldentums, ausgelöst durch die beständige Umwertung dessen, was ein Held oder eine Heldin im Kontext der Französischen Revolution und der folgenden politischen Machtwechsel gewesen war.[19] Struths Historienfotografien reihen sich in diese Entwicklung ein, indem sie zunächst ein Versprechen auf Teilhabe an einer gemeinschaftlichen Versenkung in die Darstellung einer heroischen Figur geben, diese jedoch letztlich nur abwesend oder indirekt, beispielsweise als Spiegelung, ins Bild kommt.[20]

different modes by which a piece of art evokes an effect accessible in a condensed form.[16] Like a "psychological seismograph", the large-sized photographs find their place in the tradition of history painting – a genre that has been shaped by different phases of crisis within the heroic and its presentations.[17]

Struth chose exceptionally large formats for his photographs, which earned them the title of "history photographs". In art, the history painting is the traditional genre of the heroic as it tells stories of heroes and their deeds. Ever since the 19th century, however, the history painting has also been the genre in which the crisis of the heroic is debated. This crisis was a result of the French Revolution, which replaced the individual hero with a whole population of rebelling people.[18] The artistic negotiation of the heroic can be found in the motif of the violent death of the hero, depicted by painters like Francisco de Goya, Jean Léon Gerôme (Fig. 8) or Édouard Manet, and is characterised by the decentralisation of the hero or his presentation as a corpse carelessly cast aside. Wolfgang Kemp describes this shift in art history from the heroic figure to (the absence of) its immense power as a trivialisation of heroism, caused by the constant re-evaluation of what being a hero actually meant in the context of the French Revolution and the subsequent political power shifts.[19] The large-sized photographs by Struth reflect this development in that they initially promise participation in a communal reflection on the heroic figure. However, the hero only appears indirectly, as a reflection on dark sunglasses, or he is completely absent from the picture.[20] The devaluation or the lack of a heroic figure in the picture, the absence of this magnet of attention, enhances the significance of the recipients. They become instances that weight the heroic.[21] Audiences can be hero-makers – or they can deny heroization.

Another and certainly extreme example of this meta-aesthetic reflection on the heroic is Barnett Newman's large-sized painting entitled "Vir Heroicus Sublimis", dated 1950–51 (Fig. 9), in which the hero is only mentioned in the title (which translates to "A Sublime Hero"). In this abstract painting, which consists of a red field with vertical stripes, the artist plays with an aesthetics of overwhelm, not caused by a larger-than-life figure but by the sheer size of the painting itself and the immersive effect of the colour red. In the replacement of the heroic figure by abstraction, Newman shifts the experience of the heroic from the level of the motif to the level of representation. The overwhelming effect of colour and of the painting's format is striking, even without, or rather because of the lack of a heroic figure.

The difference between heroes as motifs and heroic aesthetics is also illustrated in a particularly impressive way by the artist Andreas Gursky. In his large-format 2011 photomontage "Rückblick" (engl. Review), we see German politicians from behind (Gerhard Schröder, Helmut Schmidt, Angela Merkel and Helmut Kohl) as they sit in front of a painting by Barnett Newman (Abb. 10). This doubling of the heroic in the picture and its presence and absence addresses the political level of heroiza-

Abb. 9: Mit seiner überwältigenden Größe steht Barnett Newmans Gemälde »Vir Heroicus Sublimis« (»Ein erhabener Held«) von 1951 in der Tradition des klassischen Historienbildes. Doch statt einer heroischen Tat ist ein rotes Farbfeld ohne Gegenstandsbezug zu sehen. Erhebende Wirkung erzielen nunmehr die schiere Größe und das Bildmaterial Farbe, nicht die Identifikation mit einer heroischen Figur. Ästhetiken mit heroischer Wirkmacht können in der Kunst fortleben, auch wenn keine Held:innen zu sehen sind.

Fig. 9: With its overwhelming size, Barnett Newman's 1951 painting "Vir Heroicus Sublimis" ("A Sublime Hero" in Latin) is meant to portray a historical event. But instead of depicting heroic deeds, all we can see is a vast expanse of the colour red – with no reference to an object. Its impressive effect on the viewer is achieved by its sheer size and use of colour, as opposed to identifying a heroic figure. Aesthetics that exert heroic power can live on in art, even if there are not any heroes to be seen.

Die Abwertung oder das Fehlen einer heroischen Figur im Bild, die nicht länger Magnet der Aufmerksamkeit ist, wertet die Bedeutung der Rezipient:innen auf: Sie werden zu Instanzen, die das Heroische gewichten.[21] Publika können nicht nur Heldenmacher:innen sein, sondern sie können Heroisierung auch verweigern. Ein weiteres und durchaus extremes Beispiel für diese metaästhetische Reflexion über das Heroische ist Barnett Newmans ebenfalls großformatiges Gemälde »Vir Heroicus Sublimis« von 1950/51 (Abb. 9), in dem der Held nur noch allgemein im Titel genannt wird (übersetzt: »Ein erhabener Held«). In seinem abstrakten Gemälde, bestehend aus einem roten Farbfeld mit senkrechten Streifen, spielt der Künstler mit einer überwältigenden Ästhetik, die sich nicht länger durch eine überlebensgroße Figur, sondern durch die Größe des Bildes selbst und die eindringliche Wirkung der roten Farbe ergibt.

Abb. 10: Auch Andreas Gurskys großformatige Fotografie »Rückblick« (2015) befasst sich mit der Tradition des Historienbildes. Gursky inszeniert die (heute) ehemaligen Bundeskanzler:innen Gerhard Schröder, Helmut Schmidt, Angela Merkel und Helmut Kohl beim Betrachten des abstrakten Gemäldes von Barnett Newman. Als Rückenfiguren sind sie selbst keine heroischen Figuren, sondern Teil einer ästhetischen Überwältigung durch ein großformatiges Gemälde. So werden die Betrachter:innen der Fotografie einerseits Zeug:innen heroischer Affizierung; andererseits können sie die Mechanismen von Heroisierungsprozessen kritisch-distanziert reflektieren.

Fig. 10: Andreas Gursky's large-format photograph »Review« (2015) also depicts a type of historical image. Gursky poses former German Chancellors Gerhard Schröder, Helmut Schmidt, Angela Merkel and Helmut Kohl looking at the abstract painting by Barnett Newman. Seen only from behind, the politicians are not meant to portray heroic figures themselves, but are rather part of an aesthetic overload caused by the large-format painting. As a result, viewers observing the photograph become witness to the fascination of heroism; they can also critically and remotely reflect on the mechanisms of heroization processes.

tion processes as a possible method of overarching power structures and ironically breaks with their immersive effect. On a motif level, an overwhelming aesthetics juxtaposes the portrayal of prominent personalities, who in turn offer themselves as figures of identification to the recipients of the painting. The actual viewers of Gursky's photograph are thus confronted with the artistic methods and the figural presentation of the heroic as two separate areas. The picture medium itself becomes a hero-maker (as does the audience); its motifs and aesthetics evoke heroization processes. In addition, the photographed picture raises the question of a continued survival of the heroic in an epoch of new media.

Indem die Abstraktion die figurale Darstellung ablöst, verschiebt Newman die Erfahrung des Heroischen von der Ebene des Motivs auf die der Darstellungsweise. Die entgrenzende Wirkung von Farbe und Format ist überwältigend, und zwar ohne dass eine heldische Figur auftritt.

Die Differenz zwischen Held:innen als Motiv und heroischer Ästhetik hat zudem besonders eindrücklich der Künstler Andreas Gursky verdeutlicht. In seiner großformatigen Fotomontage »Rückblick« (2011) platzierte er die Rückenansichten deutscher Politiker:innen (Gerhard Schröder, Helmut Schmidt, Angela Merkel und Helmut Kohl) so, als würden die vier vor einem Gemälde von Barnett Newman sitzen (Abb. 10). Die Verdopplung des Heroischen im Bild in seiner An- und Abwesenheit thematisiert die politische Ebene von Heroisierungsprozessen als Teil übergeordneter Machtstrukturen und bricht ironisch ihre ästhetische Sogwirkung. Auf der Ebene des Motivs steht eine überwältigende Ästhetik der Darstellung bekannter Persönlichkeiten gegenüber, die sich wiederum den Rezipient:innen des Bildes als Identifikationsfiguren anbieten. Den eigentlichen Betrachter:innen von Gurskys Fotografie werden dadurch die künstlerischen Stilmittel und die figürliche Darstellung des Heroischen als zwei voneinander getrennte Bereiche vor Augen geführt. Das Medium Bild tritt ebenso wie das Publikum als ein Heldenmacher auf und evoziert durch Motiv und Ästhetik Heroisierungsprozesse. Zudem stellt das fotografierte Bild die Frage nach dem Weiterleben des Heroischen im Zeitalter neuer Medien.

Struths »Audience 7, Florence 2004« thematisiert die Bedeutung der Gattung der Historienmalerei für das Aufrufen einer Erwartungshaltung im Kontext heroischer Darstellung. Die Fotografie zeigt die Wirkmacht heroischer Medialisierung jedoch als eine, die sowohl überwältigen als auch ausbleiben kann. Anders als bei Newman werden die Betrachter:innen nicht selbst emotional angesprochen, sondern die Wirkmacht des David als Heros wird beobachtbar. In dieser Hinsicht ähnelt Struths Spiel mit bildinterner und -externer Wirkung demjenigen Gurskys. Heroisierung wird deutlich als ein relationales Gefüge von Held:innen und ihrem Publikum und insofern als ein Akt der äußeren Zuschreibung. Der Blick auf die Reaktionen des Museumspublikums thematisiert die »technisch-medialen Bedingungen der Produktion von bildlicher Evidenz«, also der Bezeugung von Held:innen und ihrer medialen Vermittlung.[22] Die Wirkmacht des Heroischen erweist sich folglich als ein Ergebnis des Zusammenspiels aus heroischer Darstellung (in Motiv und Stil), dem Präsentationskontext des Werkes (z. B. in einem Museum) und der emotionalen Teilhabemöglichkeit an einem geteilten Wahrnehmungserlebnis.[23] Je nach Rezeptionssituation lösen Held:innen unterschiedliche Reaktionen aus, manche lassen sie kalt; ihre gemeinschaftsbildende Wirkung ist zeit- und situationsabhängig. In bestimmten Kontexten hält sich das Heroische jedoch äußerst hartnäckig.

Struth's "Audience 7, Florence 2004" addresses the significance of the genre of history paintings for the evocation of the heroic in the realm of certain presentation contexts. In his photography, the artist reflects on the power of heroic aesthetics as something that can overwhelm as well as fail to affect an audience. In contrast to Newman, the viewers of Struth's photographs are not directly addressed; rather, the emotional power of David as a heroic figure becomes observable. In this regard, the way Struth plays with the picture's internal and external affective arrangements is similar to Gursky's. Heroization is illustrated as a relational fabric of heroes and their audiences depending on reciprocal acts of external attribution. The focus on the reactions of the visitors addresses the "technical and/or media-related conditions of the production of visual evidence", that is, of the attestation of heroes and the way they are presented in the media.[22] The power of the heroic therefore proves to be the result of the synergy between heroic presentation (in motif and style), the context a work is presented in (e.g. museum) and the opportunity for emotional participation in an aesthetic arrangement.[23] Depending on the reception situation, heroes spark various responses, or none at all; their community-building effect depends on time and situation. In specific contexts, however, the heroic stubbornly persists.

Anmerkungen

1. Bröckling 2019.
2. Fried 2008, 148.
3. Ebd.
4. Gelz u. a. 2015, hier S. 136.
5. Ebd, 138.
6. Hubert 2013, 211.
7. Asch und Butter 2016b, 11.
8. Feitscher 2021.
9. Die unbeobachtete Betrachtung der Wirkmacht von Bildern interessierte bereits den Kunstkritiker Diderot: Bexte 2005, 299.
10. Gelz u. a. 2015, 138.
11. Carlyle 1901. Hier wird explizit die männliche Form verwendet. Vor allem indigene Kulturen haben ein anderes Weltverständnis, das nicht auf kolonialem Heroentum aufbaut.
12. Bröckling 2019.
13. Ebd.
14. Weski 2017, 11–17.
15. Enwezor 2017, 304.
16. Ebd., 308.
17. Ebd.
18. Wedekind 2014, 238.
19. Kemp 1985, 111.
20. Söntgen 2007, 49–68.
21. Busch 2014, 228.
22. Belting 2005, 120.
23. Das Verhältnis von Realitätsnähe und Fotografie ist komplex und kann hier nur angedeutet werden. Dieser Artikel bezieht sich auf die Rolle von Fotografien im Kontext von menschlichem Leid wie Krieg und Terror. Nach Hana Gründler drängt Gewalt darauf hin, Bild zu werden. In der Sichtbarwerdung des Leids in der Fotografie verlangt das Grauen nach einer aktiven Auseinandersetzung. Hierdurch werden die Betrachter zu (un-)moralischen Voyeuren. Vgl. Gründler 2019, 203.

Notes

1 Bröckling 2019.
2 Fried 2008, 148.
3 Ibid.
4 Gelz et al. 2015, here p. 136.
5 Ibid, 138.
6 Hubert 2013, 211.
7 Asch and Butter 2016b, 11.
8 Feitscher 2021.
9 The unobserved observation of the power of pictures already roused the interest of art critic Diderot: Bexte 2005, 299.
10 Gelz et al. 2015, 138.
11 Carlyle 1901. Here, the male form is explicitly used. Especially indigenous cultures have a different understanding of the world, one which does not build on colonial heroism.
12 Bröckling 2019.
13 Ibid.
14 Weski 2017, 11–17.
15 Enwezor 2017, 304.
16 Ibid., 308.
17 Ibid.
18 Wedekind 2014, 238.
19 Kemp 1985, 111.
20 Söntgen 2007, 49–68.
21 Busch 2014, 228.
22 Belting 2005, 120.
23 The relation between realism and photography is complex and can only be touched upon here. The article refers to the role of photographs in the context of human suffering, e.g. in war and terror. According to Hana Gründler, violence seeks to become a picture. In making suffering visible, photography demands active involvement with the horrific. Thus, viewers become (im)moral voyeurs. Cf. Gründler 2019, 203.

© 2024 Anne Hemkendreis, Publikation: Wallstein Verlag; DOI https://doi.org/10.46500/83535581-003 | CC BY-NC-ND 4.0

Vera Marstaller

MEDIALISIERUNG

Gesten

Helden sind das Ergebnis einer Verwandlung. Erst, wenn ein Publikum von ihrem außerordentlichen Einsatz und ihrer Handlungsmacht überzeugt ist, wenn davon erzählt wird, dass sie Grenzen überschritten und mutig (gegen sich selbst oder andere) gekämpft haben, erst dann können sie den einen als Vorbild, den anderen zur Abschreckung dienen. Damit Helden Helden werden, muss von ihnen berichtet werden.[1] Sei es durch mitreißende Reden, kunstvolle Gemälde, epische Texte, spannende Filme – Heroisierung bedarf der medialen Vermittlung.

Medialisierungen sind wie Gesten des Zeigens. Wie der Finger, der in eine Richtung weist, lenken sie die Wahrnehmung ihres Publikums von etwas ab und rücken anderes an dessen Stelle. Heroisierungen lassen aus, um zu betonen. Ist etwa ausschließlich die männliche Form gewählt, werden Held:innen anderer Geschlechter nicht in Betracht gezogen.[2] Medialisierungen geben als Zeigegesten Handlungsanweisungen, wie das von ihnen Dargestellte verstanden und wie damit umgegangen werden soll.

Körper

Lässig liegt Lionel Messi auf dem Boden und richtet den Oberkörper auf. Das rechte Bein ist gestreckt, das linke aufgestellt. Der linke Arm ruht auf dem linken Knie, der Zeigefinger deutet nach vorne (Abb. 1). Die Fingerspitze berührt beinahe den ebenfalls ausgestreckten Zeigefinger des gegenüber in der Luft schwebenden Diego Maradona. Beide tragen das argentinische Trikot. Gänzlich nackte Spieler der Nationalmannschaft umringen Maradona in engem Körperkontakt. Die kurzen Hosen der beiden Hauptfiguren lassen muskulösen Beinen, die kurzärmligen Trikots wohlgeformten Unterarmen freien Raum. Maradonas muskelgestählte Brust zeichnet sich unter dem Trikot deutlich ab. Die Männer sind fit, stark und sexy. Die ausgestreckten Zeigefinger im Bild lenken die Aufmerksamkeit des Publikums jeweils auf Maradona und Messi, aber erst das Publikum hat die Macht, die beiden in Helden zu verwandeln.

Heroisierende Medialisierungen sind kontrovers. Den einen wird der Fingerzeig zum Heldenbeweis, den anderen nicht. Nackte Haut kann im Allgemeinen als ein Symbol für heroische Nacktheit gelesen werden, Ekel hervorrufen oder völlig kalt lassen. Maradonas Körperkontakt mit nackten Männern kann manche daran er-

Vera Marstaller

MEDIALISATION

Gestures

Heroes are the result of a transformation. Only when an audience has become convinced of their extraordinary commitment and agency, when stories are told about how they crossed borders or how they fought bravely (against themselves or others); only then is it possible for heroes to act as one man's role model and another man's deterrent. For heroes to become heroes, their stories have to be told.[1] Be it in rousing speeches, artistic paintings, epic texts or gripping films – heroization needs to be communicated through media.

Medialisations are like demonstrative gestures. Like a finger pointing in a specific direction, they divert the perception of the audience from one thing and direct it towards another. Heroizations omit in order to emphasise. If, for example, an exclusively male form is chosen, heroes of other genders are not considered.[2] As demonstrative gestures, medialisations give instructions for (re)action, telling the viewer how the thing they depict should be understood and dealt with.

Body

Lionel Messi is in a reclining pose on the ground, his upper body slightly raised. His right leg is extended, the left one bent. His left arm rests on his left knee, and he is pointing forwards with his left index finger (Fig. 1). The tip of his finger almost touches the similarly extended index finger of Diego Maradona, who is floating opposite him in the air. Both are wearing Argentinian football jerseys. Nude players of the national football team surround Maradona, maintaining close physical contact. The two protagonists' legs are only partly covered by their shorts, revealing muscular legs, and their short-sleeved jerseys mean their wellshaped forearms are on show. Maradona's muscular chest is clearly visible beneath his jersey. The men are fit, strong and sexy. The extended index fingers in the painting direct the audience's attention to Maradona and Messi respectively, but it is the audience itself who has the power to turn these two figures into heroes.

Heroizing medialisations are controversial. To some, this kind of 'pointing finger' is proof of heroism – to others, it is not. Bare skin can be read as a symbol of heroic nudity, or cause disgust, or even cause no reaction at all. Maradona's physical contact with the nude men around him may remind some viewers of the fact

Abb. 1: Finger erschaffen Helden. Das Deckenkunstwerk in einer Trainingshalle des Sportvereins Sportivo Pereyra Club Barracas in Buenos Aires (2014) ist eine Adaption von Michelangelos Fresko »Die Erschaffung Adams«. Lässig liegt Lionel Messi gegenüber einer Gruppe weiterer argentinischer Fußballspieler, die sich um Diego Maradona scharen. Die abgebildeten Männer sind fit, stark und sexy. Die ausgestreckten Zeigefinger im Bild lenken die Aufmerksamkeit des Publikums jeweils auf Maradona und Messi und weisen beide als Helden aus.

Fig. 1: Fingers create heroes. This work of ceiling art in a training facility at the Sportivo Pereyra Club Barracas in Buenos Aires (2014) is an adaptation of Michelangelo's fresco "The Creation of Adam". Lionel Messi is casually seated opposite a group of Argentinian footballers gathered around Diego Maradona. The men depicted are fit, strong and sexy. The outstretched index fingers in the image draw the audience's attention to Maradona and Messi respectively and identify both as heroes.

innern, dass Homosexualität ein schwieriges Thema für den Fußball darstellt. Wer Bilder von Maradona kennt, weiß, dass im Deckengemälde seine äußere Erscheinung einem Ideal angepasst wurde, dem er selbst nicht entsprach. Diese Beschönigung kann seine Heroisierung verstärken – oder auch unglaubhaft werden lassen.

Die Art und Weise, in der Heroisierungen medialisiert werden, beeinflusst deren Überzeugungskraft. Das gilt auch für die bildliche Darstellung von Körpern, Gesten und Handlungen.[3] In Jacques-Louis Davids Gemäldeentwurf zum Ballhausschwur

Abb. 2: Hände erschaffen Helden. Zentrale Figur in Jacques-Louis Davids Gemäldeentwurf zum Ballhausschwur von 1791 ist Jean-Sylvain Bailly, Präsident der französischen Nationalversammlung, der mit erhobener rechter Hand den Schwur verliest. Wie in einer gemeinsamen Bewegung richten die um ihn herum gruppierten Abgeordneten ihre Schwurhände auf ihn. Der Künstler medialisiert Bailly als heroischen Anführer und zugleich alle mit ihm im Schwur Vereinten als heroisches Kollektiv.
Fig. 2: Hands create heroes. The central figure depicted in Jacques-Louis David's sketch of the Tennis Court Oath (1791) is Jean-Sylvain Bailly, President of the French National Assembly, who is reading out the oath with his right hand raised. As if in a united movement, the parliamentarians grouped around him direct their oath hands at him. The artist medialises Bailly as a heroic leader and, at the same time, all those united with him in the oath as a heroic collective.

that homosexuality is a difficult topic in football. Anyone who has seen pictures of Maradona knows that his physical appearance in the ceiling painting has been made to fit an ideal that he did not meet in real life. This beautification can augment a heroization – or make it seem less believable.

The way heroizations are medialised impacts their persuasiveness. This also holds true for the pictorial presentation of bodies, gestures and actions.[3] In Jacques-Louis David's sketch for the Tennis Court Oath, for example, Jean-Sylvain Bailly, President of the French National Constituent Assembly, is depicted standing slightly el-

MEDIALISATION

etwa ist Jean-Sylvain Bailly, der Präsident der französischen Nationalversammlung, erhöht in der Mitte stehend dargestellt, während er eine Hand zum Schwur erhoben hat (Abb. 2). Auch die um ihn herum gruppierten Abgeordneten beteiligen sich durch ihre Handbewegung an diesem Eid von historischer Bedeutung. Doch zeigt der Künstler die Mehrzahl der Anwesenden so, dass sie ihre Hände nicht nach oben, sondern Richtung Bailly ausstrecken. Wie beim Zeigefinger sind die Bewegungen der Hände Teil einer Medialisierung, die Bailly als Helden, aber mit ihm alle im Schwur Vereinten als heroisches Kollektiv präsentiert.[4]

Medien

Gemälde in Museen sprechen nicht alle Betrachter:innen gleichermaßen an. Im öffentlichen Raum errichtete Denkmäler, die seit der Antike ein beliebtes Medium für Heroisierungen sind, können wie ein Beiwerk im Park erscheinen und nur geringe Aufmerksamkeit erlangen. Sie können ebenso Wut und Denkmalsturz provozieren. Schiere Größe eines Mediums, etwa das ca. 500 m² umfassende Deckengemälde, das Messi und Maradona zeigt, oder der »Ballhausschwur«, der mit einer Größe von rund 100 m² zeitgenössisch gängige Maße eines Gemäldes übersteigen sollte, versinnbildlicht die Grenzüberschreitung der Helden. Auch Multimedialität überschreitet Grenzen: Nachdem Messi dazu beigetragen hatte, dass die argentinische Mannschaft 2022 Fußballweltmeister wurde, fanden Fotografien des acht Jahre zuvor entstandenen Deckengemäldes auf zahlreichen Social-Media-Kanälen Verbreitung und bezeugten Messis Heldenstatus. Anders gesagt: Unterschiedliche Medien erreichen verschiedene Publika zu verschiedenen Zeiten an verschiedenen Orten und entfalten unterschiedliche Wirkungen; Multimedialität kann Heroisierungen verstärken.

Untersicht, etwa in der Darstellung auf einem Deckengemälde, lässt Held:innen größer und das Publikum kleiner erscheinen. Doch Heroisches muss nicht zwangsläufig mit Größe verknüpft werden. Nationalsozialistische Propagandafotografien waren als Schnappschüsse auf Augenhöhe aufgenommen worden, um das Heldentum von Wehrmachtsangehörigen im Kriegseinsatz authentisch zu bezeugen (Abb. 3). Auch eine bescheiden wirkende Wahl von Material und Form kann heroische Lesarten aufrufen. Das »Memorial to Heroic Self-Sacrifice« im Londoner Postman's Park beispielsweise verankert Geschichten von Held:innen des Alltags, die Menschenleben gerettet haben, im öffentlichen Raum: Statt Statuen erinnern schlichte Gedenktafeln ohne Bildnisse an ›einfache‹ Menschen, die zu Held:innen wurden (Abb. 4). Wie wir von Held:innen erfahren, hängt auch davon ab, welche Medien genutzt werden.

»Kleidung, Schmuck, Insignien, Rüstungen und Prothesen«[5] können die Körper in etwas Neues verwandeln, z.B. in einen Heldenkörper, dessen Attribute als Wesensmerkmale deutbar sind. Verehrer:innen, die sich kleiden wie ihre Idole, tun

evated in the centre, one hand raised in oath (Fig. 2). The delegates grouped around him mirror his hand gesture and thus also participate in this historically significant oath. However, the artist has depicted the delegates in such a way that the majority have their hands outstretched towards Bailly rather than upwards. Like the footballers' index fingers, these hand gestures are part of a medialisation – one that presents Bailly as a hero and all those mirroring his oath as a heroic collective.[4]

Media

Paintings in museums do not appeal to all viewers equally. Monuments erected in public spaces, a popular medium for heroizations since antiquity, may appear like a mere embellishment to a park and attract little attention. Equally, they can incite anger and end up being toppled. The sheer size of a medium epitomises the way heroes themselves transgress boundaries – the over 500 m² ceiling painting showing Messi and Maradona, for example, and the around 100 m² Tennis Court Oath painting both exceed the dimensions common for a painting of their era. Multimediality, too, crosses boundaries: After Messi helped the Argentinian team win the 2022 FIFA World Cup, photographs of the ceiling painting, which had been made eight years earlier, gained widespread circulation on various social media channels, attesting to Messi's status as a hero. In other words: Different media appeal to different audiences in different locations and at different times, causing different effects; multimediality can enhance heroizations.

   A worm's eye view, such as is used in ceiling paintings, renders heroes larger and the audience smaller. But the heroic is not necessarily linked to size. National Socialist propaganda photographs were taken at eye level so as to authentically attest to the heroic bravery of Wehrmacht soldiers in war operations (Fig. 3). In a similar vein, a seemingly modest choice of material and shape can invoke heroic interpretations. The "Memorial to Heroic Self-Sacrifice" in Postman's Park in London, for example, embeds in a public space the stories of everyday heroes who saved lives. Instead of statues, simple memorial plaques remind viewers of 'ordinary' people who became heroes (Fig. 4). How we learn about heroes also depends on the sort of media used.

   "Clothing, jewellery, insignia, armour and prosthetics"[5] can turn the body into something new, for example into a heroic body whose attributes can be interpreted as characteristic features. Admirers who dress like their idols do so as a means of heroization and in order to recognise each other. Fans wearing football jerseys with Maradona's name on it keep their hero present and visible in everyday life, sharing in his greatness. Frida Kahlo, a 20th century Mexican painter, is considered a feminist hero by some. It is her fans' shared admiration for Kahlo that makes them feel

Abb. 3: Fotos erschaffen Helden. Angehörige der Propagandakompanien fotografierten den Kampf der Wehrmacht im Zweiten Weltkrieg. Sowohl der Wehrmacht als auch dem Reichsministerium für Volksaufklärung und Propaganda unterstellt, bestand ihre Aufgabe in der Heroisierung der deutschen Soldaten. Fotografisches Mittel waren Schnappschüsse auf Augenhöhe, die das Heldentum von Wehrmachtangehörigen im Kriegseinsatz authentisch bezeugen und zudem deutlich machen sollten: Die Fotografen befanden sich in derselben Situation wie die Fotografierten.

Fig. 3: Photos create heroes. Members of the Wehrmacht Propaganda Companies photographed Wehrmacht soldiers fighting in the Second World War. Reporting to both the Wehrmacht and the Reich Ministry for Public Enlightenment and Propaganda, their task was to heroize German soldiers. The photographic technique used was snapshots taken at eye level, which were intended to authentically bear witness to the heroism of Wehrmacht soldiers in the war effort and also make it clear that the photographers were in the same situation as the people being photographed.

dies als Mittel der Heroisierung und um sich gegenseitig zu erkennen. So halten Fans in Fußballtrikots mit Maradonas Namen ihren Helden im Alltag präsent und sichtbar und partizipieren an seiner Größe. Frida Kahlo, eine mexikanische Künstlerin des 20. Jahrhunderts, gilt für manche als feministische Heldin. In der gemeinsamen Verehrung für Kahlo fühlen sie sich zusammengehörig, stark und ›empowered‹. Das zeigen sie öffentlich, indem sie sich mit unverkennbaren Kahlo-Merkmalen zurechtmachen: zusammengewachsene Augenbrauen, Damenbart, Blumen im Haar und farbenfrohe Kleidung. Kahlo war nach einem Unfall auf ein Stützkorsett angewiesen. Ihr unbedingter Wille, Schmerz und Leiden nicht ihr Leben dominieren zu lassen, macht sie auch zu einer Identifikationsfigur für Menschen mit körperlichen Beeinträchtigungen (Abb. 5 und 6).

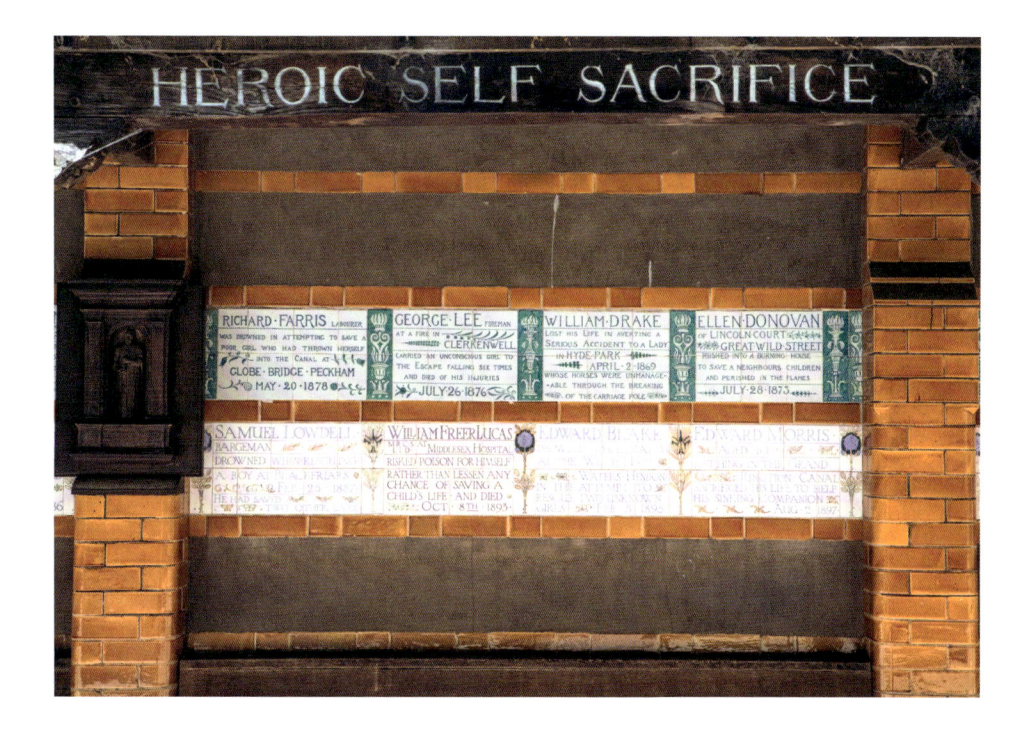

Abb. 4: Keramiktafeln erschaffen Held:innen. Auch eine bescheiden wirkende Wahl von Material und Form kann heroische Lesarten aufrufen. Das »Memorial to Heroic Self-Sacrifice« (1900) im Londoner Postman's Park verankert Geschichten von Held:innen des Alltags im öffentlichen Raum: Statt Statuen erinnern schlichte Gedenktafeln ohne Bildnisse an »einfache« Menschen, die beim Versuch starben, andere zu retten.

Fig. 4: Ceramic plaques create heroes. Even a seemingly modest choice of material and design can evoke heroic interpretations. The "Memorial to Heroic Self-Sacrifice" (1900) in London's Postman's Park anchors stories of everyday heroes and heroines within a public space. Instead of statues, simple memorial plaques without any portraits commemorate "ordinary" people who died trying to save others.

connected, strong and empowered. They show this publicly by styling themselves with distinctive Kahlo features: monobrow, facial hair, flowers in their hair and colourful clothing. Kahlo was forced to wear a support corset following an accident. Her absolute determination not to let pain and suffering dominate her life still makes her a positive role model for people with physical impairments today (Fig. 5 and 6).

Abb. 5: Bunte Kleidung und Blumen im Haar erschaffen die Heldin. Anlässlich des 110. Geburtstags der mexikanischen Künstlerin Frida Kahlo rief das Dallas Museum of Art 2017 dazu auf, sich als Frida zu verkleiden. Rund 1.000 Frida-Kahlo-Fans erschienen mit unverkennbaren Merkmalen: zusammengewachsene Augenbrauen, Damenbart, Blumen im Haar und farbenfrohe Kleidung. Ihre gemeinsame Verehrung für die Identifikationsfigur Kahlo trug auch dazu bei, sich zusammengehörig, stark und »empowered« zu fühlen.

Fig. 5: Colourful clothes and flowery hairpieces create the heroine. To mark what would have been Mexican artist Frida Kahlo's 110th birthday in 2017, the Dallas Museum of Art called upon the public to dress up as Frida. Around 1,000 Frida Kahlo fans turned up with unmistakable characteristics: unibrows, lady beards, flowers in their hair and colourful clothing. Their shared admiration for Kahlo as a figure of identity also helped them feel a sense of belonging, strength and empowerment.

Orte

Neben der Multimedialität versinnbildlicht Multimodalität heroische Grenzüberschreitung. Multimodalität meint das sinnstiftende Zusammenspiel verschiedener Kanäle, etwa, wenn Schriftgröße und Wort gemeinsam die Bedeutung formen – und damit die Grenzen einzelner Kanäle überschritten werden.[6] Orte, an denen die medialen Vermittlungen des Heroischen statthaben, tragen zu Multimodalitäten bei. Das gilt für Publikationsorte (etwa Fotografien innerhalb einer Biografie) oder für geografische Orte (etwa eine Prachtstraße in einer Stadt oder der Küchentisch zu Hause). Orte sind zeitgebunden: Zeitungen erscheinen an konkreten Tagen; Denkmäler bleiben für einen längeren Zeitraum, können aber auch genau deswegen an Aufmerksamkeit verlieren. Das Deckengemälde von Messi und Maradona ist alltäglich in der Turnhalle des Sportivo Pereyra Clubs Barracas in Buenos Aires zu sehen (Abb. 7). Indem der Künstler Michelangelos Fresko »Die Erschaffung Adams« in der Sixtinischen Kapelle zitiert (Abb. 8), wird die Sporthalle sinnbildhaft zu einem heiligen Fußballtempel, in dem diejenigen, die unter den Augen ihrer Helden trainieren, sich inspiriert fühlen und darauf hoffen können, irgendwann selbst in das Heldenpantheon aufgenommen zu werden.

Durch das Zusammenspiel verschiedener Zeiten und Orte können Medialisierungen Spaß und Ernst vereinen: Dass Maradonas Hand mit der Hand Gottes gleichgesetzt wird, hat für das Publikum auch eine unterhaltsame Seite. Schließlich sei

Abb. 6: Superman erschafft die Heldin – und Frida Kahlo erschafft Superwoman. In Memes werden bereits bekannte Bilder mit anderen visuellen Anteilen versehen, um damit neue Bedeutung zu generieren. Auch in diesem Graffito verweist das von Superman bekannte »S« auf Frida Kahlos Oberteil, dass sie nicht nur Vorbild, sondern auch Heldin ist. Doch auch das Bildnis von Kahlo verändert die Bedeutung des »S« – das damit weniger für Superman, eher für Superwoman steht. Kahlos Mimik ahmt das Zwinker-Smiley nach, das in Nachrichten auf Social Media auch eine sexualisierte Konnotation hat – und schafft damit eine intime, auch erotische Nähe zu den Betrachter:innen.

Fig. 6: Superman creates the heroine – and Frida Kahlo creates the superwoman. Memes add different visual elements to familiar images in order to create new meanings. In this graffito, the "S" on Frida Kahlo's top, familiar from Superman, indicates that she is not only a role model but also a heroine. Conversely, the portrait of Kahlo also changes the meaning of the "S" – it now stands less for Superman and more for Superwoman. Kahlo's facial expressions mimic the winking smiley emoji, which can also convey sexual connotations in messages on social media – and thus creates an intimate, erotic closeness with the viewer.

Places

The heroic transgression of boundaries is epitomised not only by multimediality, but also by multimodality. Multimodality is the meaningful synergy of different channels of representation, for example when font size and words together form a meaning, thus crossing the boundaries of individual channels.[6] The places where the heroic is imparted contribute to multimodality. This can apply to publication contexts (e.g. photographs in a biography) or to geographical places (e.g. a boulevard in a city or the kitchen table at home). Places are tied to a particular time: Newspapers are published on specific days; monuments may remain in place for a longer period but may therefore also cease to attract attention. The ceiling painting of Messi and Maradona can be seen every day in the sports hall of the Sportivo Pereyra Club Barracas in Buenos Aires (Fig. 7). By referencing Michelangelo's fresco "The Creation of Adam" in the Sistine Chapel (Fig. 8), the sports hall becomes, symbolically, a holy football temple. Those who train under the eyes of their heroes will feel inspired and hope to be included themselves in the heroes' pantheon one day.

By combining different times and places, medialisations can also unite fun and seriousness. For the audience, there is an entertaining aspect to the fact that Maradona's hand is put in equivalence with the hand of god. After all, according to Mara-

Abb. 7: Ein Sportverein erschafft den Helden. Indem das Deckengemälde Michelangelos Fresko »Die Erschaffung Adams« in der Sixtinischen Kapelle zitiert, wird die Sporthalle sinnbildhaft zu einem heiligen Ort des Fußballs. Diejenigen, die unter den Augen ihrer Helden trainieren, können sich inspiriert fühlen und darauf hoffen, irgendwann selbst in den Heldenhimmel aufgenommen zu werden.

Fig. 7: A Sport Club creates the hero. By referencing Michelangelo's fresco "The Creation of Adam" in the Sistine Chapel, this ceiling painting symbolises the sport facility as a sacred place for football. Those who train under the eyes of their heroes can feel inspired and hope to be accepted into "hero heaven" themselves one day.

nach Maradonas Aussagen das Tor, mit dem er per Handspiel 1986 die argentinische Mannschaft zum 2:1-Sieg gegen Großbritannien und letztlich zur Weltmeisterschaft geführt hatte, zur Hälfte seinem eigenen Kopf und zur Hälfte der »Hand Gottes« zu verdanken gewesen.[7] Später fügte er hinzu, es sei als Rache an Großbritannien zu verstehen angesichts der militärischen Auseinandersetzung, die beide Nationen vier Jahre zuvor um die Falkland- bzw. Malvinas-Inseln geführt hatten. Mit dieser Politisierung stellte Maradona sich selbst als ausführende Gewalt göttlicher Macht und damit den Sieg im Fußballspiel als (gottgewollte) Rache für die zahlreichen Toten dar.[8]

Maradonas sprichwörtlich gewordene »Hand Gottes« kann also als Verweis auf die Kolonialisierung und die Unabhängigkeitskämpfe in Lateinamerika und auch insofern als Sieges- und Machtgeste gelesen werden. Austragungsort des Fußballspiels, an dem die »Hand Gottes« zum Einsatz kam, war das Estadio Azteca ge-

Abb. 8: Die Hand Gottes erschafft den Menschen. Michelangelos Fresko »Die Erschaffung Adams«, um 1511 (der Titel stammt allerdings von Giorgio Vasari), in der Sixtinischen Kapelle im Vatikan ist eines der meistreproduzierten Kunstwerke. Im Fingerzeig von Gott auf Adam ist ein Teil der biblischen Schöpfungsgeschichte visualisiert.
Fig. 8: The hand of God creates man. Michelangelo's fresco "The Creation of Adam", ca. 1511 (the title was actually coined by Giorgio Vasari), in the Sistine Chapel in the Vatican is one of the world's most reproduced works of art. Part of the biblical story of Genesis is visualised by God pointing his finger at Adam.

dona, the goal with which he led the Argentine team to a 2:1 victory over Britain in 1986, ultimately winning the World Cup, was thanks half to his own head and half to the "Hand of God".[7] He later added that it was to be understood as an act of revenge exacted on Great Britain in light of the military conflict between the two nations over the Falkland Islands respectively Malvinas four years earlier. Through this politicisation, Maradona presents himself as a power executing God's will, and the victory in the game of football as (God-ordained) revenge for the numerous dead.[8]

The proverbial "Hand of God" of Maradona can also be interpreted as a reference to colonialisation and to the fights for independences in Latin America, and, thus, as a gesture of victory and power. The venue of the game that saw the "Hand of God" in action was the Estadio Azteca, whose name commemorates the inhabitants of Mexico prior to the arrival of the Europeans. The stadium is located in the Coyoacán district of Mexico City. Coyoacán is also where Frida Kahlo was born. At the time of the Football World Cup, public adoration of Kahlo had become something of a

wesen, dessen Name an die Einwohner:innen Mexikos vor der Ankunft der Europäer erinnert. Das Stadion liegt im Stadtteil Coyoacán von Mexiko-Stadt. Coyoacán wiederum ist auch der Geburtsort von Frida Kahlo. Ihre Verehrung war zur Zeit der Fußball-Weltmeisterschaft unter anderem durch eine 1983 erschienene Biografie von Hayden Herrera weltweit zu einer regelrechten Fridomanía angewachsen. Im Vordergrund standen Kahlos Zerrissenheit zwischen einer europäischen und einer indigenen Herkunft. Für Feministinnen stand Kahlo zudem für den Kampf gegen geschlechtsspezifische Gewalt, der sie selbst ausgesetzt gewesen war, und den Widerstand gegen Heteronormativität, der sie aufgrund ihres Aussehens und ihrer Affären mit Frauen nicht entsprochen hatte. Geschlechterbezogene Gewalt und binäre Geschlechterordnung sind heute wiederum Themen der politischen Aufklärung, die geschlechtsspezifische Gewalt in Lateinamerika als Resultat des europäischen Kolonialismus analysiert[9] – deutlich etwa in westlichen Medialisierungen, die das Heroische mit männlicher Eroberungskraft und entjungfernder Maskulinität assoziierten.[10] In Bezug auf sexualisierte Gewalt verkörpert Diego Maradona genau diese Seite: Im Zuge der #MeToo-Debatte wurden 2020 Vorwürfe publiziert, er habe sich der Vergewaltigung und des Menschenhandels schuldig gemacht. Und wie die Fridomanía und Coyoacán hat somit auch die #MeToo-Debatte ihren Anteil an seiner (De-)Heroisierung.

Urheber:innen

In mediale Vermittlungen sind die Positionen ihrer Urheber:inen mit eingeschrieben. Mit dem Philosophen Michel Foucault lässt sich auf dieser Ebene fragen: Wer spricht und bürgt für die Glaubwürdigkeit heroisierender Medialisierungen?[11] Während des Zweiten Weltkrieges heroisierte die deutsche Kriegsberichterstattung auch die Kriegsberichterstatter selbst, da im Sinne der Propaganda nur echte Helden von echten Helden berichten könnten. Claus Schenk Graf von Stauffenberg, Ausführender des Attentats auf Adolf Hitler am 20. Juli 1944, war in den Worten Hitlers ein Verräter. Für die 1955 gegründete Bundeswehr wurde Stauffenbergs Handeln zum Vorbild für das Prinzip der Inneren Führung, das der Gewissenstreue des »Staatsbürgers in Uniform« Vorrang vor einem geleisteten Eid verleiht, sofern ein Befehl verbrecherisch ist oder gegen die Menschenwürde verstößt (Abb. 9). Mit der Heroisierung Stauffenbergs war die Möglichkeit verbunden, sich von der nationalsozialistischen Vergangenheit abzugrenzen. Der Sportverein Sportivo Pereyra Club Barracas bezieht sich in seinen Social-Media-Accounts auf aktuelle soziale Bewegungen in Argentinien.[12] Dazu gehören feministische Kämpfe gegen geschlechtsspezifische Gewalt genauso wie dekolonial-politisch motivierte Erinnerungen an die Kolonialgeschichte Argentiniens. Das Maradona und Messi zei-

world-wide Fridomania, partly thanks to a 1983 biography by Hayden Herrera. The biography focussed on Kahlo's inner strife between her European and her indigenous origins. For feminists, Kahlo also represented the fight against gender-based violence, which she herself had experienced, and resistance of heteronormativity, a concept she did not conform to, as evidenced by her appearance and her romances with women. Today, gender-based violence and the gender binary are again topics of political enlightenment, which analyses gender-based violence in Latin America as a result of European colonialism[9] – evident, for example, in western medialisations which associate the heroic with male power and conquering, and a specific type of deflowering masculinity.[10] With reference to sexual violence, Maradona embodies exactly this aspect: In the context of the #MeToo debate, allegations of rape and human trafficking were raised against him in 2020. And thus, the #MeToo debate, too, plays a part in his (de-)heroization – as do Fridomania and Coyoacán.

Authors

The way something is presented in the media always reveals something about the position of the author. In this aspect, one can ask with the philosopher Michel Foucault: Who speaks and therefore vouches for the credibility of heroizing medialisations?[11] During World War II, German war reporting heroized the war correspondents themselves because – in keeping with propaganda statements – only true heroes could report on true heroes. According to Hitler, Claus Schenk Graf von Stauffenberg, the man who attempted to assassinate Adolf Hitler on 20 July 1944, was a traitor. For the Bundeswehr, established in 1955, the actions of Stauffenberg, however, became the model for their principles of leadership development and civic education, according to which the moral conscience of a "citizen in uniform" takes precedence over the sworn oath when an order is criminal or violates human dignity (Fig. 9). The heroization of Stauffenberg offered an opportunity to distance oneself from the Nazi past. In its social media accounts, the Sportivo Pereyra Club Barracas references current social movements in Argentina,[12] among them the feminist fights against gender-specific violence as well as decolonial politically motivated reminders of the colonial history of Argentina. The ceiling painting showing Maradona and Messi serves as the club's profile picture. In this way, decolonialisation is once again linked to the heroization of Maradona, but this time, also to the resistance against gender-based violence – which hides Maradona's violent side.

gende Deckengemälde erscheint als Startprofilbild. So wird erneut das Thema Dekolonialisierung mit der Heroisierung von Maradona verknüpft, diesmal aber auch der Widerstand gegen geschlechterbasierte Gewalt – wodurch Maradonas gewalttätige Seite ausgeblendet wird.

Praktiken

Mit Medialisierungen sind Praktiken verbunden. Dies betrifft nicht nur die Produktion und Rezeption. In Neapel beispielsweise können massenhaft Magnete eines »Santo Diego« als Souvenir für Kühlschränke gekauft werden. Auch die Bezeichnung »Fußballgott« verleiht der Michelangelo-Adaption Glaubwürdigkeit. Beides versetzt den Fußballspieler in göttliche Sphären. Durch den Zustand, gleichzeitig Teil der sozialen Ordnung zu sein wie auch aus ihr herauszuragen, sind Held:innen nah und fern zugleich. In der Verbindung zu ihnen können auch ihre Verehrer:innen einen Zugang zu entfernten Sphären, etwa dem Göttlichen, empfinden. Wie die Held:innen selbst sind Verehrer:innen das Resultat eines Verwandlungsprozesses: Durch Verehrungsrituale verwandeln sie sich zu einer Art Glaubensgemeinschaft.

Doch wer einmal Held war, kann schnell fallen. Das gilt in der Postmoderne zum Beispiel für Eroberer und Konquistadoren. Ihre Statuen werden gestürzt und die nach ihnen benannten Straßen umbenannt – letztlich ist auch die Entfernung heroisierender Medialisierungen eine Form der Medialisierung. In vielen Fällen von Denkmalstürzen und Straßenumbenennungen werden neue Denkmäler errichtet, neue Straßennamen verwendet und die alten Held:innen durch neue ersetzt. Die Attraktionskraft dieser neuen Heroisierungen kann sich verstärken, indem bekannte Formen beibehalten, aber unter neuen Vorzeichen eingesetzt werden. Doch auch hier gilt: Das Publikum macht die Held:innen.

Publikum

Heroische Medialisierung präsentiert Menschen und Figuren so, dass sie für ein Publikum zu Held:innen werden können. »Held:in« ist damit ein Wort, das Beziehungen bezeichnet. Der Begriff »Medialisierung« bezieht sich auf Handlungszusammenhänge, an deren Ende erst Menschen zu Held:innen werden, indem sie in Relation zu einem Publikum, seinen Werten und Überzeugungen stehen. Diese Handlungen vollziehen Menschen, die an einem spezifischen Ort zu einer spezifischen Zeit leb(t)en. Wer wen wie, wann, warum, wo und wozu heroisiert, was ausgelassen und worüber und über wen geschwiegen wird, ist in die Heroisierungen mit eingeschrieben. Wird von Held:innen vor allem dann erzählt, wenn sie in be-

Abb. 9: Soldaten erschaffen den Helden. Im Hof des Berliner Bendlerblocks wurden Oberst Claus Schenk Graf von Stauffenberg und andere Beteiligte des Attentatversuchs auf Adolf Hitler noch in der Nacht des 20. Juli 1944 hingerichtet. Das Gedenken am Ehrenmal gehört heute zur Traditionspflege der Bundeswehr.

Fig. 9: Soldiers create the hero. In the Bendlerblock courtyard in Berlin, Colonel Claus Schenk Graf von Stauffenberg and others involved in the attempted assassination of Adolf Hitler were executed on the night of 20 July 1944. Today, commemoration at the memorial is part of the Bundeswehr's "Traditionspflege" (cultivating of tradition).

Practices

Medialisations are linked to practices. This applies not only to production and reception. In Naples, for example, you can buy an array of fridge magnets of "Santo Diego" as souvenirs. Likewise, the designation "God of Football" lends credibility to the Michelangelo adaptation. Both lift the footballer into heavenly spheres. The state of being part of the social order and simultaneously standing out of it makes heroes appear close and yet far away. It is in the veneration of them that admirers themselves can find access to remote spheres, such as the divine. Like their heroes, the admirers are the result of a process of transformation. Rituals of veneration turn them into a sort of religious community.

sonderem Maße maskulin, agil, erotisch, attraktiv, stark und also echte Muskelpakete, vielleicht weiß, heterosexuell und nicht BIPoC sind? Wenn das Publikum entscheidet, wer Held:in ist und wer nicht, dann liegt die Antwort auf diese Frage vor allem bei denjenigen, denen von Held:innen erzählt wird.

Anmerkungen

1 Sonderforschungsbereich 948 2019b.
2 Vgl. Mommertz 2015.
3 Feitscher 2019; zu den Gesten vgl. Marstaller und Safaian 2023, 3-7.
4 Vgl. Gölz 2019a, 8.
5 Feitscher 2019.
6 Ruchatz 2023, 117.
7 Achilles 2006.
8 Maradona 2007, 127-128.
9 Lugones 2010.
10 Hemkendreis 2023.
11 Foucault 1988, 7.
12 Twitter-Account von »Sportivo Peyrera«, URL: twitter.com/sportivopereyra?lang=de, etwa twitter.com/SportivoPereyra/status/1545806330035838978/photo/1 und twitter.com/SportivoPereyra/status/1501231841415548928/photo/1 [31. Mai 2023].

But he who was once a hero can fall quickly. In postmodernism, this applies to conquerors and conquistadors. Their statues are being toppled, streets named in their honour are being renamed – ultimately, even the removal of heroizing medialisations is a form of medialisation. In many cases where statues are toppled and streets are renamed, new statues are erected and new street names are used – and the old heroes are replaced by new ones. The force of attraction of these new heroizations can become more intense when known forms are maintained but used under new circumstances. However, the truth is: It is the audience who makes a hero.

Audience

Heroic medialisation presents humans and figures in such a way that they can become heroes for an audience. Thus, "hero" is a word that denotes a relationship. The term "medialisation" refers to correlations of actions, only at the end of which do human beings become heroes by being related to the audience, its values and convictions. These actions are performed by humans who (have) lived in a specific place at a specific time. Who was heroized by whom, where, why, how and into what, what was ignored and who or what has been left unmentioned, is inherent in the heroization. Are heroes primarily talked about if they are particularly masculine, agile, erotic, attractive, strong and therefore real musclemen, possibly white, heterosexual and not black, indigenous, or a person of colour? If it is the audience who decides who is a hero and who is not, then the answer to that question primarily rests with those who are told about heroes.

Notes

1   Sonderforschungsbereich 948 2019b.
2   Cf. Mommertz 2015.
3   Feitscher 2019; for gestures cf. Marstaller and Safaian 2023, 3-7.
4   Cf. Gölz 2019a, 8.
5   Feitscher 2019.
6   Ruchatz 2023, 117.
7   Achilles 2006.
8   Maradona 2007, 127-128.
9   Lugones 2010.
10 Hemkendreis 2023.
11 Foucault 1988, 7.
12 Twitter account of "Sportivo Peyrera", URL: twitter.com/sportivopereyra?lang=de, etwa twitter.com/SportivoPereyra/status/1545806330035838978/photo/1 and twitter.com/SportivoPereyra/status/1501231841415548928/photo/1 [last accessed on 31 May 2023].

© 2024 Vera Marstaller, Publikation: Wallstein Verlag; DOI https://doi.org/10.46500/83535581-004 | CC BY-NC-ND 4.0

Johanna Pink

POLARISIERUNG

»Putin – ein Held dieser Zeit« titelte die ägyptische staatliche Zeitung *al-Ahrām* anlässlich des Staatsbesuchs des russischen Präsidenten im Februar 2015, illustriert unter anderem mit einem Bild, das Vladimir Putin mit nacktem Oberkörper und einem Gewehr in der Hand präsentierte.[1] Die Berichterstattung, die Putin als geradlinigen und aufrechten Kämpfer für russische Interessen, gegen tschetschenische Terroristen und »mehrheitlich jüdische« Oligarchen präsentierte, war sicher nicht frei von kurzfristigen Hoffnungen auf russische Investitionen, aber sie spiegelte auch eine Tendenz wider, die bis heute Medien und öffentliche Meinung in der islamischen Welt und vielen weiteren Ländern außerhalb des »globalen Nordens« prägt. »Starke Männer« wie Putin oder auch der türkische Präsident Recep Tayyip Erdoğan, die als Gegner der Vereinigten Staaten und/oder der Europäischen Union gelten, werden dort nicht selten als Helden wahrgenommen, als diejenigen, die »dem Westen« die Stirn bieten: Es ist gerade ihr Potenzial zur Polarisierung, das Verehrung auslöst (Abb. 1). Diese Verehrung – die recht losgelöst von ihrem tatsächlichen politischen Handeln ist – ist nicht nur unabhängig davon, wieviel Kritik diese Personen in europäischen und amerikanischen Medien erfahren, sondern diese Ablehnung durch die Gegenseite oder das, was als solche wahrgenommen wird, steigert die Heroisierung eher noch. In einer Freund-Feind-Erzählung, die Gut und Böse klar unterscheidbar macht, ist des einen Feind nicht nur des anderen Freund, sondern gar des anderen Held.

Warum polarisieren Held:innen?

Dieses Beispiel verweist auf einen allgemeineren Befund, der sich an zahllosen anderen Beispielen von Greta Thunberg bis Osama bin Laden festmachen lässt: Held:innen polarisieren. Sie polarisieren, weil sie in einem bereits polarisierten Kontext – der nicht selten eine Vorbedingung dafür ist, dass sie überhaupt heroisiert werden – spezifische Werte symbolisieren oder eine bestimmte Gemeinschaft repräsentieren (Abb. 2 und 3). Sobald die Grenzen dieser Gemeinschaft verlassen werden und sobald wir es mit Menschen zu tun haben, die diese Werte nicht teilen, kehrt sich die Heroisierung schnell in ihr Gegenteil um. Soldaten für ihren Kampf um die Nation zu ehren, kann zum Beispiel nur funktionieren, wenn sowohl der bewaffnete Kampf als auch die betreffende Nation mit recht großer Einhelligkeit positiv besetzt sind. Dass dies keine Zwangsläufigkeit besitzt, kann man an der

Johanna Pink

POLARISATION

Egypt's *al-Ahrām* state newspaper ran a full-page article headlined "Putin – a hero of our time" on the occasion of the Russian president's state visit there in February 2015. It was illustrated with a picture of a bare-chested Vladimir Putin, rifle in hand, among other images.[1] The coverage, portraying Putin as a straightforward, upright defender of Russian interests and fighter against Chechen terrorists and "mostly Jewish" oligarchs, was almost certainly written partly in the hope of attracting Russian investment in the near future. But it also reflected a tendency that remains strong in media and public opinion in the Islamic world and many other countries outside the 'Global North': 'Strongmen' such as Putin and the Turkish president Recep Tayyip Erdoğan, who are considered opponents of the United States and/or the European Union, are often perceived as heroes in these countries because they confront the West. It is precisely their ability to polarise that earns them admiration (Fig. 1). This admiration – which is quite detached from their actual political activities – not only remains unaffected by the amount of criticism they receive in European and US media, it is in fact intensified by it. The rejection of a hero figure by the opposing side (or what is perceived to be the opposing side) actually strengthens the degree of heroization. In a 'friend or foe' narrative that enables a clear distinction between good and evil, one person's enemy is not just another person's friend, but even their hero.

Abb. 1: Kaffeebecher als politisches Statement und Form der Heroisierung: die Allianz der »Starken Männer«. Porträts des russischen Präsidenten Putin, des syrischen Präsidenten al-Assad und des Hisbollah-Führers Nasrallah in einem Souvenirladen in der syrischen Hauptstadt Damaskus, Februar 2022.
Fig. 1: Coffee mugs representing a political statement and a form of heroization: An alliance of "strong men". This picture shows coffee mugs bearing images of Russian President Putin, Syrian President al-Assad and Hezbollah leader Nasrallah in a souvenir store in the Syrian capital of Damascus, February 2022.

Abb. 2: Öffentlicher Protest verstärkt die Polarisierung innerhalb einer ohnehin als polarisiert empfundenen Situation. Hier blockieren Protestierende eine der Hauptverkehrsstraßen von Manchester in ihrer Forderung nach mehr Klimaschutz. Die Heroisierung Greta Thunbergs trägt zur Gemeinschaftsstiftung bei. Ein Plakat zeigt die Klimaaktivistin als Heiligen Franziskus.
Fig. 2: A public protest increases polarisation in a situation that is already perceived to be very polarised. In this photo, protesters are blocking one of Manchester's main thoroughfares, demanding more climate protection. The heroization of Greta Thunberg continues to contribute to a communal cause. One poster has even replaced an image of St Francis with "St Greta".

Skepsis gegenüber Militarismus und Flaggen sehen, die sich in der jungen Bundesrepublik, vor allem im Zuge der 68er-Bewegung, einstellte. Ebenso sind Klimaaktivist:innen nur für diejenigen heroisierbar, die den Klimawandel als Tatsache akzeptieren und den Kampf gegen ihn als drängend empfinden. Für alle anderen sind sie bestenfalls Störenfriede, die die Schule schwänzen oder, schlimmer noch, den Weg zur Arbeit blockieren. In dem Maße, wie Held:innen Identifikationsfiguren einer Verehrer:innengemeinschaft sind, verfügen sie über das Potenzial, außerhalb dieser Gemeinschaft lächerlich gemacht, angegriffen oder gar dämonisiert zu werden. Und in dem Maße, in dem sie von außen angegriffen werden, können sie – zum Beispiel über Opfererzählungen – wiederum die Verehrer:innengemeinschaft stärken und einen.

Heroisierung benötigt ein Gegenüber. Denn Held:innen gelingt es in den seltensten Fällen, Werte oder Errungenschaften zu repräsentieren, die so universell sind, dass sie von nahezu allen geteilt werden. Sie werden zu Held:innen, weil sie – real oder imaginiert – einem »Feind die Stirn bieten«, ob dieser Feind nun durch Mineralölkonzerne, eine gegnerische Armee, einen personalisierten Widersacher, eine Epidemie, die »letzte Grenze« des Weltalls oder »den Westen« als globale Hegemonialmacht repräsentiert wird (Abb. 4). Damit lädt der/die Held:in all diejenigen, die sich demselben Feind gegenübersehen, zur Solidarisierung und in der Folge zur Verehrung ein – was erklärt, warum sich so viele Menschen in der islamischen Welt mit Putin und nicht etwa den muslimischen Tschetschen:innen identifizieren, denn sie betrachten ihn als Gegner eines gemeinsamen Feindes, zum Beispiel der USA oder der NATO. Allerdings schlägt die Heroisierung bei all jenen, die der vermeintlichen oder tatsächlichen Gegenseite zugehören, leicht in ihr Gegenteil um: Tschetschen:innen sind weniger empfänglich für die Heroisierung Putins als die Menschen im weit ent-

Why do heroes polarise?

This example refers to a more general finding that applies to countless other examples, from Greta Thunberg to Osama bin Laden: heroes polarise. They polarise because they symbolise specific values or represent a specific community in an already polarised context – which is often a prerequisite for their being heroized in the first place (Fig. 2 and 3). As soon as we leave this community and ask individuals who do not share these values, the heroization is quickly reversed. Honouring soldiers for their selfless struggle for their nation, for instance, only works if both the armed conflict and the respective nation are widely positively connotated. The scepticism toward militarism and national flags in the early days of the Federal Republic of Germany, especially during the movement of 1968, shows that this is not always the case. Similarly, climate activists can only be heroized by those who accept climate change as a fact and feel that the fight against it is urgent. For everyone else, they are – at best – troublemakers who are skipping school or, worse still, blocking commuter traffic. Heroes that act as role models for a community of admirers equally have the potential to be ridiculed, attacked or even demonised outside this community. And as they are attacked from the outside, they can strengthen and unite their community of admirers accordingly, for instance through victim narratives.

 A heroization requires an opponent. Heroes are rarely able to represent values or achievements so universal that they are shared by almost everyone. They become heroes because they – either in reality or in the imagination of their admirers – 'con-

Abb. 3: Je größer die Heroisierung auf der einen Seite, desto größer oft der Hass auf der anderen. Er zielt nicht selten auf eine Verächtlichmachung der von anderen verehrten Personen ab. Dieser Instagram-Post von Dezember 2019 vergleicht Greta Thunberg mit einem Ork und bezeichnet sie als »Klimakobold« (»climate goblin«).

Fig. 3: The greater the heroization of an individual on one side, the greater the hostility from the other. This hostility is often aimed at belittling people revered by others. In this Instagram post from December 2019, Greta Thunberg is compared to an orc and referred to as a "climate goblin".

fernten Ägypten; umgekehrt kann Distanz Heroisierungen vereinfachen. Die polarisierende Wirkung von Held:innen ist somit auch eine Frage der Perspektive, und ein Perspektivwechsel kann erhellend sein.

Eroberer, Schlächter, Opfer

Für Perspektivwechsel bietet sich die Figur Dschingis Khans (gest. um 1227) an. Mit Bezug auf das Territorium, das er unter seine Kontrolle brachte, war er einer der größten Eroberer der Menschheitsgeschichte. Gleichzeitig ist er vor allem in der Geschichtsschreibung Europas, das den Mongolen notorisch unterlegen war, als grausamer Schlächter verewigt. Und noch im Februar 2023 nutzte ein Abgeordneter aus Colorado diesen Mythos, um gegen das Fehlen eines Abtreibungsverbots zu polemisieren: Die Barbarei Dschingis Khans sei nichts gegen die Barbarei massenhafter Abtreibungen.[2] Wie auch immer man zu dieser politischen Instrumentalisierung von Geschichtsmythen steht – das Bild Dschingis Khans als Massen-

Abb. 4: Gemeinschaften gründen sich auf gemeinsame Werte oder Errungenschaften – oder auch, wie diese Karikatur von 2019 andeutet, auf das gemeinsame demonstrative Nicht-Teilen von Werten, die die Gegenseite für existenziell und unveräußerlich hält.

Fig. 4: Communities are based on shared values or achievements – or, as this 2019 cartoon suggests, on the common occurrence of not sharing values that the other side considers existential and inalienable. [Cartoon: "No way! Human Rights Day just happens to fall on "Saint Whosie-Whatsit's Day"! (Suggesting that these politicians disregard human rights so much that they don't even make the effort to pretend to acknowledge Human Rights Day.)]

mörder ist nicht unberechtigt, denn die Eroberungszüge, die ihn zum Herrscher eines riesigen Reiches machten, forderten zahllose Opfer.

Die Erinnerung an Dschingis Khan wurde und wird bis heute weitgehend dadurch bestimmt, welche der beiden Perspektiven auf sein Wirken im Fokus steht: die der Eroberung oder die der Opfer. In Zentralasien galt Dschingis Khan über Jahrhunderte als Vorbild, und als sich einige Generationen nach ihm Timur (1336-1405) erneut zum Herrscher eines riesigen Reiches machte, das sich von Indien bis Anatolien erstreckte, legitimierte er sich über die Einheirat in Dschingis Khans Abstammungslinie. Noch die Dynastie der Moguln, die von Timur abstammten und vom 16. bis 18. Jahrhundert über weite Teile Indiens herrschten, bezeichnete sich als »Gurkani«-Dynastie – die Dynastie der »Schwiegersöhne«.[3] Dies ist die Per-

front an enemy'. Whether the enemy is oil companies, a foreign army, a personal adversary, an epidemic, the 'final frontier' of the universe, or 'the West' as a global hegemonic power, the important thing is its role as the hero's opponent (Fig. 4). It allows the hero to invite all those who see themselves as facing the same enemy to express their solidarity and therefore their admiration. This explains why so many people in the Islamic world support Putin rather than the Muslim Chechens because they see him as the opponent of a common enemy, e. g. the United States and NATO. However, for all those who belong to the hero's alleged or actual opponent's side, heroization can easily incite opposite emotions. Chechens are less likely to heroize Putin than people in far-away Egypt, which shows that distance can facilitate heroization. The polarising effect of heroes is therefore also a question of perspective, and a change of perspective can be enlightening.

Conquerors, butchers, victims

The figure of Genghis Khan (deceased circa 1227) provides a good example of how heroization is subject to changing perspectives. In terms of the territory he acquired for his empire, he was one of the greatest conquerors in human history. But he has also been immortalised as a cruel butcher, especially in the historiography of Europe, the continent which the Mongols so famously defeated. In February 2023, a Congressman from Colorado used this myth to polemicise against the lack of an abortion ban, by stating that the barbarism of Genghis Khan was nothing compared to the barbarism of mass abortion.[2] Irrespective of how one sees this political instrumentalisation of historical myths, the image of Genghis Khan as a mass murderer is not unwarranted; the conquests that made him ruler of a huge empire claimed countless victims.

To this day, the memory of Genghis Khan has been largely determined by two differing views: The view from the perspective of the conquerors, and the view from the perspective of the victims. In Central Asia, Genghis Khan was considered a role model for centuries. Several generations later, when Timur (1336–1405) became the ruler of a huge empire extending from India to Anatolia, he sought legitimacy partly through marrying into Genghis Khan's line of descent. Even the Mughal dynasty, which was descended from Timur and ruled over large parts of India from the 16th to the 18th century, referred to itself as the "Gurkani" dynasty – the dynasty of the "sons-in-law".[3] This is the conquerors' perspective. The European memory of Genghis Khan and Timur, on the other hand, comes from the perspective of the victims, or of the defeated. The famous painting "The Apotheosis of War" by Vasily Vasilyevich Vereshchagin (1842–1904), which shows a mountain of skulls (Fig. 5), was inspired by Timur's conquests and dedicated to "all great conquerors: those of the past, the present, and of the future".[4] Modern Mongolia, meanwhile, which became

spektive der Eroberer; die europäische Erinnerung an Dschingis Khan wie auch an Timur ist hingegen die der Opfer oder zumindest der Unterlegenen. Das berühmte Gemälde »Die Apotheose des Krieges« von Wassili Wassiljewitsch Wereschtschagin (1842–1904), das einen Schädelberg darstellt (Abb. 5), war inspiriert von Timurs Eroberungen, gewidmet »allen großen Eroberern: den vergangenen, den gegenwärtigen und den zukünftigen«.[4] Die moderne Mongolei wiederum, in den 1990er Jahren unabhängig vom sowjetischen Einfluss geworden, suchte nach einer Identifikationsfigur, die gegenüber den übermächtigen Nachbarn Russland und China den eigenen historischen Geltungsanspruch repräsentierte; doch bedrohlichen Expansionismus konnte und wollte sie nicht ausstrahlen, und so wurde Dschingis Khan vor allem als Begründer mongolischer Staatlichkeit heroisiert (Abb. 6).[5]

Abb. 5: »Apotheose des Krieges« nannte der russische Militärmaler Wassilij Wassiljewitsch Wereschtschagin sein 1871 entstandenes Gemälde: Auch ein siegreicher Eroberer wie Timur baut seine Zukunft auf Tod und Zerstörung auf. Das Gemälde ist ein Hauptwerk der Staatlichen Tretjakow-Galerie in Moskau. Als ein Mann in der sibirischen Stadt Tomsk im März 2022 mit einer Kopie des Bildes gegen den Einmarsch russischer Truppen in die Ukraine protestierte, wurde er festgenommen und anschließend zu einer Geldstrafe verurteilt.

Fig. 5: *Russian military painter Vasily Vasilyevich Vereshchagin entitled his 1871 painting, dedicated to all great conquerors, "Apotheosis of War". Even a victorious conqueror like Timur based his future on death and destruction. This painting is a major work of art in the State Tretyakov Gallery in Moscow. In March 2022, a man in the Siberian city of Tomsk protested against the invasion of Ukraine by Russian troops with a copy of the painting; he was arrested and subsequently sentenced to pay a fine.*

Diese Umfunktionierung eines polarisierenden in einen weniger kontroversen Helden kann gelingen; sie hat in diesem Fall aber auch deswegen funktioniert und sogar einen gewissen Einfluss auf die europäische Geschichtsschreibung ausgeübt, weil es keine Opfergemeinschaften gibt, die die Anerkennung des Leids ihrer Vorfahren einfordern. Das liegt nicht lediglich an der zeitlichen Distanz. Christoph Kolumbus' Status als heroischer Entdecker etwa wird heute mehr denn je angefochten, weil gerade heute indigene Gemeinschaften in Amerika eine Stimme haben und fordern, dass die Gewalt, die seinen Entdeckungsreisen inhärent war und von ihnen ausgelöst wurde, nicht nur anerkannt, sondern ins Zentrum der Erinnerung an Kolumbus gerückt wird (Abb. 7).[6]

Abb. 6: Dschingis Khan (reg. 1206–1227) begründete das mongolische Reich und dehnte es durch Eroberungszüge auf ein riesiges Territorium aus. Anlässlich der 800-Jahr-Feiern zur Reichsgründung erhielt er 2006 ein monumentales Denkmal vor dem Parlamentsgebäude in Ulaanbaatar, der Hauptstadt der Mongolei. Die Berufung auf Dschingis Khan als Begründer mongolischer Staatlichkeit rückt die von ihm ausgeübte Gewalt aus dem Fokus der Wahrnehmung. Gleichzeitig verkörpert Dschingis Khan den historischen mongolischen Geltungsanspruch. Dies ist ein Versuch, die jahrzehntelange Abhängigkeit von der Sowjetunion erinnerungspolitisch den Jahrhunderten unabhängiger Staatlichkeit unterzuordnen, auch als Geste gegenüber der aktuellen Machtpolitik Chinas und Russlands.

Fig. 6: Genghis Khan (ruled: 1206–1227) founded the Mongolian Empire and conquered vast swathes of territory. In 2006, to mark the 800th anniversary of the Empire's founding, he was honoured with a monumental memorial in front of the Parliament Building in Ulaanbaatar, the capital of Mongolia. Referencing Genghis Khan as the founder of Mongolian statehood shifts the focus of attention away from the violence he inflicted. At the same time, Genghis Khan embodies Mongolians' historical claim to existing as a legitimate people. This is an attempt to make decades of dependence on the Soviet Union subordinate to centuries of independent statehood in terms of commemorative politics, as well as a gesture towards the current political power of Russia and China.

independent from Soviet influence in the 1990s, was searching for a role model that would legitimise its own historical validity over its powerful neighbours Russia and China. The country could not and did not want to radiate belligerent expansionism, however, so it heroized Genghis Khan as the founder of Mongolian statehood rather than as a conqueror of other lands (Fig. 6).[5]

POLARISATION

Aufopferung, Einsatz, Ziele

Neben der kompletten Ausblendung der Opferperspektive gibt es noch eine andere Form der Heroisierung gewaltsamen Heldentums, die es der Polarisierung innerhalb der eigenen Gemeinschaft entzieht: Sie gilt dem Einsatz für eine Sache, der ein so hoher moralischer Wert zugeschrieben wird, dass dieser die Opfer auf beiden Seiten rechtfertigt – insbesondere dann, wenn die Held:innen selber Opfer erbringen. Dies trifft zum Beispiel weitgehend auf die nachträgliche Bewertung der Rolle der Alliierten im Zweiten Weltkrieg zu. Selbst hier gibt es jedoch Grenzen: So stand der britische Luftwaffenmarschall Arthur Harris, auch bekannt als »Bomber Harris«, nicht nur in Deutschland aufgrund der Flächenbombardements deutscher Städte in der Kritik, sondern er war auch in Großbritannien umstritten, weil unter seiner Führung die britische Luftwaffe hohe Verluste zu verzeichnen hatte. Für die Verehrer von »Bomber Harris« wogen die Erfolge des Bombenkrieges die Verluste unter den eigenen Piloten allerdings auf, insbesondere, da bis zum 6. Juni 1944 der Bombenkrieg anstelle eines sehr viel verlustreicheren Landkrieges geführt wurde (Abb. 8 und 9).[7]

Nur selten liegen die Dinge jedoch so vergleichsweise klar wie beim Kampf gegen Hitler – und auch dort liegen sie ja nur im Nachhinein klar, denn zu Lebzeiten wurde Hitler bekanntlich durchaus heroisiert, und selbst heute ist dies noch nicht undenkbar, wie die deutsche Neonazi-Szene ebenso zeigt wie die Kontroverse um ein Café mit Nazi-Dekor im Indonesien der 2010er Jahre oder die Interviewaussage einer ägyptischen Schauspielerin, die sich im Jahr 2014 einen Präsidenten wünschte, der »stark wie Hitler« sei.[8] Auch – und vielleicht gerade – die Antwort auf die Frage, ob das Ziel eines Krieges als gut und wertvoll zu definieren sei, ist eine Frage der Perspektive. Nicht nur im Fall Adolf Hitlers kann ein Blick auf Subkulturen oder ins Ausland das Bild einer einhelligen Ablehnung schnell ins Wanken bringen. So berichtete die italienische Journalistin Francesca Borri 2017 von den Malediven, die Kämpfer des IS gälten dort breiten Bevölkerungsschichten als Helden. Die Malediven waren damals das muslimische Land mit dem proportional zur Bevölkerung höchsten Anteil von Kämpfern des »Islamischen Staates« (IS) in Syrien und dem Irak. Die jungen Männer, die sich auf die Reise machten, träumten von Gemeinschaft, Gerechtigkeit und dem Kampf für die Unterdrückten. Der IS erschien ihnen als Ausweg aus der Perspektivlosigkeit eines verarmten und korrupten Landes. Viele von ihnen lebten von Kriminalität; für sie stellte die Reise nach Syrien nicht die Überschreitung der Grenze zur Gewaltbereitschaft dar, sondern sie sahen diese Reise vielmehr als Gelegenheit, bereits vorhandene Gewaltbereitschaft in den Dienst einer »guten Sache« zu stellen.[9]

Gewaltbereitschaft ist jedoch keine Voraussetzung für diese Form der Polarisierung. Auch gewaltlose Held:innen polarisieren dann, wenn Dissens über die Ziele,

Such transformations of a polarising hero into a less controversial hero can have success. In this case it worked, and even influenced European historiography to a certain extent because there were no victim communities demanding recognition for the suffering of their ancestors. This is not only because Genghis Khan was from the distant past. Christopher Columbus' status as a heroic explorer, for instance, is being challenged today more than ever because indigenous communities in America have been given a voice. They are demanding that the violence inherent in and triggered by his expeditions must not only be acknowledged, but should also be the main focus in any remembrance of Columbus (Fig. 7).[6]

Sacrifices, commitment, objectives

Besides the complete suppression of the victim's perspective, there is another form of the heroization of violent actions that remove them from polarisation within the hero's own community: That is to focus on the hero's commitment to a cause that is seen as having a moral value so high that it justifies sacrifices on both sides – particularly if the sacrifices are made by the heroes themselves. This largely applies, for example, to the retrospective evaluation of the actions of the Allies during World War II – although even in this case there were mixed opinions. Arthur Harris, the British Air Force Marshal also known as 'Bomber Harris', was not only criticised in Germany for the area bombing of German cities in 1945. He was also controversial in Britain because the Royal Air Force suffered heavy losses under his command. But for the admirers of 'Bomber Harris',

Abb. 7: Auch Helden haben ein Verfallsdatum. Christoph Kolumbus, seit Jahrhunderten als heroischer Entdecker verehrt, polarisiert die heutige Erinnerungskultur. Die in den Amerikas ansässigen Völker hatten Kultur und eine lange Geschichte, längst bevor sie von einem Europäer »entdeckt« wurden. Nicht nur Angehörige dieser Völker fordern eine kritische Neubewertung dieser »Entdeckung«, die millionenfaches Leiden und Sterben zur Folge hatte. Das Bild zeigt den Versuch, 2020 die Kolumbus-Statue in St. Paul (Minnesota) zu stürzen.

Fig. 7: Even heroes have an expiry date. Christopher Columbus, revered for centuries as a heroic explorer, is now polarised in modern-day culture. Indigenous peoples living in the Americas hundreds of years ago had their own culture and history long before they were "discovered" by Europeans. Both members inside and outside of these communities are calling for a critical reassessment of this "discovery", which resulted in mass suffering and millions of deaths. This picture from 2020 shows protesters attempting to topple Columbus' statue in St Paul, Minnesota.

Abb. 8/9: Die Bilder zeigen Szenen von Mai und Oktober 1992. In Anwesenheit der Königinmutter festlich eingeweiht, war das Denkmal für »Bomber Harris« schon kurze Zeit später Ziel heftigen Protests. Auch wenn in Großbritannien kein Zweifel daran besteht, dass Arthur Harris zur Zeit des Zweiten Weltkriegs auf der »richtigen Seite« stand, polarisiert die Wahl seiner Mittel.

Fig. 8/9: These pictures show scenes from May and October 1992. The memorial shown, commemorating British Air Officer Commanding-in-Chief Arthur "Bomber" Harris, was inaugurated in the presence of Queen Elizabeth The Queen Mother, but soon became the target of fierce protests. Even though the most of the population in Great Britain believes that Harris fought for the "right side" during the Second World War, his choice of actions has polarised opinions.

die sie vertreten, herrscht. Die Heroisierung einer Klimaaktivistin wie Greta Thunberg wirkt auf Gegner:innen klimapolitischer Maßnahmen in höchstem Maße provozierend, auch weil mit ihr moralische Forderungen verbunden sind, die sie nicht bereit sind zu erfüllen. Dass andere Menschen nicht nur eine andere Meinung haben, sondern sogar bereit sind, für diese Position Opfer zu bringen und – wie im Fall der Klimaaktivist:innen – diese auch von anderen einzufordern, macht es Gegner:innen schwer, indifferent zu bleiben; sie reagieren nicht selten mit Hass oder Wut. Heroisierungen und Angriffe auf Held:innen können in solchen Fällen seismographische Wirkung haben: Sie bringen eine bestehende Polarisierung zum Vorschein.

the success of the bombing campaigns outweighed losses among British pilots, especially since the bombing campaigns replaced the much costlier land war that had raged up until 6 June 1944 (Fig. 8 and 9).[7]

It is rare, however, that things are as black and white as in the fight against Hitler. And even here, they are only clear in retrospect, because Hitler was, as we know, heroized in his lifetime. Even today, he is still a hero for certain individuals, as the German neo-Nazi movement has shown, as well as the controversy over a café with Nazi decorations in Indonesia in the 2010s, and the 2014 interview statement of an Egyptian actress who hoped for a president who was "strong like Hitler".[8] The answer to the question as to whether a war's objective can be defined as good and valuable is also highly dependent on perspective. A closer look at subcultures or other countries can quickly undermine the idea of a unanimous demonisation, not only in the case of Adolf Hitler. In 2017, for example, the Italian journalist Francesca Borri reported that, in the Maldives, IS fighters were seen as heroes by broad sections of the population. At that time, the Maldives were the Muslim country with the highest proportion of "Islamic State" (IS) fighters in Syria and Iraq. The young men who set out on their journey there dreamed of community, justice and fighting for the oppressed. They saw the IS as a way out of the hopelessness of an impoverished and corrupt country. Many of them were already living a life of crime, so the journey to Syria did not constitute the initiation into a life of violence. Instead, they saw the journey as an opportunity to put their existing propensity to violence into the service of a "good cause".[9]

A willingness to use violence is not a prerequisite for this form of polarisation, however. Non-violent heroes can also polarise if there is disagreement about the objectives they are pursuing. The heroization of a climate activist such as Greta Thunberg is highly provoking to opponents of climate policy measures, not least because activists are expressing moral demands that the opponents reject. The fact that other people not only have a different opinion but are even willing to make sacrifices for it and to demand the same from others, as in the case of the climate activists, means opponents struggle to remain indifferent. Their response is often one of hatred or anger. In these cases, heroizations and attacks on heroes can have a seismographic effect because they reveal an existing polarisation.

Non-violence, age, gender

In certain contexts, it is non-violence itself that polarises people, namely those who regard violence as unavoidable. They would see a policy of non-violence as giving in to the enemy, as submission, as the opposite to the kind of confrontation that is inherent to heroizations. Decolonisation, for instance, was a context in which

Gewaltlosigkeit, Alter, Geschlecht

In bestimmten Kontexten ist es die Gewaltlosigkeit selbst, die polarisiert, nämlich dann, wenn vielen Akteuren Gewalt als unausweichlich erscheint. Sie sehen Gewaltlosigkeit als Einknicken vor dem Gegner, als Unterwerfung, als Gegenteil des »Die-Stirn-Bietens«, das Heroisierungen innewohnt. Die Dekolonisierung war ein derartiger Kontext, in dem viele Gegner:innen der Kolonialherrschaft überzeugt waren, dass Gewalt unvermeidlich sei und Gewaltlosigkeit niemandem außer der Kolonialmacht nütze.[10] Selbst Mahatma Gandhis (1869–1948) Philosophie der Gewaltlosigkeit war in Indien nicht so unstrittig, wie es die spätere Geschichtsschreibung scheinen ließ; er konkurrierte mit gewaltbereiten Akteuren wie Bhagat Singh (1907–1931), der aufgrund der Ermordung eines britischen Polizisten im Alter von 23 Jahren erhängt wurde und bereits in den 1930er Jahren Gegenstand breiter populärer Heroisierung war (Abb. 10).[11]

Als polarisierend können aber auch persönliche Merkmale des Helden oder der Heldin wirken, so etwa Geschlecht und Alter. Um noch einmal auf Greta Thunberg zurückzukommen: Was sie in den Augen ihrer Verehrer:innen mutig und kämpferisch erscheinen lässt, wirkt auf manch andere empörend. Ein Schulmädchen erdreistet sich, den Erwachsenen die Leviten zu lesen, anstatt vorschriftsmäßig fünf Tage in der Woche die Schule zu besuchen! Bei Malala Yousafzai, der jungen pakistanischen Paschtunin, die wegen ihre Einsatzes für Mädchenbildung von den Taliban angeschossen wurde, ließen sich ähnliche Reaktionen beobachten, und identitätspolitische Aspekte

Abb. 10: Bhagat Singh gehörte zu einer Gruppe von drei jungen indischen Attentätern, die von der britischen Kolonialjustiz zum Tode verurteilt und 1931 hingerichtet wurden. Die drei waren 22 und 23 Jahre alt. Vor allem ihre Jugend und die schweren Strafen tragen dazu bei, dass sie bis heute in Indien und Pakistan als Freiheitskämpfer und Märtyrer verehrt werden, die angesichts eines übermächtigen Unrechtssystems das größtmögliche Opfer gegeben haben. Ihre Gewaltbereitschaft tut der Verehrung keinen Abbruch.

Fig. 10: Bhagat Singh was one of three young Indian assassins who were sentenced to death by the British Colonial Judiciary and executed in 1931. They were all between 22 and 23 years old. Their young age and harsh sentences are the main reasons why they are still honoured today in India and Pakistan – as freedom fighters and martyrs who made the greatest possible sacrifice in the face of an overpowering system of injustice. Their willingness to use violence does not diminish their veneration.

many opponents of colonial rule were convinced that violence was inevitable, and that non-violence was of no use to anyone other than the colonial power.[10] Even Mahatma Gandhi's (1869–1948) philosophy of non-violence was not as undisputed in India as later historiography has portrayed. He was competing with violent individuals such as Bhagat Singh (1907–1931), who was hanged for murdering a British policeman at the age of 23, and who was already the subject of widespread popular heroization in India in the 1930s (Fig. 10).[11]

The personal characteristics of a hero, such as gender and age, can also be polarizing factors. To return to Greta Thunberg once more: characteristics that make her appear courageous and determined in the eyes of her admirers can seem outrageous to others. A schoolgirl showed the audacity to reprimand adults – instead of attending school five days a week, as per the rules. Similar reactions were to be observed in the case of Malala Yousafzai, the young Pakistani Pashtun who was shot by the Taliban because of her activism for girls' education. The polarisation was further intensified by aspects related to identity politics. In the eyes of many Pakistani, the admiration she experienced in the Western world, including the Nobel Peace Prize she was awarded as the youngest ever recipient, and her transformation into a feminist made her an agent of American neo-colonialism – a neo-colonialism that encroached on other countries' right of self-determination under the guise of defending women's rights. In India, on the other hand, reactions to her were hostile because of her defence of women's right to wear a headscarf.

Abb. 11: »Girls' education is a climate solution« – »If girls are not allowed in schools, they can't school strike« – »Believe in science & fight for girls' right to learn it« – Slogans einer Klimademonstration, die im Juni 2022 in Stockholm stattfand. Die Gesichter dieser Aktion waren die ugandische Klimaaktivistin Vanessa Nakate, Malala Yousafzai, die aus Pakistan stammende Menschenrechtsaktivistin und jüngste Nobelpreisträgerin, und die schwedische Klimaaktivistin Greta Thunberg (von links nach rechts). Jung, weiblich, selbstbewusst, global vernetzt und überzeugt von der eigenen Botschaft – auf Gegner:innen wirkt dies provozierend.

Fig. 11: "Girls' education is a climate solution" – "If girls are not allowed in schools, they can't school strike" – "Believe in science & fight for girls' rights to study it". These were slogans from a climate protest that took place in Stockholm in June 2022. The faces belonging to this campaign were Ugandan climate activist Vanessa Nakate, Pakistani-born human rights activist and youngest Nobel Prize winner Malala Yousafzai and Swedish climate activist Greta Thunberg [pictured from left to right]. Young, female, self-confident, globally networked and convinced of their own message – all of these characteristics have a provocative effect on those who oppose them.

POLARISATION

trugen noch zusätzlich zur Polarisierung bei: Die Bewunderung, die sie in der westlichen Welt erfuhr, der Friedensnobelpreis, den sie als jüngste Person aller Zeiten erhielt, und ihr Wandel zur Feministin machten sie in den Augen vieler Pakistani zur Agentin eines amerikanischen Neokolonialismus, der unter dem Deckmantel der Verteidigung der Frauenrechte in das Selbstbestimmungsrecht anderer Länder eingreife. In Indien wiederum wurde sie wegen ihres Einsatzes für die Freiheit, ein Kopftuch zu tragen, angefeindet. In den Attacken auf beide junge Frauen waren sexistische Untertöne überdeutlich. Die Polarisierung scheint zuzunehmen, sobald der Held oder die Heldin bezüglich Geschlecht, Herkunft, Hautfarbe oder Religion nicht den Erwartungen entspricht. Dies macht ihn oder sie zur Identifikationsfigur für die einen, zum Hassobjekt für die anderen (Abb. 11). Vielleicht – um zum Ausgangspunkt dieser Überlegungen zurückzukehren – sind Putin und die ›starken Männer‹ das Kehrbild dieses Phänomens: Die Inszenierung von Männlichkeit und der Dominanz der gesellschaftlichen Mehrheit über Außenseiter und Minderheiten übt offenbar hohe Anziehungskraft auf ihre Verehrer:innen aus und wirkt auf ihre Gegner:innen in gleichem Maße abstoßend.

Anmerkungen

1 ʿImāra 2015.
2 Gage 2023.
3 Conermann 2006, 7.
4 Kantarbaeva-Bill 2017.
5 Kaplonski 2004.
6 Lopenzina 2021.
7 Hughes 2021.
8 Masr 2014.
9 Borri 2017.
10 Fanon 1968, 34–105.
11 Pink 2018.

The sexist undertones in the attacks on both young women are unmistakable. Polarisation seems to increase whenever the hero fails to meet certain expectations in terms of gender, origin, skin colour or religion. This makes them a role model for some, and an object of hatred for others (Fig. 11). To return to the starting point of these considerations, it is possible that Putin and other 'strongmen' are an inverted version of this phenomenon: their performance of masculinity and commitment to the dominance of a social majority over outsiders and minorities is obviously very attractive to their admirers, while equally repulsive to their opponents.

Notes

1. ʿImāra 2015.
2. Gage 2023.
3. Conermann 2006, 7.
4. Kantarbaeva-Bill 2017.
5. Kaplonski 2004.
6. Lopenzina 2021.
7. Hughes 2021.
8. Masr 2014.
9. Borri 2017.
10. Fanon 1968, 34–105.
11. Pink 2018.

© 2024 Johanna Pink, Publikation: Wallstein Verlag; DOI https://doi.org/10.46500/83535581-005 | CC BY-NC-ND 4.0

Stefan Tilg

KAMPF

Kämpfe verschiedener Art sind ein fundamentales Bewährungsfeld des Heroischen. In Kämpfen werden Leistungen vollbracht, auf die sich Heroisierungen berufen. Helden kämpfen, mit Waffen, Worten oder Werten.

Merkmale und Heroisierungsweisen

Ein erstes wesentliches Merkmal des Kampfes ist dabei, dass er destabilisiert. Es handelt sich um ein potenziell umstürzlerisches Problemlösungsverhalten, um einen ereignisreichen, oft gewalttätigen Moment der Be-Streitung und Neu-Aushandlung von Machtverhältnissen. Aus solchen krisenhaften Situationen gehen gern Helden hervor. Das kann im Kleinen zum Beispiel eine Protestaktion von Klima-Aktivist:innen sein, die in ihrem Kampf gegen fossile Energieträger und deren Lobbys den Verkehr zum Erliegen bringen. Von manchen für ihre Anfechtung von Machtverhältnissen verteufelt, werden sie von anderen gerade deswegen zu Held:innen ausgerufen (Abb. 1). Ähnliches, wenn auch in größerem Maßstab, passiert, wenn zum Beispiel Gemeinschaften ihre Identität aus einem kriegerischen Helden(zeit)alter bzw. einem ›heroic age‹ herleiten, in dem heroische Individuen das Alte bekämpften, um etwas Neues zu schaffen. In diesem Sinn bewunderte Hegel etwa Alexander den Großen, Caesar und Napoleon als die großen weltgeschichtlichen Individuen, die im Kampf einer neuen Ordnung Bahn brachen. Im ›vernünftigen‹, stabilen und unkämpferischen Beamtenstaat seiner Gegenwart dagegen könne es keine Helden mehr geben.

Sich im Kampf bewähren heißt auch Besonderes können und jedenfalls auf irgendeine Art besser zu sein als das bekämpfte Gegenüber. Das zweite Merkmal des Kampfes ist damit der Antagonismus: Jemand kämpft gegen jemanden oder etwas. Zumindest im Wesenskern des Kampfes sind es immer genau zwei Parteien, die einander bekämpfen und die Oberhand über den jeweils anderen erlangen wollen. Nicht zu Unrecht gilt daher häufig der Zweikampf als das Urbild aller Kämpfe. Wer aus einem Kampf als Held hervorgeht, ist aus irgendeinem Grund besser als der andere. Ob es darüber hinaus Dritte gäbe, die *noch* besser als der Held wären, ist angesichts der Funktion des kämpfenden Paars als Verstehens- und Inszenierungseinheit eher nebensächlich. Entscheidend für eine Heroisierung ist vielmehr, dass der Konflikt größere, symbolhafte Bedeutung in einer Gemeinschaft gewinnt und die Leistung eines der Kontrahenten gegenüber dem anderen betont wird. Ent-

Stefan Tilg

FIGHTING

Fights of different types are a fundamental testing ground of the heroic. Fighting involves a performance that forms the basis of heroization. Heroes fight – with weapons, words or values.

Characteristics and ways of heroization

One of the first important characteristics of fighting is that it results in destabilisation. Fighting is a potentially subversive way of solving problems – an eventful and often violent moment of dispute and renegotiation of power structures. It is from these crisis situations that heroes often emerge. On a low level, for instance, this could be a protest by climate activists bringing traffic to a standstill in their fight against fossil energy sources and the relevant lobby groups. While some of these activists are condemned for challenging power structures, others are proclaimed heroes for the very same reason (Fig. 1). Something similar happens, albeit on a larger scale, when communities derive their identity from a war-like 'heroic age', in which heroic individuals fought the old order to create something new. In this sense, Hegel admired Alexander the Great, Caesar and Napoleon as great individuals of world history who won ground in the fight for a new order. In the reasonable, stable and peaceful 'civil servant state' of his time, however, there could no longer be heroes.

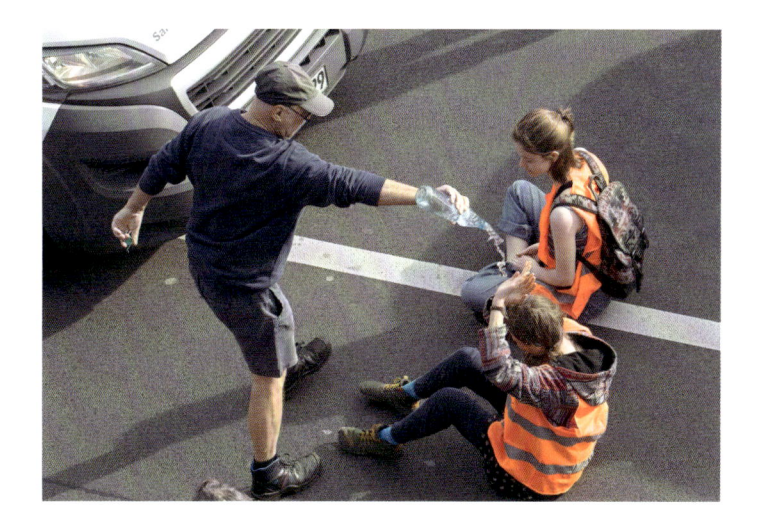

Abb. 1: Ein Verkehrsteilnehmer überschüttet zwei Aktivist:innen der Letzten Generation bei einer Blockade auf der Autobahn 100 mit Wasser (2023). Zum Zeitpunkt der Abfassung des Essays waren die disruptiven Protestaktionen der Letzten Generation in aller Munde. Sie können im Kleinen für die Bestreitung und Neuaushandlung von Machtverhältnissen stehen, die allen physischen oder ideologischen Kämpfen zugrunde liegen.

Fig. 1: A car driver pours water over two Last Generation activists during a blockade on the M-100 in 2023. At the time of writing this essay, the Last Generation's disruptive protests were the talk of the town. On a small scale, these actions are supposed to represent the contestation and renegotiation of power relations that underlie everyday physical and/or ideological struggles.

sprechend polarisierend können sich Helden- und Feindbilder dann auch gegenüberstehen und sich gegenseitig bedingen.

Der Sieg im Kampf ist allerdings nicht in jedem Fall Voraussetzung für Heroisierungen. Siege helfen, aber es gibt eben auch die ›moralischen Sieger‹, die ›tragischen Helden‹ und diejenigen, die für die Unbedingtheit ihres Wollens heroisiert werden. Die vielen Helden verlorener Schlachten von Leonidas und seinen Spartanern bei den Thermopylen bis zu Andreas Hofer und seinen Tirolern am Bergisel legen davon Zeugnis ab. Mut, Moral, Teilerfolge und den Sieg ›eigentlich verdient‹ zu haben, können als heroische Leistung im Kampf anerkannt werden (Abb. 2).

Ein auffälliges historisch-kulturelles Merkmal des Kampfs ist darüber hinaus seine emphatisch maskuline Codierung. Kämpfende Frauen wurden von den Amazonen bis zu modernen Boxerinnen häufig als Anomalie wahrgenommen. Auch wenn sich die Gender-Stereotype in jüngerer Zeit verstärkt wandeln, bleibt doch auffällig, dass gerade die blutigsten, gefährlichsten und körperlichsten Auseinandersetzungen nach wie vor stark männlich besetzt sind. Während man etwa im Klimakampf oder dem Tennissport von weiblichen Heldinnen kaum überrascht sein wird, gelten Soldatinnen auf dem Schlachtfeld oder Athletinnen im Kampfsport in den Augen vieler nach wie vor als Normbruch. Als klassische Männerdomäne zeichnet der Kampf mitverantwortlich für die Maskulinität traditioneller Heldenfiguren.

Begriffliche Weite und existenzielle Nähe

Die Begriffe »Kampf« und »kämpfen« eignen sich aus mehreren Gründen besonders gut für das Sprechen über Helden. Sie werden sowohl in der Alltagssprache als auch in der Fachsprache benutzt. Sie evozieren ein ganzes Wortfeld von weiteren Begriffen wie »(Wett)streit«, »Heldentat«, »Krieg« und »Agonalität«, die dem Heroischen nahestehen. Und sie können fast nach Belieben auf alle Lebensbereiche übertragen werden, in denen Konflikte oder Auseinandersetzungen eine profilierte Rolle spielen: Man trägt Kämpfe nicht nur im Krieg, sondern zum Beispiel auch im Sport, in Weltanschauungen oder im politischen Rededuell aus. Begriffe des Kämpfens können damit die ganze historische, kulturelle und situative Vielfalt von Heroisierungen und Heldenfiguren abbilden.

Schließlich ist es auch nicht unerheblich, dass der metaphorisch erweiterte Gedanke vom heroischen Kämpfen einen Anknüpfungspunkt in der Lebenswirklichkeit praktisch aller ›normalen‹, nicht-heroisierten Individuen finden kann. Vom antiken Philosophen Seneca stammt das geflügelte und in unzähligen Variationen verbreitete Wort »Leben heißt kämpfen« (Vivere … militare est). Diese Sentenz gibt Seneca in den *Epistulae morales* (96,5) seinem in seinen Augen verhätschelten Adressaten Lucilius mit, um ihm bewusst zu machen, dass das Leben nur lebenswert ist,

Proving oneself in a fight also means having a special ability, or being better in some way than the opponent. The second characteristic of fighting is therefore antagonism: somebody is fighting against someone or something. In essence, fighting always involves exactly two parties fighting each other, each of them attempting to gain the upper hand over the other. Therefore, it is not without reason that the duel is often considered the archetype of all fights. An individual emerging from a fight as a hero is, in some aspect, stronger than their opponent. In view of the role of the two fighting individuals as a unit of understanding and staging, it is nearly irrelevant whether any third party may be *even better* than the hero. What is more decisive for heroization is that the conflict gains symbolic significance in a community and that the performance of one of the opponents versus the other is emphasised. Images of heroes and enemies can therefore confront each other in an accordingly polarising and interdependent way.

However, winning a fight is not a precondition for heroization in every case. Victories help, but there are also 'moral winners', 'tragic heroes', and those who are heroized for their tremendous determination. The many heroes of lost battles, ranging from Leonidas and his Spartans in the Battle of Thermopylae to Andreas Hofer and his Tyroleans at the Bergisel hill, bear witness to this. Courage, morale, partial success and 'having deserved' victory can be considered a heroic performance during a fight (Fig. 2).

Beyond this, a conspicuous historical-cultural feature of fighting is its emphatic masculine coding. Fighting women, ranging from the Amazons to modern female boxers, are often perceived as an anomaly. Although gender stereotypes have been changing in recent times, it remains striking that the most bloody, dangerous and physical conflicts are still heavily male-dominated. While we are not surprised to

Abb. 2: Der spartanische König Leonidas (2006 im Spielfilm »300« dargestellt von Gerard Butler) war ein griechischer Feldherr, der 480 v. Chr. mit einer sehr kleinen Truppe den Thermopylen-Pass gegen eine Übermacht der heranrückenden Perser verteidigte. Der harte Kern dieser Truppe sollen 300 Spartaner gewesen sein. Ihr aufopferungsvoller Kampf, bei dem alle starben, wurde bald heroisiert. Noch heute gelten Leonidas und seine Spartaner als Musterbeispiel eines (verlorenen) heroischen Kampfes.

Fig. 2: The Spartan King Leonidas (portrayed in the 2006 film "300" by Gerard Butler) was a Greek general who defended the Thermopylae Pass against an overwhelming army of advancing Persians with a very small troop in 480 BC. The core of this troop is said to have been 300 Spartans. Their self-sacrificing battle, in which they all died, was heroized soon after. Even today, Leonidas and his Spartans are regarded as a prime example of a (lost) heroic battle.

Abb. 3: Düsseldorf, Sonntag, 5. April 2020. Bei frühlingshaften Temperaturen gehen Menschen auf der Rheinuferpromenade spazieren, es ist die Zeit des ersten Corona-Lockdowns in Deutschland. Ein großes Banner dankt allen »Helden des Alltags«. So wie der Alltag hinsichtlich bestimmter Herausforderungen heroisierbar ist, müssen auch die dabei ausgefochtenen Kämpfe nicht überlebensgroß sein. Die Metapher vom »Leben als Kampf« etwa suggeriert eine gewisse Heroisierung der elementaren existenziellen Herausforderungen jedes Lebens.

Fig. 3: Düsseldorf, Sunday, 5 April 2020: People are strolling along the Rhine promenade in lovely weather during the first coronavirus lockdown in Germany. A large banner hanging in the background thanks the "everyday heroes". Just as day-to-day life can be heroised in terms of certain challenges, the battles we fight do not have to be larger than life. The metaphor "life as a struggle", for example, suggests a certain heroisation of the elementary existential challenges we experience every day.

wenn wir seine Verwerfungen mutig annehmen. Seneca benutzt militärisches Vokabular (*militare* heißt wörtlich »als Soldat [*miles*] kämpfen«, »Kriegsdienst [*militia*] leisten«), will aber als notorischer Pazifist bestimmt nicht wörtlich sagen, dass ein gutes Leben ein Leben als Soldat sei. Vielmehr nutzt er das metaphorische Potenzial von Kampfbegriffen, um Lucilius eine Art existenzielle Heroik des Alltags zu empfehlen (Abb. 3). Diese zeichnet sich nach dem Vorbild des Kriegers durch Tatendrang, Konflikt- und Leidensbereitschaft aus, Eigenschaften, die im Text sehr deutlich mit Männlichkeit assoziiert werden. In dem unter anderem als Rollenmodell empfohlenen *vir fortis* (wörtlich »tapferer Mann«) steckt sowohl die Männlichkeit als auch nach einem damals häufigen römischen Sprachgebrauch der »Held«. Der allgemeine Gedanke einer kämpferischen Lebensgestaltung dürfte aber zu allen Zeiten kein abwegiger und eine Grundlage für die Bewunderung herausgehobener Heldenfiguren gewesen sein, die schon schwerere Kämpfe bestritten hatten.

Eine kleine Typologie des heroischen Kämpfens

Die Breite und Metaphorik des Kampfbegriffs bringt es mit sich, dass heroisches bzw. heroisiertes Kämpfen auf vielen verschiedenen Sinnebenen stattfindet. Ganz grundsätzlich lässt sich, wenn auch nicht immer trennscharf, der eher physisch ausgetragene Kampf vom eher geistig geführten unterscheiden.

Unter den physischen Kämpfen ragt der Kampf auf Leben und Tod als der ernsteste, erbittertste, mit dem größten Einsatz und der größten Opferbereitschaft geführte heraus. Das archetypische Milieu für solche Kämpfe ist der Krieg, der selbst

find female heroines in the climate fight or the sport of tennis, female soldiers on the battlefield or female athletes in martial arts are still seen by many as breaking the norm. As a classic male domain, fights are partly responsible for the masculine character of traditional heroes.

Conceptual breadth and existential relevance

For several reasons, the terms 'fight' and 'fighting' are particularly suitable for talking about heroes. They are used both in everyday language and in professional jargon. They evoke an entire semantic field of other terms, such as 'competition', 'heroic deed', 'war' and 'agonality', which are related to the heroic. These can be applied to nearly all areas of life where conflicts or confrontations play a prominent role: Fights are not only carried out in war, but also, for instance, in sports, in world views and in political debates. Concepts of fighting can therefore reflect the entire historical, cultural and situational diversity of heroizations and heroes.

It is significant that the metaphorically extended idea of heroic fighting has a connection to the everyday lives of nearly all 'normal' and 'non-heroized' individuals. The phrase "to live is to fight" (vivere … militare est), which is used in countless variations, was coined by the ancient philosopher Seneca. Seneca, in his *Epistulae Morales* (96,5), shares this aphorism with his addressee Lucilius, whom he regarded as spoiled, to teach him that life is only worth living if we bravely embrace its struggles. Seneca uses military vocabulary (*militare* literally means 'fighting as a soldier [*miles*]', 'performing military service [*militia*]'), but – as a notorious pacifist – he certainly does not want to say that a good life means living as a soldier. Instead, he uses the metaphorical potential of combat terms to recommend to Lucius a type of existential heroism in everyday life (Fig. 3). Following the example of the warrior, this existential heroism is characterised by a thirst for action and a readiness for conflict and suffering – qualities which are clearly associated with masculinity in the text. The concept *vir fortis* (literally 'brave man'), which is, among other things, recommended as a role model, suggests both masculinity and the notion of a 'hero' (which is a common meaning of the Latin phrase). The general idea of a militant way of life, however, would not have seemed far-fetched at any time, and it would also have served as a basis for the admiration of prominent heroic individuals, who had already gathered experience in other fights.

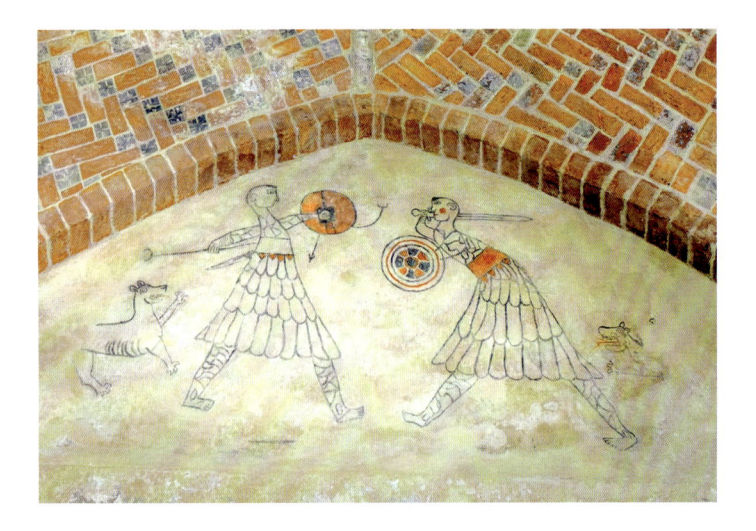

Abb. 4: Jedem Kampf liegt archetypisch ein Zweikampf, also eine Auseinandersetzung zwischen genau zwei Parteien zugrunde. Das liegt auch daran, dass sich Zweikämpfe besonders gut verstehen und inszenieren lassen. In Homers Epos *Ilias* wird dies in zahlreichen sogenannten *Aristien* ausgeführt, also Zweikämpfen zwischen einzelnen herausragenden Kämpfern der Griechen und der Trojaner. Das Deckengemälde der Dorfkirche von Westerwijtwerd, Niederlande, zeigt im 14. Jahrhundert Hektor und Achill im Kampf.

Fig. 4: One could argue that every fight is archetypically based on a duel, i.e., a confrontation between exactly two parties. This can be attributed to the ease with which duels are understood and staged. In Homer's epic poem Iliad, this concept is realised in numerous so-called aristeiai, duels between individual outstanding fighters among the Greeks and the Trojans. The painted 14th-century ceiling in the village church of Westerwijtwerd, Netherlands, shows Hector and Achilles in combat.

auch wieder einen Kampf von (zumindest in der Regel und im Kern) zwei Parteien darstellt. Von Homers Epos *Ilias*, das den Kampf um Troja literarisch beschreibt, bis zu den faktischen militärischen Konflikten der Gegenwart bieten Kriege einen Schauplatz für Heroisierungen (Abb. 4). Das Epos als heroisches Genre par excellence in Literatur und Film lebt von Schlachten und den persönlichen Schicksalen, die damit verwoben werden. Die Bedeutung des Heroischen in Sprache und Symbolik rund um Kriege wird uns gerade in der Gegenwart angesichts des russischen Angriffs auf die Ukraine wieder in Erinnerung gerufen. Orden wie der 2010 neu belebte russische Suworow-Orden (benannt nach dem russischen General Alexander Wassiljewitsch Suworow, 1730–1800) beschwören eine heroische militärische Tradition; im Gegenzug intensivierte sich die Verleihung des an sich nicht auf die Domäne des Kriegs festgelegten »Held der Ukraine«-Ordens in den Kriegsjahren der Annexion der Krim (2014) und des Angriffs auf die gesamte Ukraine (2022) auf sprunghafte Weise durch die Auszeichnung von Soldaten und Offizieren (Abb. 5).

Von hier aus ist der Begriff des ›Nationalhelden‹ nicht weit. Politische Gemeinschaften nehmen Nationalhelden in Anspruch, um ihre Identität zu festigen und im stärksten Fall sogar von diesen Helden herzuleiten. Das gelingt oft am besten, wenn Letztere in kriegerischen Verhältnissen und unter Einsatz ihres Lebens im Kampf für die spätere Nation dargestellt werden. Literarisch ist dieser Fall in der westlichen Tradition modellhaft in Vergils *Aeneis* grundgelegt, in der Aeneas als Stammvater der Römer die Voraussetzungen für das römische Imperium schafft. Was Aeneas in der Antike für die Römer ist, sind im Spätmittelalter zum Beispiel Jeanne d'Arc für Frankreich oder der

A small typology of heroic fighting

The breadth and metaphorics of the concept of fighting mean that heroic or heroized fighting takes place on many different semantic levels. Generally, although a clear separation is not always possible, the more physical fights can be distinguished from fights that happen on a mental level.

Among the physical fights, fights to the death stand out as the most serious and fierce, the ones led with the greatest commitment and the greatest willingness to make sacrifices. The archetypal environment for these fights is war, which itself represents a fight between two parties. From Homer's *Iliad*, which describes the battle for Troy in a literary way, to the actual military conflicts of the present, wars offer a stage for heroizations (Fig. 4). As the heroic genre par excellence in literature and film, the epic is based on battles and the fates of individuals involved in them. The significance of the heroic in language and symbolism in the context of real warfare has recently become again apparent in view of the Russian invasion of Ukraine. Decorations such as the Russian Order of Suvorov (named after Russia's General Alexander Vasilyevich Suvorov, 1730–1800), which was revived in 2010, are intended to invoke a heroic military tradition. In return, Ukraine has rapidly intensified the frequency with which it is awarding the 'Hero of Ukraine' decoration (which can in principle also be awarded to civilians) to soldiers and officers in the years of the annexation of Crimea (2014) and the attack on Ukraine as a whole (2022) (Fig. 5).

Abb. 5: Der Konnex von Krieg, Kampf und Heroisierung war gerade nach dem Ende des Zweiten Weltkriegs vielen Deutschen suspekt. Mit der »Zeitenwende« des Ukraine-Krieges scheint das Konzept kriegerischen Heldentums wieder mehr Akzeptanz zu finden. Dass global gesehen der Kampf im Krieg besonders häufig heroisiert wurde, stand nie in Frage. Die 2022 ausgegebene ukrainische Briefmarke erinnert an eine häufig als heldenhaft angesehene Tat ukrainischer Soldaten in den ersten Tagen des Krieges: Statt sich zu ergeben, behaupteten sie ihren Posten auf der Schlangeninsel und funkten, »Russisches Kriegsschiff, f*ck dich«.

Fig. 5: *For many Germans, the connection between war, fighting and heroization has been seen as questionable – especially since the end of the Second World War. However, the Ukraine War has acted as a sort of "turning point" to these doubts; it seems to have made the concept of war heroism more acceptable again. On a global scale, the connection between heroization and combat in war has never been doubted. This Ukrainian stamp, issued in 2022, commemorates an act by Ukrainian soldiers in the early days of the war which has often been regarded as heroic: Instead of surrendering, they stood their ground on Snake Island and radioed, "Russian warship, f*ck you".*

Türkenkämpfer Skanderbeg für Albanien. Kämpfer für die nationale Freiheit haben gute Chancen, zu ›Nationalhelden‹ zu werden, sei es im Kampf gegen die Habsburger wie Wilhelm Tell, gegen europäische Kolonisatoren wie Simón Bolívar oder im Widerstand gegen die Nationalsozialisten wie Charles de Gaulle.

Von Carl von Clausewitz ist das berühmte Diktum überliefert, dass der Krieg nichts anderes als ein erweiterter Zweikampf sei. Wie eingangs festgestellt, liegt eine Idee von Zweikampf allen Kämpfen zugrunde. Sogar das deutsche Wort »Kampf« kommt wahrscheinlich als frühe Entlehnung aus lateinisch ›campus‹ von dem für Zweikämpfe abgesteckten »Feld«. Wenn nun tatsächlich Zweikämpfe im Wortsinn inszeniert werden, wohnt ihnen aufgrund der Zuspitzung des Kampfs auf zwei Individuen ein besonderes Heroisierungspotenzial inne. Von der epischen ›Aristie‹ bis zum Western-Duell der Cowboys werden Zweikämpfe medial ohne Rücksicht auf historische Plausibilität zur Veranschaulichung von gewaltsamen Konflikten eingesetzt.

Nimmt man den Zweikampf Mann gegen Mann als Normalfall an, kann man den Kampf Mann gegen Drache oder sonstiges wildes Urwesen als eine zwar phantastische, aber auch modernen Menschen stets griffbereite und in vielen Kulturen anzutreffende Variante ansehen. Jason im Kampf um das Goldene Vlies, der Heilige Georg und der Siegfried der Nibelungensage sind nur einige bekannte Drachentöter der europäischen Tradition. Ihr Sieg über das Urwesen symbolisiert jeweils auch einen Sieg von Ordnung und Zivilisation über Chaos und Barbarei. Dass man ihre Geschichte auch ›gegen den Strich‹ als Festigung patriarchaler Machtstrukturen lesen kann, ist offensichtlich, wenn man bedenkt, dass die den männlichen ›Kulturheroen‹ entgegengesetzten chthonischen Wesen oft weiblich bzw. weiblich konnotiert sind (Abb. 6).

Eine entfernte Variante des Zweikampfs auf Leben und Tod mag man schließlich auch noch im menschlichen Kampf gegen Naturgewalten finden. Dass sich hier besonders Feuerwehrleute (engl. fire fighters) für Heroisierungen eignen, liegt vermutlich daran, dass sie im Gegensatz etwa zu Helfer:innen bei Erdbeben, Überschwemmungen oder Lawinenabgängen nicht ›nur‹ ein Rennen gegen die Zeit nach einer nicht beeinflussbaren Katastrophe bestreiten, sondern einen aktiven Kampf führen, dessen Ausgang offen ist. Ähnliches lässt sich zum Beispiel im ›Bodenkampf‹ gegen Epidemien und Pandemien beobachten: 2014 hat etwa das global rezipierte *Time Magazine* die »Ebola fighters« – also jene Ärzt:innen, Pfleger:innen, Fahrer:innen etc., die ihr Leben aufs Spiel setzten, um in den afrikanischen Krisengebieten die Ausbreitung des Ebola-Virus zu verhindern – als »Person of the Year« ausgezeichnet und sich dabei heroischer Bilder bedient. Die Begründung der Wahl wurde eingeleitet mit dem Satz: »›Not the glittering weapon fights the fight‹, says the proverb, ›but rather the hero's heart‹«.[1]

Immer noch physisch, aber nicht mehr auf Leben und Tod geführt ist der sportliche Wettkampf. Dass auch dieser ernst und erbittert ausgetragen werden kann,

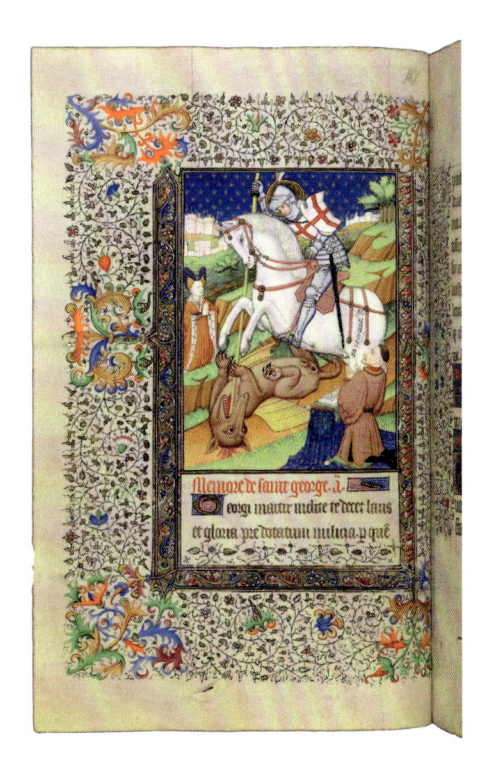

Abb. 6: Der Drachenkampf ist ein oftmals wiederkehrendes Element indoeuropäischer Heldenerzählungen. Er symbolisiert die Überwindung von Chaos und die Etablierung von Zivilisation. Die erfolgreichen Drachenkämpfer werden als Kultur-Helden heroisiert. Dabei sind die Drachenkämpfer typischerweise männlich, die mit der Erde verbundenen Drachenwesen aber zumindest weiblich konnotiert. Den Erzählungen vom Drachenkampf sind insofern häufig auch patriarchale Machtstrukturen eingeschrieben. In dieser Darstellung des 15. Jhs. tötet der Heilige Georg einen weiblichen Drachen.

Fig. 6: Slaying dragons is a frequently recurring element found in Indo-European heroic tales. It symbolises overcoming chaos and the establishing of civilisations. Successful dragon slayers are depicted as cultural heroes. They are typically male, whereas the dragons or dragon-like creatures tend to have female connotations. In this respect, patriarchal power structures are often embedded in tales of dragon fighting. In this 15th century image, St George is slaying a female dragon.

There is no great leap between receiving such decorations and being called a 'national hero'. Political communities use the term 'national heroes' to consolidate or – in the strongest case – even to establish their identity. This is often best achieved if the latter are portrayed in a state of war and while risking their lives for the future nation during combat. In literary terms, a prime example of this in the Western tradition is Virgil's *Aeneid*, in which Aeneas, as forefather of the Romans, lays the foundations for the Roman Empire. Aeneas' role for the Romans in ancient times corresponds, for example, to that of Joan of Arc for France and Skanderbeg, the anti-Ottoman rebel commander, for Albania in the late Middle Ages. Fighters for national freedom have good chances of becoming national heroes, be it in the fight against the Habsburgs like William Tell, against European colonisers like Simón Bolívar, or in the French Resistance against the Nazis, like Charles de Gaulle.

Carl von Clausewitz famously said that war is nothing but an extended duel. As stated earlier, all fights are fundamentally based on the concept of the duel. Even the German word 'Kampf' (fight) is probably an early derivation from the Latin term *campus*, referring to the 'field' used for duels. When duels are actually staged in the literal sense of the word, they have a particular potential for heroization because the fight focuses on two individuals. From the epic 'aristeia' to the Western mov-

Abb. 7: Alex Tate aus Großbritannien läuft bei den ersten Invictus Games zum Sieg im 100-Meter-Lauf der Herren, Ambulant IT1. Die Invictus Games sind ein internationaler Sportwettkampf für Soldaten und Soldatinnen, die im Dienst dauerhafte Beeinträchtigungen an Körper oder Seele davontrugen. Initiiert von Prinz Harry, finden sie seit 2014 nach dem Vorbild der US-amerikanischen Warrior Games statt. »Invictus« (lat. »unbesiegt«, »unbesiegbar«) deutet auf den doppelten kämpferischen Impetus hin: Nicht nur haben sich die Soldaten dem Kampf für ihre jeweiligen Gemeinschaften gewidmet, auch nach ihrer Verletzung kämpfen sie weiter – in der sportlichen Arena und gegen alle Hindernisse, die ihr verändertes Leben mit sich bringt.

Fig. 7: Great Britain's Alex Tate sprints to victory in the men's 100 metre race at the first Invictus Games, Outpatient IT1. The Invictus Games are an international sports competition for ex-soldiers who have suffered permanent physical or mental impairments during their military service. Initiated by Prince Harry, the Games have been taking place since 2014 and are modelled on the USA's "Warrior Games." "Invictus" (Latin for "undefeated", "invincible") suggests a double combative impetus: Not only have the soldiers dedicated themselves to fighting for their respective countries and communities, they also continue to fight after their injuries – both in the sporting arena and against all the obstacles that have changed their lives.

steht außer Frage. Rituale wie der Handschlag, der Trikottausch, sogar der konventionalisierte ›trash talk‹ vor oder nach einem Wettkampf sowie festgelegte Regeln verweisen jedoch darauf, dass es hier um einen eingehegten Kampf geht, der grundsätzlichen Spielcharakter hat und bei dem nicht existenzielle Werte auf dem Spiel stehen. Das Paradigma des Zweikampfs scheint am deutlichsten im ›Kampfsport‹ wie zum Beispiel dem Boxen durch; zu verschiedenen Graden sind aber alle wettkampfmäßig betriebenen Sportarten antagonistisch als Kampf gegen andere Parteien angelegt: als Mann gegen Mann bzw. Frau gegen Frau wie im Tennis, als Mannschaft gegen Mannschaft wie im Fußball oder als eine:r gegen alle wie (zumindest in der Grundidee) beim Radfahren, wobei sich auch hier wieder oft duale Rivalitäten herausbilden wie die zwischen Lance Armstrong und Jan Ullrich bei der Tour de France – auf der englischen *Wikipedia* kann man eine sehr lange »list of sports rivalries« quer durch die verschiedensten Sportarten nachlesen. Über diese agonale Grundkonstellation hinaus sind Sportler:innen immer dann besonders für Heroisierungen geeignet, wenn sie den von Seneca angedeuteten existenziellen Kampf mit sich selbst (*vivere militare est*) ins Außerordentliche steigern, sich überwinden, an ihre Grenzen gehen, sie überschreiten etc. Einen symbolisch besonders verdichteten Fall stellen dabei Wettkämpfe von versehrten oder kranken Sportlern wie die nach dem Vorbild der US

ie cowboy duels, fights between two individuals are used in the media to illustrate violent conflicts, regardless of historical plausibility.

Assuming the duel between two men is the default confrontation, the fight between a man and a dragon or other wild primordial being is an imaginary variant, albeit one that modern humans are familiar with and that is present in many cultures. Jason in the fight for the Golden Fleece in Greek mythology, Saint George in Christian legend and Siegfried in the *Nibelungenlied* represent just a few well-known dragon slayers from the European tradition. Their victory over primordial beings symbolises the victory of order and civilization over chaos and barbarism. Howver, their stories can also be read against the grain as a consolidation of patriarchal power structures, considering that the chthonic beings opposing the male 'cultural heroes' are often female or have a female connotation (Fig. 6).

Finally, human fights against the forces of nature can also be interpreted as a remote variant of the duel to the death. Firefighters are particularly suitable for heroizations, which is probably because they – in contrast to rescue workers helping after earthquakes, floods or avalanches – do not 'only' race against time following an uncontrollable disaster, but engage in an active fight with an uncertain outcome. Similar heroic portrayals can be observed during the 'ground combat' against epidemics and pandemics: In 2014, for instance, the globally read *Time Magazine* used heroic images to honour the 'Ebola fighters' as 'Person of the Year' – i.e. the physicians, nurses, drivers, etc. who risked their lives to prevent the spread of the Ebola virus in Africa's crisis regions. The explanation of the decision started with the following sentence: "'Not the glittering weapon fights the fight', says the proverb, 'but rather the hero's heart'."[1]

Sporting competitions are still physical, but they are no longer a life-or-death situation. There is no doubt that these competitions can also be carried out seriously and fiercely. However, rituals such as handshakes, jersey swaps, certain sets of rules and even conventional 'trash talks' before or after a competition indicate that this is a restricted fight over non-existential values with a generally playful character. The paradigm of the duel seems most obvious in 'martial arts' such as boxing. However, to different degrees, all competitive sports have an antagonistic design as fights against another party: man against man, or woman against woman in tennis, for example, or team against team as in football, or one against all as in cycling (at least in the essential idea, although, here too, dual rivalries often emerge, such as that between Lance Armstrong and Jan Ullrich during the Tour de France). The English *Wikipedia* entry on sports rivalries provides an extensive list of such rivalries across a wide range of sports. Beyond this basic 'agonistic' situation, athletes are particularly suited for heroizations when one also considers the existential struggle they endure with themselves (*vivere militare est*), as indicated by Seneca, when they increase it to a maximum and push

Warrior Games ins Leben gerufenen Invictus Games dar. Die hier antretenden kriegsversehrten Soldaten kämpfen als Sportler nicht nur gegen andere, sondern auf gewisse Weise auch gegen ihre persönlichen körperlichen und psychischen Herausforderungen (Abb. 7).

Wettkämpfe verschiedener Art können natürlich auch auf geistiger Ebene geführt werden. Ein besonders agonales Setting lag dabei stets dem Kampf mit Worten zugrunde. Schon in der *Ilias* werden neben physischen Gefechten auch Wort-Zweikämpfe ausgetragen, zum Beispiel im initialen Streit zwischen Agamemnon und Achill um die Kriegsgefangene Briseis. Berühmt wurden später auch die formalisierten Rede-Agone im Drama, v. a. bei Euripides, und das Konzept des Rede-Duells ist zum Beispiel aus Talkshows und Podiumsdiskussionen bis heute wohlbekannt. Ins Künstlerische gewendet, begegnet es als Dichter- und Sängerwettkampf, von dem aus römischer Kaiserzeit stammenden *Certamen Homeri et Hesiodi* (*Wettstreit zwischen Homer und Hesiod*) über den Sängerkrieg auf der Wartburg bis hin zum zeitgenössischen *battle rap* (Abb. 8).

Dass Sprache als ›Waffe‹ in Konflikten eingesetzt werden kann und so besonders privilegiert ist, das physische Konzept des Kampfes ins Intellektuelle zu erweitern, bewahrheitet sich auch beim Kampf mit Werten. Wenn Weltanschauungskämpfe wie der Kulturkampf, der Klassenkampf oder der Geschlechterkampf nicht gerade physisch-aktionistisch geführt werden, ist sprachliche Argumentation oder Polemik ihr bevorzugtes Mittel. Der Übergang zu physischer Gewalt ist dabei oft flie-

Abb. 8: Der Sängerkrieg auf der Wartburg ist eine Sammlung mittelhochdeutscher Sangspruchgedichte, die einen fiktiven Dichter-Wettkampf auf der thüringischen Wartburg inszenieren. Der im 13. Jh. entstandene Kern wurde bis zum Ausgang des Mittelalters erweitert und später vielfach literarisch und künstlerisch adaptiert. Am bekanntesten ist wohl Richard Wagners Oper »Tannhäuser und der Sängerkrieg auf der Wartburg« (1843), die den Stoff vom Sängerkrieg mit dem früher getrennten Stoff der Tannhäuser-Sage verbindet. Moritz von Schwinds Zeichnung entstand 1837, er hatte den Auftrag zur Ausmalung von Räumen der Wartburg erhalten.

Fig. 8: The Sängerkrieg ("Minstrel Contest") of 1207, which is said to have taken place at the Wartburg Castle in the German State of Thuringia, is a collection of Middle High German song poems that depict a fictional competition between poets and minstrels. The centrepiece, which dates back to the 13th century, was expanded until the end of the Middle Ages and later adapted in many literary and artistic styles. Richard Wagner's opera "Tannhäuser und der Sängerkrieg auf der Wartburg" (1843) is probably the best known adaptation, combining the material from the Sängerkrieg with the previously separate material from the legend of Tannhäuser, another German poet and minstrel. Moritz von Schwind's painting, pictured here, was completed in 1837 when he was commissioned to decorate rooms in the Wartburg Castle.

themselves to their limits and beyond. A case with particularly strong symbolism in this context is the competition between athletes with physical disabilities, such as in the Invictus Games, which follow the example of the US Warrior Games. The injured war veterans competing as athletes in these games are not only fighting against others, but essentially also against their own physical and mental challenges (Fig. 7).

Different kinds of competitions can, of course, also be carried out on a mental level. Fights with words always have a particularly agonistic setting. Besides physical battles, duels with words were also already carried out in the *Iliad*, for instance in the initial dispute between Agamemnon and Achilles over Briseis as a prisoner of war. Later on, the formalised verbal duels in drama also became popular, especially with Euripides, and the concept of the war of words is well-known to this day, for example from talk shows and panel discussions. From an artistic perspective, it occurs as a competition between poets and singers, ranging from the *Certamen Homeri et Hesiodi* (*Contest of Homer and Hesiod*) from the Roman imperial period through to the singer's contest at Wartburg castle and contemporary battle rap (Fig. 8).

The fact that language can be used as a weapon in conflicts, which extends the physical concept of fighting to the intellectual domain, is also true regarding the fight over values. If ideological fights such as culture wars, class war, or the battle of the sexes are not carried out in a physical manner, then verbal argumentation

ßend, wie etwa am Beispiel des Black Power Movement und seiner ambivalenten Helden wie Malcolm X deutlich wird.

Ein in Ernsthaftigkeit, Häufigkeit und heroisierenden Folgen nicht zu unterschätzender Typus des Kämpfens ist schließlich derjenige, der auf gekränkter persönlicher Ehre und auf Streitlust (dem englischen *fight-picking*) beruht. In früheren Zeiten auch gern in Form eines Duells auf Leben und Tod ausgetragen, ist dieser Typus heute eher als ein mediales Ereignis zwischen großen Egos bekannt, die sich in ihren jeweiligen Revieren in die Quere kommen und sich gegenseitig provozieren. Ein Beispiel wäre die an einen infantilen Sandkastenkampf erinnernde Rivalität von Unternehmern wie Elon Musk und Jeff Bezos um die Vorherrschaft im Bereich der Raumfahrt, die gerade durch die sozialen Medien vielfach multipliziert und verstärkt wurde und so zur heroisierenden Verehrung oder Verachtung der beiden Persönlichkeiten maßgeblich beitrug (Abb. 9).

Fazit

Insgesamt zeigt sich der Kampf als ein Schlüsselkonzept, das auf vielfältige Weise in Heroisierungsprozesse eingebunden ist. Auf wörtlicher oder metaphorischer Ebene fördert seine destabilisierende, antagonistische Struktur den Umsturz und die Neuordnung von Machtverhältnissen auf Kosten eines oder mehrerer Gegner. Als Träger dieses Geschehens tritt in der sozialen Wahrnehmung häufig eine Heldenfigur hervor, deren Kampf als heroisch gedeutet wird. Dass diese Figur traditionell so häufig ein Mann ist, hat nicht zuletzt mit der kulturellen Codierung des Kampfs als männlicher Domäne zu tun.

Anmerkungen

1   Gibbs 2014.

Notes

1   Gibbs 2014.

or polemics are the preferred instrument. The boundaries between verbal and physical violence can be blurred, as in the case of the Black Power movement and its ambivalent heroes, such as Malcolm X.

Finally, there is a type of fighting whose gravity, frequency and potential to heroize its winners should not be underestimated: the fighting caused by personal humiliation and the temptation to pick a fight. In former times, this type of fight was often carried out as a life-or-death duel. Today, however, it is better known as a media event involving two large egos that get in each other's way in their respective territories and provoke each other. One example reminiscent of a childish sandpit fight was the rivalry between entrepreneurs Elon Musk and Jeff Bezos for dominance in space travel. The rivalry was particularly reinforced through social media, which then significantly fuelled either heroizing admiration or contempt for the two personalities (Fig. 9).

Abb. 9: Ob Musk gegen Bezos oder Musk gegen Zuckerberg: Ein weltweites Publikum verfolgt ihre öffentlich ausgefochtenen Zweikämpfe mit Staunen, mokiert sich über die Protagonisten – und heroisiert die Unternehmer-Milliardäre doch für Eigenschaften, die als Bedingung ihres wirtschaftlichen Erfolgs wahrgenommen werden: Kampfgeist, Durchsetzungsvermögen, Wagemut, Risikofreude und eine gewisse Fähigkeit, sich um die Meinung der Öffentlichkeit nicht zu scheren.

Fig. 9: Whether it's Musk versus Bezos or Musk versus Zuckerberg, global audiences watch their public duels in awe. They mock the protagonists – and yet heroize these entrepreneurial billionaires for qualities that are perceived as a prerequisite for their economic success: A fighting spirit, assertiveness, daring, a willingness to take risks and a certain ability to not give a damn about public opinion.

Conclusion

On the whole, fighting appears as a key concept that is involved in heroization processes in many different ways. On both literal and metaphorical levels, its destabilising, antagonistic nature promotes the overthrow and reorganisation of power structures at the expense of one or more opponents. In terms of social perception, the carrier of this process often emerges as a hero figure whose fight is interpreted as heroic. The fact that this figure is traditionally so often a man has to do, not least, with the cultural coding of fighting as a male domain.

© 2024 Stefan Tilg, Publikation: Wallstein Verlag; DOI https://doi.org/10.46500/83535581-006 | CC BY-NC-ND 4.0

Tobias Schlechtriemen

GRENZÜBERSCHREITUNG

Heldengeschichten erzählen nicht nur von großen Taten, sondern auch von den Grenzüberschreitungen, die damit einhergehen: Wenn Herkules mit bloßen Händen den Löwen erwürgt, wenn Chesley B. Sullenberger ein Passagierflugzeug auf dem Hudson River notlandet, wenn Antigone gegen Kreons Verbot ihren Bruder bestattet, wenn Alexander der Große bei seinem Feldzug den Hindukusch überquert und weite Teile des Perserreichs erobert (Abb. 1), oder wenn Melli Beese gegen alle Widerstände eine Pilotin wird – dann überschreiten sie alle dabei Grenzen (Abb. 2). Die Grenzüberschreitung kennzeichnet alle heroischen Figuren.[1] Dabei sind die Grenzen, die sie überschreiten, durchaus verschieden: Es handelt sich um geografische Grenzen, aber auch um die Grenzen, die durch Normen und Gesetze gezogen sind, oder um die Grenzen dessen, was als normal und erwartbar gilt. Wären die Held:innen nicht zu Krieg und Abenteuer ausgezogen, sondern zuhause geblieben, hätten sie sich an die geltenden Regeln gehalten oder einfach nur das getan, was alle tun, dann wäre ihr Verhalten nicht aufgefallen, hätte nicht die öffentliche Aufmerksamkeit erregt und man würde sie letztendlich auch nicht als Heldinnen und Helden verehren.

Abb. 1: Die Verehrung Alexanders des Großen (356–323 v. Chr.) überschritt viele Grenzen: Er wurde nicht nur in seiner Heimat, sondern auch dort heroisiert, wo er als Eroberer Fuß fasste. Das ägyptische Goldmedaillon zeigt ihn mehr als 500 Jahre nach der Eroberung mit der Binde des Gottes Dionysos über der Stirn und dem Widderhorn. Das Widderhorn symbolisiert, dass er von Zeus Ammon, dem Widdergott, als sein Sohn ausgerufen wurde. Insofern überschritt Alexander zudem die Grenzen des Menschlichen, indem er als Gott verehrt wurde.

Fig. 1: The veneration of Alexander the Great (356–323 BC) spanned many borders. He was not only heroized in his homeland, but wherever he established himself as a conqueror, too. More than 500 years later, this Egyptian medaillon shows him wearing a headband bearing the Greek god Dionysus and a ram's horn. The ram's horn symbolises that he was proclaimed by Zeus Ammon, the ram god, as his son. In this respect, Alexander also transcended human limitations by being worshipped as a god.

Wenn sie erst einmal Heldenstatus erreicht haben und man ihnen Denkmäler errichtet, von ihnen in Schul- und Geschichtsbüchern berichtet, erwecken Held:innen den Eindruck, als seien sie schon immer als solche etabliert gewesen und gehörten

Tobias Schlechtriemen

CROSSING BOUNDARIES

Heroic stories do not only tell of great deeds but also of the transgression of boundaries that comes with them: When Hercules strangles a lion with his bare hands, when Chesley B. Sullenberger performs an emergency landing with a passenger aircraft on the Hudson River, when Antigone buries her brother despite being forbidden to do so by Creon, when Alexander the Great crosses the Hindu Kush during his campaign and conquers large parts of the Persian Empire (Fig. 1), or when Melli Beese becomes a pilot against all opposition (Fig. 2) – they all cross boundaries. All heroic figures cross boundaries.[1] The boundaries they cross are quite diverse: They are geographical boundaries but also boundaries set by norms and laws, or the boundaries of what is considered normal and expectable. Had heroes stayed at home rather than setting out for war and adventure, had they adhered to the existing rules, or had simply done what anybody else would have done, their behaviour would have not stood out. They would not have attracted the attention of the public and ultimately they would not have ended up being venerated as heroes.

Once they have achieved heroic status and memorials have been erected for them, textbooks and history books tell of them, it seems like they have always been established as part of the

Abb. 2: Melli Beese (1886–1925) war zu ihrer Zeit eine unkonventionelle Erscheinung. Mehrere Fluglehrer weigerten sich, sie als Schülerin anzunehmen, oder brachen die Ausbildung ab; das Fliegen galt als »ein Männern vorbehaltenes Terrain«. Trotz aller Widrigkeiten erwarb Beese am 13. September 1911 ihre Fluglizenz (Nr. 115). Ihre im folgenden Jahr gegründete eigene Flugschule musste sie zu Beginn des Ersten Weltkriegs wieder schließen, weil ihr Mann Franzose war. Von diesem Rückschlag erholte sie sich nicht. 1925 setzte sie ihrem Leben ein Ende. Heute sind nach der Pionierin der Luftfahrt Kindergärten, Schulen, Straßen und auch Flughafenlounges benannt – im Bild diejenige in Berlin-Tempelhof.

Fig. 2: Melli Beese (1886–1925) was an unconventional individual in her day. Several flight instructors refused to accept her as an aviation student – or simply cancelled her training. Back then, flying was considered "a field reserved for men". Despite these adversities, Beese obtained her flying licence (No. 115) on 13 September 1911. She had to close her own flying school, which she founded the following year, at the beginning of the First World War because her husband was French. She did not recover from this setback and took her own life in 1925. Today, kindergartens, schools, streets and airport lounges are named after the aviation pioneer – the photograph shows the lounge in Berlin-Tempelhof.

Abb. 3: Als Rosa Parks am 1. Dezember 1955 in Montgomery (Alabama) im Bus sitzenblieb, statt ihren Platz für einen Weißen zu räumen, verletzte sie formal die Beförderungsbedingungen. Nach einem mehr als einjährigen Boykott des öffentlichen Nahverkehrs durch die Schwarze Bevölkerung entschied der Oberste Gerichtshof in dritter Instanz, dass die systematische Benachteiligung Schwarzer durch rassistische Regeln der öffentlichen Busunternehmen in Alabama verfassungswidrig sei. Das Bild zeigt eine Skulptur von Rosa Parks in einem historischen Bus des National Civil Rights Museums in Memphis (Tennessee).

Fig. 3: When Rosa Parks refused to give up her seat for a white passenger on a bus in Montgomery, Alabama, on 1 December 1955, she formally violated transport regulations. After a subsequent public transportation boycott by the black population that lasted more than a year, the Supreme Court ruled in the third instance that the systematic discrimination against black people by racist rules put in place by public bus companies in Alabama was unconstitutional. This picture shows a sculpture of Rosa Parks on a vintage bus at the National Civil Rights Museum in Memphis, Tennessee.

seit jeher zum Bestand des kulturellen Kanons. In diesem Zustand erregen sie selten die Gemüter und führen ein eher befriedetes Dasein. Dabei gerät schnell aus dem Blick, dass sie ebenso eine andere, konflikthafte Seite aufweisen: Sie sind durchaus in der Lage, Unruhe zu stiften und Streit auszulösen. Ihre Taten werden – gerade anfangs – nicht von allen bewundert und als »heroisch« wahrgenommen. Im Gegenteil: Oftmals gibt es darüber auch Empörung und die Forderung, ein solches Verhalten zu sanktionieren. Ob Edward Snowdens Veröffentlichung der Geheimdienstdokumente ein bewundernswerter und mutiger Dienst für die Allgemeinheit war oder nicht viel eher »Spionage und Diebstahl von Regierungseigentum«, wie die Anklage der US-Regierung gegen ihn lautet, bleibt durchaus umstritten. Und so gehört es zu Held:innen, dass sie Gesetze brechen und gegen geltende Normen verstoßen. Mit dieser transgressiven Seite kommen die streitbaren Facetten heroischer Figuren zur Sprache.

Gesellschaftliche Grenzen

Nimmt man gezielt die Grenzüberschreitung in den Blick, lässt sich darüber die heroische Figur mit ihrem gesellschaftlichen Kontext verbinden. Man schaut dann nicht nur auf die Einzelfigur, sondern bezieht das soziale Setting mit ein, in dem sich ihre Heldentat abspielt. Denn bei jeder Grenzüberschreitung stellt sich die Frage, *welche* Grenze überschritten wurde: die Grenze, die rechtlich durch ein bestimmtes Gesetz festgelegt ist (Abb. 3), die Grenze einer sozialen Norm, die gesellschaftlich gesetzt ist, oder die Grenze dessen, was man von einer Person in einer bestimmten Situation

cultural canon since time immemorial. In this state, they rarely spark any outrage and lead a rather peaceful existence. It tends to be forgotten that they also have a different, conflicting side to them: They are more than capable of disturbing the peace or causing an argument. Their deeds are – especially in the beginning – not necessarily unanimously admired and perceived as heroic. On the contrary: they often spark outrage and demands that such behaviour should be sanctioned. Whether Edward Snowden's public release of intelligence documents was an admirable and brave service for the public or rather "espionage and theft of government property", as the U. S. government's charge states, remains disputed. Part of being a hero is breaking the established laws and norms. With this transgressive side, the disputable aspects of heroic figures are brought up.

Societal boundaries

Focusing specifically on boundary transgression allows us to connect the heroic figure with their social context. This approach allows us to pay attention not only to the individual figure but also to the social setting in which the heroic deeds take place. Every crossing of a boundary raises the question: which boundary has actually been crossed? The boundary legally defined by a certain law (Fig. 3), the boundary of a social norm that has been set by society, or the boundary of what would be expected from a certain person in a certain situation. All these boundaries are defined by orders and ideas that are valid in the society in question and are binding to all its members under normal circumstances.

The transgression of a boundary by the hero marks exactly the spot where the extraordinary deed of an individual is connected to a social order. And the deed itself is only extraordinary, exceptional, an exemption because it contrasts with order, rules and ordinary behaviour as such.[2] Greta Thunberg, sitting on the ground in front of the Swedish parliament with a cardboard sign, seems rather vulnerable and lacking in any significant power at first glance. A young girl determinedly and resolutely taking a stand for environmental protection and, in her subsequent appearances, making demands in a brave and eloquent fashion in front of a greater political public, however, becomes extraordinary when considering the backdrop of the established image of a child, and a female one at that (Fig. 4). The significance of the heroic deed can therefore not be understood without simultaneously considering the rules and norms broken through the deviating behaviour of the hero. Especially the strong public reaction to the deed can only be understood if the social context is taken into consideration. The colossal effect that the seemingly unassuming actions of Greta Thunberg had can be understood in this way. The image of the girl with the yellow rain coat and a cardboard sign went around the world. Her protest did

erwarten würde. Alle diese Grenzziehungen sind durch Ordnungen und Vorstellungen bestimmt, die in der betreffenden Gesellschaft gelten und für alle Mitglieder unter normalen Umständen verbindlich sind.

Die Grenzüberschreitung der Heldin oder des Helden markiert nun genau die Stelle, an der die außerordentliche Tat einer Einzelperson mit der gesellschaftlichen Ordnung verbunden ist. Und die Tat ist ja auch nur deshalb außerordentlich, exzeptionell, eine Ausnahme, weil sie sich von der Ordnung, der Regel, dem üblichen Verhalten als solche absetzt.[2] So wirkt Greta Thunberg, die als Fünfzehnjährige mit ihrem Pappschild vor dem schwedischen Parlament auf dem Boden sitzt, erst einmal eher verletzlich und ohne starke Handlungsmacht. Aber dass ein junges Mädchen so beharrlich und konsequent für Umweltschutz eintritt und bei den folgenden Auftritten in einer größeren politischen Öffentlichkeit so mutig, eloquent und fordernd agiert, ist vor dem Hintergrund des etablierten Bildes von Kindern und insbesondere Mädchen außergewöhnlich (Abb. 4). Was die heroische Tat bedeutet, lässt sich folglich nicht verstehen, wenn man nicht gleichzeitig bedenkt, welche Regeln und Normen durch das abweichende Handeln der Heldin oder des Helden gebrochen werden. Vor allem lässt sich die mitunter heftige soziale Reaktion darauf nur verstehen, wenn man den gesellschaftlichen Kontext bedenkt. Das gilt auch für die enorme Wirkung, welche die zunächst unscheinbare Aktion von Greta Thunberg erzielte. Das Bild des Mädchens mit seinem gelben Regenmantel und seinem Pappschild ging um die Welt. Ihr Protest initiierte nicht nur die globale Jugendbewegung *Fridays for Future*, sondern auch die starke Ablehnung, die sich etwa in den zahllosen Hasskommentaren in sozialen Medien äußerte.[3] Die starke Resonanz – und Polarisierung – hängt auch damit zusammen, dass der Umgang mit dem Klimawandel eine Frage ist, die viele Menschen in der Gegenwartsgesellschaft umtreibt. Zudem stellt Thunberg als politisch agierende junge Frau traditionelle Maskulinitätsvorstellungen in Frage. Überhaupt werfen ihre Aktionen die Frage auf, wie ein adäquates politisches Handeln angesichts des Klimawandels aussehen könnte. Weil dies brennende gesellschaftliche Fragen sind, kann sie als einzelne Person mit der zunächst relativ harmlosen Grenzüberschreitung eines Schulstreiks eine solch enorme Wirkung hervorrufen. Wer also die Bedeutung einer Heldentat verstehen will, darf nicht nur auf die beeindruckende Aktion der heroischen Figur schauen, sondern muss genauso den gesellschaftlichen Kontext einbeziehen, in dem sie sich abspielt.

Die Grenzüberschreitung als Auslöser

Schaut man sich genauer an, wie eine Heldin oder ein Held zu einer solchen oder einem solchen wird, dann stehen die Heldentat und die mit ihr einhergehende

not only initiate the global youth movement *Fridays for Future* but also strong rejection, expressed in countless hate postings on social media.[3] The strong resonance – and polarisation – that met Thunberg's actions also has something to do with the fact that dealing with climate change is a question weighing on many people's minds in contemporary society. Furthermore, as a politically active young woman, Thunberg also challenges traditional perceptions of masculinity. Her actions raise questions about the shape adequate political action in the face of climate change could take. Because these are such pressing social issues, she, as an individual, can trigger a tremendous impact with the seemingly harmless transgression of a school strike. Understanding the significance of a heroic deed means considering the social context in which it takes place and not only focussing on the impressive action of the heroic figure itself.

Abb. 4: Auch in Schweden besteht Schulpflicht für alle Kinder und Jugendlichen bis 16 Jahren. Als Greta Thunberg in der neunten Klasse im Jahr 2018 begann, jeden Freitag in den »Schulstreik für das Klima« zu treten, übertrat sie (bzw. übertraten ihre Eltern) dieses Gesetz. Thunberg schloss die Schule mit hervorragenden Noten ab; die von ihr inspirierte weltweite Klimabewegung *Fridays for Future* wird bis heute von Schüler:innen und Studierenden geprägt.

Fig. 4: In Sweden, school attendance is compulsory for all children and adolescents up to the age of 16. When in 2018, Greta Thunberg began to go on "school strike for the climate" every Friday in Year 9, she (or rather her parents) broke this law. Thunberg graduated from school with excellent grades, and the global climate movement Fridays for Future *that she inspired is still being organised by pupils and students today.*

Crossing boundaries as a trigger

Upon closer inspection of how heroes gain their status, it becomes evident that it all starts with the heroic deed and the boundary that it crosses. When pilot Chesley B. Sullenberger is informed shortly after take-off from the New York airport LaGuardia that both engines of his passenger aircraft had failed he is forced to act quickly. He decides against instructions given by air control and does not return or set course to a nearby airport. Instead, he makes an emergency water landing on the Hudson River. Such a manoeuver is neither intended for emergencies nor is it very likely to succeed – no one had been successful in such a landing before. Sullenberger manages to land the aircraft on the water, avoiding bridges and fer-

Grenzüberschreitung am Anfang. Als der Pilot Chesley B. Sullenberger darüber informiert wird, dass kurz nach dem Start am New Yorker Flughafen LaGuardia beide Triebwerke seines Passagierflugzeugs ausgefallen sind, muss er schnell handeln. Er entscheidet sich gegen die Anweisungen des Towers, zurückzufliegen oder einen nahegelegenen Flughafen anzusteuern. Stattdessen führt er eine Notwasserung auf dem Hudson River durch. Ein solches Manöver ist für den Notfall weder vorgesehen, noch ist es besonders aussichtsreich – in dieser Form ist eine solche Landung bis zu diesem Zeitpunkt noch niemandem geglückt. Sullenberger gelingt es, das Flugzeug auf dem Wasser zwischen den Brücken und Fähren – und eineinhalb Kilometer vom Times Square entfernt – zu landen. Alle 155 Insassen werden gerettet. Bereits in den ersten Berichten ist von einem »Wunder vom Hudson« die Rede und Sullenberger wird als Held gefeiert (Abb. 5).[4] Die amerikanische Verkehrsbehörde (*National Transportation Safety Board*) setzt sich allerdings anschließend mehr als ein Jahr lang mit dem Ereignis und dessen Bewertung auseinander, bis auch sie zu dem Schluss kommt, dass Sullenberger richtig gehandelt habe. Man stelle sich jedoch vor, wie sein Handeln von allen Seiten bewertet worden wäre, wenn die Notwasserung nicht geglückt wäre. Man hätte ihm sicherlich vorgeworfen, dass er die Anweisungen des Towers nicht befolgt habe.[5] Der Fall zeigt exemplarisch, dass am Anfang des Heroisierungsprozesses eine Grenzüberschreitung steht – hier entscheidet sich Sullenberger zu einem Vorgehen, das in den Luftfahrtregeln nicht vorgesehen und so auch zuvor niemandem gelungen ist. Direkt nach der Grenzüberschreitung ist es erst einmal völlig offen, wie die soziale Reaktion darauf ausfallen, inwiefern die Person dafür heroisiert wird oder nicht. In Sullenbergers Fall erfolgt sie prompt und eindeutig positiv. Das ist aber längst nicht bei allen Grenzüberschreitungen der Fall.

Bei Sullenberger handelt es sich um ein reales Ereignis und eine reale Person. Über Zuschreibungen, die dann auch medial verbreitet werden, wird er als Held bezeichnet und gefeiert. Bei solchen realen Ereignissen ist es nicht vorhersehbar, wie die soziale Reaktion auf die Grenzüberschreitung ausfallen wird. In fiktiven Heldengeschichten ist zumindest sicher, dass am Ende die Heldin oder der Held auch als solcher wahrgenommen wird – das gilt auch dann, wenn es zur Dramatik der Erzählung gehört, dass dieser Status erst errungen werden muss. Denn: Die Grenzüberschreitung bildet ein wesentliches Element, auch von fiktiven Heldengeschichten. Der Literaturwissenschaftler Jurij Lotman geht noch grundsätzlicher davon aus, dass *alle* Geschichten im Kern eine Grenzüberschreitung enthalten.[6] Erst dadurch, dass die Hauptfigur eine Grenze überschreitet, kommt die Geschichte in Gang. Alle Geschichten erzählen somit von einer Grenzüberschreitung und ihren Folgen. Auch bei Lotman gibt es verschiedenste Grenzen, die überschritten werden können: zwischen der Heimat und der Fremde, zwischen Land und Meer oder zwischen Dies- und Jenseits. Orpheus etwa überwindet die Grenze, welche die Welt der

ries, and only one and a half kilometres from Times Square. All 155 passengers were saved. The first reports on the incident already started referring to it as the "Miracle on the Hudson" and Sullenberger was hailed as a hero (Fig. 5).[4] However, the American *National Transportation Safety Board* subsequently discussed and evaluated the incident and its outcome for over a year until they, too, reached the conclusion that Sullenberger had made the right call. Just imagine how his actions would have been appraised by all sides if the emergency water landing had not been successful. He would no doubt have been blamed for not following the instructions of air control.[5] This example demonstrates that the heroization process always begins with the transgression of boundaries – in this case, Sullenberger decided to proceed in a way that was not recommended by aviation law and had never been achieved in this fashion by anyone before him. In the direct aftermath of the transgression, the social response and potential heroization of the person remains undecided. In the case of Sullenberger, the response was quick and decisively positive. This is, however, not the case with all transgressions of boundaries.

In the Sullenberger case, it was a real event and a real person. His character is labelled and celebrated as heroic by others, including the media. For real events such as this one, it is impossible to predict what the social reaction to the transgression will be. With fictional hero's tales, it is at least certain that by the end of the tale the heroes will be perceived as such – even if the story's dramatics mean that this status has to be earned first. The transgression of boundaries

Abb. 5: Der Unterlauf des Hudson River in New York City wird von zahlreichen Brücken überspannt und ist ein vielgenutzter Wasserverkehrsweg. Notwasserungen von Flugzeugen sind so riskant, dass sie in Pilotenschulungen nicht unterrichtet werden. Nachdem die Triebwerke seines Flugzeugs ausgefallen waren, entschied sich Flugkapitän Chesley B. Sullenberger 2009 unter extremem Zeitdruck und entgegen den Anweisungen für eine Notlandung auf dem Hudson. Die sichere Landung von Flug 1549 auf dem Hudson war jedoch so außergewöhnlich, dass sie als nicht wiederholbar gilt – wahrscheinlich nicht einmal von Sullenberger selbst.

Fig. 5: The lower section of the Hudson River in New York City is spanned by several bridges, and it is also a busy waterway. Emergency landings by aircraft in bodies of water ("ditching") are so risky that they are not taught in pilot training courses. After his aircraft's engines failed, Captain Chesley B. Sullenberger decided to make an emergency landing on the Hudson in 2009, under extreme time pressure and against instructions from the groundcrew. However, he safely landed Flight 1549 on the Hudson. This feat was so extraordinary that it is considered unrepeatable – probably not even by Sullenberger himself.

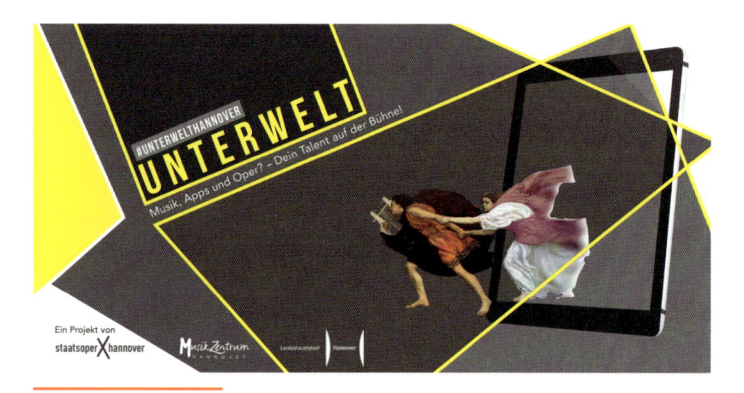

Abb. 6: Der mythische Sänger Orpheus konnte mit seinem Gesang die Grenzen zwischen belebter und unbelebter Natur überwinden und sogar Steine rühren. Am Tag seiner Hochzeit mit Eurydike starb diese an einem Schlangenbiss. Um sie ins Leben zurückzuholen, überschritt Orpheus die Grenze von Diesseits und Jenseits und ging zu Eurydike ins Totenreich. Doch ihm gelang Eurydikes Rettung nicht. Als er daraufhin der Liebe zu Frauen abschwor, wurde er von wütenden Mänaden zerrissen. Obgleich sein Körper zerstört war, blieb seine Stimme erhalten.

Fig. 6: Orpheus, a figure in Greek mythology, was able to overcome the boundaries between animate and inanimate nature with his singing; he even managed to move stones with his voice. On the day of his wedding to Eurydice, she died of a snakebite. To bring her back to life, Orpheus crossed the divide between this world and the afterlife and found Eurydice in the Realm of the Dead. But he did not succeed in rescuing her. As a result, he renounced his love for women, whereupon he was torn apart by angry maenads. Although his body was destroyed, his voice was preserved.

Lebenden vom Reich der Toten trennt, um seine geliebte Eurydike wieder ins Leben zurückzuholen (Abb. 6).[7] Die heroische Grenzüberschreitung, also der Fall einer positiv bewerteten Grenzüberschreitung, sei ein »moralisch reguliertes Abweichen«, so der Soziologe Niklas Luhmann. Das habe den Vorteil, dass man »durch *Übertreffen der erwartbaren Leistungen* beide Wege zugleich begehen [könne]: den der Konformität und den der Abweichung«[8].

Die Überschreitung des Gesetzes

Nicht selten initiieren Held:innen etwas Neues. Daher rührt auch ihre Nähe zu Künstler:innen, Gründungsfiguren und nicht zuletzt der Figur des Gesetzgebers. Um ein neues Gesetz zu begründen, muss allerdings ein altes ersetzt werden. Und an dieser Stelle setzen Held:innen nicht auf die langsamen Mühlen demokratischer Verfahren. Sie wären auch nicht bereit, Kompromisse einzugehen. Stattdessen ändern sie die Dinge aus eigener Kraft und ohne demokratische Abstimmung.[9] Aus Sicht der überkommenen Gesetzgebung handelt es sich dabei um einen unrechtmäßigen Gesetzesbruch. So heißt es über Lykurg, den mythischen Gesetzgeber Spartas, dass er in einem Staatsstreich die Macht zunächst gewaltsam an sich gerissen habe (Abb. 7). Nachdem einmal die Macht in seinen Händen lag, etablierte er eine neue Verfassung, in der die Herrschaft auf viele verteilt wurde. Er selbst hungerte sich anschließend zu Tode und wurde posthum für seine Tat verehrt. Wenn der Gesetzgeber heroisiert wird, beinhaltet dies auch einen heiklen Aspekt: Denn es handelt sich nicht nur um den Begründer des neuen Gesetzes, sondern zugleich um die Person, die rück-

is a key element – even in fictional stories regarding heroes. Literary scholar Jurij Lotman holds the even more fundamental believe that *all* stories contain a crossing of a boundary at their core.[6] Only when the main character crosses a boundary does the story gain momentum. Therefore, all stories contain boundary crossings and their consequences. In Lotman's works too, there are many different boundaries that can be crossed: between the homeland and foreign land, between land and sea or between present life and past life. Orpheus, for example, crosses the border between the world of the living and the world of the dead in order to bring his beloved, Eurydice, back to life (Fig. 6).[7] The heroic crossing of a boundary, meaning one that is perceived as positive, is a "morally regulated deviation," according to sociologist Niklas Luhmann. This offers the advantage that one could "walk both paths, that of conformity and that of deviation, at the same time by *exceeding the effort that is to be expected*"[8].

Crossing legal boundaries

Frequently heroes initiate something new. They are therefore closely linked to artists, founding figures and, not least, the character of the lawmaker. In order to establish a new law, an old one has to be replaced, however. And in this case, heroes do not rely on the slow wheels of democratic procedures – nor are they willing to compromise. Instead, they bring about change through their own efforts and without a democratic consensus.[9] From the perspective of legislation, this is an unlawful overstepping of boundaries. Such is the case for Lycurgus, the mythical lawmaker of Sparta, who is said to have violently seized power through a coup d'état (Fig. 7). Once power was in his hands, he established a new constitution in which rule was distributed among many. He subsequently starved himself to death and was posthumously revered for his deeds. The heroization of a legislator also contains a tension: They are not just the person who established a new law, but also the person who was ruthless enough to break the old. From the perspective of the newly established legal system, the hero's act of establishing this new system is of course exemplary. His ruthless transgression of a legal boundary, however, should not be emulated henceforth. Due to his demise, Lycurgus was no longer a threat to his new order. Even in the form of the lawmaker, the heroic figure incorporates subversive potential by crossing a boundary. Sometimes it is also the discrepancy between law and norm that provides the starting point for a heroic deed. Antigone is very much aware that she is violating the law of King Creon that states that Polynices is not to be buried as he has committed treason. But it is the divine norm to bury her brother and she considers this to be of a higher importance – and is ready to accept the consequences (Fig. 8).

Abb. 7: Lykurg riss in einem Staatsstreich die Herrschaft an sich, um eine neue Staatsform zu begründen: eine Gesetzesherrschaft, in der die Macht in den Händen vieler liegt. Nach der Zusage der Spartaner, bis zu seiner Rückkehr nichts zu verändern, hungerte er sich in Delphi zu Tode, um seine Reformen dauerhaft zu sichern. Darstellungen von Lykurg befinden sich unter anderem im Brüsseler Justizpalast und im Kapitol in Washington. Der Held, der alle traditionellen Vorstellungsgrenzen menschlichen Zusammenlebens überschritt, indem er eine Volksherrschaft durch seinen eigenen Tod sicherte, steht nun für die Herrschaft demokratischer Gesetze auf der Grundlage demokratischer Verfassungen.

Fig. 7: Lycurgus seized power in a coup d'état in order to establish a new form of government – a rule of law in which power would rest in the hands of the many. After the Spartans promised not to make any changes to his reforms until his return from battle, he starved himself to death in Delphi in order to permanently secure his new form of government. Representations of Lycurgus can be found in the United States Capitol and the Palace of Justice in Brussels. A hero who transcended all traditional notions of human co-existence by securing the people's rule through his own death now stands for the power of democratic laws on the basis of democratic constitutions.

sichtslos genug war, mit dem alten Gesetz zu brechen. Vorbildlich aus Sicht der neu begründeten Rechtsordnung ist folglich der Gesetzgebungsakt des Helden, seine skrupellose Grenzüberschreitung sollte hingegen fortan nicht nachgeahmt werden. Lykurg stellt durch seinen Tod keine solche Gefahr mehr für die neue Ordnung dar. Auch in der Form des Gesetzgebers wohnt der heroischen Figur durch die Grenzüberschreitung folglich ein subversives Potential inne. Manchmal ist es auch der Widerspruch zwischen Gesetz und Norm, der den Ausgangspunkt einer heroischen Tat bildet. So ist Antigone sehr wohl klar, dass sie gegen das Gesetz des Königs Kreon verstößt, das besagt, dass Polyneikes nicht bestattet werden dürfe, weil er Landesverrat begangen habe. Aber es ist die göttliche Norm, den Bruder zu bestatten, und die erachtet sie für sich als wichtiger – und ist bereit, die Folgen dafür in Kauf zu nehmen (Abb. 8).

Abb. 8: Die antike Figur Antigone missachtet die weltliche Weisung des Königs, um ein göttliches Gebot zu befolgen (Gemälde von 1825). Sie nimmt dafür die Todesstrafe in Kauf. Diese heroische Grenzüberschreitung gewinnt noch an Bedeutung durch den Umstand, dass Antigone eine Frau ist. Denn Frauen hätten der Weisung des Stärkeren zu gehorchen und nicht gegen Männer aufzubegehren, so heißt es in der antiken Tragödie, die Antigones Namen trägt. Heute wird Antigone vor allem als bestärkendes Vorbild im Kampf um Menschenrechte, gegen Unterdrückung und soziale Ungleichheiten interpretiert.

Fig. 8: *The ancient Greek figure Antigone disobeyed her king's secular instructions in order to fulfil a divine commandment (1825 painting). She accepted the death penalty for doing so. This heroic transgression is made even more significant by the fact that Antigone is a woman. According to the ancient tragedy that bears Antigone's name, women must obey their masters and may not rebel against men. Today, Antigone is primarily interpreted as an encouraging role model in the fight for human rights – against oppression and social inequality.*

Normative Überschreitungen

Das Verhalten der Gesellschaftsmitglieder orientiert sich nicht nur an rechtlichen Regelungen, sondern auch an Verhaltensnormen. Obwohl diese nicht unbedingt schriftlich fixiert sind, ist dennoch allen klar, dass sie gelten und dass es sanktioniert wird, wenn sie nicht eingehalten werden. Heldinnen und Helden weisen auch hier eine Eigenwilligkeit auf. Sie zeugt davon, dass Held:innen sich nicht in erster Linie an den normativen Erwartungen der anderen orientieren und vielmehr bereit sind, die mit dem abweichenden Verhalten verbundenen Schwierigkeiten auf sich zu nehmen. So ist Melli Beese immer wieder damit konfrontiert, dass das Fliegen als »Männersache« gilt. Sie akzeptiert jedoch nicht die Abgrenzung dieser Männerdomäne. Stattdessen bricht sie aus bürgerlichem Hause kommend mit den Erwartungen, die an sie gestellt werden, kämpft für ihre Leidenschaft und erwirbt gegen alle Widerstände als erste Frau in Deutschland eine Fluglizenz. Heroisiert wurde sie dann aber vor allem für ihre Weltrekorde beim Fliegen, die sie bald darauf aufstellte.

Die Überschreitung des Erwartbaren

Was als eine außerordentliche Leistung empfunden wird, hängt auch davon ab, was zu einer bestimmten Zeit und in einem bestimmten gesellschaftlichen Kontext als normal und erwartbar gilt. Diese Erwartung muss deutlich überschritten werden. In diesem Sinne stellt Greta Thunbergs beharrlicher Einsatz für den Umweltschutz eine deutliche Überschreitung des Erwartbaren dar. Eine weitere Form, in der Erwartbarkeiten überschritten werden, zeigt sich, wenn Menschen ihr eigenes Leben für andere riskieren. Dies trifft auch auf viele Taten von als »Alltagsheld:innen« bezeichneten Personen zu, wie die Aktion des Bahnmitarbeiters Mayur Shelke, der am 27. April 2021 im indischen Vangani einen sechsjährigen Jungen in letzter Sekunde von den Gleisen rettet, bevor der Zug einfährt (Abb. 9). Es kann von keinem Menschen erwartet werden, dass sie oder er das eigene Leben für andere riskiert. Insofern überschreitet die heroische Opferbereitschaft die Grenzen des normalerweise Erwartbaren.

Gesetze, Normen und Erwartungshaltungen werden insbesondere dann sichtbar, wenn sie überschritten werden. Im Fall von Heldinnen und Helden bewertet zumindest ein genügend großer Teil der Gesellschaft ihre Überschreitung als einen positiven, bewunderns- und gegebenenfalls auch nachahmenswerten Akt. Das bedeutet allerdings, dass in der Folge die entsprechenden Grenzziehungen neu ausgehandelt werden. So hat Snowdens Whistleblowing in vielen Staaten dazu geführt, dass die Überwachungsmöglichkeiten der Geheimdienste öffentlich diskutiert und schließlich eingeschränkt wurden – auch wenn seine eigene Grenzüberschreitung in den

Normative transgressions

The behaviour of the members of a society is not solely guided by legal provisions but also by behavioural norms. Even though they are not necessarily written down, their existence is clear to everyone, as is the fact that not adhering to them will be sanctioned. Heroes exhibit a unique trait in this case as well. They do not necessarily orientate themselves around the normative expectations of others, but often rather prefer to take responsibility for the issues linked to their deviating behaviour. In Melli Beese's case, she is continuously confronted with the fact that aviation is a "male domain". She does not, however, accept the demarcation of this male domain. Instead, as a woman coming from a middle-class home, she breaks with the expectations tied to her person, fights for her passion and, despite much resistance, acquires a pilot's license – the first woman in Germany to do so. However, her heroization began only when she started setting world records in aviation shortly afterwards.

Crossing the boundaries of the expectable

What is perceived as an extraordinary accomplishment also depends on what is considered normal and expectable at a certain time and in a certain social context. This expectation has to be significantly exceeded. In this sense, Greta Thunberg's persistent commitment for the protection of the environment represents a significant exceedance of the expectable. Another shape the exceeding of the expectable can take is when people risk their own lives for others. This is also true for many of the deeds of those referred to as "everyday heroes". For example, railway employee Mayur Shelke who, on 27 April 2021, rescued a six-year-old boy from the tracks just seconds before a train entered the station in Vangani, India (Fig. 9). It cannot be expected of anyone that they risk their own life for somebody else. Thus, the heroic willingness to make a sacrifice exceeds the boundaries of what is usually expected.

Laws, norms and expectations become especially visible when they are exceeded. In the case of heroes, at least a sufficiently large part of society considers their transgressions of boundaries as a positive, admirable act that is potentially even worthy of being imitated. This does, however, mean that as a consequence the boundaries in question have to be renegotiated. Thus, Snowden's act of whistleblowing has led to public debates about secret services' surveillance powers, and even led to these powers being reigned in in many countries – even though his own transgression continues to be handled as a criminal offence in the U. S. and is being prosecuted accordingly. The heroic overstepping of boundaries, there-

USA weiterhin als Straftat gilt und entsprechend verfolgt würde. Heroische Grenzüberschreitungen lösen insofern nicht selten gesellschaftliche Veränderungsprozesse aus. Vor diesem Hintergrund lassen sich Heroisierungsprozesse auch als Arbeit an gesellschaftlichen Grenzen (*boundary work*) begreifen. Umgekehrt deuten heroische Figuren, wenn sie auftreten, in der Regel auf gesellschaftlichen Wandel hin.

Abb 9: Das Kind einer blinden Frau war 2021 vom Bahnsteig gestürzt und drohte vom ankommenden Zug überrollt zu werden. Mayur Shelke erfasste in Sekunden die Situation und reagierte ohne Rücksicht auf seine eigene Sicherheit. Für diesen grenzüberschreitenden Einsatz, seine blitzschnelle Reaktionsfähigkeit und sein selbstloses Agieren wurde er als Held gefeiert. Dass das Geschehen von einer Kamera aufgezeichnet worden war und über Soziale Medien verbreitet wurde, trug zu Shelkes weltweiter Verehrung bei.

fore, frequently ends up triggering processes of change in a society. Against this backdrop, processes of heroization can also be considered *boundary work* on the boundaries of society. In turn, the occurrence of heroic figures usually indicates societal change.

Fig 9: A blind woman's child had fallen from the platform in 2021 and was in danger of being run over by an oncoming train. Mayur Shelke, a platform worker, analysed the situation in seconds and reacted without regard for his own safety. He was celebrated as a hero for his quick reaction and selflessness. The fact that the incident was recorded on camera and shared on social media contributed to Shelke's worldwide admiration.

Anmerkungen

1 Schlechtriemen 2018; Bröckling 2020, 29–32.
2 Held:innen können Ordnungen außerdem neu setzen, durch ihren kompromisslosen Einsatz stabilisieren oder aber eben durch Grenzüberschreitungen in Frage stellen. Zu allen drei Aspekten vgl. Bröckling 2020, 29–32. Im Krieg werden mit der Bereitschaft zum Töten Grenzüberschreitungen zur Regel. Dann sind es Deserteur:innen, die sich von der Regel absetzen.
3 Vgl. Safaian 2022.
4 Ausführlicher zur Grenzüberschreitung und Heroisierung von Sullenberger vgl. Schlechtriemen 2021.
5 Die Bewertung einer grenzüberschreitenden Tat ist allerdings nicht immer und nicht allein an deren Gelingen gebunden. Oftmals sind es vornehmlich das unbedingte Wollen und die gutgeheißene moralische Motivation, die zählen.
6 Lotman 1972, 340–347.
7 Auch der eigene Körper kann zu einer Grenze werden, die dann etwa zum Geistigen hin überschritten wird. Dann geht es entsprechend auch nicht um körperliche, sondern geistige Leistungen, die bewundert werden. Zum Modell des Geisteshelden vgl. Gaehtgens und Wedekind 2009.
8 Beide Luhmann 1995, 92.
9 Deswegen kann es nach Hegel im ausgebildeten Staat mit Verfassung, Beamtentum und Verwaltung keine Held:innen mehr geben. Hegel 1986, 236–255.

Notes

1 Schlechtriemen 2018; Bröckling 2020, 29–32.
2 Heroes can also establish new orders, stabilise them through their uncompromising effort, or, on the other hand, challenge them by transgressing boundaries. For all three aspects cf. Bröckling 2020, 29–32. In war, through the willingness to kill, crossing boundaries becomes the norm. It is deserters that then pose as an exemption to the rule.
3 Cf. Safaian 2022.
4 For more details on the boundary crossing and heroization of Sullenberger cf. Schlechtriemen 2021.
5 The appraisal of a deed that transgresses boundaries is, however, not always and not solely tied to the success of said deed. Oftentimes, it is mainly the unconditional will and the approved moral motivation that count.
6 Lotman 1972, 340–347.
7 Even one's own body can become a boundary that is then crossed towards the intellectual sphere. Accordingly, it is not physical accomplishments that are venerated then but intellectual ones. For the model of the intellectual hero cf. Gaehtgens and Wedekind 2009.
8 Both Luhmann 1995, 92.
9 For this reason heroes cannot exist in a fully developed state with a constitution, officialdom and administrative authority according to Hegel. Hegel 1986, 236–255.

© 2024 Tobias Schlechtriemen, Publikation: Wallstein Verlag; DOI https://doi.org/10.46500/83535581-007 | CC BY-NC-ND 4.0

Dorna Safaian

HANDLUNGSMACHT

Held:innen handeln. Nicht, dass andere das nicht auch tun. Aber Held:innen tun es intensiver, schneller, effektiver und vor allem wirkungsvoller und bedeutsamer. Wo andere abwarten, machen sie den ersten Schritt. Während andere zögern oder resignieren, greifen sie entschlossen zu. Woran andere zerbrechen: Das halten sie aus. Wovor viele zurückschrecken, das packen sie tatkräftig an und überschreiten dafür Grenzen. Was sie in die Hand nehmen, macht Geschichte. Kurzum: Sie sind das Gegenteil von Mittelmaß und niemals Spielball des Zufalls oder der Umstände. – So erzählen es Filme, Romane, Epen, Bilder und Berichte, der Stoff, aus dem Held:innen sind. Sie präsentieren ein vielfältiges Bild heroischer Figuren und ihrer Taten. Seien es die Opferbereitschaft der Antigone im gleichnamigen Drama von Sophokles, die Abenteuer der Superheld:innen in Action- und Science-Fiction-

Abb. 1: Helden zeichnen sich dadurch aus, dass sie große Taten zum Wohle anderer vollbringen. Das gilt auch für fiktive Figuren wie Spider-Man, der mit seinem Körper einen Zug und die Passagiere rettet (»Spider-Man 2«, 2004).
Fig. 1: Heroes are generally characterised by performing great deeds for the benefit of others. This also applies to fictional characters such as Spider-Man, who uses his superhuman body to save passengers on a speeding train ("Spider-Man 2", 2004).

Dorna Safaian

AGENCY

Heroes act. It's not that others would not. But heroes act more intensively, faster, and more effectively and meaningfully. Where others wait, they take the first step. Where others hesitate or give up, they resolutely take action. That which breaks others, they endure. What others are afraid of, they tackle boldly, transgressing boundaries in the process. Their actions become history. In short: heroes are the opposite of mediocrity, never a plaything of chance or circumstance. All of this is what films, novels, epic stories, pictures, and reports say is the fabric heroes are made of. These media present a multifaceted picture of heroic figures and their deeds – be it Antigone's willingness to sacrifice herself in the eponymous drama by Sophocles, the adventures of the superheroes in action and science fiction films (Fig. 1) or the tenacity of a resistance hero such as Martin Luther King Jr. Acting heroically can take many forms. It can manifest itself in an event, in a decision or in an attitude, but it can also mean enduring an evil – or (not) saying certain words at a specific point in time. Whichever action is heroized, what all heroes have in common is that something extraordinary and potent is attributed to them. They strike us as strong, empowered and effective – as subjects with agency.

Intentionality and orientation towards values

Heroes act confidently and resolutely. Chance occurrences, mishaps or unconscious responses may come their way, but will not deter them from their path. They are presented as figures who act consciously, willingly and intentionally. The "subjective sense"[1], which, according to the sociologist Max Weber, every action has for the actor, is in the case of heroes "a *specific* intention."[2] This intention may be a virtue, like the benefit of the community, or an ideological motive; whichever way, it is a higher value that the figures fight or maybe even sacrifice themselves for. For Max Weber, this "value-rational acting" is determined by "a conscious belief in the value for its own sake of some ethical, aesthetic, religious or other form of behaviour". Personal risks do not daunt heroes. They are prepared to make sacrifices, "independently of the prospects of success"[3] – and they act autonomously, that is, they decide for themselves what they do. They reject instructions from authorities if they do not coincide with their own moral concept, and the environments they find themselves will not dampen their determination. In heroic stories, social restraints, economic conditions or family entanglements are not impediments to action, but

Filmen (Abb. 1) oder die Beharrlichkeit eines Widerstandshelden wie Martin Luther King. Heroisch handeln kann vieles bedeuten. Es kann sich in einem Ereignis, einer Entscheidung oder einer Haltung manifestieren; es kann aber auch bedeuten, ein Übel zu ertragen – oder zu einem bestimmten Zeitpunkt etwas Bestimmtes (nicht) zu sagen. Welche Handlung auch immer heroisiert wird: Allen Held:innen ist gemeinsam, dass ihnen etwas Außergewöhnliches und Weitreichendes zugeschrieben wird. Sie erscheinen uns als stark, sich selbst ermächtigend und wirkungsvoll; als Subjekte, die Agency, also Handlungsmacht haben.

Intentionalität und Orientierung an Werten

Held:innen handeln souverän und entschlossen. Zufälle, Missgeschicke, unbewusste Reaktionen können ihnen begegnen und widerfahren, sie aber nicht von ihrem Weg abbringen. Vielmehr werden sie als bewusst, willentlich und absichtsvoll agierende Figuren dargestellt. Der »subjekte Sinn«[1], den nach dem Soziologen Max Weber jede Handlung für den Handelnden hat, ist im Falle der Held:innen »eine *bestimmte* Intention.«[2] Es kann eine Tugend sein, das Wohl der Gemeinschaft oder ein ideologisches Motiv, jedenfalls ist es ein höherer Wert, für den sich die Figur einsetzt, vielleicht sogar opfert. Für Max Weber zeichnet sich dieses »wertrationale« Handeln »durch bewußten Glauben an den – ethischen, ästhetischen, religiösen oder wie immer sonst zu deutenden – unbedingten *Eigenwert* eines bestimmten Sich-verhaltens« aus. Persönliche Risiken schrecken Held:innen nicht ab. Sie handeln opferbereit, »unabhängig vom Erfolg«[3] – und autonom, das heißt, sie bestimmen ihr Tun selbst. Anweisungen von Autoritäten lehnen sie ab, wenn sie nicht mit ihren Wertvorstellungen übereinstimmen; auch das Umfeld, in das sie eingebettet sind, scheint ihren einmal gefassten Willen nicht erschüttern zu können. Soziale Zwänge, ökonomische Bedingungen oder familiäre Verstrickungen sind in Heldengeschichten keine Handlungshemmnisse, sondern Widerstände, an denen sich Handlungsmacht entzündet. Die Balance zwischen Struktur, im Sinne von Ausgangsbedingungen des Handelns, und individuellem Handlungsvermögen – eine soziologische Grundsatzdiskussion – kippt in ihnen zugunsten von Agency. Held:innen sind in Geschichten Treiber, nicht Getriebene. Antigone, die Protagonistin des antiken Dramas, ist dafür ein geradezu idealtypisches Beispiel. Ihr tyrannischer Onkel Kreon, König von Theben, verbietet per Gesetz die Bestattung ihres Bruders Polyneikes. Dieser war gegen Theben in den Krieg gezogen und gefallen. Wer nun den Feind begraben würde, solle mit dem Tode bestraft werden. Anstatt sich diesem Gesetz zu beugen, wie es ihre Schwester Ismene tut, entscheidet sich Antigone für ein höheres, über dem Irdischen stehendes Gesetz zu »mühn und handeln«.[4] Sie bestattet und betrauert ihren Bruder, und sie bekennt dies ohne Furcht

resistance that sparks agency. In sociology, the balance between pre-given structure and individual agency is a central discussion. In hero narratives, the balance is clearly tipped in favour of agency. Heroes are drivers of action, not driven by it. Antigone, the protagonist of the classical drama, is an almost perfect example of this. Her tyrannical uncle Creon, King of Thebes, prohibits by law the burial of her brother Polynices. He had gone to war against Thebes and had fallen. Creon decreed that he who buried the enemy was to be punished with death. Instead of bowing to this decree like her sister Ismene, Antigone decides to "strive and act"[4] for a higher, eternal law. She buries and mourns her brother, and admits it, unafraid of Creon. Her brave and transgressive act ultimately ends her uncle's rule and dramatically restructures the family hierarchy. Sophocles makes his heroine an active and powerful figure whose actions, in a situation of mourning and suppression, "exceed all bounds"[5], in the words of Ismene (Fig. 2).

Abb. 2: Eine »Antigone unserer Zeit« nannte die Philosophin Donatella Di Cesare Carola Rackete, Kapitänin des Seenotrettungsschiffs Sea-Watch 3. Rackete lief 2019 den Hafen von Lampedusa mit aus Seenot geretteten Menschen an, obwohl die italienischen Behörden ihr das untersagt hatten. Ungehorsam ist eine Form der Handlungsmacht.

Fig. 2: *Philosopher Donatella Di Cesare called Carola Rackete, captain of the Sea-Watch 3 rescue ship, an "Antigone of our time". Rackete sailed to the port of Lampedusa in 2019 to rescue people at sea, even though the Italian authorities had forbidden her from doing so. Disobedience is a form of agency.*

Concentration and uniqueness

Heroes are as unique as their deeds. In heroic tales, it is often only one single character whose actions have a major influence on the course of events. That is the case in Sophocles' tragedy, too. Hesitant Ismene refuses to bury her brother with Antigone but later wants to share in her sister's death sentence. Antigone rejects that. Her extraordinary agency stays unshared until the end, she alone remains the heroine, and she is the one who makes the ultimate sacrifice.

What applies to fictional narratives often holds true for heroizations in historical discourses. There, too, agency is concentrated in one character, who forms the engine of the story while others involved in the action remain in the background, if

vor Kreon. Ihre mutige, grenzüberschreitende Tat beendet schließlich die Herrschaft ihres Onkels und ordnet die familiäre Architektur auf dramatische Weise neu. Sophokles entwirft seine Heldin als eine tatkräftige und wirkmächtige Figur, deren Handeln in einer von Trauer und Unterdrückung geprägten Situation, wie Ismene sagt, »alle Maße sprengt« (Abb. 2).[5]

Konzentration und Einzigartigkeit

So singulär wie ihre Taten sind auch die Held:innen. In heroischen Erzählungen ist es oft eine einzelne Figur, deren Handeln den Lauf der Dinge maßgeblich beeinflusst. So auch in Sophokles' Tragödie. Die zögerliche Ismene weigert sich, ihren Bruder mit Antigone zu begraben, will aber später das Todesurteil mit ihr teilen. Ihre Schwester lehnt das ab. Antigones außerordentliche Handlungsmacht bleibt bis zum Schluss ungeteilt, sie alleine bleibt die Held:in, sie bringt das ultimative Opfer.

Was für fiktionale Erzählungen gilt, trifft häufig auch auf Heroisierungen in historischen Diskursen zu. Auch hier konzentriert sich die Handlungsmacht auf eine Figur, die den Motor der Geschichte bildet, während andere an der Handlung Beteiligte in den Hintergrund rücken, sofern sie überhaupt in Erscheinung treten. Ein Beispiel aus den Naturwissenschaften: Der Mikrobiologe Louis Pasteur (1822–1895) wird unter anderem für die Entwicklung der Pasteurisation und von Impfstoffen heroisiert und in seiner Heimat Frankreich als Nationalheld verehrt (Abb. 3). Dass seine Mitarbeiter:innen, andere Forscher:innen, die Medien und andere Faktoren seine wissenschaftlichen Experimente prägten, wird dabei ausgeblendet.[6] Komplexe Prozesse, die sich unter ganz bestimmten Bedingungen in einem Netzwerk von Einflüssen abgespielt haben, werden auf diese Weise verdichtet, vereinfacht und persona-

Abb. 3: Dass die meisten Helden ihre großen Taten angeblich allein und aus eigener Kraft vollbringen, wird durch Denkmäler eindrucksvoll vermittelt. So auch dasjenige für Louis Pasteur in Arbois (1901), wo er übergroß und weit über die Köpfe der Passanten hinweg in die Ferne blickt.

Fig. 3: The idea that most heroes accomplish their feats alone and by their own means is impressively conveyed by monuments around the world. One such monument is the one to Louis Pasteur in Arbois (1901). It portrays him oversized and gazing into the distance far above the heads of passers-by.

they are mentioned at all. Here is an example from the natural sciences: Microbiologist Louis Pasteur (1822–1895) is heroized for developing the pasteurisation process as well as vaccines, and is revered as a national hero in his homeland of France (Fig. 3). That fact that his employees, other scientists, the media and other factors shaped his scientific experiments is largely ignored.[6] Complex processes that unfolded under very specific conditions in a network of influences are thus condensed, simplified and personalised. As a result, what shines through in the media and in public memory is the image of an exorbitant individual achievement – the structures, influences, cooperation projects and technologies as other players with agency remain hidden.

This concentration of agency can also occur in groups that are heroized as a unit, such as in European chivalry. This class of mounted warrior, which emerged in the 11th century, is a "heroic collective", whose "appearance is dominated by the heroic group identity, behind which the identity of its individual members recedes".[7] As such communities are not homogeneous, they "depend on association with a specific act – the heroic deed"[8] – which creates and stabilises their collective identity. Myths and legends of the fearless fight against a superior enemy establish and legitimize their rank and reputation. The deed of a single knight – who does not appear as an individual anymore, but rather a type[9] – is put on the assets side of the entire collective. The bold action of an individual represents the bravery of all those in the unit, who in their entirety stand out from an environment perceived as ordinary, passive, helpless and unheroic. The same holds true in reverse. The reputation of the collective is bestowed to the individual knight, regardless of his deeds. Ideas of heroic agency are thus transferable: from the individual to the group and vice versa (Fig. 4).

Abb. 4: Nicht nur einzelnen Personen, sondern auch Gruppen kann heroische Handlungsmacht zugeschrieben werden. Dies gilt für das mittelalterliche Rittertum ebenso wie für das Kommando Spezialkräfte der Bundeswehr. Schon die Zugehörigkeit zu einem solchen Kollektiv ist heroisierbar.

Fig. 4: Heroic power can be attributed to both individuals and groups. This applies to medieval chivalry as well as to the Special Forces Command of the German Armed Forces. Simply belonging to such a collective can also be heroized.

lisiert. In der medialen Berichterstattung und im Gedächtnis der Öffentlichkeit glänzt dann das Bild einer exorbitanten Einzelleistung – Strukturen, Einflüsse, Kooperationen und Technologien bleiben dagegen als Träger von Handlungsmacht im Dunkeln.

Dass sich diese Konzentration von Agency auch auf Gruppen beziehen kann, die als Einheit – quasi als ein Körper – heroisiert werden, zeigt das Beispiel des europäischen Rittertums. Der im 11. Jahrhundert aufkommende Stand der Reiterkrieger ist ein »heroisches Kollektiv«, dessen »Auftritt von der heroischen Gruppenidentität dominiert wird, hinter der die Identität ihrer Mitglieder zurücktritt«.[7] Da solche Gemeinschaften nicht homogen sind, sind sie »von der Assoziierung mit einer bestimmten Tat – der Heldentat – abhängig«[8], die ihre kollektive Identität stiftet und stabilisiert. Sagen und Legenden vom todesmutigen Kampf gegen eine feindliche Übermacht begründen und legitimieren ihren Rang und Ruf. Dabei wird die Tat eines einzelnen Ritters – der nicht mehr als Individuum, sondern als Typus erscheint[9] – auf das Aktivitätskonto des gesamten Kollektivs gebucht. Die kühne Tat des einen steht für den Heldenmut aller, die sich in ihrer Gesamtheit von einer Umwelt abheben, die demgegenüber als alltäglich, passiv, wehrlos und unheroisch erscheint. Umgekehrt gilt das Gleiche. Das Ansehen des Kollektivs geht auch auf den einzelnen Ritter über, unabhängig von seiner Tat. Vorstellungen von heroischer Handlungsmacht sind also übertragbar: vom Einzelnen auf das Ganze und vice versa (Abb. 4).

Agonalität

Ritter wären keine Helden ohne mächtige Feinde, auch Antigone nicht ohne den König von Theben. Heldengeschichten blenden vieles aus, sie bündeln Handlungsmacht auf eine Gruppe oder Figur, mit der Ausnahme ihrer Gegenspieler:innen: »Neben den Helden sind sie die Einzigen, deren Agency nicht abgedunkelt wird.«[10] Die polare, in Freund und Feind geteilte Welt der Held:innen ist das Biotop, in dem ihre Aktivitäten wachsen und sich entfalten. In harmonischen Zuständen oder an schwachen Widerständen kann man nichts beweisen. Ist der Gegner dagegen mächtig oder bedrohlich, so erscheint auch seine Überwindung unerwartet und außeralltäglich, also heroisch. Der Kampf, die direkte Konfrontation zum Beispiel mit dem unsichtbaren »Feind« der Mikroben oder dem Kriegsgegner ist dabei nur ein Modell des heroischen Kräftemessens. Handlungsmacht kann auch »auf den Kampf gegen sich selbst verschoben«[11] werden und sich im bewussten Ertragen eines Zustandes manifestieren. Im Ersten Weltkrieg etwa geriet das Primat des Angriffs angesichts neuer Waffen- und Verteidigungstechniken ins Wanken. »Durchhalten« war die neue Devise der Kriegspropaganda.[12] Nicht mehr Wagemut und physische Aktivität, sondern die »Willens- und Nervenstärke des Soldaten«[13] wurden zum Gradmesser des Heldentums. Was wie Untätigkeit und Passivität aus-

Agonality

Knights would not be heroes without powerful enemies – neither would Antigone without the King of Thebes. Although heroic tales generally ignore many individuals and concentrate agency in one group or character, the hero's opponent marks an exception to the rule. "Apart from the heroes, they are the only ones whose agency is not toned down."[10] The polarised world of the heroes, divided as it is into friend and foe, is the habitat in which their activities grow and unfold. Nothing can be proved under harmonic conditions or when resistance is weak. If the opponent is powerful or threatening, in contrast, overcoming him is unexpected and extraordinary, that is, heroic. However, the fight, the direct confrontation with the invisible "enemy", e.g. the microbes, or the wartime enemy, is only one model of the heroic trial of strength. Agency can also be "shifted to the battle against oneself"[11] and manifest itself in the conscious endurance of a specific situation. In World War I, the

Abb. 5: Unter heroischem Handeln wird oft körperliche Aktivität verstanden. Aber auch das Ertragen einer Gefahr kann heroisiert werden: zum Beispiel im Krieg ruhig zu bleiben – wie der Protagonist im Film »1917« von 2019 – während ringsherum Chaos und Panik ausbrechen.

Fig. 5: We often understand heroic action as physical exertion. But other means of facing danger can also be heroized. For example, remaining calm in war – like the protagonist in the 2019 film "1917" – while chaos and panic break out on all sides.

AGENCY

sieht, ist »internalisierte Agonalität« (Abb. 5).[14] Der Gegner wird nach innen verlagert, zum Schauplatz des Kampfes werden der eigene Körper und seine Bedürfnisse. Es muss aber nicht immer ein menschlicher Akteur sein, mit dem die antagonistische Konstellation gebildet wird. Als sich die schwedische Schülerin Greta Thunberg im Jahr 2018 weigerte, freitags zur Schule zu gehen, um gegen die Klimapolitik zu protestieren, wurde sie damit zur Heldin einer klimabewussten Jugend und Öffentlichkeit. Die aus dieser Protestform hervorgegangene Bewegung *Fridays for Future* entfaltete ihre Attraktivität und politische Wirkung in der Anfangsphase unter anderem im Ungehorsam gegenüber der gesetzlichen Schulpflicht. Seien es solche institutionellen Widerstände, eine gegnerische Kriegspartei oder das eigene Selbst als Bewährungsfeld: In der Spannung von Gegensätzen lädt sich Handlungsmacht heroisch auf.

Bilder der Handlungsmacht

Held:innen bewegen Menschen. Sie faszinieren, werden nachgeahmt und verehrt, nicht nur wegen ihrer Heldentaten, sondern auch wegen ihres Auftretens und ihrer Inszenierung. Sie sind ästhetische Phänomene, die als Figuren in der medialen Berichterstattung, in Fotografie und Malerei immer auch über ihre sinnliche Ebene wirken. Nicht selten tragen sie auch Attribute und Embleme am Körper oder werden mit Symbolen inszeniert, die an vergangene Vorstellungen von Heldentum anknüpfen. Handlungsmacht, schreiben die Soziolog:innen Mustafa Emirbayer und Anna Mische, ist ein von der Vergangenheit geprägter Prozess, der auf die Veränderung der Zukunft gerichtet ist.[15] Dass das auch mit künstlerischen Mitteln gelingen kann, zeigen die *Tom's Men*-Figuren des finnischen Zeichners Touko Laaksonen (1920–1991). In den 1950er Jahren, als Homosexuelle in Europa gesetzlich diskriminiert und als verweichlicht geschmäht wurden, erfand er Figuren, die als Muskelprotze an gängige Vorstellungen von draufgängerischer Männlichkeit anknüpften (Abb. 6). Indem sie an heroische Typen wie den Kämpfer, Krieger und Retter erinnerten, machten die *Toms* Homosexualität publikumswirksam. Das Bild des wehrhaften, kampfbereiten Mannes mit XXL-Bizeps und prallen Waden eröffnete der Schwulenbewegung neue Vorstellungs- und Handlungsräume in der Mehrheitsgesellschaft. Es schuf die Aussicht auf Anerkennung durch den Rückgriff auf heroische Vorbilder wie den gestählten Körper des antiken Herkules – ästhetischer Heroismus als Vehikel des Befreiungskampfes.

Handlungsmacht muss nicht immer mit der Konstruktion eines neuen kollektiven Selbstverständnisses einhergehen, sie kann sich auch in einem Objekt verdichten. Im Vietnamkrieg zwischen den USA und Nordvietnam avancierte beispielsweise die Kalaschnikow zum heroischen Zeichen der Guerillakämpfer:innen des

primacy of attack as heroic distinction began to fade in light of new weapons and defence techniques. "Perseverance" was the new name of the game in war propaganda.[12] Bravery and physical activity were no longer the yardsticks of heroism, replaced instead by "the soldiers' strength of will and nerve"[13]. What looks like inactivity and passiveness is instead "internalised agonality" (Fig. 5).[14] The hero no longer confronts the opponent in the physical world, but in their own mind. The hero's own body becomes the battlefield. However, the antagonist does not necessarily have to be another human being. When the Swedish schoolgirl Greta Thunberg refused to go to school on Fridays in 2018 in an act of protest against the government's climate policy, she became the heroine of an environmentally conscious younger generation and public. In the early days, the movement *Fridays for Future*, which emerged from this form of protest, had its appeal and political effect in its defiance of compulsory school attendance. Whether the opposing side is institutional resistance, an opposing warring party or the individuals' own self, it takes tension between opposites for agency to become heroically charged.

Images of agency

Heroes move people. They fascinate, they are imitated and revered, not only because of their heroic deeds but also because of their appearance and the way they present and express themselves. They are aesthetic phenomena, who as figures in media coverage, in photography and in painting always also produce an effect by way of their sensory characteristics. They often carry emblems on their body or particular attributes may be visible in their appearance. They may be portrayed with symbols that are associated with past ideas of valour. According to the sociologists Mustafa Emirbayer and Anna Mische, agency is "a process that is shaped by the past and geared to changing the future".[15] That this can be represented by artistic means, too, is illustrated by the *Tom's Men* figures by Finnish artist Touko Laaksonen (1920–1991). In the 1950s when gay people were being legally discriminated against and were reviled as effeminate, he created homoerotic art featuring beefcake figures that drew on popular images of daredevil masculinity (Fig. 6). By evoking heroic types, such as the fighter, the warrior and the saviour, the *Toms* gave homosexuality public appeal. Laaksonen's utilisation of the image of the macho alpha male with XXL biceps and muscular calves in his portrayal of gay men opened up new spheres of imagination and action for the gay movement in mainstream society. The pictures created the possibility of acceptance for homosexuality by associating gayness with accepted heroic role models, as embodied by the toned body of Hercules for example. Laaksonen's art used aesthetic heroism as a weapon in the fight for gay liberation.

Vietcong. Die Propagandabilder zeigten kämpferische Frauen, die ein »Awtomat Kalaschnikowa« entschlossen in den Händen hielten. Sie sollte die Handlungsmacht symbolisieren, die Nordvietnam durch die Mobilisierung der gesamten Bevölkerung gegenüber der technisch überlegenen, von Männern geführten US-Armee gewonnen haben sollte (Abb. 7). Als starke und wartungsfreundliche Waffe wurde das »AK« aber auch in anderen Guerillakämpfen eingesetzt und avancierte durch seine Inszenierung zur Ikone der Handlungsmacht eines als anti-imperialistisch und anti-amerikanisch verstandenen Widerstands. Heroische Agency ist, wie diese Fälle zeigen, nicht nur eine Erzählweise: Sie ist auch ein visuelles Phänomen, mit dem sich Vorstellungen von Selbstermächtigung, Souveränität und Wirksamkeit verbinden.

Abb. 6: Mit seinen betont maskulinen *Tom of Finland*-Figuren (1973) schrieb der Zeichner Touko Laaksonen Homosexuellen in einer Zeit, in der sie gesetzlich diskriminiert und stigmatisiert wurden, heroische Wirksamkeit zu.

Fig. 6: Illustrator Touko Laaksonen's emphatically masculine Tom of Finland *characters (1973) attributed heroic power to homosexual individuals at a time when they were legally discriminated against and stigmatised.*

Soziale Funktionen

Heroische Handlungsmacht erzählt das Unwahrscheinliche in faszinierender Form. Was in der Alltagswirklichkeit nicht vorkommt, wird in heroischen Inszenierungen als anschauliche und bewegende Geschichte oder als Bild präsentiert. Zufälle, Absurditäten, körperliche Beschwerden und Alltagsbelastungen, die das menschliche Leben prägen, scheinen das Handeln der Held:innen nicht einzuschränken. Auch Abhängigkeiten, Hilfsbedürftigkeit und die Notwendigkeit, mit anderen zusammenzuarbeiten, werden in Heldengeschichten ausgeklammert oder kleingeredet. Solche Erzählungen sind getragen von der Vorstellung, dass eine einzelne Person Geschichte macht und aus eigener Kraft den Lauf der Dinge verändern kann. Mit anderen

Agency does not necessarily have to be accompanied by the construction of a new collective identity; it can also be concentrated in an object. In the Vietnam War between the USA and North Vietnam, the Kalashnikov, for example, became a heroic symbol of the guerrilla fighters of the Vietcong. Propaganda images showed female combatants resolutely holding an "Awtomat Kalaschnokowa" in their hands. It acted as a symbol of the agency that North Vietnam had apparently gained by mobilising its entire population over the technically superior, male-dominated U.S. Army (Fig. 7). As a powerful and easy to use weapon, the "AK" was used in other guerrilla wars too, and the prominence it gained soon made it into an icon of the agency of resistance movements that were interpreted as anti-imperialistic and anti-American. As these examples illustrate, heroic agency is not only a narrative mode: it is also a visual phenomenon that is associated with ideas of self-empowerment, sovereignty and effectiveness.

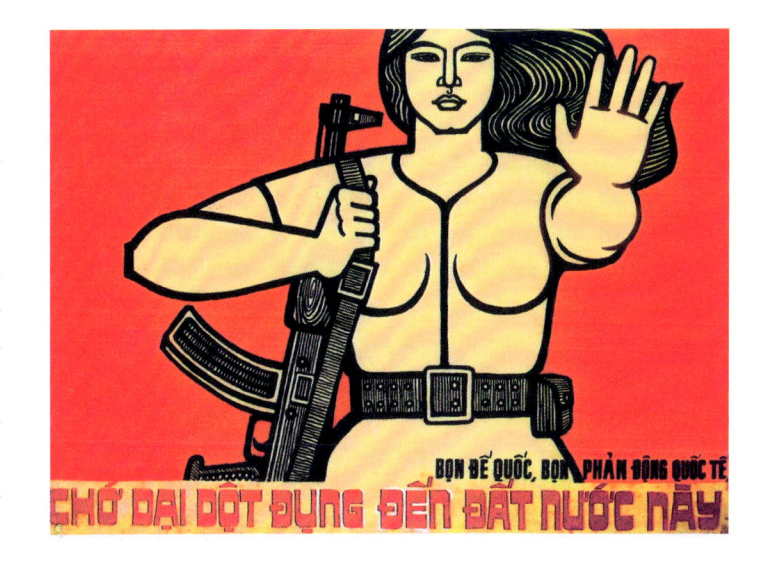

Abb. 7: Heroische Agency verkörpert sich nicht nur in Figuren, sondern kann sich auch in Attributen ausdrücken. Die Kalaschnikow, die die Kämpferinnen in den Propagandaplakaten des Vietcong tragen, steht für Wehrhaftigkeit, Stärke und Tatkraft. Das Plakat von 1977 warnt »Kolonialisten und internationale Verräter« davor, sich Vietnam aneignen zu wollen.

Fig. 7: Heroic agency is not only embodied in figures, but can also be expressed in attributes. The Kalashnikov, which female fighters carried in Vietcong propaganda posters, stands for defence, strength and energy. The 1977 poster warns "colonialists and international traitors" against trying to take over Vietnam.

Social functions

Heroic agency makes the improbable captivating. Things far-removed from daily life can be presented in a vivid and moving tale or picture. Chance events, absurdities, physical complaints and the strains of the everyday that shape most humans' lives do not restrict heroes' actions. Being dependent on others, asking for help or cooperating with others are likewise ignored or trivialised in heroic tales. Such narratives are pervaded by the idea that a single individual can make history and change the course of events on their own. In other words: They reduce complexity and offer simple answers to the question of who is responsible for innovation, transformation and other societal changes. They offer guidance. Situations

Worten: Sie reduzieren Komplexität und geben einfache Antworten auf die Frage, wer für Neuerungen, Wandel und andere gesellschaftliche Veränderungen verantwortlich ist. Damit bieten sie Orientierung. Was sonst überwältigend sein könnte, stellen sie als nachvollziehbare Kette von Ereignissen und Handlungen dar, für die eine Figur oder Gruppe ursächlich stehe. Daran knüpft eine weitere Funktion an: Heroische Handlungsmacht hat Vorbildcharakter. Sie ist nicht nur einflussreich, weil sie als solche dargestellt und wahrgenommen wird, sie ist auch wirksam, weil sie das Publikum bewegt, beeindruckt und zum Nachahmen auffordert.

Anmerkungen

1 Weber 2013, 149.
2 Aurnhammer und Klessinger 2018, 130.
3 a.a.O. Weber 2013, 175.
4 Sophokles 2013, 8.
5 Ebd., 9.
6 Vgl. Schlechtriemen 2019.
7 Gölz 2022.
8 Ebd.
9 Vgl. ebd.
10 Bröckling 2020, 41.
11 Müller und Oberle 2020.
12 Vgl. ebd.
13 Ebd.
14 Ebd.
15 Vgl. Emirbayer und Mische 1998, 963.

that would otherwise be overwhelming are presented as a comprehensible chain of events and actions caused by a group or an individual. This is where another function ties in: heroic agency is a role model. It is influential not only because it is portrayed as potent. It is also effective because it moves and impresses the audience, and invites imitation.

Notes

1. Weber 2013, 149.
2. Aurnhammer and Klessinger 2018, 130.
3. loc.cit. Weber 2013, 175.
4. Sophocles 2013, 8.
5. Ibid., 9. English version taken from Antigone (Orig.) as translated by Gilbert Murray.
6. Cf. Schlechtriemen 2019.
7. Gölz 2022.
8. Ibid.
9. Cf. ibid.
10. Bröckling 2020, 41.
11. Müller and Oberle 2020.
12. Cf. ibid.
13. Ibid.
14. Ibid.
15. Cf. Emirbayer and Mische 1998, 963.

Olmo Gölz

EINSATZ

Der Einsatz als bestimmendes Element des Heroischen

Wesensmerkmal des Heroischen ist, dass Held:innen als Ausnahmeerscheinungen wahrgenommen werden und insofern als außerordentlich gelten.[1] Im Falle mythologischer oder fiktionaler Figuren, von Herkules bis Superman, steht deren Außerordentlichkeit nicht in Frage. Sie sind bereits als Helden angelegt, wenn sie als Figuren entworfen werden; schon die Blickrichtung auf sie bestimmt ihren Ausnahmestatus (Abb. 1), von etwaigen Superkräften ganz zu schweigen. Die Bedingung der Ausnahme als Regel des Heroischen gilt jedoch auch im realen Leben. Sie gilt gänzlich unabhängig von der gesellschaftlichen Größe der heroisierten Figur, gleich ob es sich um Nationalheld:innen handelt oder um lediglich im privaten Rahmen verehrte Personen, die eigenen Eltern womöglich. Die Verehrung ist stets an die Auffassung geknüpft, dass es nicht normal war, was diese Personen geleistet haben, dass ihre Handlungen nicht als selbstverständlich erschei-

Abb. 1 : Die Titelminiatur einer mittelalterlichen Handschrift des »Belial« von Jacobus de Teramo zeigt den Autor sowie den Auftraggeber der Handschrift, Herzog Ludwig I. von Pfalz-Zweibrücken. Ludwig galoppiert auf einem Schimmel durch die Landschaft vor Burg Trifels. Er ist als ritterlicher Held angelegt, der zu einer Heldenreise aufbricht. Wohin diese Reise gehen soll, ist dabei unerheblich. Entscheidend ist, dass er als Held erkennbar ist, obwohl er noch keine Heldentat vollbracht hat. Die Blickrichtung auf die Figur bestimmt ihren Ausnahmestatus unabhängig von der Frage nach ihrem Einsatz.

Fig. 1: This miniature of a medieval manuscript from Jacobus de Teramo's "Belial" shows the author and the manuscript's patron, Duke Ludwig I of Palatinate-Zweibrücken. Ludwig is galloping through the countryside in front of Trifels Castle on a grey horse. He is depicted as a chivalrous hero setting off on a heroic journey. Where this journey will take him is irrelevant. The decisive factor is that he is recognisable as a hero, even though he has not yet accomplished any heroic deeds. The focus on a character determines their exceptional status, notwithstanding their commitment.

Olmo Gölz

COMMITMENT

Commitment as a determining element of the heroic

The characteristic feature of the heroic is that heroes are perceived as exceptional and are therefore considered extraordinary.[1] In the case of mythological or fictional figures, from Hercules to Superman, their extraordinary character is beyond dispute. They were designed as heroes the moment their characters were conceived; even the perspective from which they are looked upon defines their status as exceptions (Fig. 1), not to mention any superpowers they may have. The condition of being an exception – a rule of the heroic – applies in real life, too, however. It applies regardless of the social significance of the heroized figure – be it a national hero or a person revered only in private, one's own parents for example. Veneration is always tied to the notion that these persons did something out of the ordinary, that their actions are not self-evident, and that their deeds should therefore not be considered as commonplace. Humans only become heroes when other humans agree that they did more than could be expected of them. It is this deviation from expectation which brings about the moral evaluations that mark a person who is considered extraordinary as a hero – another important criterion.[2]

From a real world focused perspective, whether a figure is extraordinary is determined not by the figure's design, as it is in case of godly Hercules and extra-terrestrial Superman with their superhuman powers, but by that figure's specific act or deed, a deed that could not reasonably be expected of them. It is this deed that leads to their heroization. However, the keyboard of the heroic offers a multitude of mechanisms for heroization that appear to be completely different from each other. In a specific historical moment, a deed may be considered self-evident for a group of people which in another place, at another time and in another constellation would be interpreted as an extraordinary heroic act. It is not always the same deeds that are rewarded with hero status. On the other hand, both low-impact deeds and those with great socio-political explosive power and import can be considered extraordinary. The self-sacrificing commitment of parents may spark, on a smaller scale, the same heroizing veneration as the revolutionary surrender of one's own life that precedes a new state order. Consequently, heroizations are personalised and depend on space and time, and the question of extraordinariness cannot necessarily be answered by looking at the effects and the momentousness of the underlying actions, but rather by looking at the actors themselves and the contexts within which they act (Fig. 2 and 3).

nen und ihre Taten daher nicht als gewöhnlich zu gelten haben. Menschen werden erst dann zu Held:innen, wenn andere Menschen sich darin einig sind, dass erstere mehr taten, als von ihnen erwartbar gewesen wäre. Durch die Abweichung von der erwartbaren Norm werden jene moralischen Bewertungen erst hervorgerufen, die als weiteres wichtiges Kriterium die als außerordentlich geltenden Menschen als Held:innen markieren.[2]

Aus einer solchen auf die reale Welt fokussierenden Perspektive orientiert sich die Feststellung der Ausnahme nicht am Entwurf einer Figur, wie beim göttlichen Herkules oder außerirdischen Superman mit ihren übermenschlichen Kräften, sondern an der spezifischen, nicht erwartbaren Handlung oder Tat, die zur Heroisierung einer Person führt. Die Klaviatur des Heroischen bietet aber zahlreiche, völlig unterschiedlich scheinende Mechanismen der Heroisierung an. Es kann in einem bestimmten historischen Moment für einen bestimmten Personenkreis eine Tat als selbstverständlich gelten, die in einer anderen Konstellation zu einer anderen Zeit oder an einem anderen Ort als außerordentliche, heroische Handlung interpretiert wird. Es werden nicht stets dieselben Taten mit dem Held:innenstatus belohnt. Andererseits können sowohl Handlungen von nur geringer Reichweite als außerordentlich gelten als auch Taten mit hoher gesellschaftspolitischer Sprengkraft und Tragweite. Der aufopferungsvolle Einsatz von Eltern kann im kleinen Rahmen ebenso heroisierende Verehrung nach sich ziehen wie die revolutionäre Hingabe des eigenen Lebens, die einer neuen staatlichen Ordnung vorausgeht. Heroisierungen sind also einerseits personen-, orts- und zeitgebunden, zum anderen ist die Frage nach der Außerordentlichkeit nicht zwingend über die Wirkung und Strahlkraft der zugrundeliegenden Taten ermittelbar, sondern vor allem über den Blick auf die Akteure selbst und die Kontexte, in denen sie handeln (Abb. 2 und 3).

Auch fiktionale Figuren oder Superheld:innen können Entbehrungen ertragen müssen, ihre Außerordentlichkeit ist jedoch bereits in der Figur angelegt. Sie bilden von vornherein den Fokus der Erzählung und heben sich so von jenen ab, von denen nicht erzählt wird. Menschen der realen Welt hingegen stehen nicht von sich aus im Mittelpunkt heroischer Erzählungen und haben nicht die Möglichkeit, ihre Außerordentlichkeit über Superkräfte zu belegen. Sie müssen sich viel mehr noch als fiktionale oder mythologische Figuren über Taten beweisen. Damit sie zu Held:innen aufsteigen können, müssen diese Taten als Ausnahmetaten erscheinen, als Taten eben, die deswegen nicht erwartbar sind, weil sie einen besonders großen Einsatz abverlangen. So ist es erst die Frage nach dem persönlichen Einsatz, die hilft, profane Bewunderung (etwa für einen starken Körper, fast so wie jener des Herkules) von der heroisierenden Verehrung zu unterscheiden: Zum Helden wird in unserer Gegenwart eigentlich eher jene Person, die sich zum Wohle anderer in eine Gefahr begibt, ohne auf die eigene Überlegenheit vertrauen zu dürfen – ganz im Gegensatz zu Herkules oder Superman also. Held:innen bringen ein Opfer, und

Abb. 2/3: Vergleichbare Taten können in unterschiedlichen historischen Kontexten zu völlig anderen Bewertungen führen. In früheren Jahrhunderten lieferten Wale wichtige Rohstoffe. Walfänger wurden dafür heroisiert, dass sie sich den Gefahren der offenen See aussetzten, um mit den Walen einen mächtigen Gegner zu besiegen (Gemälde von 1708). Mit der Neubewertung des Walfangs haben sich auch die Maßstäbe der Heroisierung geändert. Nicht der Fang, sondern der Schutz der Wale gilt heute vielen als Ziel, das einen großen Einsatz lohnt. Heute sind es die Umweltaktivist:innen, die dafür heroisiert werden, dass sie den Naturgewalten trotzend ihr Leben riskieren, um sich einem mächtigen Gegner entgegenzustellen – den Walfangflotten (2006).

Fig. 2/3: Similar actions can lead to completely different judgements in different historical contexts. Back in the day, whales provided important raw materials to human beings. Whalers were heroized for exposing themselves to the dangers of the open sea in order to defeat the whales – seen then as powerful opponents (1708 painting). As whaling has been re-evaluated by society, standards of heroization have also changed. Today, it is not catching whales, but protecting them that is considered by many to be a worthwhile goal. It is now the environmental activists who are heroized for risking their lives in defiance of the forces of nature in order to confront their own powerful opponents: whaling fleets (2006).

Fictional characters or superheroes may have to suffer privations, too, but their extraordinariness is already inscribed in their character. They are the focus of the narrative right from the start and thus set themselves apart from those who play no role in the story. Real-world people, in contrast, do not automatically take centre stage in heroic tales and do not have the opportunity to prove their extraordinariness through superpowers. Even more than fictional or mythological figures, they

COMMITMENT

es ist dieser persönliche Einsatz, der ihre Taten als mehr-als-erwartbar und somit außerordentlich erscheinen lässt.

Es mag archetypische Taten geben, welche Dauer, Form und Tragweite von Heroisierungen bestimmen. Die Rettung von Hilfsbedürftigen unter Einsatz des eigenen Lebens lässt etwa ganze Berufszweige in den Sog des Heroischen geraten.[3] Verbunden werden die ganz unterschiedlichen Heroisierungsprozesse allerdings erst über eine Frage, die der Blickrichtung der jeweiligen Verehrer:innen folgt: Wie hoch war der *Einsatz* der verehrten Person? Und häufig kann hinzugesetzt werden: deren Einsatz *für uns* – sei es für die eigene Gemeinschaft, für übergeordnete moralische Werte oder sogar für eine ›bessere Welt‹. Über diese Fragen werden zahlreiche Phänomene des Heroischen erst in einen Zusammenhang gesetzt. An der Antwort auf diese Fragen misst sich die Heroisierung von Eltern ebenso wie die von Feuerwehrleuten oder Märtyrern, die neue Religionen stiften.

Der Einsatz des eigenen Lebens: Das Selbstopfer

Auf einer Skala, welche die Dimensionen des persönlichen Einsatzes definiert, markiert das finale Selbstopfer den äußersten Referenzpunkt. Es kann schwerlich mehr an eine Sache gesetzt werden als das eigene Leben. Die Person, von der behauptet wird, dass sie in selbstloser Absicht ihr Leben für das Wohl Anderer oder ein (noch) höheres Gut eingesetzt habe, kann zudem kaum *ohne* einen moralisch wertenden Blick betrachtet werden. Der Mechanismus der posthumen Heroisierung von Menschen, deren Tod als Sterben für eine bestimmte Gemeinschaft gedeutet wird, scheint beinahe unausweichlich. Dies liegt nicht nur an der Bewunderung, die ihrem Mut entgegengebracht werden kann. Es ist vielmehr auch dem Bedürfnis der Hinterbliebenen geschuldet, im Extremfall einen ›sinnlosen‹ Tod in einen sinnhaften Einsatz umzudeuten. Die Auffassung, dass jemand »für uns« gestorben ist, kann Trost spenden und zugleich dazu auffordern, dem Andenken der Person gerecht zu werden, indem ihre vermeintliche Sache weiter vertreten wird. Mit der Heroisierung ist in diesen Fällen somit auch eine Verpflichtung der Gemeinschaft gegenüber den Idealen verbunden, die das Selbstopfer erst sinnvoll erscheinen lassen (Abb. 4).

Wichtig für die heroische Erzählung ist aus dieser Perspektive nicht, dass die Person wirklich ihr Leben geben wollte – das wäre überhaupt nur in den seltensten Fällen unzweifelhaft ermittelbar –, sondern wichtig ist ausschließlich, dass ihr Sterben in diesem Sinne erzählt und erinnert wird: als ultimativer Einsatz für eine Sache, mit der Bereitschaft, sich zu opfern. Im Idealfall des aktiven Selbstopfers wird dies durch die Entscheidungs- und Handlungsmacht der heroisierten Person in Bezug auf ihren eigenen Tod verdeutlicht.

have to prove themselves through deeds. For them to ascend to hero status, their deeds have to come across as exceptional acts – feats, that is which could not be expected of them due to the great personal commitment they require. Thus, it is the question of personal commitment that helps to differentiate between worldly admiration (for example for a strong body, almost like that of Hercules) and heroizing veneration: In today's world, a hero is most likely to be someone who puts themselves in danger for the good of many, without being able to rely on their own superiority – unlike Hercules or Superman. Heroes make a sacrifice – and it is this sort of personal commitment that means their actions exceed expectations and are therefore extraordinary.

There may be certain archetypal deeds that determine the duration, shape and scope of heroizations. Rescuing people in need while risking one's own life, for example, makes whole professional branches come under the pull of the heroic.[3] However, the various heroization processes are linked by one question posed from the perspective of the admirers: How great was the *commitment* of the revered person? And it is often possible to specify: how great was their commitment *for us* – be it for one's own community, for superior moral values or even for a 'better world'. It is this question that establishes a connection between the many phenomena of the heroic. The answer to this question is the yardstick for the heroization of parents as much as it is for firefighters or martyrs who found new religions.

Putting one's own life at stake: the self-sacrifice

On a scale that defines extent of personal commitment, the hero's final self-sacrifice marks the highest point. It is hard to put more at stake than one's own life. The person who has selflessly risked their life for the well-being of others or an (even) higher good can hardly be regarded *without* moral appraisal. The mechanism of posthumous heroization of people whose death is interpreted as a death for the good of a particular community seems almost inevitable. This is not only due to the admiration their bravery is met with. It is much more due to the desire of those left behind to, in the most extreme case, reinterpret a 'pointless' death as a meaningful event. The notion that someone has died "for us" can offer consolation and at the same time be a call to honour the person's memory by continuing to advocate for their supposed cause. Heroization in these cases also implies an obligation of the community to adhere to the ideals that made the hero's self-sacrifice appear meaningful in the first place (Fig. 5).

What is relevant for the heroic narrative from this perspective is not that the person truly sought to lose their life – only in the rarest of cases would it be possible to prove that beyond doubt – but that their death is told and remembered this

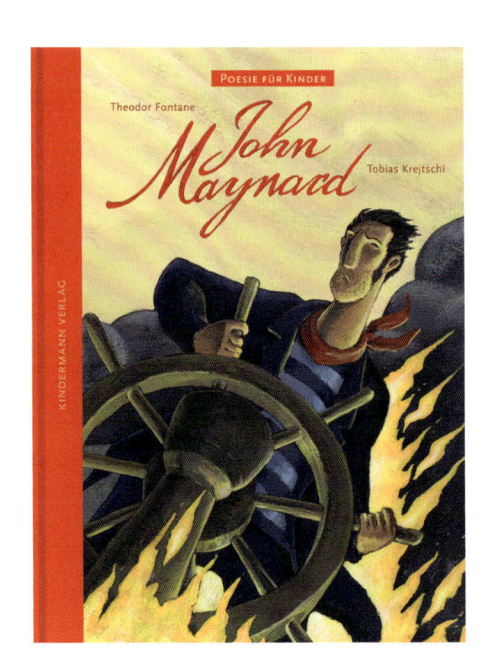

Abb. 4: Am 10. August 1841 sank der Raddampfer »Erie« auf dem Weg nach Buffalo. Der tapfere Steuermann Luther Fuller harrte bis zuletzt auf seinem Posten aus und starb bei seinem Versuch, die Menschen an Bord zu retten. Seine Figur ist Vorlage für Theodor Fontanes berühmtes Gedicht »John Maynard«, wo es heißt: »John Maynard war unser Steuermann, / Aus hielt er, bis er das Ufer gewann, / Er hat uns gerettet, er trägt die Kron', / Er starb für uns, unsre Liebe sein Lohn.« Zentral für die Heroisierung Luther Fullers alias John Maynards ist also, dass er sein Leben »für uns« eingesetzt hat. Bereits Kinder lernen, dass der Einsatz des eigenen Lebens zum Wohle anderer gesellschaftlich positiv bewertet wird.

Fig. 4: On 10 August 1841, the paddle steamer "Erie" sank on its journey to Buffalo. The brave helmsman Luther Fuller stayed at his post until the end and died trying to save the people on board. His story is the inspiration for Theodor Fontane's famous poem "John Maynard", which reads: "John Maynard was our helmsman, / He held out 'til he reached land, / He wanted to save us, he wears the crown, / He died for us, our love is his renown." The central aspect of Luther Fuller's (alias John Maynard) heroization is that he laid down his life "for us". Even children learn that committing one's own life for the well-being of others is socially valued in a positive way.

Ein Ausstellungsbeispiel kann dies verdeutlichen: Die schiitische Glaubensauffassung des Islam gründet sich maßgeblich auf die Auffassung, dass Imam al-Husayn, der Enkel des Propheten Muhammad, bei der Schlacht von Kerbala im Jahre 680 willentlich und im Bewusstsein um seinen bevorstehenden Tod in den Kampf gezogen sei und damit sein Leben für ein höheres Ideal eingesetzt habe.[4] Das Martyrium des Prophetenenkels wird im ›Kerbalaparadigma‹ (Abb. 5) als ein aktives Selbstopfer erinnert und nicht etwa als ein passives Erdulden. Sein Einsatz geht damit über das hinaus, was von einem gewöhnlichen Menschen erwartet werden kann. Dies gilt vielleicht sogar in gesteigerter Form für jeden seiner Gefolgsleute, die für ihn und seine Ideale in derselben Schlacht ihr Leben ließen, obwohl Imam al-Husayn ihnen am Vorabend der Schlacht die Wahl gelassen haben soll, zu gehen.

An dieser Frage, jener nach der aktiven Inkaufnahme des eigenen Todes, scheidet sich, ob ein Martyrium in einer heroisierenden Rahmung erzählt wird oder lediglich in Begrifflichkeiten der Viktimisierung. Nicht jedes Martyrium ist heroisch; die Heroisierung macht sich am *Einsatz* fest, an der Frage, ob es sich um ein aktives Selbstopfer für ein höheres Gut handelte. Zudem darf die Bereitschaft zum

Abb. 5: Nach schiitischer Auffassung wurde der Enkel des Propheten Muhammad, al-Husayn in der Schlacht von Kerbala 680 CE zum Märtyrer, weil er sein Leben für ein höheres Ideal eingesetzt hatte. Zentrale Figur dieses Gemäldes (spätes 19. / frühes 20. Jahrhundert) ist sein Halbbruder al-Abbas, der ebenfalls in der aussichtslosen Schlacht sein Leben riskierte und zum Märtyrer wurde. Der Erzählung zufolge riskierte er seinen Tod auch, um die Frauen und Kinder der Gemeinschaft zu schützen und in der Wüste mit Wasser zu versorgen. Al-Abbas' Heroisierung stützt sich darauf, dass er sich anders hätte entscheiden und das Schlachtfeld verlassen können. Seine Treue zu al-Husayn beglaubigt wiederum dessen Kampf als der Heroisierung umso würdiger.

Fig. 5: According to Shiite belief, al-Husayn, grandson of the Prophet Muhammad, was martyred in the Battle of Kerbala in 680 CE because he had risked his life for a higher cause. The central figure in this painting (late 19th / early 20th century) is his half-brother al-Abbas, who likewise risked his life in the hopeless battle and became a martyr. According to the tale, he also risked his death to protect the women and children of the community and to provide them with water in the desert. Al-Abbas' heroization is based on the fact that he could have made a different decision to leave the battlefield. His loyalty to al-Husayn, in turn, authenticates his half-brother's battle as all the more worthy of heroization.

way: as the ultimate commitment to a cause, including the willingness to sacrifice their life. In the case of active self-sacrifice, i.e. the ideal case, this is illustrated by the power of the heroized person's decision-making and their own agency with regards to their death.

Here is an example to illustrate this point: The Shia interpretation of Islam is founded essentially on the notion that Imam al-Husayn, grandson of the Prophet Muhammad, went willingly into battle at Karbala in 680 and in full knowledge of his

COMMITMENT

Abb. 6: Die Inschrift auf diesem 1925 eingeweihten Berliner Denkmal für gefallene deutsche Soldaten des Ersten Weltkriegs lautet: »Wir starben, auf dass Deutschland lebe, so lasset uns leben in euch!« Die Nation stehe also in der Schuld der Verstorbenen. Die Erinnerung an gefallene Soldaten ist häufig mit der Botschaft verknüpft, dass die Verstorbenen ihr Leben eingesetzt hätten, damit alle anderen Angehörigen ihrer Nation einerseits überleben und andererseits auch ihr Leben genau so führen können, wie sie es nun tun. Über Kriegshelden wird eine sittliche Pflicht der Überlebenden und Nachgeborenen aufgerufen, ihr Andenken zu wahren und die Gesellschaft zu schützen, für die sie ihr Leben gegeben hätten.

Fig. 6: The inscription on this Berlin memorial dedicated in 1925 to fallen German soldiers during the First World War reads: "We died so that Germany may live, so let us live within you!" The nation is therefore indebted to those who died. The memory of fallen soldiers is often linked to the message that the deceased had sacrificed their lives so that all other members of their nation could survive, on the one hand and, on the other, live their lives exactly as they do now. War heroes are called upon to fulfil the moral duty of survivors and those born after them to preserve their memory and protect the society for which they supposedly gave their lives.

Selbstopfer nicht durch die ausdrückliche Absicht, sterben zu wollen, oder durch andere, egoistische Motive überschattet werden: Jemandem, der einen sinnlosen Tod sucht, sein ›Opfer‹ ostentativ im Voraus ankündigt oder primär nach Ruhm oder Einlass ins Paradies strebt, kann kaum Heldenstatus zugeschrieben werden.[5] Der Soziologe Farhad Khosrokhavar hat für solche unheroischen Fälle, die nicht mehr als Märtyrertum oder Selbstaufopferung um der Gemeinschaft willen bezeichnet werden können, den Begriff der »Martyropathie« geprägt, weil eine selbstbezogene tödliche Logik an die Stelle jener Logik tritt, die das Selbstopfer als Einsatz für das Leben anderer begreift.[6]

Erzählungen über heroische Selbstopfer haben wichtige soziale Funktionen, die noch weit über die bereits angesprochene rückwirkende Legitimierung eines Verlustes hinausgehen. Insbesondere kann der Verweis auf den Einsatz des eigenen Lebens einer Person für eine Gemeinschaft zu deren vielschichtiger Mobilisierung führen, denn solche heroischen Opfererzählungen appellieren implizit oder explizit an die anderen Mitglieder der Gemeinschaft, sich in Zukunft ebenso selbstlos für die Gemeinschaft zu engagieren. Die Botschaft der Verstorbenen lautet immer: ›Ich habe mein Leben eingesetzt, damit ihr euer Leben führen könnt.‹ Oft wird folglich der Topos der Schuld als sittliche Pflicht beschworen, indem behauptet wird, die Lebenden stünden für immer in der Schuld der Held:innen, die sich für sie geopfert haben (Abb. 6).[7]

imminent death, thus consciously sacrificing his life for a higher ideal.[4] The martyrdom of the Prophet's grandson is remembered in the 'Karbala Paradigm' (Fig. 5) as an active selfsacrifice rather than passive endurance. His commitment thus surpasses that which can be expected of an ordinary man. Maybe the same holds true all the more for his followers, who in the same battle gave their lives for him and his ideals, although Imam al-Husayn is said to have left them the freedom, on the eve of the battle, to leave.

It is this question – the question of active acceptance of one's own death – that decides whether an ordeal is told of within a heroizing framework or rather within a narrative of victimization. Not every martyrdom is heroic; heroization is defined through *commitment*, through the question of whether there has been an active self-sacrifice for a higher cause. Also, the willingness to sacrifice oneself must not be overshadowed by a desire to die in exchange for spiritual reward, or by any other, selfish motives. Someone who seeks a meaningless death, ostentatiously announcing his "sacrifice" beforehand or primarily seeking fame or access to Paradise, can hardly be credited with being a hero.[5] Sociologist Farhad Khosrokhavar has coined the term "martyropathy" for such unheroic cases that cannot be called martyrdom or self-sacrifice for the community anymore because a self-centred deathly logic has replaced the logic that interprets the self-sacrifice as a service for the life of others.[6]

Narratives about heroic self-sacrifices have an important social function that goes well beyond the above-mentioned retrospective legitimisation of a loss. Reference to the fact that a single person put their life at stake for a community can in particular cause a multi-layered mobilisation of that same community, as such heroic narratives of sacrifices implicitly or explicitly appeal to the other community members to commit themselves to the community in a similarly selfless fashion in the future. The message of the deceased is always: 'I gave my life so you may live yours.' As a result, the topic of guilt as a moral obligation is often evoked by insinuating that the living will forever be in debt to the heroes who sacrificed themselves for them (Fig. 6).[7]

Commitment as social risk: the personal sacrifice

Risking one's own life automatically opens oneself up to the mechanisms of heroization because this commitment is generally understood as an act that exceeds what can legitimately be expected of a person. Yet it is also an extreme case of the heroic. Readiness to make a sacrifice does not necessarily have to lead to death and can also be utterly independent of a physical dimension. The commitment that renders a deed extraordinary and as an exceedance of expectations can also

Der Einsatz als soziales Risiko: Das persönliche Opfer

Der Einsatz des eigenen Lebens öffnet sich zwar einerseits gleichsam automatisch den Mechanismen der Heroisierung, weil dieser Einsatz regelmäßig als mehr-als-erwartbar begriffen wird, er ist allerdings zugleich lediglich ein Extremfall des Heroischen. Die Bereitschaft, ein Opfer zu bringen, muss nicht zwangsläufig im Tod enden und kann sich zudem gänzlich von einer rein körperlichen Dimension lösen. Der Einsatz, der eine Handlung als außerordentlich und so nicht erwartbar qualifiziert, kann auch wirtschaftlicher, sozialer oder politischer Natur sein. Häufig sind es die Gefahr des wirtschaftlichen Abstiegs oder das soziale Risiko, die Handlungen als ausnahmslos mutig und nicht erwartbar erscheinen lassen. Freilich können auch verschiedene Risiken zusammenkommen: Der Deserteur setzt sein Leben aufs Spiel – er tut dies aber zunächst, um zu überleben. Im Falle des Überlebens ist das Risiko der Ächtung und des damit verbundenen sozialen Abstiegs die Herausforderung, die das restliche Leben prägen kann. Zu einer Heroisierung lädt das so noch nicht ein, denn der Grund für die Ächtung ist ja zunächst die unterstellte Feigheit davor, für die Gemeinschaft einstehen zu wollen. Allerdings: Was, wenn die moralische Bewertung des Systems, für das der Deserteur sich weigerte einzustehen,

Abb. 7: Die Stadt Kassel erinnert mit dieser Gedenktafel aus dem Jahr 1987 an diejenigen Kasseler Soldaten, die sich während der NS-Zeit dem Kriegsdienst verweigerten und dafür verfolgt wurden. Dass die sogenannte Fahnenflucht von offizieller Seite positiv sanktioniert und sogar heroisiert wird, ist vor dem Hintergrund der nachträglichen Neubewertung der NS-Zeit möglich. Was im historischen Moment als Feigheit oder Verrat aufgefasst wurde, wird in der Rückschau als Einsatz des eigenen Lebens gegenüber Unrecht und Tyrannei bewertet. Das persönliche Risiko der Deserteure tritt hier in den Vordergrund und der soldatische Ungehorsam wird moralisch positiv bewertet.

Fig. 7: With this memorial plaque from 1987, the city of Kassel commemorates soldiers from Kassel who refused to do military service during the Nazi regime and were persecuted for it. The fact that this act of desertion is officially sanctioned and even heroized is possible against the background of the subsequent re-evaluation of the Nazi regime. What was seen as cowardice or betrayal at the time is seen in retrospect as risking one's own life in the face of injustice and tyranny. The personal risk of the deserters takes centre stage here, and military disobedience is viewed in a morally positive light.

Abb. 8: Dieser Stich von ca. 1806 zeigt George Washington in Uniform mit den Insignien der Society of the Cincinnati; er steht auf einem Sockel mit der Aufschrift »Erster im Krieg, Erster im Frieden und Erster in den Herzen seines Landes«. Im Hintergrund ist eine Schlacht aus dem Revolutionskrieg dargestellt. Dieser eher kriegerisch erscheinende Washington hält in seiner Hand ein Dokument, bei dem es sich wohl um die Rückgabe seines Kommandos handelt – eine Handlung aus dem militärischen Kontext, die seinen Amtsverzicht in Friedenszeiten spiegelt.

Fig. 8: This engraving (ca. 1806) shows George Washington in uniform with the Society of the Cincinnati's insignia. He is standing on a pedestal with the inscription "First in war / first in peace / and / first in the hearts of / his country". A battle from the Revolutionary War is depicted in the background. This rather warlike figure of Washington is holding a document in his hand, which is probably the resignation of his command – an act taken from the military context reflecting his abdication of office during peacetime.

be of an economic, social or political nature. It is often the risk of economic decline or social risk that makes deeds appear brave and unexpected. Of course, various risks can combine: The deserter, for example, risks their life – but they do so in an attempt to survive. If they do survive, the risk of ostracism and the associated social disadvantages constitute a challenge that can shape the rest of their life. This alone does not yet qualify them for heroization because the initial reason for the ostracism is their alleged cowardice and not the act of standing up for their community. However, what if the moral evaluation of the system the deserter refused to comply with changes? The complicated way Wehrmacht deserters were dealt with in Germany after 1945 illustrates how the idealisation of the self-sacrifice for the community may conflict with the admiration afforded the personal sacrifice in the shape of social risk – albeit only if the sacrifice is made for a higher cause (Fig. 7).

This example once again highlights the necessity of looking closely at the specific context in order to assess *what* is considered a heroic personal sacrifice, *when*, and *for* and *by* whom: In what context is the potential hero's act considered a risk to their personal good committed for the benefit of the community?

This is illustrated by another example: Much of the heroic status of George Washington (Fig. 8) derives from the fact that he – being the first President of the United States of America – in 1796 voluntarily denied himself a third term in office al-

sich ändert? Der komplizierte Umgang mit den Deserteuren der Wehrmacht nach 1945 zeigt, wie die Überhöhung des Selbstopfers für die Gemeinschaft mit der Bewunderung für das persönliche Opfer in Gestalt des sozialen Risikos konfligieren kann – allerdings eben nur, wenn das Opfer für eine höhere Sache erbracht wurde. Hier also der Verweigerung der Mittäterschaft (Abb. 7).

Dieses Beispiel deutet einmal mehr auf die Notwendigkeit, die jeweiligen Kontexte genau in den Blick zu nehmen, um bewerten zu können, was wann von wem durch wen als ein heroisierbares persönliches Opfer bewertet wurde – als Einsatz eines persönlichen Gutes zum Wohle der Gemeinschaft also.

Dies veranschaulicht noch ein weiteres Ausstellungsbeispiel: Der heroische Status George Washingtons (Abb. 8) gründet maßgeblich darauf, dass der erste Präsident der Vereinigten Staaten von Amerika im Jahre 1796 freiwillig auf eine dritte Amtszeit verzichtete, obwohl sie ihm sicher war. Rückblickend mag dieser Verzicht nicht als übermäßiges Opfer, sondern als demokratische Selbstverständlichkeit interpretiert werden. Allerdings ist es – und daher rührt sein Heldenstatus – erst Washingtons Beispiel selbst, das den Verzicht auf Macht und ihre friedliche Übergabe in die Hände eines Nachfolgers zu einer vermeintlichen Selbstverständlichkeit werden ließ.[8] In einer Zeit, in welcher global gesprochen die hegemoniale Vorstellung von Herrschaft einem monarchischen Prinzip folgte, war der Verzicht auf fortgesetzte Herrschaft nicht nur ein ungewöhnlicher und außerordentlicher Akt, sondern auch eine Handlung, die in der jungen Republik als großer persönlicher Einsatz zum Wohle der Gemeinschaft gewertet werden durfte.

Das persönliche Opfer kann somit verschiedene Formen annehmen, der Einsatz kann als Verzicht daherkommen, als zu erwartende Entbehrung oder als Risiko. In welcher Form auch immer es sich äußert, die Vorstellung, dass Held:innen Opfer bringen würden, deckt sich nicht nur mit den theoretischen Vorüberlegungen zum Einsatz als bestimmendem Element des Heroischen, sondern auch mit vielen populären Auffassungen davon, was Held:innen ausmacht. Die psychologische Forschung hat beispielsweise über empirische Erhebungen in westlichen Ländern in den letzten Jahren darauf aufmerksam gemacht, dass die breite Öffentlichkeit Opferbereitschaft zum Wohle der Gemeinschaft als einen der zentralen Aspekte ihrer Konzeptionen von Heldentum ansieht.[9] Folglich ist es auch die Ermittlung der Höhe des persönlichen Einsatzes, welche hilft, den bloßen Altruismus von jenen Handlungen zu unterscheiden, die als heroische Taten Verehrung finden.[10] Im schillernden Grenzbereich dieser Unterscheidung lassen sich wohl auch solche Konstellationen suchen, die als ›Alltagsheldentum‹ bezeichnet werden.

though he was sure to have been re-elected. In retrospect, this relinquishment of power may be interpreted as a given in a democratic state rather than an exorbitant sacrifice. However, it was Washington's example itself that made the renunciation of power after a certain length of time and the peaceful transfer of political power into the hands of a successor a supposed matter-of-course in the first place. This is the feat his status as a hero derives from.[8] In a time when the global hegemonic concept of rule was shaped by monarchical principles, forsaking continued rule was not only an uncommon and extraordinary act but also a deed that, in the young republic, could be considered proof of great personal commitment to the benefit of the community.

Personal sacrifice thus can take various forms. Commitment can take the shape of relinquishment, of a hardship to be expected or a risk. Whatever form it takes, the notion that heroes make sacrifices is not only in accord with the theoretical preliminary considerations of commitment as a determining element of the heroic, but also with many popular notions of what it is that makes a hero. Based on empirical surveys conducted in Western countries in the last few years, psychological research has drawn attention to the fact that the general public considers willingness to make a sacrifice for the benefit of the community a central aspect of their notion of heroism.[9] Consequently, determining how much an individual has personally risked is helpful in differentiating simple altruism from those actions that are admired as heroic.[10] Along the threshold of this distinction, it is surely possible to look for constellations that are referred to as 'everyday heroism'.

Commitment as mission: the expected sacrifice

What, however, do we make of those cases where commitment is also mission? When risking one's own life is an occupational hazard? If the sacrifice is *expected* rather than an extraordinary act? Firefighters risk their lives to save others professionally, at least in the eyes of the public, and so do soldiers in their role as defenders of their societies, while members of the police are exposed to constant threats to their personal safety. The condition of the extraordinariness of the heroic deed is explicitly tied to its respective context, and will thus not be the same everywhere. However, when commitment is mission, it is exactly the other way around: The typical deed is clearly defined. As regards firefighters, soldiers and the police, it is all about rescuing, protecting, safeguarding. In these cases, the mechanisms of heroization are expanded to include those collectives whose task it is to do the extraordinary things that other members of society cannot and will not do (Fig. 9). The individual takes a backseat to the heroic collective.[11] The individual person themself is afforded their heroic veneration as a member of an allegedly extraordinary col-

Der Einsatz als Auftrag: Das erwartete Opfer

Was aber, wenn der Einsatz zum Auftrag wird? Wenn selbst der Einsatz des eigenen Lebens zum Berufsrisiko wird? Wenn also das Opfer erwartbar wird und nicht mehr als außerordentlich zu bewerten ist? Feuerwehrleute riskieren zumindest in der öffentlichen Wahrnehmung berufsmäßig ihr Leben zur Rettung anderer, Soldat:innen tun dies aus der jeweiligen Perspektive zur Verteidigung ihrer Gesellschaften auch, Polizist:innen sind einem ständigen Sicherheitsrisiko ausgesetzt. Die Bedingung der Außerordentlichkeit der heroischen Tat war ja ausdrücklich an ihrer Kontextbezogenheit ausgerichtet worden und sollte eben nicht überall immer gleich sein. Im Falle des Einsatzes als *Auftrag* ist dies aber genau entgegengesetzt: Die typische Tat ist klar bestimmt. Es geht um Retten, Schützen, Sichern, um dies in Bezug auf die Feuerwehrleute, Soldat:innen und Polizist:innen zu definieren. In diesen Fällen werden die Mechanismen der Heroisierung auf die Kollektive ausgeweitet, deren Aufgabe es ist, die außergewöhnlichen Dinge zu tun, welche die anderen Mitglieder der Gesellschaft nicht tun können und auch nicht sollen (Abb. 9). Das Individuum tritt hinter das heroische Kollektiv zurück.[11] Die Person selbst erhält ihre heroische Verehrung allenfalls als Mitglied des vermeintlich außerordentlichen Kollektivs. Im Alltag aber ist ihr Einsatz erwartbar – oder eben Auftrag. Die Heroisierung des Individuums innerhalb eines solchen heroischen Kollektivs richtet sich dann allerdings erneut an der Frage aus, was hier als mehr-als-erwartbar gelten kann. Sonst gäbe es keine Tapferkeitsmedaillen.

Anmerkungen

1 Vgl. Schlechtriemen 2018, 109.
2 Gölz 2019a, 9; Luhmann 1995, 91.
3 Gölz 2019a, 12-14.
4 Vgl. Gölz 2019b.
5 Bröckling 2020, 47.
6 Khosrokhavar 2005, 60.
7 Vgl. Feitscher und Gölz 2023.
8 Butter 2016, 37-39.
9 Vgl. Rankin und Eagly 2008.
10 Vgl. Feitscher und Gölz 2023.
11 Gölz 2019a, 12.

Notes

1 Cf. Schlechtriemen 2018, 109.
2 Gölz 2019a, 9; Luhmann 1995, 91.
3 Gölz 2019a, 12-14.
4 Cf. Gölz 2019b.
5 Bröckling 2020, 47.
6 Khosrokhavar 2005, 60.
7 Cf. Feitscher and Gölz 2023.
8 Butter 2016, 37-39.
9 Cf. Rankin and Eagly 2008.
10 Cf. Feitscher and Gölz 2023.
11 Gölz 2019a, 12.

lective at best. In everyday life, however, their commitment – or their mission, that is – can be expected. The heroization of an individual within such a heroic collective depends on what can be considered to exceed expectations within that given context. Otherwise, there would not be any medals for bravery.

Abb. 9: Bei den Darstellungen der polizeilichen Eliteeinheit GSG 9 sind die Individuen nicht mehr erkennbar und sollen auch anonym bleiben. Wenn der Einsatz zum Auftrag wird, tritt die Identität des Einzelnen meist hinter die Gruppenidentität zurück. Im Falle der polizeilichen Eliteeinheit ist die Anonymität der Gruppenmitglieder sogar oberstes Gebot, um diese zu schützen. Heroisierung ist dann allenfalls als Mitglied des heroisierten Kollektivs möglich.

Fig. 9: In portrayals of the elite police unit GSG 9, individuals are usually no longer recognisable – and are even supposed to remain anonymous. When the mission becomes an order, the identity of the individual takes second place to the identity of the group. In the case of the elite police unit, the group members' anonymity is actually the highest priority in order to protect them. Heroization is then only possible as a member of the heroized collective.

© 2024 Olmo Gölz, Publikation: Wallstein Verlag; DOI https://doi.org/10.46500/83535581-009 | CC BY-NC-ND 4.0

Georg Eckert

VORBILD

Nicht jedes Vorbild stellt bereits einen Helden dar: zumindest jenseits der modischen Vereinnahmung von Alltagshelden oder der weitaus weniger ironischen Reverenz, die etwa ein ambitionierter Violinist einem bewunderten Virtuosen wie Nicolò Paganini entgegenbringen mag. Aber es ist kaum ein Held denkbar, der seinen Verehrern nicht zugleich irgendwie als Vorbild diente: ob nun aufgrund des ihm zugutegehaltenen Agierens, das nicht notwendigerweise als imitationsfähig wahrgenommen werden muss, oder aufgrund der ihm attestierten Gesinnung. Der vergewissernde Bezug auf einen Tyrannenmörder beispielsweise vermag ganz andere, etwas weniger heldenhafte Akte des Widerstandes zu legitimieren; kaum ein »ziviler Ungehorsam«, bei dem Mahatma Gandhi, Martin Luther King Jr. oder fiktive Heldinnen wie Antigone nicht mitgedacht wären. So vollzieht sich der ausgesprochene oder unausgesprochene Verweis auf derartige Vorbilder innerhalb eines Wechselverhältnisses. Ein neuer Held lässt sich kaum heroisieren, ohne dass sich seine Verehrer zu bekannten Helden-Figuren und Helden-Mustern verhielten; zugleich verleiht der neue Held vermeintlich alten Figuren und Mustern weitere Geltung. Das Abendland kommt bis heute über Archetypen wie den Einfallsreichtum des Odysseus oder den Kampfesmut des Achilles kaum hinweg, deren Imagination noch der Deutung unserer Realität dient.[1] Helden werden in den Himmel erhoben, aber vom Himmel fallen sie eben nicht.

Zu Heroisierungsprozessen gehören also hinlänglich bekannte Vorbilder. In der einen oder anderen Weise sind Helden immer nach ihnen gezeichnet, doch zugleich zeichnen Heroisierungsprozesse eben diese Vorbilder nach oder neu – es wird selbst »das Wiederholte erst durch Wiederholung, durch diesen kontingenten Akt der Selektion, dessen Kontingenz zu verdrängen ist, zum mythischen Programm«.[2] So hat der Philosoph Hans Blumenberg das Prinzip jener Mechanismen beschrieben, mit denen Vorbilder bei jedem Verweis neuerlich gemacht werden: In der Verehrung spezifischer Helden verwandeln sich nicht nur die Verehrenden, sondern auch die Verehrten. An sie zu erinnern, meint keinen Akt der Reproduktion, sondern der Rekonstruktion (Abb. 1).[3] Ein Held entsteht erst, indem seine Verehrer in je spezifischer Form an ihn appellieren. Drei Verweisungszusammenhänge, die beim Blick auf solche Prozesse der Anverwandlung und Aushandlung besonders ins Auge fallen, möchte dieser Essay erkunden. Sie sind allesamt mit Funktionen verbunden, die Helden als Vorbilder erfüllen. Heroisierungsprozesse schaffen Nähe: sowohl zum verehrten, vorbildhaften Helden als auch zu anderen, die ihn verehren. Sie stellen indes auch Distanz her: sowohl zum verehrten, vorbildhaften Helden als

Georg Eckert

ROLE MODELS

Not every role model is a hero – at least beyond the trendy appropriation of everyday heroes, or the much less ironic reverence which an ambitious violinist might have for an admirable virtuoso such as Nicolò Paganini. It is hard to think of a hero, however, who does not, in one way or another, serve as a role model for their admirers – this could be due to their reported accomplishments, which do not necessarily have to be seen as desirable of emulating, or because of the laudable convictions ascribed to them. The praise of a hero killing a tyrant, for example, can legitimise quite different and somewhat less heroic acts of resistance; there are few cases of 'civil disobedience' which do not implicitly refer to the ideas of Mahatma Gandhi, Martin Luther King Jr., or fictional heroines such as Antigone. An explicit or implied reference to such role models takes place in a context of interdependence. A new hero can hardly be heroized without their admirers reflecting on familiar heroic figures and behaviours. At the same time, the new hero increases the validity of supposedly old heroic figures and behaviours. Even today, the Western world struggles to move beyond certain heroic archetypes such as the resource-

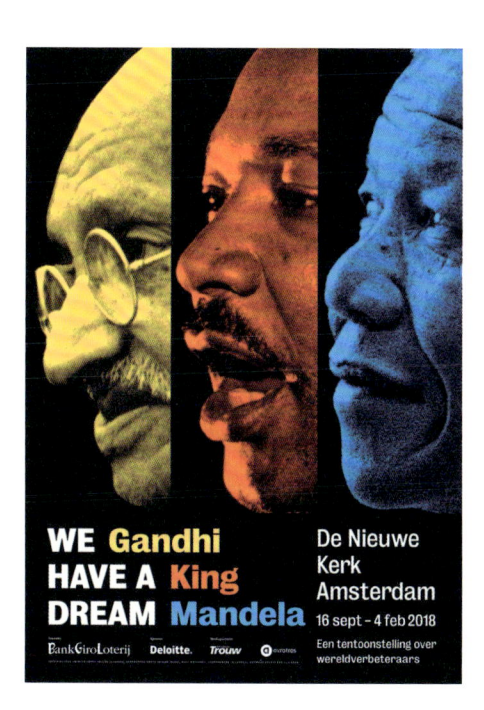

Abb. 1: Moderne Helden eines gewaltfreien Widerstandes zeigt dieses Plakat einer Amsterdamer Ausstellung aus dem Jahre 2018. Mahatma Gandhi, Martin Luther King und Nelson Mandela waren im Westen längst zu Ikonen des zivilen Ungehorsams geworden: als populäre Vorbilder auch vereinnahmt, um deren heroische Entbehrungen gerade nicht selbst erdulden zu müssen.

Fig. 1: This poster from an exhibition in Amsterdam in 2018 shows modern-day heroes engaged in non-violent forms of protest. Mahatma Gandhi, Martin Luther King Jr. and Nelson Mandela became icons of civil disobedience in the West a long time ago. They have also been adopted by many others as popular role models – so as to have someone with whom to share their heroic hardships.

auch zu denjenigen, die ihn anders oder gar nicht verehren. Zugleich legen Vorbilder in gewissem Ausmaß jene Muster fest, nach denen weitere Vorbilder gezeichnet werden: Vorbilder interagieren, Helden sind voneinander abhängig. Alltagshelden nähren neue Alltagshelden – doch diese postmoderne Begeisterung teilen andere Kulturen selbst unserer Zeit keineswegs, in denen andere Typen vorherrschen.

Vorbilder schaffen Nähe

Helden als Vorbilder auszuweisen, gehört zu mannigfachen Heroisierungsprozessen in unterschiedlichsten Umständen. Worin die postulierte Heldentat eigentlich bestehe, bedarf allerdings erst der Aushandlung. Alexander der Große beispielsweise wurde als Feldherr heroisiert, aber auch als hellenistischer Zivilisationsbringer – Bert Brecht hingegen ließ seinen *lesenden Arbeiter* fragen: »Der junge Alexander eroberte Indien. Er allein?«[4] (Abb. 2) Werden Helden als vorbildhaft empfunden respektive dargestellt, vollziehen sich stets Aneignungsprozesse und Konstruktionsleistungen. So hat es einen echten Wilhelm Tell nie gegeben – gleichwohl seit dem späten 15. Jahrhundert wechselnde Interessen des jeweiligen Publikums, diese bald als historisch statt fiktiv wahrgenommene Gestalt zu einem Nationalhelden zu stilisieren, später gar bisweilen zu einem Helden für die ganze Menschheit

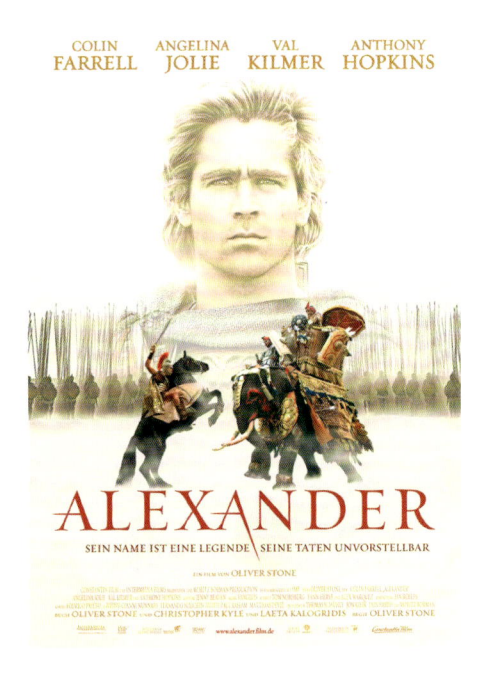

Abb. 2: Um einen Helden wie Alexander kommt die Moderne nicht herum: und sei es, wie in manchen Szenen in Oliver Stones Monumentalfilm aus dem Jahre 2004, als gebrochener Held. So blond, wie ihn Hollywood zuletzt präsentierte, war Alexander übrigens mitnichten. Selbst Vorbilder werden spezifischen Idealen nachgezeichnet.

Fig. 2: *Modernity loves a hero like Alexander the Great – even portrayed as a broken hero, like in certain scenes in Oliver Stone's monumental 2004 epic historical drama. Incidentally, Alexander the Great was by no means as fair-haired as Hollywood presented him. Even heroes are modelled on specific ideals.*

fulness of Ulysses or the fighting spirit of Achilles, whose imagination continues to shape our interpretation of reality.[1] Heroes are praised to high heaven, but they do not simply fall from the sky.

Well-known role models, therefore, are part of heroization processes. Indeed, in one way or another, heroes are always shaped after role models, although at the same time, processes of heroization can redraw and redesign these role models. Thus, "that which is repeated only becomes a mythical programme through repetition, by means of a contingent act of selection whose contingency should be suppressed."[2] Here, the philosopher Hans Blumenberg describes the principle of such mechanisms, by which role models are recreated each time they are invoked. The admiration of specific heroes not only transforms the admirers, but also those being admired. Remembering them is not an act of reproduction, but of reconstruction (Fig. 1).[3] A hero is only created when their admirers appeal to them in a specific form.

This essay aims to explore three reference contexts which become particularly apparent when examining such processes of appropriation and negotiation. They are all associated with functions performed by heroes as role models. Heroization processes create proximity – both to the admired, exemplary hero as well as between those who admire this hero. On the other hand, they also create distance – both to the admired, exemplary hero as well as between admirers and those who see the hero differently or do not even acknowledge them as such. At the same time, role models determine, to a certain extent, the patterns according to which future role models are drawn: Role models interact with each other, heroes depend on each other. For example, everyday heroes contribute to the creation of new everyday heroes. However, we need to keep in mind that other cultures do not share this postmodern enthusiasm of ours. Within these cultures, different types of hero prevail.

Role models create proximity

Identifying heroes as role models is part of numerous heroization processes within a variety of different circumstances. In such processes, however, people have to negotiate what exactly constitutes a heroic deed. Alexander the Great, for instance, was heroized as a military commander, but also as a Hellenistic bringer of civilisation. On the other hand, Bertolt Brecht made his *worker who reads* ask questions: "The young Alexander conquered India. Was he alone?"[4] (Fig. 2) Whenever heroes are perceived or portrayed as exemplary, processes of acquisition and construction are at work. For instance, there was never a real-life Wilhelm Tell. Nevertheless, since the late 15th century, changing interests among respective audiences have transformed this figure into a national hero, who gradually came to be regarded as historical rather than fictional, later even into a hero for the whole of humanity. Like

Abb. 3: Helden werden von ihren Verehrern gemacht, oftmals von rivalisierenden Gemeinschaften. Das Glasgower Derby (»Old Firm«) gewann seine Brisanz aus einer Zuordnung jenseits des Fußballs: Die einen fanden ihre Vorbilder unter den britisch-protestantischen Rangers, die anderen unter den irisch-katholischen Celtics.

Fig. 3: Heroes tend to be moulded by their admirers – often from rival communities. The Glasgow Derby ("Old Firm"), the collective name for two Scottish football clubs, drew controversy from a categorisation that went beyond football: Some found their role models among the British-Protestant Rangers, while others found them among the Irish-Catholic Celtic.

jenseits aller Nationen: wie jeder Held eine Projektionsfläche, auf der sich Vorbilder anzeichnen lassen.

Nähe herzustellen, erweist sich dabei auf zweierlei Weise als eine wesentliche Funktion von Heroisierungsprozessen. Indem Menschen sich Helden zurechtlegen, schaffen sie eine enge Verbindung sowohl zu den Heroisierten als auch zu anderen Heroisierenden. Sie bilden eine geradezu komplizenhafte Gemeinschaft, die just in der Verehrung zusammenfindet und zum Handeln im Sinne dieser Gemeinschaft motivieren soll (Abb. 3). Im Kreis um den Dichter Stefan George am Beginn des 20. Jahrhunderts ist diese doppelte Anteilnahme in besonderer Unmittelbarkeit zu beobachten. Einerseits war die Verehrung des poetischen Genies das Band, das dessen Mitglieder trotz oder wegen ihrer durchaus heterogenen Herkünfte und Ansichten verband; andererseits machte eine Zugehörigkeit zu dieser Runde insbesondere die Suggestion so attraktiv, dass die Verehrer einen obendrein exklusiven Anteil an der Größe des Verehrten haben müssten (Abb. 4) – die einschließende Wirkung ist immer die Spiegelseite der ausschließenden.

Auf andere Weise effektvoll lassen sich solche Prozesse gestalten, wo sich Heroisierte gegen ihre Vereinnahmung nicht mehr wehren können. Der antike Varus-Besieger Hermann der Cherusker firmierte in der Neuzeit immer wieder als Tugendvorbild, zu einem vornehmlich ›deutschen‹ Helden wurde er indes in zwei spezifischen Situationen erklärt.[5] In der Reformationszeit würdigten ihn Humanisten wie Ulrich von Hutten unter Rückgriff auf die wiederentdeckte *Germania* des Tacitus als Verteidiger des Vaterlandes: Römerabwehr dereinst und damals ließen sich analog inszenieren, der germanischen Zurückdrängung des antiken Imperiums entsprach die protestantische Abwendung von der römischen Papstkirche. Beides plausibilisierte sich gegenseitig.

all heroes, he became a surface onto which role models could be projected.

In this context, the establishment of proximity between hero and admirer proves to be an important function of heroization, in two ways. Firstly, when creating heroes, people establish a close connection with the heroized one. Secondly, this process creates a close connection with other individuals heroizing the same person. They form an almost conspiratorial community, united by their very admiration and with the shared aim of inspiring actions in the interest of their community (Fig. 3). This dual sense of belonging was evident with particular immediacy among the following of the poet Stefan George in the early 20th century. On the one hand, admiration of the poetic genius was the bond which united the group's members despite or because of their heterogeneous origins and views; on the other hand, belonging to this group was what made the idea so attractive that the admirers had an exclusive share in the greatness of the person they admired (Fig. 4) – the inclusive effect is always the inverse of the exclusive one.

Abb. 4: Dass Helden vorbildlich seien, ist oftmals ganz wörtlich zu nehmen: Im Marbacher Literaturarchiv finden sich viele Büsten von Stefan George und Mitgliedern des George-Kreises, die einander auffallend ähneln. Individuell sollten die Porträtskulpturen gerade nicht sein, sondern einen neuen, heroischen Dichter- und Menschentypus idealisieren. Helden-Gemeinschaften tendieren oftmals zu einem homogenen Erscheinungsbild.

Fig. 4: *The notion that heroes are "models" can often be taken quite literally. The Marbach Literature Archive contains numerous busts of German poet Stefan George and members of the "George-Kreis" (George Circle). The sculptures were not intended to be individual portraits, but to idealise a new, heroic type of poet and individual. Heroic communities often tend to have a homogeneous appearance.*

Such processes can also be shaped to great effect in other ways, in situations where the people who are heroized can no longer prevent themselves from being appropriated. In the modern period, "Hermann the Cheruscan" (Arminius), the ancient chieftain defeating Varus, was repeatedly held up as a paragon of virtue, and he was declared a primarily "German" hero on two specific occasions.[5] In the Reformation period, humanists such as Ulrich von Hutten praised him as a defender of the fatherland, drawing on the rediscovery of Tacitus' *Germania*. Defence against the Romans in the distant past and at that time could be presented as analogous; the Germanic tribes pushing back the ancient empire corresponded to the contemporary Protestant departure from the

ROLE MODELS 149

Im 19. Jahrhundert wiederum gehörten der Schriftsteller Heinrich von Kleist und der »Turnvater« Friedrich Ludwig Jahn zu den Pionieren einer neuen nationalen Helden-Verklärung, die später unter anderem im Hermannsdenkmal nahe Detmold eine kolossale Gestalt annahm. In einem egalitären nationalen Heroismus, den man auf germanische Stämme rückprojizierte, taugte Hermann nun zu einem kollektiven Vorbild: als Identifikationsfigur und Medium der Sammlung der Deutschen. Die Verehrung gerade dieses Helden bedeutete ein politisches Bekenntnis zugunsten einer kämpferischen und erst noch zu erkämpfenden Nation (Abb. 5); als Ausweis eines patriotisches Engagements verband es Bürger wie Monarchen, die sich an der Spendenkampagne des zwischen den Jahren 1838 und 1875 errichteten Denkmals beteiligten.[6] Wie sich die Deutschen ehedem gemeinsam erfolgreich der Römer erwehrt hätten, die einem seinerzeit populären Lied des Dichters Joseph Victor von Scheffel zufolge »frech geworden« waren, so hätten sie im Krieg von 1870/71 den »französischen Uebermuth« abgewiesen, wie es die Inschrift auf dem Sockel wollte.

Ähnlich spezifisch war der Kontext, in dem einer historisierenden Heroisierung des Tommaso Aniello d'Amalfi eine besondere politische Bedeutung zukam. Er hatte unter dem Namen Masaniello im Jahre 1647 einen zunächst erfolgreichen Aufstand von Neapolitanern gegen die spanische Herrschaft angeführt – und nahm im Jahre 1830 als Opernfigur neuerlich eine Hauptrolle ein: in der belgischen Revolution. So stark war die heroische Erwartungshaltung gut organisierter Separatisten in Brüssel, dass sie eine staatstragend gemeinte Aufführung von Daniel-François-Esprit Aubers historischer Oper *Muette de Portici* in ein Fanal ihres Unabhängigkeitskampfes gegen die Niederlande verwandelten: indem sich revoltierende Bürger den einfachen Fischer Masaniello, den Protagonisten der Oper, zu ihrem Vorbild als patriotischen Helden nahmen (Abb. 6). Sie erbrachten also eine signifikante Übertragungsleistung, die einen wichtigen Befund bekräftigt: »Das Vorbild existiert nicht als eine feste, vorgegebene Größe, sondern wird im Prozess der Präfiguration verändert oder als Bezugsfigur erst erschaffen«.[7]

Wie Bezugsfiguren besondere Nähe herstellen sollen, zeigen beispielsweise die »Helden der Arbeit« in sozialistischen Gesellschaften seit den 1920er Jahren. Dieser Typus verband ein disziplinierendes Moment mit einem emanzipativen – er suggerierte zumindest eine Chance, aus eigenen Arbeits-Kräften heraus einen zudem mit materiellen Vorteilen prämierten Helden-Status zu erlangen: ob nun als Arbeiter, Fabrikleiter oder Künstler. Solchen Vorbild-Konturen war die Vorstellung eingezeichnet, es diesen von weitreichender Propaganda gerühmten Helden gleichtun zu können. Sie schufen Nähe zum Helden und Nähe derjenigen untereinander, die diesen Imperativ zu beherzigen suchten (Abb. 7).

papal Roman Catholic Church. Each situation contributed towards an understanding of the other.

Then, in the 19th century, writer Heinrich von Kleist and gymnastics educator Friedrich Ludwig Jahn – known as "Turnvater" or "father of gymnastics" Jahn – were among the pioneers of glorifying Hermann as a new national hero. Later on, this construction took on a colossal form, for example in the Hermann Memorial near Detmold. In an egalitarian national heroism, which was projected back onto Germanic tribes, Hermann was now a useful collective role model, a positive figure for Germans to identify with and a medium for bringing them together. Admiration for this hero in particular was a political statement in favour of a combative nation which people were still fighting to achieve (Fig. 5); as a statement of patriotic commitment, it united both citizens and monarchs, who participated in efforts to raise money for the monument built between 1838 and 1875.[6] Just as the Germans had once come together to successfully fight against the Romans – who had "become insolent", in the words of a popular song by poet Joseph Victor von Scheffel – they had also repelled the "French haughtiness" in the war of 1870 to 1871, according to the inscription on the base of the monument.

Abb. 5: Zwei zeitlich weit voneinander entfernte Helden rahmen das Württembergische Turnfest des Jahres 1845 in Reutlingen. Nicht nur auf dieser Postkarte deuteten Zeitgenossen beide Helden als ihnen gleichermaßen nahestehende Vorbilder: Hermann der Cherusker hatte im Jahre 9 n. Chr. die Hermannsschlacht gewonnen, die wir heute eher als Varusschlacht kennen, »Turnvater« Ludwig Jahn galt als Erneuerer »germanischer« Stärke. Der Turm des Reutlinger Hausbergs Achalm verstärkt die Anmutung nationaler Wehrhaftigkeit.

Fig. 5: Two heroes from very different times characterised the Württemberg Gymnastics Festival in Reutlingen in 1845. Contemporaries have interpreted both of these heroes as similar role models before, and not only on this postcard. Namely, Hermann the Cheruscan, who won the Battle of Hermann in 9 AD (which we know today as the Battle of Varus), and Ludwig Jahn, the "father of gymnastics", regarded as someone who modernised "Germanic" strength. The tower on Achalm, Reutlingen's local mountain, reinforces the impression of national defence.

The context in which a historicising heroization of Tommaso Aniello d'Amalfi achieved special political significance was very specific, too. Under the name of Masaniello, Amalfi had led an initially successful uprising of Neapolitans against Spanish rule in 1647. In 1830, he once again played a major role, this time in the Belgian Revolution, and as an opera charac-

ROLE MODELS

Abb. 6: Die Aufführung der Oper *La Muette de Portici* in Brüssel am 25. August 1830 sollte eigentlich den Feierlichkeiten für den niederländischen König Wilhelm I. dienen. Doch hiesige Revolutionäre, die ihren ungeliebten Monarchen als Besatzer empfanden, übernahmen die Herrschaft erst über die Inszenierung und bald über den neugegründeten belgischen Nationalstaat. Sie reklamierten die Opernfigur eines neapolitanischen Fischers, der sich gegen einen fremden Tyrannen auflehnte, als Vorbild. Indem sie die Aufführung des fünften Aktes verhinderten, in dem dessen umjubelter Aufstand niedergeschlagen wird, machten sie aus der begeisterten Selbstermächtigung des Publikums ein Fanal der nationalen Unabhängigkeit.

Fig. 6: Originally, the performance of the opera La Muette de Portici *in Brussels on 25 August 1830 was intended to celebrate King William I of the Netherlands. However, local revolutionaries, who saw their unloved monarch as a coloniser, seized control of the production – and later on of the newly founded Belgian nation state. They claimed the operatic figure of a Neapolitan fisherman, who rebelled against the foreign tyrant, as their role model. By preventing the performance of the fifth act, suppressing William I's acclaimed revolt, they transformed the audience's enthusiastic feelings of self-empowerment into a beacon of national independence.*

Vorbilder schaffen Distanz

Ganz anders sind Helden-Ideale beschaffen, denen eher eine weitere Funktion innewohnt: nämlich die Verehrten zu entrücken – und so vielmehr die Grenzen der Nachahmbarkeit zu betonen oder des Grades, bis zu dem sie überhaupt wünschenswert sei. Die Heroisierung von Heiligen in Mittelalter und Früher Neuzeit etwa schuf mit aller Nähe auch Distanz; in die Nähe der angebeteten Heiligen vermochte den einzelnen Gläubigen nicht etwa eigenes Bemühen zu rücken, sondern allein göttliche Gnade, deren Gewährung er sich erhoffte. Zumal der erlösende Tod Jesu ließ sich nicht imitieren, weil ihn nur der Sohn Gottes stellvertretend für alle Menschen habe auf sich nehmen können, so jener theologische Gedankengang, den Johann Sebastian Bach in seiner »Johannes-Passion« vertonte: »Der Held aus Juda siegt mit Macht / Und schließt den Kampf. / Es ist vollbracht«.

Der bereits erwähnte George-Kreis, zu dem auch die Brüder Stauffenberg gehörten, liefert zugleich ein einschlägiges Exempel für distanzschaffende Vorbilder. Stefan George kultivierte seine Unnahbarkeit selbst, ja gerade im exklusiven kleinen

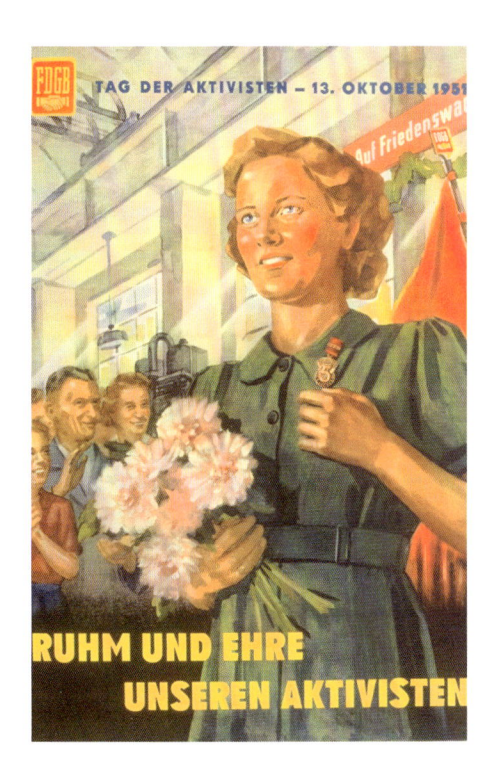

Abb. 7: Die Propaganda sozialistischer Staaten rief »Helden der Arbeit« zu Vorbildern aus. Am »Tag der Aktivisten« betrieb die DDR massenhafte Auszeichnungen, um auch andere zu besonderem Arbeitseinsatz anzutreiben. Auch eine einfache Arbeiterin konnte hier Heldenstatus erringen, so suggerierte die Propaganda.

Fig. 7: *Socialist state propaganda used to proclaim "labour heroes" as role models. On the "Day of Activists", the German Democratic Republic organised several different awards to encourage others to show special dedication to labour. The propaganda suggested that even a simple labourer could achieve heroic status.*

ter. The heroic expectations of well-organised separatists in Brussels were so high that they transformed an official performance of Daniel-François-Esprit Auber's historical opera *La muette de Portici*, intended to celebrate the king's reign, into a beacon of hope in their struggle for independence from the Netherlands. The rebelling citizens made the simple fisherman Masaniello, the opera's protagonist, their role model as a patriotic hero (Fig. 6). In this way, they engaged in significant transference, which confirms an important finding: "the model does not exist as a fixed, largely unchangeable phenomenon, but is transformed or even created through the process of prefiguration".[7]

The honorary title "hero of labour" awarded in socialist societies since the 1920s, for example, shows how figures of reference are intended to establish a particular proximity. This archetype combined a disciplinary function with an emancipatory one: it suggested that people at least had an opportunity to achieve the status of hero, which was also rewarded with material advantages, through their own efforts, whether as workers, factory managers or artists. These role models, who were much praised in propaganda, were characterised by the idea that they could be emulated. They created proximity to the hero and proximity amongst those who sought to heed this imperative (Fig. 7).

Abb. 8: Der Architekt Walter Gropius präsentierte sich als einsamer Visionär der Moderne. Dieses Foto aus dem Jahre 1933 zeigt ihn vor dem Wettbewerbsbeitrag für den Chicago Tribune Tower, den er elf Jahre zuvor gemeinsam mit Adolf Meyer eingereicht hatte. Gropius' kühn-heroischer Habitus passte zum vorbildhaft avantgardistischen Plan dieses kühl-minimalistischen Hochhauses – der ein Plan blieb. In Chicago war unterdessen ein neogotischer Bau errichtet worden.
Fig. 8: In this photo, architect Walter Gropius presents himself as a lone visionary of modernism. Taken in 1933, it shows him standing in front of what could have been the Chicago Tribune Tower, a building plan he had submitted to an interior and exterior design competition eleven years earlier together with fellow architect Adolf Meyer. Gropius' bold, heroic manner suits his exemplary avant-garde design, reflective of the cool, minimalist skyscraper – which, at the end of the day, remained just a design. A neo-Gothic-style building was built in Chicago instead.

Kreise; seine Anhänger wiederum gefielen sich in ihrer als genialisch empfundenen Distanz zur Gesellschaft. Insbesondere Selbstheroisierungen definieren sich geradezu aus ihrer Abgrenzung zu Nicht-Helden und zu solchen, die keine oder andere, aus dieser Warte defiziente Helden haben. Derlei Motivationen wie Effekte reichen von künstlerischen Avantgarden – exemplarisch die wirkungsvolle Selbstinszenierung etwa rund um das »Bauhaus«, das dessen Protagonisten wie Walter Gropius als Sammlungsort von Pionieren zu vermarkten verstanden (Abb. 8) – bis hin zum brutalstmöglichen Gegensatz etwa jener SS-Gruppenführer, die Heinrich Himmler in Posen im Oktober 1943 auf den Vernichtungskrieg einschwor: Gemeinsam habe man »das nordisch-germanische Blut bewusst auszulesen versucht, da wir von diesem Blutsteil am meisten annehmen konnten, dass er der Träger der schöpferischen und heldischen, der lebenserhaltenden Eigenschaften unseres Volkes ist«.[8]

Indem Heroisierungen bestimmte Individuen oder Gruppen hervorheben, verschaffen sie ihnen einen womöglich uneinholbaren Vorrang – so beispielsweise bei Ordensverleihungen entlang von Geschlechtergrenzen, die Helden-Status in oder außer Reichweite bringen (Abb. 9): Das im Jahre 1856 gestiftete Victoria Cross konnten als Tapferkeitsauszeichnung zunächst nur (damals selbstredend männliche) Soldaten erhalten (Abb. 10), dafür war das im Jahre 1883 von derselben Königin gestiftete Royal Red Cross anfangs allein Frauen vorbehalten.[9] Selbst in der Geschichte als egalitär entworfener, weil für individuelle Heldentaten verliehener Auszeichnungen finden sich diskriminierende Momente: Ausschließlich Männer konnten

Role models create distance

Other heroic ideals have quite different a function, namely that of establishing distance at various degrees between the admirers and the admired – and therefore placing more emphasis on the limited possibilities of imitating them, and questioning to what extent such imitation would even be desirable at all. The heroization of saints in the Middle Ages and the early modern period, for example, created distance in spite of the closeness. It was not the individual believers' own efforts but only the divine grace they hoped for which could get them closer to the revered saints. Jesus' redeeming death could not be imitated because only the Son of God as a representative of all people could bear this burden. This was the theological line of reasoning which Johann Sebastian Bach set to music in his *St John Passion*: "Der Held aus Juda siegt mit Macht /Und schließt den Kampf. / Es ist vollbracht! (The hero from Judah triumphs in his might / and brings the struggle to an end. / It is accomplished!)"

Stefan George's circle, as described above, also included the Stauffenberg brothers and provides a relevant example of role models who create distance as well. Stefan George cultivated his unapproachability himself, especially within his small exclusive group. His followers, in turn, were pleased with their distance to society, which they perceived as a sign of brilliant eccentricity. Self-proclaimed heroes are par-

Abb. 9: Königin Elisabeth II. empfing im Jahre 2018 Inhaber des Victoria Cross und des George Cross, der beiden höchsten britischen Orden: offenkundig eine weitgehend maskuline Veranstaltung. Die Verleihungspraxis dominiert bis heute die für das britische Empire konstitutive Vorstellung, dass Tapferkeit mit Kampf und Kampf mit Männlichkeit zusammenhänge. Das Victoria Cross wird seit 1856 für Mut im Angesicht des Feindes verliehen, das George Cross seit 1940 bezeichnenderweise »for non-operational gallantry or gallantry not in the presence of an enemy. This is awarded for acts of the greatest heroism or of the most conspicuous courage in circumstances of extreme danger«, so erklärt es das Cabinet Office. Auch Galanterie schreibt man selten Frauen zu.

Fig. 9: Pictured in 2018, Queen Elizabeth II can be seen sitting with recipients who had just been awarded the Victoria Cross and the George Cross, the two highest British decorations – a largely masculine affair. To this day, the award ceremony is dominated by the British Empire's fundamental notion that valour is associated with battle and battle with masculinity. The Victoria Cross has been awarded since 1856 for courage in the face of the enemy, while the George Cross has been awarded since 1940, "for non-operational gallantry or gallantry not in the presence of an enemy. This is awarded for acts of the greatest heroism or of the most conspicuous courage in circumstances of extreme danger", according to the Cabinet Office. Gallantry is also rarely attributed to women.

Abb. 10: Mit einer ebenso furcht- wie selbstlosen Attacke rettete der junge britische Unterleutnant James Hills-Johnes bei der Belagerung Delhis seine Artilleriebatterie vor einer indischen Übermacht – und bekam für seine Tapferkeit das ehrenvolle Victoria Cross verliehen. Diese Heldenszene aus dem Indischen Aufstand von 1857 idealisierte Frank Nowlan in seinem imperialen Ölgemälde aus dem Jahre 1893. Es weist vorbildhaften Heldenmut aus – und stellt dem Betrachter zugleich die Frage: Wärest auch Du bereit, allein gegen scharfe Säbel anzureiten? Zeitgenossen unserer Tage mögen einwenden: nicht für Königin, Vaterland und Empire – aber vielleicht für die Menschenrechte.

Fig. 10: With an attack that was as fearless as it was selfless, young British sub-lieutenant James Hills-Johnes saved his artillery battery from an overwhelming Indian military force during the siege of Delhi – and was awarded the Victoria Cross for his bravery. Frank Nowlan idealised this heroic scene from the Indian uprising of 1857 in his imperial oil painting from 1893, demonstrating exemplary heroism – and, at the same time, posing a question to the viewer: Would you also be prepared to fight alone against such enemies? Modern-day contemporaries might argue: Not for Queen, country or empire – but perhaps for human rights.

im Krieg von 1870/71 als Soldaten das erneuerte »Eiserne Kreuz« erhalten, in ähnlicher Gestaltung wurde zugleich ein separates »Verdienstkreuz für Frauen und Jungfrauen« vergeben.

Als selektiv erweisen sich also nicht nur die Verbindungen, die jeweils zu heroischen Ausgangsfiguren gezogen werden,[10] sondern auch der Kreis derjenigen, die sich an spezifischen Vorbildern orientieren sollen oder zur Verehrergemeinschaft zugelassen werden. Schließlich konkurrieren Vorbilder im sozialen Raum – auch, ja gerade ein- und dieselben Helden, wie in der Ausstellung unter anderem am Beispiel des Li Wenliang deutlich wird. Mit höchst gegenläufigen Heroisierungen wurde dieser im Februar 2020 an einer frühen Corona-Infektion verstorbene chinesische Arzt aufgeladen: Würdigten ihn zeitgenössische Meinungsmacher in vielen Demokratien als mutigen, regierungskritischen Whistleblower, so stellte ihn die Propaganda der chinesischen KP als selbstlosen Mitarbeiter im staatlichen Gesundheitswesen dar.

Dass eine gewisse Distanz eine wesentliche Funktion von Heroisierungen darstellen kann, Unnahbarkeit mithin ein wesentliches Moment von Heroisierungsprozessen, zeigt sich insbesondere in solchen, deren Helden gerade nicht auf Imitation angelegt sind – aus ganz unterschiedlichen Gründen. Wer nach dem Zweiten Weltkrieg in Deutschland den immer wieder anders gedeuteten 20. Juli 1944 respektive den kontrovers bewerteten Claus Schenk Graf von Stauffenberg (Abb. 11) rühmte, rief keineswegs zu neuen Staatsstreichen auf: sondern meist zu einer Art von Zivilcourage, die äußersten Widerstand eben unnötig machen wür-

ticularly prone to defining themselves by setting themselves apart from non-heroes and those who have different, deficient heroes or even no heroes at all. Such motives and effects range from avant-garde artistic movements – such as the image effectively promoted around the Bauhaus, which leading figures like Walter Gropius successfully presented as a gathering point for pioneers (Fig. 8) – to the most brutal contrast possible, such as the SS group leaders whom Heinrich Himmler called upon to commit themselves to a war of annihilation in his speech in Poznan in October 1943. Together, he said, they had "consciously tried to select the Nordic-Germanic blood, for we could best expect this section of our blood to contain the creative, heroic and life-preserving qualities of our people".[8]

By emphasising certain individuals or groups, heroization can give these individuals or groups an elevated status which may be impossible for others to attain – for example, when awards are bound to gender restrictions which offer or deny access to the status of hero (Fig. 9). The Victoria Cross, a decoration for bravery established in 1856, could initially only be awarded to soldiers (who, at that time, were of course exclusively male) (Fig. 10), while the Royal Red Cross, which was established by the same queen in 1883, was initially reserved for women only.[9] Even in the history of awards which were supposed to be egalitarian by rewarding a heroic deed regardless of gender, there are discriminatory moments: in the Franco-Prussian War of 1870 to 1871, only men now could receive the newly reissued Iron Cross, while a separate Cross of Merit for Women and Girls with a similar design was awarded to the opposite sex.

Accordingly, it is not only the associations linked to a heroic figure which prove to be selective,[10] but also the group of people who are intended to be guided by this specific role model or who are admitted to the community of admirers. After all, role models compete in a social space – even and especially when they are one and the same hero, as this exhibition illustrates with examples such as Li Wenliang. The Chinese doctor, who died of an early COVID-19 infection in February 2020, was presented as (at least) two very different versions of a heroic figure: while contemporary opinion leaders in many democracies praised him as a courageous whistle-blower critical of the government, the Chinese Communist Party's propaganda portrayed him as a selfless employee of the state healthcare system.

The fact that a certain distance between hero and admirers can be an essential function of heroization, with unapproachability featuring an essential aspect of heroization processes, is particularly evident in the heroization of heroes who were not intended to be imitated, for a wide variety of reasons. After World War II, those who praised the 20th July 1944 attempt to assassinate Hitler were by no means calling for new coups d'état. The controversial figure of Claus Schenk Graf von Stauffenberg (Fig. 11) was subject to many different interpretations over time. By appealing to his act of resistance, most people rather were calling for a gener-

Abb. 11: Für viele derjenigen, die sich gerade als Soldaten und Beamte bis zum Untergang an ihren Eid auf den »Führer« gebunden fühlten, war Stauffenberg am 20. Juli 1944 einen entscheidenden Schritt zu weit gegangen, hin zum Staatsstreich. In der kritischen Rückschau vieler anderer war dieser Schritt viel zu spät gekommen. Wieder andere diskutierten später, ob der widerständige Stauffenberg als anfänglicher Anhänger des NS-Regimes ein geeignetes Vorbild sei – und heute sagen so manche: vielleicht gerade dieser Brechung halber.

Fig. 11: In the 1940s, many people, especially soldiers and civil servants, felt bound by their oath to the "Führer" – up until their downfall. When Stauffenberg made his decision to try to assassinate the "Führer" on 20 July 1944, these individuals felt he had taken a decisive step too far – towards a coup d'état. Many others who looked back on these events with a critical eye, however, felt that this decision had been made far too late. Others later discussed whether Stauffenberg, who initially supported the Nazi regime, could even be viewed as a proper role model. Today, some critics say that this could very well be the case – precisely because of his act of rebellion.

de – verbunden teils mit Vorwürfen, teils mit Verantwortungsentlastung all jener, die einen Aufstand gegen das NS-Regime nicht gewagt hatten. Stauffenberg und andere hingegen hatten es versucht, postum wurden sie gewissermaßen zu Stellvertretern des beziehungsweise der Guten erhoben: »Sie haben vor einer empörten, zweifelnden und tief erregten Welt draußen auf jeden Fall ausgewiesen, dass es auch in unserem Volk damals Menschen gab, die nicht dem Nationalsozialismus verfallen waren«, so formulierte es Bundespräsident Gustav Heinemann in seiner Rede zum 25. Jahrestag des gescheiterten Attentates auf Hitler.[11]

Verehrung hatte nicht nur in diesem Falle eine exkulpierende Wirkung für Verehrer selbst, die allerdings auch die demonstrative Nichtverehrung weithin gepriesener Helden zu gewähren vermag. Entsprechende Ambivalenzen zwischen Nähe und Distanz zu Vorbildern der Weltkriegszeit charakterisieren noch den jüngsten Traditionserlass der Bundeswehr aus dem Jahr 2018. Seine bedingte Heroisierungsbereitschaft schwankt zwischen dem geschichtspolitischen Prinzip »Für die Streitkräfte eines demokratischen Rechtsstaates ist die Wehrmacht als Institution nicht traditionswürdig« und der heldenkompatiblen, eine Vorbildfunktion wieder ermöglichenden Einschränkung »Die Aufnahme einzelner Angehöriger der Wehrmacht in das Traditionsgut der Bundeswehr ist dagegen grundsätzlich mög-

al kind of moral courage which would render extreme resistance unnecessary. These calls were sometimes associated with accusations against those who had not dared to revolt against the Nazi regime, and sometimes with relieving them of their responsibility. Stauffenberg and others, in contrast, had tried. Posthumously, they were, to a certain extent, elevated to representatives of the good: "They showed an outraged, doubtful and deeply agitated world outside which there absolutely were people among us at that time who had not been seduced by National Socialism", said Federal President Gustav Heinemann in his speech marking the 25th anniversary of the failed assassination attempt on Adolf Hitler[11].

This was not the only case where admiration had an exculpating effect for the admirers themselves. Yet a marked lack of admiration for widely praised heroes can also offer the same effect. This kind of ambivalence between proximity and distance to role models from the World War II period still characterises the most recent Guidelines on Tradition and the Cultivation of Tradition in the Bundeswehr from 2018. Their conditional willingness to heroize varies between the principle of the politics of memory in which "for the armed forces of a democratic state governed by the rule of law, the Wehrmacht as an institution is not worthy of being included in traditions", and the hero-compatible qualifier which allows for a role model function after all: "Inclusion of indi-

Abb. 12: Der britische Präraffaelit John Everett Millais zitierte Jacques-Louis Davids Napoleon-Gemälde, als er seinen »Black Brunswicker« (1860) auf dem Weg zur Schlacht bei Quatre-Bras unweit Waterloo im Jahre 1815 porträtierte. Vor dem militärisch offenkundig vorbildhaften gegnerischen Feldherrn muss der braunschweigische Reiter freilich erst einmal seine Liebste überwinden, die ihn zurückzuhalten sucht. Dem Feldherrn heroisch nahezukommen, liegt für das Paar in diesem Moment denkbar fern.

Fig. 12: British Pre-Raphaelite John Everett Millais quoted the Napoleon painting by Jacques-Louis David when he portrayed his 'Black Brunswicker' (1860) on his way to the Battle of Quatre-Bras, not far from Waterloo in 1815. Before confronting the enemy commander, obviously an exemplary military figure, however, the Brunswick horseman must first overcome his sweetheart, who is trying to hold him back. At this moment, the lovers put aside the heroic ideal.

ROLE MODELS 159

lich. Voraussetzung dafür ist immer eine eingehende Einzelfallbetrachtung sowie ein sorgfältiges Abwägen.«[12]

In dieser sehr deutschen Geschichte steckt indes ein sehr viel allgemeineres Muster, das etwa auch in der Verherrlichung von Tyrannenmördern in anderen Zeiten zum Ausdruck kam: Sie reichte in eine »Tabuzone«[13] hinein. Heroisierbarkeit einzelner Handlungen oder eines Akteures ist keineswegs zwingend mit Appellen verbunden, diese oder gar alle seiner Handlungen nachzuahmen (Abb. 12); übermenschliche Leistungen zu erbringen, kann man gerade nicht von allen verlangen. Vielmehr vermag Heroisierung als Medium dienen, mit einem Zwiespalt umzugehen: zwischen einer Würdigung, wie ein Held in einer Ausnahmesituation verdienstvoll agiert habe, und einer Mahnung, daraus keinesfalls eine Regel werden zu lassen. In diese Richtung deuten so unterschiedliche Fälle wie diejenigen des Piloten Chesley Sullenberger, des Whistleblowers Edward Snowden oder des Frankfurter Vize-Polizeipräsidenten Wolfgang Daschner. Ihr jeweiliger – und in den letzteren beiden Fällen öffentlich heftig umstrittener – Ruhm beruhte darauf, sich aus höheren Erwägungen über geltende Regeln hinweggesetzt zu haben; der Streit darum, wie helden- und vorbildhaft ihr Handeln gewesen sei, galt freilich bis zu einem gewissen Ausmaß letztlich den Regeln selbst. Heroisierungen sind also immer auch Teil weit über sie hinausweisender gesellschaftlicher Aushandlungsprozesse. Selektiv verlaufen sie ohnehin: Dass sich viele Herrscher von frühneuzeitlichen Königen und Kaisern bis hin zu Diktatoren des 20. Jahrhunderts auf Caesar als Vorbild bezogen, bedeutete mitnichten, dass sie sich gerne ermorden lassen wollten.

Vorbilder schaffen Vorbilder

Zwischen Heroisierten und Heroisierenden besteht also eine intensive Wechselbeziehung – aber auch zwischen Heroisierten und bereits schon zuvor Heroisierten. Spezifische Gesellschaften und Gruppen hegen ihre eigenen Erwartungen daran, was zum Heldsein tauge, gebunden wiederum an heroische Erfahrungswerte. Als der preußische Generalleutnant Ludwig von Yorck im Jahr 1813 mit dem russischen Zaren eigenmächtig die Konvention von Tauroggen einging, konnte er auf jenen künftigen Ruhm noch nicht rechnen, der ihm schon im folgenden Jahr den gräflichen Namenszusatz »von Wartenburg« einbrachte. Dennoch waren Möglichkeiten seiner späteren Heroisierbarkeit in einer damals weithin bekannten Vorgeschichte angelegt. Johann Friedrich Adolf von der Marwitz, auf den sich später die Männer rund um den 20. Juli 1944 ebenso berufen sollten wie auf Generäle der Reformzeit (darunter wiederum Yorck selbst), hatte im Siebenjährigen Krieg das Exempel eines befehlsverweigernden Militärs gegeben, sein Neffe hatte diesen Ruhm auf einen Gedenkstein setzen lassen: »Wählte Ungnade, wo Gehorsam nicht Ehre brachte« (Abb. 13).

vidual members of the Wehrmacht in the Bundeswehr's traditions, however, is generally possible. This always requires a thorough analysis of individual cases and careful consideration."[12]

In this very German history, however, there is a much more general pattern which, for example, was also expressed in the glorification of tyrannicides in other times: it extended into a "taboo zone"[13]. The suitability of individual actions or actors for heroization is by no means necessarily associated with appeals to imitate any or even all of an actor's actions (Fig. 12); superhuman achievements cannot per se be demanded of everyone. Instead, heroization can be a medium in dealing with a conflict: acknowledging a hero's laudable actions in extraordinary circumstances, while cautioning against making these actions the norm. This is reflected in cases as diverse as those of pilot Chesley Sullenberger, whistle-blower Edward Snowden, or Frankfurt Vice-Chief of Police Wolfgang Daschner. Their respective fame – which, in the latter two cases, was highly controversial – was based on having, for a higher good, ignored the rules in place. Indeed, the dispute about how heroic and exemplary their actions really were was concerned, to a certain extent, with the legitimacy of the rules themselves. Heroization is therefore always part of societal negotiations which go far beyond a specific case. In any event, they are selective: the fact that many rulers, ranging from early modern kings and emperors to dictators of the 20th century, referred to Caesar as a role model certainly did not mean that they wanted to be murdered.

Role models create role models

There is an intense interrelationship between the heroized and the heroizing – but also between the heroized and those who were heroized before them. Specific societies and groups have their own expectations of what constitutes heroism, which in turn depend on heroic examples from the past. When Prussian Lieutenant General Ludwig von Yorck signed the Convention of Tauroggen with the Russian tsar in 1813, without kingly authorisation, he could not have anticipated the future renown it would earn him, already garnering him the noble rank of count with the title "von Wartenburg" in the following year. Nevertheless, signs of his future potential for heroization were already inherent in a background history, which was well known at the time. Johann Friedrich Adolf von der Marwitz, later invoked by both the men involved in the 20th July plot and by generals in the Prussian Reform Movement period (including Yorck himself), served as an example of a soldier who had refused to obey orders in the Seven Years' War. His nephew immortalised Marwitz's fame on a memorial stone: "He chose disfavour where obedience did not bring honour" (Fig. 13).

Damit ist nicht gesagt, dass Heroisierungsprozesse in allen Einzelheiten von vorgängigen Heldenerzählungen festgelegt wären. Allerdings ist damit zumindest benannt, wie sehr in unserem Alltag unzählige Narrative auf uns einwirken, was Helden ausmache oder eben nicht: von großen Entwürfen auf Pergament oder Leinwand bis hin zu kleinen Abziehbildchen aus der Werbung, von konkreten Helden als Vorbildern erster Ordnung bis hin zu sie verbindenden Heldennarrativen, sozusagen Vorbilder zweiter Ordnung. Dass man einmal etablierte Vorbilder nicht so einfach aus dem Weg räumen kann, wie es manche Statuenstürze unserer Tage suggerieren, zeigt eine Episode aus dem frühneuzeitlichen Florenz. Der Bildhauer Donatello hatte in den 1450er Jahren für das Bildprogramm des Palazzo Medici nebst dem heute ungleich bekannteren David auch eine Judith geschaffen. Gemäß alttestamentarischer Überlieferung enthauptet sie den brutalen assyrischen Feldherrn Holofernes; ursprünglich war die Figur gemeint als Allegorie des Triumphes der so tugendhaften Medici über ihre vorgeblich verkommenen Gegner wie die als despotisch ausgewiesenen Albizzi. Nach dem vorläufigen Sturz der Medici im Jahre 1494 eigneten sich aufsässige Florentiner Bürger die Statue an (Abb. 14). Die Chancen, die der Stoff ihnen bot, überwogen anscheinend die Risiken, ein Kunstwerk prominent zu plazieren, das zum Ruhm der soeben abgesetzten Dynastie geschaffen worden war. Sie versahen die Statue kurzerhand mit der Inschrift »Exemplum Salutis Publicae Cives Posuere 1495«: als Monument wehrhafter Bürger, die einer Tyrannei getrotzt hatten (»Dieses Beispiel des Gemeinwohles errichteten die Bürger 1495«) – und versetzten sie auf die Piazza della Signoria, vor den Palazzo Vecchio, den Sitz des Parlaments der Stadtrepublik.[14]

Die Medici wiederum beließen die Statue nach ihrer Rückkehr an die Macht zunächst unverändert am neuen Standort: im Kalkül, sie wieder für sich vereinnahmen zu können, wie im Wissen darum, dass Heldenerzählungen ihre eigene Dynamik aufweisen. Weil es sich um soziale Konstruktionen handelt, erweisen sie sich als flexibel und unflexibel zugleich: Ganz willkürlich lassen sie sich nicht an gewandelte Interessen anpassen – wenigstens dann, wenn sie einen mehr oder minder breiten Konsens stiften und publikumsfähig geraten sollen. Vorbilder werden in Heroisierungsprozessen immer neu gemacht, aber eben in Abhängigkeit auch von weiteren Vorbildern und der damit verbundenen Eigendynamik: An einem Heldenkanon arbeitet selbst, wer gezielt gegen einen etablierten Heldenkanon arbeitet.

Fazit: Heroisierung als Anverwandlung

Werden Helden zu Vorbildern stilisiert oder Vorbilder zu Helden, so geschieht das in einem Modus der Anverwandlung: Sie werden passend zu den jeweiligen Umständen und Interessen inszeniert. Auf diese Weise konnten sich unter anderem

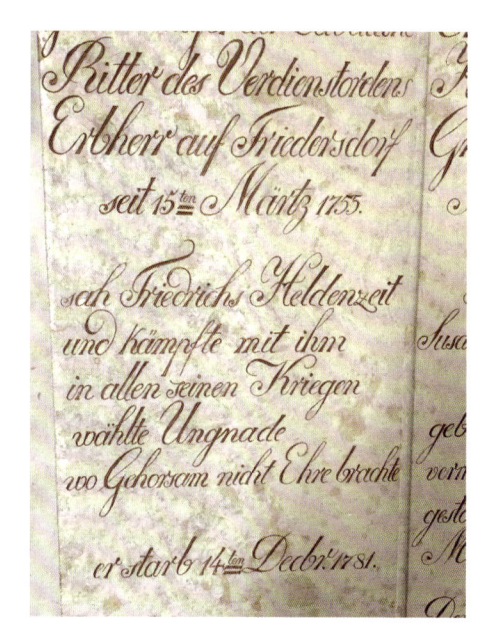

Abb. 13: Friedrich August Ludwig von der Marwitz (1777–1837) war ein altpreußischer Konservativer. Zum Vorbild, nötigenfalls sogar gegen eine ausdrückliche Order des Königs zu handeln, machte er seinen Onkel: »Sah Friedrichs Heldenzeit und kämpfte mit ihm in all seinen Kriegen. Wählte Ungnade, wo Gehorsam nicht Ehre brachte«, heißt es auf dem Gedenkstein, den der jüngere Marwitz für den älteren setzen ließ.

Fig. 13: Friedrich August Ludwig von der Marwitz (1777-1837) was a conservative officer and politician from Old-Prussia. He turned to his uncle as a role model, even acting against explicit orders from the King where necessary. "[He s]aw Friedrich's heroic actions and fought alongside him in all his wars. [He c]hose disgrace where obedience did not bring honour," says the memorial stone slab dedicated to him.

This does not mean that all aspects of heroization processes are defined by earlier heroic narratives. However, it indicates the extent to which countless narratives about what does and does not constitute a hero influence us in our everyday lives. This can range from large-scale visions on parchment, canvas, or cinema screens to advertising stickers; from specific heroes serving as first-order role models, to the heroic narratives connected to them – second-order role models, so to speak. An incident from early modern Florence shows that it is not quite as easy to do away with established role models as today's toppling of statues might suggest. In the 1450s, the artist Donatello created the bronze sculpture *Judith and Holofernes* for the Palazzo Medici's collection, along with the bronze sculpture *David*, which is now much more famous. According to the Old Testament, Judith be-

Abb. 14: Das biblische Motiv der Judith, die Holofernes köpft, eignet sich für ganz unterschiedliche Zwecke. Donatellos elegante Statue hatten die Medici in Auftrag gegeben, um sich als vorbildhafte Tyrannenbesieger zu inszenieren; nach dem Sturz der Medici aber machten sich Florentiner Bürger diese alttestamentarische Erzählung zu eigen und versahen das Kunstwerk im Jahre 1495 mit einer neuen Widmung an das Gemeinwohl.

Fig. 14: The biblical scene depicting Judith beheading Holofernes can be used for very different purposes. The Medici commissioned this elegant statue from Donatello in order to present themselves as heroes conquering tyrants. After their downfall, however, Florentine citizens adopted this narrative and, in 1495, re-dedicated the work of art to the common people.

Hermann Göring und Thomas Mann im Zweiten Weltkrieg gleichermaßen, doch zu gegensätzlichen Zwecken auf das Vorbild der Spartaner an den Thermopylen berufen; beide legten sich Leonidas und seine Männer als Legitimationsfiguren zurecht.[15] In solchen Appellen überlagern sich Heroisierungsprozesse: Sich auf ein Vorbild zu beziehen, bedeutet bereits, an der niemals abgeschlossenen Konstruktion des Vorbilds mitzuwirken. Schließlich geschieht es immer in spezifischer und selektiver Weise – teils aktiv und willentlich, teils dem nicht weiter hinterfragten Sinn nach, den weithin bekannte Heldenerzählungen stiften. Vorbilder stehen immer in Relation zu weiteren Vorbildern. Auch darüber vermögen sie ebenso Nähe wie Distanz zwischen Verehrenden und Verehrten herzustellen, zwischen Verehrenden und Verehrenden, zwischen Verehrten und Verehrten.

headed the brutal Assyrian general Holofernes. Originally, the figure was meant to be an allegory for the triumph of the ever so virtuous Medici over their supposedly degenerate rivals such as the Albizzi, thus accusing them of being despots. After the temporary overthrow of the Medici in 1494, rebellious Florentine citizens took possession of the statue (Fig. 14). The opportunities presented by the piece apparently outweighed the risks of prominently displaying a work of art created to honour the dynasty which had just been deposed. They simply fitted the statue with the inscription "Exemplum Salutis Publicae Cives Posuere 1495" ("This example of the common good was put up by the citizens in 1495"), making it a monument to stalwart citizens who had fought against tyranny – and then moved it to the Piazza della Signoria in front of the Palazzo Vecchio, the seat of the parliament of the Florentine Republic.[14]

After their return to power, the Medici initially left the statue at its new location in order to reclaim the symbol for themselves, and in the knowledge that heroic narratives have their own dynamics. Because they are social constructs, they are simultaneously flexible and inflexible: they cannot be adapted arbitrarily to changed interests, at least not if they are to create a relatively broad consensus and appeal to the public. Role models are always created anew in heroization processes, but are also contingent on other role models and the associated dynamics. Even those who specifically work against an established canon of heroes are working on a canon of heroes.

Conclusion: Heroization as appropriation

If heroes are stylised as role models or role models as heroes, this occurs in a mode of appropriation: they are presented in a manner suitable for the relevant circumstances and interests. In this way, Hermann Göring and Thomas Mann, among others during World War II, both invoked the Spartans at the Battle of Thermopylae as role models, but for opposite purposes. Both of them used the figures of Leonidas and his men as legitimation for their positions.[15] In such appeals, processes of heroization overlap: referencing a role model already means participating in constructing this very role model, a process which is going on ever and ever. Ultimately, this process is always performed in a specific and selective way – at times actively and deliberately, at others in accordance with the meaning provided by well-known heroic narratives which are not then examined further. Role models always exist in relation to other role models. This is also a way in which they are able to establish proximity and distance between themselves and their admirers, between admirers and other admirers, and between themselves and other role models.

Anmerkungen

1 Zur Präsenz solcher Helden im zeitgenössischen Antikenfilm siehe exemplarisch Lindner und Steffensen 2023.
2 Blumenberg 2014, 11.
3 Feitscher 2021.
4 Brecht 1967.
5 Zur Geschichte: Doyé 2001.
6 Tacke 1995, 172.
7 Sonderforschungsbereich 948 2022c.
8 Himmler 1943, 148.
9 Zum Wandel des britischen Ordenswesens siehe Harper 2020.
10 von den Hoff u. a. 2018.
11 Heinemann 1969.
12 Bundesministerium der Verteidigung 2018, 6.
13 Zwierlein 2020, 66.
14 Herzner 1980.
15 Zahlreiche weitere Wendungen dieser Rezeption analysiert Albertz 2006.

Notes

1. For examples of the presence of such heroes in contemporary historical films, see Lindner and Steffensen 2023.
2. Blumenberg 2014, 11.
3. Feitscher 2021.
4. Brecht 1967.
5. On the history: Doyé 2001.
6. Tacke 1995, 172.
7. Sonderforschungsbereich 948 2022c.
8. Himmler 1943, 148.
9. On the change of the British award system, see Harper 2020.
10. von den Hoff et al. 2018.
11. Heinemann 1969.
12. Bundesministerium der Verteidigung 2018, 6.
13. Zwierlein 2020, 66.
14. Herzner 1980.
15. Albertz 2006 analyses numerous other variations on this perception.

© 2024 Georg Eckert, Publikation: Wallstein Verlag; DOI https://doi.org/10.46500/83535581-010 | CC BY-NC-ND 4.0

Joachim Grage

MASKULINITÄT

Der Held als Mann – der Mann als Held

Welches Geschlecht haben Helden? Im *Deutschen Wörterbuch* der Brüder Grimm, dem historischen Belegwörterbuch der deutschen Sprache, findet man unter der maskulinen Form des Wortes einen ausführlichen, mehr als vier Spalten umfassenden Eintrag. Die Bedeutungserläuterungen zeigen, dass Helden hier ausschließlich männlich gedacht sind. Das ist in Anbetracht des grammatischen Geschlechts zunächst nicht verwunderlich und liegt wohl auch daran, dass als Hauptbedeutung der »durch tapferkeit und kampfgewandtheit hervorragende krieger«[1] genannt ist – Helden werden demnach ursprünglich und vornehmlich auf den Schlachtfeldern gemacht, und dort kämpfen in der Regel Männer. Später wird – neben zahlreichen anderen Bedeutungen – auch die Bezeichnung ›Held‹ für denjenigen genannt, »der in irgend einem gebiete etwas ausgezeichnetes, hervorragendes leistet« (Abb. 1). Hier sind ja durchaus Bereiche vorstellbar, zu denen auch Frauen Zugang haben und in denen sie durch herausragende Leistungen hervortreten könnten, aber in allen Belegstellen handelt es sich auch hier um Männer. Diese Bedeutung wird zudem als Folge einer Übertragung aus dem Militärischen auf andere Bereiche des menschlichen Lebens eingestuft.

Doch es gibt auch einen Eintrag für das Femininum ›Heldin‹. Dieser ist gerade einmal eine Viertelspalte lang und nennt als Bedeutungen lediglich »die heldin eines schauspiels, eines romans, einer geschichte, einer begebenheit« sowie die »schauspielerin, die heldenrollen gibt«[2]. Heldinnen existieren demnach nur in der Literatur und auf der Bühne, nicht aber im wirklichen Leben.

In der Sprache manifestiert sich immer auch das kulturelle Gedächtnis von Gesellschaften. Es war eher ein Zufall, dass der 10. Band des Grimm'schen Wörterbuches, in dem das Lemma »Held« verzeichnet ist, 1871 erschien, im Jahr des Sieges über Frankreich, der zahlreiche Kriegshelden hervorbrachte. Aber bis heute ist das Heroische »eine primär männliche Domäne«,[3] und was heroisch ist, gilt oft auch als männlich. So sind traditionelle Vorstellungen von Männlichkeit von dem geprägt, wodurch Helden glänzen – und andersherum. Helden sind Vorbilder für Männer (Abb. 2). Sie generieren Erwartungen an Männer, sich heroisch zu verhalten, selbst wenn nicht jeder ein Held werden kann oder darf, denn »ein Volk von Helden würde unweigerlich dessen Untergang herbeiführen.«[4] Für Männer, die diesen Erwartungen nicht entsprechen oder sich ihnen gar verweigern, gibt es dagegen viele geschlechtsspezifische despektierliche Ausdrücke, die noch nicht im Grimm'schen Wörterbuch stehen: Sie werden heute als ›Weicheier‹, ›Warmduscher‹ oder ›Schattenparker‹ bezeichnet.

Joachim Grage

MASCULINITY

The hero as a man – the man as a hero

What is the gender of heroes? In the *German Dictionary* by the Brothers Grimm, the comprehensive historical dictionary of the German language, the masculine form of the word 'hero' has an entry spanning over four columns. The definitions here indicate that a hero is perceived exclusively as a masculine entity. Considering the gender of the noun in German, this may not at first seem particularly surprising, and may also be due to the fact that the chief definition provided is that of a "warrior standing out because of his bravery and skilfulness of fighting".[1] Heroes, it seems, are made on the battlefield, and it is usually men who fight there. At a later date – and in addition to many other definitions in the Grimms' dictionary – the term 'hero' is also assigned to those "delivering something excellent, extraordinary in any area" (Fig. 1). It is not beyond the realms of imagination that some of these areas could be accessible to women and could therefore be areas where they too could stand out for their exceptional achievements. However, all references solely refer to men. The military meaning also seems to be transferred to other areas of human life.

Nevertheless, there is one entry for the feminine variation of the German noun for hero. It makes up a mere quarter of a column, simply listing "the heroine of a play, a novel, a story, an event" or the "actress playing the role of a heroine".[2] According to the dictionary, feminine heroes only exist in literature and on stage, not in real life.

Language is where the cultural memory of societies manifests itself. It was mere coincidence that the 10th volume of the Grimms' dictionary, containing the lemma 'hero', was published in 1871, the year which saw victory over France and with it the creation of numerous war heroes. But even today, heroism is a "primarily masculine domain"[3], and what is heroic is often also regarded as being masculine. For example, traditional concepts of masculinity are characterised by the very aspects that make heroes shine – and vice versa. Heroes are role models for men (Fig. 2). They generate expectations of men to behave heroically, even though not everyone can or is allowed to become a hero, as "a people of heroes would invariably cause its own doom".[4] For men who do not meet these expectations or even oppose them, there is a multitude of gender-specific contemptuous expressions which cannot be found in the Grimms' Dictionary: today, they would be called 'wusses', 'wimps' or 'scaredy-cats'.

Abb. 1: »Kein Stand nicht, auch das weibliche Geschlecht nicht, ist ausgeschlossen. Gleichheit besteht in der Walhalla; hebt doch der Tod jeden irdischen Unterschied auf!« König Ludwig I. von Bayern (1786–1868) wollte offenbar, dass »rühmlich ausgezeichnete Teutsche« beiderlei Geschlechts in das durch ihn gegründete Gedenkmonument aufgenommen werden. Dennoch sind nur 13 der 160 Geehrten Frauen. An der Ostwand ist eine einzige Frau dargestellt – Viktoria, Personifikation der Siege, die durch Männer errungen wurden.

Fig. 1: "No class is excluded – not even the female sex. Equality prevails in Valhalla; death cancels out every earthly difference!" With this quote, King Ludwig I of Bavaria (1786–1868) evidently wished to include "gloriously distinguished Germans" of both sexes in the memorial monument he founded. Nevertheless, only 13 of the 160 figures honoured are women. The eastern wall only shows one woman: Victoria, the personification of victories won by men.

Heroische Qualitäten

Welche Eigenschaften für typisch männlich oder weiblich gehalten werden, variiert kulturell, sozial, historisch und individuell. Selbst wer persönlich der Überzeugung ist, dass es gar keine geschlechtsspezifischen Charaktereigenschaften oder Verhaltensweisen gibt, wird einräumen müssen, dass diese als stereotype Zuschreibungen sehr wohl existieren. Um die geschlechtliche Dimension bestimmter Eigenschaften einzuschätzen, ist daher nicht entscheidend, was man selbst für männlich oder weiblich hält, sondern vielmehr das, wovon man glaubt, dass es die meisten anderen darüber denken oder fühlen.

Abb. 2: In 18 Suworow-Militärschulen in Russland bereiten sich 14- bis 18-jährige Jungen auf den Schulabschluss vor. General Suworow, gefeierter Held der Türken- und der napoleonischen Kriege, wird ihnen dabei als Vorbild präsentiert. Er verkörpert die russische Kriegskunst, glänzende Siege gegen mächtige Gegner, militärisches Genie, Größe und Macht des Imperiums. Suworow wurde zum Maßstab für Heldentum in unterschiedlichen politischen Systemen, vom Zarenreich über die Sowjetunion zur Zeit Stalins bis zum heutigen Russland unter dem Präsidenten Putin.

Fig. 2: In 18 Suvorov military schools in Russia, 14–18-year-old boys are preparing to graduate. General Suvorov, a celebrated Russian hero during the Turkish and Napoleonic wars, is presented to them as a role model. He epitomises the Russian art of war: Brilliant victories against powerful opponents, military genius and an empire's power and greatness. Suvorov became a symbol of heroism in different political systems – from the Tsarist Empire, to the Soviet Union during Stalin's time, to today's Russia under President Putin.

Heroic qualities

Which characteristics are regarded as typically masculine or feminine differs depending on cultural, social, historical and individual contexts. Even people who are of the personal opinion that gender-specific character traits or patterns of behaviour do not exist, will have to concede that as stereotypical associations they clearly do. To evaluate the gender dimension of certain characteristics, the decisive factor is not what one regards as masculine or feminine oneself, but rather what one believes most people think or feel is masculine or feminine.

Nicht alle heroischen Qualitäten – also solche Eigenschaften und Verhaltensweisen, die Personen im Zuge von Heroisierungsprozessen zugeschrieben werden[5] – gelten aber in diesem Sinne als maskulin. Stärke, Mut, Tapferkeit, Entschlussfreudigkeit und Handlungsbereitschaft mögen allgemein als männlich assoziiert werden, Eigenschaften wie Opferbereitschaft, Geduld und Ausdauer werden dagegen häufig auch mit Feminität in Verbindung gebracht. Helden sind also nicht unbedingt Super-Männer, die alle stereotypen Eigenschaften ihres Geschlechts in sich vereinen. Wenn Helden sich dadurch auszeichnen, dass sie mehr leisten, als gemeinhin erwartet wird, so kann dieses ›Mehr‹ auch bedeuten, dass sie die Erwartungen, die an ihr Geschlecht gestellt werden, nicht uneingeschränkt erfüllen und sich in entscheidenden Situationen nicht so männlich verhalten, wie es zu erwarten wäre, dafür aber den Mangel an heroischer Männlichkeit durch ein Mehr in Bezug auf andere Eigenschaften kompensieren. Dennoch werden männliche Helden am Ende in der Regel als Repräsentanten ihres Geschlechts gefeiert.

Das männliche Gewaltmonopol

Nicht von ungefähr versteht das Grimm'sche Wörterbuch den Helden in erster Linie als Krieger. In vielen Heldentaten spielt physische Gewalt eine zentrale Rolle. Der Kampf, den Helden zu bestehen haben, wird oft mit Waffen oder Fäusten geführt und zielt darauf ab, Gegner zu verletzen oder auszuschalten, insbesondere im so wichtigen heroischen Bewährungsfeld des Krieges. Selbst wer im Kampf unterliegt, kann als Held gefeiert werden, schon allein weil er sich dem Kampf tapfer ausgesetzt hat (Abb. 3). Physische Gewaltausübung ist »eine zentrale Ressource für Heroisierungsprozesse«.[6] Die enge Verbindung von Männlichkeit und Heldentum hat auch darin ihre Ursache, dass »Männer und Frauen [...] in unterschiedlichem Maße über die (Macht-)Ressource Gewalt [verfügen]«.[7] Gewalt gilt als Domäne von Männern, was sich nicht zuletzt darin zeigt, »dass die überwiegende Zahl der Gewaltverbrechen weltweit von Männern verübt wird«.[8] Das männliche Gewaltmonopol ist ebenso Ursache wie Ausdruck eines männlichen Herrschaftsanspruchs, der lange Zeit als selbstverständlich hingenommen wurde: Er richtet sich nicht nur und häufig gar nicht in erster Linie gegen Frauen, sondern zunächst gegen andere, in Machtkämpfen unterlegene Männer.

Die Soziologin Raewyn Connell hat in einer einflussreichen Studie darauf hingewiesen, dass es stets verschiedene Formen von Männlichkeiten gibt, je nachdem, welche Altersgruppen, sozialen Schichten oder kulturellen Milieus man gerade betrachtet. Diejenige Form von Männlichkeit, »die in einer gegebenen Struktur des Geschlechterverhältnisses die bestimmende Position einnimmt«,[9] bezeichnet sie als ›hegemoniale Maskulinität‹. Hegemonial ist diese Maskulinität in doppeltem

Not all heroic qualities – i.e., such qualities and patterns of behaviour which are attributed to people in the course of heroization processes[5] – are regarded as being masculine per se, though. While strength, courage, bravery, initiative, and willingness to take action may generally be connoted with masculinity, characteristics such as willingness to make sacrifices, patience and stamina are frequently associated with femininity. This means that heroes are not necessarily super-men who unite all the stereotypical characteristics of their sex in one person. If heroes are distinguished as people who exceed expectations, this 'exceedance' could also mean that they do not abide by the expectations of their sex, and that in decisive situations they may not behave as masculinely as they would be expected to. They may compensate for this deviation from the masculine heroic with 'exceedance' in other characteristics. Nevertheless, in general male heroes are ultimately celebrated as representatives of their sex.

Men's exclusive right to use force

It is no coincidence that the Grimms' Dictionary firstly and foremostly perceives the hero as a warrior. Physical violence plays a central role in many heroic deeds. The fight which heroes have to win is often conducted with weaponry or fists with intent to maim or completely eliminate the opponent, particularly in the vital heroic performance field of warfare. Even those who are defeated can be celebrated as heroes, simply because they went into battle bravely (Fig. 3). Physical exertion of violence is "a central resource for heroization processes".[6] The close connection between masculinity and heroism is also partly caused by the fact that "men and women have access to the (power) resource of violence to different degrees".[7] Force is regarded as the domain of men, which is not lastly illustrated by the fact "that the vast majority of violent crimes worldwide are committed by men".[8] The male monopoly on the use of force is the cause as well as the expression of a male claim to power which has been taken for granted for a long time. It is not only, and often not even principally, directed against women but rather against other men, who are to be defeated in power struggles.

In an influential study, the sociologist Raewyn Connell pointed out that there are always various forms of masculinity, depending on which age groups, social groups or cultural environments are under consideration. She calls the form of masculinity "that occupies the hegemonic position in a given pattern of gender relations"[9] a 'hegemonic masculinity'. This masculinity is hegemonic in a double sense, as it both "guarantees (or is taken to guarantee) the dominant position of men and the subordination of women"[10] and maintains a position of domination over other forms of masculinity (Fig. 4). Those heroes who utilise force affirm the continuation of a

Abb. 3: Am 8.12.1914 sank im Seegefecht bei den Falklandinseln beinahe das gesamte deutsche Ostasiengeschwader, darunter auch der Kleine Kreuzer Leipzig. Mehrere Zeitungen berichteten, ein Matrose habe noch im Sinken die Kriegsflagge der Kaiserlichen Marine emporgehalten: »Und als die Welle den Kopf bedeckt, / Aus dem Wasser ein Arm noch die Fahne streckt. / Er läßt sie nicht, er nimmt sie hinein; / Sie soll auch im Tod sein Begleiter sein.« Hans Bohrdts Gemälde »Der letzte Mann« wurde tausendfach kopiert und adaptiert. Die Wahrheit war wohl prosaischer: »Viele über Bord gesprungen, erfroren, ertrunken. 9 Uhr geht das Schiff mit Kommandant unter«, lautet ein Augenzeugenbericht. Von mehr als 300 Besatzungsmitgliedern überlebten nur 18.

Fig. 3: On 8 December 1914, nearly the entire German East Asia Fleet, including the small cruiser "Leipzig", sank during the Battle of the Falkland Islands. According to several newspapers, a sailor was observed holding the Imperial Navy's battle flag as he sank. "And as the wave covers his head, / An arm still reaches out from the water, flag in hand / He does not abandon it, but rather embraces it; / It shall be his companion even in death." Hans Bohrdt's painting "The Last Man" has been copied and adapted thousands of times. The truth was, however, probably more prosaic. "Many jumped overboard, froze to death or drowned. At 9 o'clock in the morning, the ship sank with her Captain," reads one eyewitness report. Of more than 300 crew members, only 18 survived.

Abb. 4: Der »Hercules Farnese« bzw. dessen verlorenes griechisches Vorbild kann als Prototyp hegemonialer Männlichkeit gelten. Die Künstlerin Ulrike Rosenbach zeigte ihre Rauminstallation »Herakles – Herkules – King Kong. Die Vorbilder der Mannsbilder« 1977 auf der documenta 6. In der Endlosschleife des Videos haucht Rosenbach immer wieder das Wort »Frau«. Sie verstand die Arbeit als Auseinandersetzung mit einem überlieferten männlichen Machtbild.

Fig. 4: "Hercules Farnese", or rather his long-lost Greek original, can be considered the prototype of hegemonic masculinity. Artist Ulrike Rosenbach presented her interpretation of the statue called "Herakles – Herkules – King Kong. Die Vorbilder der Mannsbilder" (Heracles – Hercules – King Kong. Role models of the male image) at documenta 6, a large art exhibition held in Kassel, Germany, in 1977. Throughout the video's endless loop, Rosenbach repeatedly whispers the word "woman". She intended the piece to be an examination of the traditional male image of power.

certain concept of ideal masculinity in physical strength and assertiveness, and strengthen the male claim to dominance over women, even though this is rarely the explicit objective or intention of their 'heroic deed'.

Heroic bodily features and sexual attractiveness

Usually, men are regarded as male due to their physical characteristics. This is especially because heroic deeds are often linked to a significant bodily commitment, meaning that the heroic is particularly ingrained in the body. When the inconspicuous average citizen mutates into a superhero, he grows muscles which make his spe-

Sinne, insofern sie einerseits »die Dominanz der Männer sowie die Unterordnung der Frauen gewährleistet (oder gewährleisten soll)«[10] und andererseits eine Vormachtstellung gegenüber anderen Formen von Maskulinität behauptet (Abb. 4). Gerade diejenigen Helden, die Gewalt einsetzen, bekräftigen das Fortbestehen einer bestimmten Vorstellung von idealer Männlichkeit, die sich auf körperliche Stärke und Durchsetzungskraft bezieht, und sie affirmieren den Herrschaftsanspruch von Männern gegenüber Frauen, auch wenn dies gar nicht Ziel oder Zweck ihrer ›Heldentat‹ ist.

Heroische Körperlichkeit und sexuelle Attraktivität

Männer werden in der Regel aufgrund körperlicher Merkmale als Männer betrachtet. Gerade weil Heldentaten oft mit einem besonderen Körpereinsatz verbunden sind, ist das Heroische dem Körper eingeschrieben. Wenn der unauffällige Durchschnittsbürger zum Superhelden mutiert, wachsen ihm Muskeln, die schon äußerlich seine besonderen Kräfte sichtbar machen. Im Alltag ein schmächtiger Seemann, schwillt Popeye der Bizeps, sobald er sein Superfood Spinat isst – erst dann ist er bereit zur Heldentat (Abb. 5).

Helden repräsentieren oft ein männliches Körperideal. In der Antike wurden athletische Helden nackt dargestellt, wobei ihren Darstellungen aber auch Aspekte von Schwäche und Widersprüchlichkeit eingeschrieben sein konnten. So zeigt der Hercules Farnese (die römische Kopie einer griechischen Statue aus dem 4. Jahrhundert v. Chr.) einen muskulösen, starken Helden im Moment der Inaktivität oder der Ratlosigkeit. Als die monumentale Statue in den römischen Caracalla-Thermen aufgestellt war, setzte der trainierte Körper des Hercules gleichwohl Maßstäbe für die männlichen Besucher der Badeanlage, die dort ihre Körper pflegten. In der Neuzeit wurde der nackte männliche Heldenkörper zunehmend ästhetisiert und als Schönheitsideal betrachtet – noch heute ist das ein Geschäftsmodell für Fitness-Center, die ihren Kunden versprechen, sich mit ausreichendem Training und Muskelaufbau einen Heldenkörper verschaffen zu können, der ihnen Selbstvertrauen gibt und sie zu glücklicheren und erfolgreicheren Menschen macht.

Heroische Figuren besitzen eine »intensivierte Attraktionskraft«: Sie können »unmittelbar auf Menschen einwirken und emotionale Reaktionen hervorrufen«.[11] Daher kann heroische Körperlichkeit auch als Kapital auf dem Feld der Sexualität eingesetzt werden, und zwar nicht nur bei dem Teil der Verehrer:innenschaft, der von den maskulinen Reizen erotisch angesprochen wird, sondern auch bei potentiellen Konkurrenten. Der entblößte männliche Heldenkörper gilt nicht nur als schön, er kann auch sexy sein. Die Bilder, die Vladimir Putin in wilder Natur mit nacktem Oberkörper zu Pferde zeigten, sollten wohl auch Wählerinnen ansprechen

Abb. 5: Was mag den jungen Australier im Jahr 1940 bewogen haben, sich Popeye auf die Brust tätowieren zu lassen? Der bauernschlaue Matrose ist ein Mann von der Straße, ehrlich und unverstellt. Seine erstaunliche Stärke zieht er aus Spinat, den er bei Bedarf direkt aus der Dose verschlingt. Popeye ist ein maskuliner Held, stark und unkompliziert, aber gegenüber seiner Herzensdame ergeben bis zur Unterwürfigkeit. Er entspricht damit in klischeehafter Verzerrung einem Männlichkeitsideal seiner Zeit.

Fig. 5: What could have motivated this young Australian to get Popeye tattooed on his chest in 1940? The shrewd cartoon sailor, popular in the '30s and '40s, is a street-wise guy – honest and straightforward. He mostly draws his astonishing strength from spinach, which he devours straight from the can whenever he needs it. Popeye is a type of masculine hero – strong and uncomplicated, but devoted to his sweetheart to the point of submissiveness. In a clichéd distortion, he therefore corresponds to the masculine ideal of his time.

cial powers visible. A weedy sailor in everyday life, Popeye's biceps swell whenever he eats his superfood spinach – only then is he ready to accomplish heroic deeds (Fig. 5).

Heroes often represent an ideal of a male body. In antiquity, athletic heroes were depicted naked, with signs of weakness and inconsistency also inscribed in their representations. The Farnese Hercules (the Roman copy of the original Greek statue dating from the 4th century BC), for example, shows a muscular, strong hero in a moment of inactivity or perplexity. When the monumental statue was placed at the Baths of Caracalla in Rome, Hercules' toned body set the standards for the male baths visitors and their own bodies. In modern times, the naked male heroic body has become more and more utilised as an aesthetic concept and ideal of beauty – today, this is a business model for fitness centres who promise their clients that they may achieve the body of a hero with sufficient training and muscle building, thus giving them more self-confidence and making them happier and more successful individuals.

Heroic types possess an "intensified attractive power". They can "affect people directly and evoke emotional responses".[11] Heroic bodily features may therefore also be considered an asset in the field of sexuality, not only among the portion of male and female admirers erotically attracted by masculine appeal but also among potential competitors. The exposed male heroic body is not only regarded as beautiful, it may also be sexy. The images depicting a bare-chested Vladimir Putin horse-riding are probably intended to appeal to female voters and emphasise the physical fitness of the Russian president compared to other men – he portrays himself as a 'strong man' in a macho

MASCULINITY

Abb. 6: Vladimir Putins Selbstdarstellung beruht wesentlich auf dem Image des »echten Mannes«, der durch physische Fitness, rücksichtslose Entschlusskraft und Durchsetzungsfähigkeit glänzt. Bilder von Putin bei »männlichen« Hobbys wie Reiten oder Jagen (wie hier 2009) sind inzwischen selten geworden – auch der besttrainierte Männerkörper verliert mit über 70 Jahren an heroischer Attraktionskraft.

Fig. 6: Vladimir Putin's self-presentation is primarily based on the image of a "real man" – someone who is physically fit, ruthlessly decisive and assertive. Images of Putin pursuing "manly" hobbies such as horse riding or hunting (like this one from 2009) have now become rare – even the most well-trained male body loses its heroic appeal over the age of 70.

und gegenüber anderen Männern die körperliche Fitness des russischen Präsidenten behaupten – hier inszeniert er sich als ›starker Mann‹ mit Macho-Attitüde und zugleich als Gegenbild des durchschnittlichen russischen Mannes, der mit Alkoholexzessen, Gewaltausbrüchen und Seitensprüngen die Geduld seiner Ehefrau strapaziert (Abb. 6).[12] Wenn sich Emmanuel Macron im Wahlkampf gegen Marine Le Pen im Jahr 2022 betont locker auf einem Sofa fläzend fotografieren lässt, mit ausgebreiteten Armen, gespreizten Beinen und mit offenem Hemd, das den Betrachter:innen den Blick auf seine Brustbehaarung gewährt (Abb. 7), dann inszeniert er sich nicht nur als besonders maskulin, sondern bedient dabei auch Codes des Heroischen: Er präsentiert sich als dynamisch, handlungsfähig und souverän. Der Sexappeal wird im Kampf um die Macht im Staate eingesetzt. Selbst diejenigen, die das weder sexy finden noch für Staatsmänner als angemessen betrachten, bestätigen mit ihren Reaktionen, dass sie auf die Erotisierung der Macht und der (Staats-)Gewalt angesprungen sind. Die erotische heroische Selbstinszenierung scheint Macrons Kampagne genützt zu haben: Aus der Stichwahl gegen seine Gegnerin ging er als Sieger hervor.

Der binarisierende Effekt des Heroischen

»Die heroische Geschlechterordnung ist binär und lässt kaum Raum für Zwischenlagen«, so der Soziologe Ulrich Bröckling.[13] Helden bekräftigen die herrschenden

© Foto: Soazig de la Moissonnière (Offizielle Fotografin von Emmanuel Macron / Instagram – https://www.instagram.com/p/Ccc0oBLLTVP)

Abb. 7: In raumgreifender Pose, jederzeit bereit aufzuspringen, sitzt der französische Präsident Emmanuel Macron auf dem Sofa. Das aufgeknöpfte Hemd signalisiert Lässigkeit, das daraus herausquellende Brusthaar Virilität. Kurz vor der Stichwahl um das Präsidentenamt 2022 zeigte sich Macron als die junge, vitale und vor allem männliche Alternative zu Marine Le Pen.

Fig. 7: French President Emmanuel Macron is sitting on a sofa, arms and legs spread expansively, ready to spring to his feet at a moment's notice. His unbuttoned shirt signals nonchalance, his exposed chest hair, virility. Shortly before the second ballot in the 2022 presidential election, Macron presented himself as a young, energetic and, above all, masculine alternative to Marine Le Pen.

posture and simultaneously as a counter-image of the average Russian male who taxes the patience of this wife through alcohol excesses, violent outbreaks and affairs (Fig. 6).[12] Photos of Emmanuel Macron released during his election campaign against Marine le Pen in 2022 see him sitting casually on a sofa with arms and legs spread wide, and an unbuttoned shirt allowing a glimpse of his chest hair (Fig. 7). Such images are deliberate attempts not only to highlight the president's masculinity but also his heroic qualities: Macron is presenting himself as dynamic, capable of taking action and self-assured. Sex appeal can be used in the struggle for power within a state. Even those who find this picture neither sexy nor regard it as appropriate for a statesman, react in a way which confirms that they have been drawn in by the erotisation of power and (state) authority. The erotic and heroic-self-portrayal seems to have paid off for Macron's campaign: he emerged victorious in the runoff election against his opponent.

MASCULINITY

Abb. 8: Groß, blond und blauäugig: Obwohl Adolf Hitler dem Ideal des angeblich perfekten Deutschen selbst gar nicht entsprach, vermochte er bei vielen deutschen Frauen eine an Hysterie grenzende Verehrung zu erwecken.
Fig. 8: Tall, blond and blue-eyed. Although Adolf Hitler himself did not meet this ideal of a supposedly perfect German, he was able to inspire adoration bordering on hysteria in many German women.

Vorstellungen darüber, dass es von Natur aus genau zwei Geschlechter gibt, die sich fundamental voneinander unterscheiden und zwischen denen ein Machtgefälle herrscht. Frauen stellen in vielen Heldenerzählungen entweder diejenigen dar, die der männliche Held zu beschützen hat, oder diejenigen, die dem Protagonisten Verehrung und Bewunderung entgegenbringen, seine Tat als außerordentlich preisen und ihm dadurch erst seinen Heldenstatus verleihen (Abb. 8). Die enge Verbindung zwischen Maskulinität und Heldentum und die Ausrichtung idealer Männlichkeit am Modell des Helden untermauern Herrschaftsansprüche von Männern gegenüber Frauen. Zwar können Helden Gesellschaftsordnungen ins Wanken bringen, ihr Effekt auf die Geschlechterordnung ist dagegen eher stabilisierend.

Teil dieser naturhaft verstandenen Geschlechterordnung ist auch, dass sich das erotische Begehren auf das jeweils andere Geschlecht zu richten hat. Männliche Homosexualität wurde (und wird auch heute noch häufig) als »ein[e] bestimmt[e] Weise der innerlichen Verkehrung des Männlichen und des Weiblichen charakterisiert«.[14] Damit ist sie eine potenzielle Herausforderung für das Heroische. Solange Homosexualität nicht als Perversion, sondern lediglich als Praktik verstanden wurde, war das kein Problem oder konnte gar den Heldengeschichten eine weitere faszinierende Facette hinzufügen, wie im Falle von Achilles und Patroklos, David und Jonathan oder Alexander und Hephaistion. Spätestens im Laufe des 19. Jahrhundert aber, als man die sexuelle Orientierung als Teil der persönlichen Identität zu verstehen begann, konnte der Verdacht der Homosexualität am maskulinen Image des Helden kratzen. Als der dänische Schriftsteller Klaus Rifbjerg im Jahr 2002 dem norwegischen Polarforscher Fridtjof Nansen (Abb. 9) in einem Roman eine homosexuelle Affäre mit einem anderen Teilnehmer seiner Nordpolexpedition

The binarising effect of the heroic

According to sociologist Ulrich Bröckling, "the heroic gender order is binary and hardly leaves any space for intermediate layers".[13] Heroes confirm the predominant ideas that sex is inherent and binary, and that the two sexes differ fundamentally from each other and have a power difference between them. In many heroic narratives, women are either those in need of protection by the male hero or those admiring and worshipping the protagonist, praising his deeds as extraordinary and thus endowing him with heroic status (Fig. 8). The close connection between masculinity and heroism and the orientation of ideal masculinity along the model of the hero underpin claims of dominance of men over women. Although heroes can shake up social orders, their effect on the gender order is a stabilising one.

A part of this inherent gender order is also the idea that erotic desire should be directed at the opposite sex. Male homosexuality was regarded as (and is still frequently regarded today as) "a certain way of internal reversal of the masculine and the feminine".[14] This makes it a potential challenge for the heroic. During the period when homosexuality was not regarded as a perversion but just as a practice, it did not pose a problem to the heroic, and could even add another fascinating layer to the hero stories, as was the case with Achilles and Patroclus, David and Jonathan or Alexander and Hephaestion. However, over the course of the 19th century, as sexual orientation started to be viewed as part of one's personal identity, the suspicion around homosexuality had the power to undermine the masculine image of the hero. When in 2002 the Danish writer Klaus Rifbjerg published a novel, mentioning a homosexual affair the Norwegian polar explorer Fridtjof Nansen (Fig. 9) allegedly had with another participant in his north pole expedition, Norway became very indignant – the mere suggestion that their national hero could have shared his libido with another man in the eternal ice was too much for many Norwegians. Another indicator for the overbearing power of the traditional heroic gender order is the fact that homosexuality is still a taboo subject in many types of sports which have an extremely masculine image and a large heroic potential, such as men's football.

Female Masculine Heroism?

Heroizations mainly appear in male-connoted domains of society, particularly where competition, willingness to fight and hierarchic structures exist. This does not automatically exclude women from the sphere of heroism but impedes their access to a heroic status. The example of flight pioneer Melli Beese, who got a pilot's licence as the first woman in Germany and set a number of records as 'first woman' – but

andichtete, war die Empörung in Norwegen groß – allein die Vorstellung, dass der Nationalheld seine Libido im ewigen Eis mit einem anderen Mann geteilt haben könnte, empfanden viele als Zumutung. Auch dass Homosexualität in Sportarten mit einem extrem maskulinen Image und einem großen Heldenpotential wie dem Männerfußball noch immer tabuisiert wird, ist ein Zeichen für die Wirkungsmacht der traditionellen heroischen Geschlechterordnung.

Weibliches maskulines Heldentum?

Heroisierungen treten überwiegend in männlich konnotierten Domänen der Gesellschaft auf, dort, wo Wettbewerb, Kampfbereitschaft und Hierarchien herrschen. Das schließt Frauen nicht automatisch aus der Sphäre des Heroischen aus, erschwert ihnen aber den Zugang zum Heldenstatus. Das Beispiel der Fliegerpionierin Melli Beese, die als erste Frau in Deutschland einen Pilotenschein machte und einige weitere Rekorde als ›erste Frau‹ aufstellte, in der Heldengeschichte der Fliegerei aber lange vergessen war, macht deutlich, dass es Frauen oft erschwert wird, in männlich dominierte und heroisch auratisierte Berufsfelder vorzudringen und dass sie, wenn sie dort erst einmal angekommen sind, einem erhöhten Legitimationsdruck ausgesetzt sind.

Frauen können heroisiert werden, müssen dafür aber oft wie Männer auftreten, maskuline Eigenschaften annehmen oder die Erwartungen an Weiblichkeit enttäuschen. So treten sie beispielsweise wie Jeanne d'Arc als Jungfrau in Erscheinung, brechen als kämpferische Amazonen das männliche Gewaltmonopol auf (was für männliche Krieger wiederum den Einsatz von Gewalt gegen Frauen rechtfertigt) oder inszenieren sich in Männerkleidung und in maskulinen Posen wie Katharina die Große. Weibliches Heldentum geht also offenbar häufig einher mit ›weiblicher Maskulinität‹ (Abb. 10).[15] Selbst heroisierte Frauen, die durch eine besonders aufopferungsvolle Care-Arbeit hervortreten, wie Florence Nightingale oder Mutter Teresa, und die insofern als hyper-feminin gelten mögen, wurden ›nur‹ symbolisch Mütter und erfüllten insofern wie viele andere Heldinnen nicht die Weiblichkeitsideale ihrer Zeit. Zugleich bestätigt aber ihre Heroisierung als aufopferungsvolle Frauen wiederum die bestehende binäre Geschlechterordnung. Gerade an Held:innen (männlichen wie weiblichen!) zeigt sich, dass Geschlecht als soziale Kategorie ein Konstrukt ist und körperlich inszeniert werden muss – und dass das Heroische die bestehende Geschlechterordnung eher festigt als aufbricht.

Doch insbesondere im Zuge der homosexuellen Emanzipationsbewegungen des 20. Jahrhunderts spielen Heroisierungen eine wichtige Rolle. Das Coming Out und der Kampf gegen Vorurteile lassen sich auch als Heldengeschichte erzählen. Der inzwischen etablierte Kanon von »LGBTQ-Held*innen« reicht »von Sappho bis

Abb. 9: Die Polarregionen waren um 1900 Orte, an denen maskuline Helden gemacht wurden. Hier trotzten Männer den Gewalten der Natur und zeigten selbst im Tod heroische Größe. Diesem Männlichkeitsideal folgt die Darstellung des im Schneesturm sterbenden Lawrence Oates (1880–1912), Mitglied von Robert Falcon Scotts Terra-Nova-Expedition zum Südpol. Nach vier Monaten in Schnee und Eis war er zu erschöpft, um weiterzumarschieren. Um seinen Kameraden nicht zur Last zu fallen, verließ er den Unterschlupf während eines Schneesturms mit den Worten »Ich gehe ein wenig heraus und werde wohl eine Weile weg sein.« – Er ging in den sicheren Tod.

Fig. 9: Around the year 1900, masculine heroes were often defined in the Earth's polar regions. Here, men defied the forces of nature and demonstrated heroic greatness – even in death. This depiction of Lawrence Oates (1880-1912), a member of Robert Falcon Scott's Terra Nova expedition to the South Pole, dying in a snowstorm reflects this era's ideal of masculinity. After four months wandering through the snow and ice, he was too exhausted to march on. In order to avoid being a burden to his comrades, he left their shelter during a snowstorm, declaring: "I'm going out for a bit and will probably be gone for a while". He walked straight to his certain death.

had nevertheless been long forgotten in the heroic history of aviation – illustrates that woman are often hindered in their progression in male-dominated and heroically glamourised career fields, and that even once they have succeeded in entering them, they are put under increased pressure of legitimisation.

Women may be heroized but in order to achieve this status they often have to behave like men, adopt masculine characteristics or disappoint the ideals of femi-

Abb. 10: Melli Beese (1886–1925) wuchs in einem privilegierten, wohlhabenden Elternhaus auf, das ihr eine breitgefächerte Ausbildung ermöglichte. Die Pilotenlizenz allerdings musste sie sich als Frau gegen männliche Vorurteile hart erkämpfen. Um sich in der damaligen Männerdomäne Luftfahrt durchzusetzen, glich sich Beese bei Bedarf auch äußerlich dem Bild des männlichen Piloten an.

Fig. 10: Melli Beese (1886-1925) grew up in a privileged, wealthy home that allowed her to receive a wide range of education. However, as a woman, she had to fight hard for her pilot's licence in the face of male prejudice. In order to assert herself in the male-dominated world of aviation at the time, Beese adapted her appearance to the image of a male pilot whenever necessary.

Freddy Mercury und Ellen deGeneres«.[16] Ebenso haben die modernen Frauenbewegungen ihre Heldinnen hervorgebracht. Wenn also die binäre Geschlechterordnung selbst zum Kampfplatz wird, kann das Heroische auf diesem Feld durchaus subversiv sein (Abb. 11).

ninity. For instance, they appear as a virgin like Jeanne d'Arc, break the male monopoly on the use of force as aggressive Amazons (which in turn justifies male warriors' use of violence against them) or dress in men's clothing and strike masculine poses like Catherine the Great. Female heroism seems frequently to go hand in hand with 'female masculinity' (Abb. 10).[15] Even heroized women who distinguish themselves by nursing patients with particular devotion, like Florence Nightingale or Mother Teresa, and who might thus be regarded as hyper-feminine, 'only' became symbolic mothers and not biological mothers, joining the category of many other heroines who did not meet the ideals of femininity of their times. Simultaneously, their heroization as devoted women confirms the existing binary gender order. The example of heroes and heroines demonstrates that gender as a social category is a construct and needs to be physically portrayed – and that the heroic stabilises rather than breaks that gender order.

However, in the course of the homosexual emancipation movements of the 20th century, heroization processes played an important role. The idea of coming-out and fighting prejudices are perfect material for a heroic narrative. The now well-established canon of "LGBTQ heroes" encompasses Sappho to Freddy Mercury and Ellen deGeneres.[16] Likewise, the modern women's movements have established their heroines. This means that if the binary gender order itself becomes a battle arena, the heroic can indeed be subversive in this field (Fig. 11).

Abb. 11: Geehrt als Mensch, Mann und Held: Der 25-jährige Transmann Malte C. stellte sich 2022 schützend vor eine Gruppe von Besuchern des Christopher Street Days in Münster, als ihn der Schlag eines 20-jährigen Angreifers zu Boden streckte. Der Aufprall auf dem Kopfsteinpflaster hatte eine schwere Verletzung zur Folge, an der er wenige Tage später starb.

Fig. 11: Recognised as a person, a man and a hero: 25-year-old trans man Malte C. stood protectively in front of a group of visitors to Christopher Street Day 2022 in Münster when he was knocked to the ground by a 20-year-old attacker. He died a few days later as a result of injuries sustained from his head hitting the cobblestones.

Anmerkungen

1. held, m. Deutsches Wörterbuch von Jacob Grimm und Wilhelm Grimm, digitalisierte Fassung im Wörterbuchnetz des Trier Center for Digital Humanities, Version 01/23. www.woerterbuchnetz.de/DWB?lemid=H05741 [14. Juli 2023].
2. heldin, f. Deutsches Wörterbuch von Jacob Grimm und Wilhelm Grimm, digitalisierte Fassung im Wörterbuchnetz des Trier Center for Digital Humanities, Version 01/23. www.woerterbuchnetz.de/DWB?lemid=H05950 [14. Juli 2023].
3. Bröckling 2020, 36.
4. Rousseau 2009, 119.
5. Vgl. Feitscher 2022.
6. Gölz und Brink 2020, 19.
7. Meuser 2002, 73.
8. Gölz und Brink 2020, 18.
9. Connell 2015, 130.
10. Ebd.
11. Sonderforschungsbereich 948 2019a.
12. Zu Putins Männlichkeitsinszenierungen vgl. Arend 2023, 14.
13. Bröckling 2020, 37.
14. Foucault 1983, 47.
15. Der Begriff stammt von Jack Halberstam; vgl. Halberstam 1998.
16. Vgl. das Jugendbuch *Queer Heroes*, Sicardi und Tanat-Jones 2020.

Notes

1. held, m. Deutsches Wörterbuch von Jacob Grimm und Wilhelm Grimm, digitised version in the dictionary network of Trier Center for Digital Humanities, Version 01/23. www.woerterbuchnetz.de/DWB?lemid=H05741 [14 July 2023].
2. heldin, f. Deutsches Wörterbuch von Jacob Grimm und Wilhelm Grimm, digitised version in the dictionary network Trier Center for Digital Humanities, Version 01/23. www.woerterbuchnetz.de/DWB?lemid=H05950 [14 July 2023].
3. Bröckling 2020, 36.
4. Rousseau 2009, 119.
5. cf. Feitscher 2022.
6. Gölz and Brink 2020, 19.
7. Meuser 2002, 73.
8. Gölz and Brink 2020, 18.
9. Connell 2005, 76.
10. Connell 2005, 77.
11. Sonderforschungsbereich 948 2019a.
12. On Putin's stagings of masculinity cf. Arend 2023, 14.
13. Bröckling 2020, 37.
14. Foucault 1983, 47.
15. The term was coined by Jack Halberstam; cf. Halberstam 1998.
16. Cf. young adult fiction book *Queer Heroes*, Sicardi and Tanat-Jones 2019.

© 2024 Joachim Grage, Publikation: Wallstein Verlag; DOI https://doi.org/10.46500/83535581-011 | CC BY-NC-ND 4.0

Frank Reichherzer

MIT DEM FUßBALL DURCHS NIEMANDSLAND
Suchfelder des Heroischen in der Sinnlosigkeit des Massenkrieges.
Ereignis: »The best kicked goal in history«

Frank Edwards' Plan ging auf. Mit schnellen Atemstößen blies er Luft in einen Fußball. Es war der 25. September 1915, frühmorgens in Nordfrankreich, nahe dem Bergbaustädtchen Loos, das der kommenden Schlacht ihren Namen gab. Edwards war es entgegen den Befehlen seiner Vorgesetzten gelungen, einen Ball mit in die vorderste Stellung der *London Irish Rifles* zu nehmen. Man kann nur erahnen, welche Anspannung in den Gräben geherrscht haben mag. Plötzlich ertönte ein Pfiff, das Zeichen für den Beginn des sekundengenau geplanten Angriffs auf die deutschen Stellungen. Für Frank Edwards war es gleichsam der Anpfiff für seinen Abschlag ins Niemandsland – und wohl trotz des einsetzenden Abwehrfeuers auch eine Erlösung von der Anspannung der letzten Stunden und Tage. Mit den Worten »Play up, London Irish!« soll er über die Brustwehr des Grabens dem Ball hinterher ins Niemandsland gesprungen sein.

Beobachter berichten von einer Gruppe Soldaten, die einer Wolke aus Chlorgas folgend, umgeben von Granateinschlägen und Gewehrkugeln, einen Fußball passend und dribbelnd sich den deutschen Stellungen näherten (Abb. 1). Französische Soldaten, die dem Angriff aus ihren Stellungen zusahen, schwankten in ihrer Bewertung zwischen »Wahnsinn« und todesverachtender »beau geste«. Patrick MacGill, Teilnehmer und Chronist der Schlacht – im Frieden Schriftsteller und im Krieg Feldsanitäter bei den *Irish Rifles* – erzählt davon, wie der Ball nach dem Vorstoß zerschossen in einem Stacheldrahtverhau vor den deutschen Stellungen gefunden wurde. In den Augen des Kriegsberichterstatters des *Daily Telegraph*, Philip Gibbs, war dies »the best-kicked goal in history«.

Nicht nur der Ball, auch die *Irish Rifles* hatten mehr als das Erwartbare erreicht. Doch Planungsfehler wie das zu langsame Nachführen von Kräften und fehlende Artillerieunterstützung ließen den Einbruch in die deutschen Stellungen nicht zum erhofften Durchbruch werden. Zwei Wochen später hatten die deutschen Gegenangriffe die Briten wieder auf ihre Ausgangsstellungen zurückgeworfen. Am Ende der Schlacht waren auf beiden Seiten 75.000 Menschen tot, verwundet oder gefangen genommen. Das Ergebnis der Kämpfe war ein mit hohen Opferzahlen erkaufter Ausgangszustand. Das »Tor« – und somit die Heroisierung der Tat einiger unbekannter

Frank Reichherzer

WITH A FOOTBALL THROUGH NO MAN'S LAND
Searching for the Heroic in the Senselessness of Mass Warfare.
Event: "The Best-Kicked Goal in History"

Frank Edwards' plan worked. With a few quick puffs, he had inflated a football. It was early in the morning of 25 September 1915, close to the mining town of Loos in northern France, which would give its name to the upcoming battle. Against the orders of his superiors, Edwards had succeeded in bringing a ball right up to the most forward position of the *London Irish Rifles*. We can only guess at the tension that must have prevailed in the trenches. All of a sudden, a whistle sounded, indicating the start of the attack on German positions, planned to the second. For Edwards, it was also the kickoff whistle for his punt into no man's land – and in spite of the defensive fire that was already starting, it was probably also a moment of relief from the tension of the last hours and days. He is said to have shouted "Play up, London Irish!" as he jumped over the trench parapet and followed the ball into no man's land.

Observers later described how a group of soldiers, following a cloud of chlorine gas and surrounded by firing grenades and rifle bullets, passed and dribbled a football as they approached the German positions (Fig. 1). The French soldiers watching the attack from their positions described the action variously as "madness" and a death-defying "beau geste". Patrick MacGill, participant in and chronicler of the battle – an author in peacetime and a stretcherbearer for the *Irish Rifles* during the war – reported how, after the advance, the ball – now riddled with bullets – was found in a barbed-wire entanglement in front of the German positions. In the eyes of *Daily Telegraph* war correspondent Philip Gibbs, this was "the bestkicked goal in history".

Not only the ball but the *Irish Rifles*, too, had achieved more than could be expected. However, planning errors such as the slow supply of forces and lack of artillery support meant that the breakthrough into the German positions did not materialise as hoped. Two weeks later, German counterattacks pushed the British back into their initial positions. At the end of the battle, a total of 75,000 people had been killed, wounded or taken captive. The fighting had resulted in nothing more than a return to their original position, and had cost them many lives. With losses high and failure evident, the "goal" – and thus, the heroization of the deed of some unknown *London Irish* soldiers – quickly came to be publicly glorified as a symbol of

Abb. 1: Sergeant Harry Tyres war bei den *London Irish* bekannt für seine Cartoons, mit denen er das Leben in den Schützengräben und die Einsätze seiner Einheit kommentierte. Seine Zeichnung von kickenden *Tommies* in der Schlacht wirkt wie eine groteske Überblendung von Todesgefahr und Normalität.
Fig. 1: Sergeant Harry Tyres was known among the London Irish for his cartoons commenting on life in the trenches and the operations carried out by his unit. His drawing of Tommies kicking a football in battle appears like a grotesque superimposition of mortal danger and normality.

Soldaten der *London Irish* – wurde gerade im Zuge der Verluste und des Misserfolgs in der Öffentlichkeit schnell zu einem Sinnbild der Opferbereitschaft für die Nation und als Marker der überlegenen Charakterstärke und Willenskraft des britischen Soldaten (v)erklärt (Abb. 2).[1]

Die von Frank Edwards und anderen etablierte Performance im Spannungsfeld von Wahnsinn und Courage lädt Handlungsmacht heroisch auf. Schlachtfelder werden somit auch zu Suchfeldern des Heroischen. Sie ermöglichen es, sich dem Heroischen als einem kulturellen Phänomen anzunähern, anhand dessen sich Sinn und Sinnlosigkeit des Krieges und damit auch die Funktionen von Heroisierungen mit all ihren eingebauten Ambiguitäten thematisieren lassen.

Sporting Warriors: Die Suchfelder Medialisierung und Männlichkeit

Es sprangen nur wenige Soldaten mit Bällen aus den Gräben und rannten kickend gegen die feindlichen Stellungen an. Millionen taten dies ohne Sportgeräte. Trotzdem sind ›football charges‹ ein zentraler Bestandteil der kollektiven britischen Erinnerung an den Ersten Weltkrieg. Vermittelt über den Sport konnten etablierte Muster heroischer Tugenden und Heldentaten des »einfachen« britischen Soldaten fixiert und in Geschichten erzählt werden, die die Wirklichkeit des industrialisierten Krieges nicht liefern konnte. Der einfache Soldatenheld – so die Botschaft – hat in schwierigsten Situationen nicht immer gesiegt, aber Lebensmut, Optimismus, Zusammenhalt und nicht zuletzt Coolness und Witz bewiesen und verkörperte so wesentliche Elemente der zeitgenössischen Vorstellung vom britischen ›Nationalcharakter‹. Damit bedienten Aktionen wie die ›football charges‹ das Bedürfnis nach Selbstver-

the willingness to sacrifice oneself for the nation and as a marker of the British soldier's superior strength of character and willpower (Fig. 2).[1]

The action performed by Frank Edwards and others was an act that lay somewhere between madness and courage, an instance in which their agency became heroically charged. Battlefields thus become sites for the search of the heroic, too. They make it possible to approach the heroic as a cultural phenomenon. Culture can be used to explore the sense and senselessness of war and the functions of heroizations, with all their intrinsic ambiguities.

Sporting warriors: the search fields of medialisation and masculinity

Only a few soldiers jumped out of the trenches with footballs and charged on the enemy positions while kicking and passing. But throughout the war millions did so without sports equipment. Nevertheless, the 'football charges' are a central element of the collective British memory of World War I. Through sport, established patterns of heroic virtues and the heroic deeds of the 'ordinary' British soldier could be recorded and narrated in stories which had nothing to do with the everyday reality of industrial warfare. The ordinary soldier hero, so the message goes, may not always have been victorious in difficult situations, but demonstrated prowess, courage, optimism, solidarity and, last but not least, a certain coolness and wit,

Abb. 2: Auch die bekannte Schlachtenmalerin Elizabeth Southerden Thompson (1846–1933), bekannt als »Lady Butler«, verewigte die ›football charge‹ von Loos. Das Bild war Teil einer Serie von Aquarellen, in denen Butler Szenen festhielt, für die Soldaten das Victoria Cross verliehen bekommen hatten. Nach der Schlacht von Loos wurde die höchste britische Auszeichnung elfmal verliehen. Frank Edwards und seine Mitspieler waren nicht unter den mit Orden zertifizierten Helden. Dass sich ihr Angriff mit Fußbällen in der Bilderserie befindet, verweist aber auf ansonsten verborgene Formen des Heroischen und macht sie sichtbar.

Fig. 2: *Even the well-known war artist Elizabeth Southerden Thompson, known as "Lady Butler" (1846-1933), immortalised the football charge of Loos. The painting was part of a series of watercolours in which Butler captured scenes that had earned soldiers the Victoria Cross. After the Battle of Loos, Britain's highest honour was awarded eleven times. Frank Edwards and his teammates were not among the heroes awarded the Order. However, the fact that their attack, involving footballs, is included in this series points to otherwise hidden forms of heroism and makes them visible.*

gewisserung einer durch den Krieg tief verunsicherten Gesellschaft, auch lange über die Kriegszeit hinaus.

Sport ist mehr als nur körperliche Betätigung. Er ist eingewoben in vielfältige kulturelle und gesellschaftliche Zusammenhänge. Sportliche Aktivitäten bereiten nicht nur Freude und halten den Körper fit, sondern machen auch Unsichtbares sichtbar. Besonders in Großbritannien, dem ›Mutterland des modernen Sports‹, war diese Funktion allgegenwärtig. Sportlichkeit stand für die Charakterbildung und Eignung des Einzelnen sowie für die Gesamtheit der britischen Nation. Sport und Sportanalogien waren daher ein mächtiges Werkzeug, um Konflikte und Kriege zu beschreiben, zu deuten und medial einzuordnen. Der Sport und der Krieg waren wechselseitig austauschbare Heroisierungsmaschinen. Die Figur des ›sporting warrior‹ hatte sich um 1900 tief in die britische Kultur als Leitbild für soldatisch-kriegerische Männlichkeit eingeschrieben. Doch in der Verherrlichung des ›greater game‹ verzerrt die oft verwendete Gleichung ›Sport = Krieg‹ die Realität des Krieges, blutige Kämpfe, Verstümmelungen und das Sterben bis ins Groteske.[2] In der Wirklichkeit des Krieges haben sportlich gerahmte heroische Tugenden wie *fair play* keinen Platz. »Das Letzte, was sich Soldaten auf dem Schlachtfeld wünschen, ist« – worauf Ulrich Bröckling hinweist – »ein fairer Kampf.«[3]

Trotzdem oder gerade deswegen spielte der Sportkult während des Ersten Weltkriegs eine bedeutende Rolle in den britischen Streitkräften. In den Warteräumen des Krieges waren Sport und Spiele ein willkommener Zeitvertreib. Insbesondere der Fußball war ein wesentlicher Teil der Erlebnis- und Erfahrungswelten des Krieges. Matches wurden von den Soldaten und der Armeeführung von spontanen Kicks bis hin zu organisierten Turnieren genutzt (Abb. 3). Sport diente zur körperlichen Ertüchtigung, zur taktischen Ausbildung für den Kampf, als Spektakel sowie zur Rehabilitation von Kriegsversehrten. In der Kriegspropaganda wurden vermeintlich britische Werte wie Männlichkeit und Tapferkeit, Fairplay, Wagemut und Initiative gegen unsportliche und damit unmännliche Kriegsführung, Gräueltaten und Hinterlistigkeit des Gegners sowie die ›teutonische Obrigkeitshörigkeit‹ süffisant ins Feld geführt. Sport war also nicht nur eine gängige Alltagspraxis. Er stellte den Soldaten einen reichhaltigen Symbolhaushalt für je eigene Sinnzuschreibungen und Rahmungen ihrer Erlebnisse und Handlungen zur Verfügung.[4]

Zwischen Heroismus und Eskapismus: die Suchfelder Kampf und Handlungs(ohn)macht

Die frontalen Angriffsverfahren der ersten Hälfte des Krieges führten zu hohen Verlusten und selten zu Durchbrüchen. Ein schnelles Ende der Kämpfe war nicht in Sicht. Das Wort ›Abnutzung‹ stand für viele Tote und die Aussicht auf einen langen Krieg.

and thus has embodied crucial elements of the contemporary notion of the British 'national character'. Actions like the 'football charges' thus satisfied the need for self-assurance in a society deeply unsettled by war, even long after the war was over.

Sport is more than physical exercise. It is a thread woven into the fabric of various cultural and societal relations. Sporting activities do not only spark joy and keep you fit, but also render the invisible visible. This function was omnipresent especially in Great Britain, the 'mother country of modern sports'. Sportsmanship was linked with character formation and the capability of an individual as well as of the entire British nation. Sport and sport analogies were therefore powerful tools for describing, interpreting and classifying armed conflicts and wars in the media. Sports and war were interchangeable heroization devices. By 1900, the figure of the sporting warrior had become deeply entrenched in British culture as the model of military masculinity. However, in the glorification of the 'greater game' the popular equation of 'sports = war' often grotesquely distorted the reality of war with its bloody fighting, maiming and death.[2] There is a way heroic virtues can be framed in a sports metaphor, e.g. fair play. But in the reality of war: "The last thing soldiers wish for on the battlefield," says Ulrich Bröckling, "is a fair fight."[3]

Nevertheless (or precisely for that reason), the sporting cult played a major role in the British Armed Forces during World War I. Sport and games were welcome diversions during the tedious waiting for battle. Football in particular was an essential element of the world of experience associated with war. Matches were initiated by soldiers and the military leadership alike, be it spontaneous kickabouts or organised tournaments (Fig. 3). Sport served the purposes of physical exertion and tactical combat training, as well as providing entertainment and as a way to rehabilitate war veterans. War propaganda smugly juxtaposed allegedly British values, such as masculinity and bravery, fair play, brav-

Abb. 3: Ein paar mehr oder weniger Beteiligte, einen Ball, ein Feld und Material für ein Tor – viel braucht es nicht, um Fußball spielen zu können. Von spontanen Kicks hinter der Front wie auf diesem Foto bis hin zu länderspielartigen Wettkämpfen: Der Fußball war vor allem in den britischen Streitkräften allgegenwärtig.

Fig. 3: A few more or less talented players, a ball, a pitch and material for a goal – it doesn't take much to play football. From spontaneous dribbling behind the front line, as shown in this photo, to international competitions: Football was ubiquitous, especially in the British Armed Forces.

WITH A FOOTBALL THROUGH NO MAN'S LAND

Es verwundert daher nicht, dass die Soldaten die Angriffe nicht nur als gefährlich, sondern auch als sinnlos empfanden. Fremdbestimmung, Todesängste und Nervosität dominierten die Zeit vor der Schlacht und konnten in eigensinnige Formen von Handlungsmacht überführt werden. Patrick MacGill liefert in seiner Bewertung der ›football charge‹ seines Regiments einen Hinweis auf eine Bewältigungsstrategie:

> The instinct of self-preservation is the strongest in created beings, and here we see hundreds of men whose premier consideration was their own personal safety moving forward to attack with the nonchalance of a church parade. Perhaps the men who kicked the football across were the most nervous in the affair. Football is an exciting pastime, it helped to take the mind away from the crisis ahead, and the dread anticipation of death was forgotten for the time being. But I do not think for a second that the ball was brought for that purpose.[5]

Hier tritt nicht der ›sporting warrior‹ auf die Bühne und inszeniert die Identität von ›sporting spirit‹ und ›fighting spirit‹. Vielmehr kommt bei MacGill für einen Augenblick das Unsagbare zum Vorschein, um dann sofort wieder zu verschwinden: die Hilflosigkeit und Ohnmacht der Soldaten gegenüber der Realität des industriellen Massenkrieges. Das Kicken eines Fußballs ermöglichte es den Soldaten, die Realität des Schlachtfelds mit der Imagination des Spielfelds zu tauschen. Der Handlungsmacht vortäuschende Akt konnte helfen, Nervosität und Ängste zu bekämpfen, Widerstände zu überwinden und von den Schrecken des Krieges und der unmittelbaren Gefahr des eigenen Todes abzulenken, um gerade so todesmutig den Angriff zu führen und – beabsichtigt oder nicht – das symbolische Material für Heroisierungsprozesse zu liefern (Abb. 4).

Zeitgenössische Quellen belegen, dass Soldaten in vielen Situationen versuchten, die in ihrer Fremdheit monströsen Kriegslandschaften mit einer ihnen bekannten und weit verbreiteten Logik des Spielfelds zu verstehen.[6] Als Realitätswandler konnte sportliche Aktivität für einen Moment die Wirklichkeit, den Schrecken des Krieges, mit einem Ausschnitt des Friedens vertauschen und eine Auszeit vom Krieg ermöglichen. Diese Form der Wirklichkeitsvertauschung galt vor allem für die Zeit nach und zwischen den Gefechten, aber auch im Kampf selbst.[7] Der Augenzeugenbericht eines Teilnehmers der Schlacht, abgedruckt im *Weekly Dispatch*, verdeutlicht diese Inversion, wenn er das Spiel von Frank Edwards und seinen Kameraden beschreibt, »als ob« sie auf ihrem heimatlichen Sportplatz in London spielen würden.

Die ›football charges‹ waren somit eine extreme Form der Realitätsflucht – eine Auszeit vom Kämpfen mitten im Kampf. Vor dem Hintergrund einer mehr oder weniger ausgeprägten Tötungshemmung des Menschen konnte das Kicken der Bälle nicht nur von der drohenden eigenen Todesgefahr, sondern auch von der Tötung der gegnerischen Soldaten ablenken. Der Fußball diente der Distanzierung, als in-

ery and initiative, with the enemy's unsportsmanlike and therefore unmanly warfare, atrocities, deceitfulness and their 'Teutonic obedience to authority'. Sport was therefore much more than a common everyday practice. It also provided soldiers with an ample kit of symbols to make sense of – and frame – their own experiences and actions.[4]

Between heroism and escapism: the search fields of fighting, agency and impotence

The frontal attacks of the first half of the war often resulted in high losses and rarely in any meaningful advances. A rapid end to the fighting was not in sight. The term 'attrition' signified high numbers of casualties and the prospect of a long war. It is therefore not surprising that for the soldiers, the attacks seemed not only dangerous but also pointless. Fear of death and nervousness dominated the time before the battle and could be translated into wilful forms of agency. In his assessment of the 'football charges' of his regiment, Patrick MacGill hints at one of their coping strategies:

> The instinct of self-preservation is the strongest in created beings, and here we see hundreds of men whose premier consideration was their own personal safety moving forward to attack with the nonchalance of a church parade. Perhaps the men who kicked the football across were the most nervous in the affair. Football is an exciting pastime, it helped to take the mind away from the crisis ahead, and the dread anticipation of death was for-

Abb. 4: Der Maler Richard Caton Woodville Jr. (1856–1927) hielt eine weitere ›football charge‹ in einem Bild fest. Hier stürmen die *East Surreys* mit Fußbällen gegen die deutschen Stellungen an der Somme 1916 an. Das vielfach in britischen Zeitungen abgedruckte Bild stand, wie bei diesem Beispiel in Kombination mit der in typischer Manier verfassten Heldenballade, für erste sinngebende Umformungen der historischen Ereignisse in Heldengeschichten.

Fig. 4: The painter Richard Caton Woodville Jr. (1856–1927) captured another football charge. His painting shows the East Surreys charging the German defences on the Somme in 1916 with footballs. The painting was frequently printed in British newspapers and, as in this example in combination a heroic ballad written in a typical manner, stood for the first meaningful transformation of historical events into heroic stories.

dividueller Abwehrmechanismus, als Imprägnierung gegenüber der Brutalität und Grausamkeit des Krieges. In einer militärischen Organisation, die auf Befehl und Gehorsam ausgerichtet war, bot das Spiel mit dem Ball in einer Situation mit hohem Todes- und Verletzungsrisiko einen Rest individueller Agency: Selbstbestimmung, Widerständigkeit, Autonomie und Zivilität.[8] Eskapismus und mobilisierender Heroismus schlossen sich hier nicht aus, sondern formten in ihren Wechselwirkungen eine eigene komplexe Form der Heroisierung des in die Situation geworfenen Soldaten und zivilen Bürgers. Als Kriegsfreiwilliger oder Wehrpflichtiger ist der Soldatenheld des Massenkrieges nicht nur der, der nur erduldet, sondern der, der Ohnmacht in Handlungsmacht verwandelt und auch während des Horrors des Krieges in seiner Identität als ziviler Mensch intakt bleibt, um sich gleichzeitig auf spielerische Art als Soldat dem Krieg und dem Tod zu stellen. Statt den Sport dazu zu nutzen, durch seine Gleichsetzung mit dem Krieg den Krieg zu verharmlosen, nutzten die Soldaten den Sport dazu, den Krieg wenigstens zeitweise zu verdrängen. Die Geste trägt somit Elemente der Verweigerung gegenüber dem Krieg in sich und verdeutlicht so die in der Oszillation zwischen Todesmut und Eskapismus erkennbar werdende Doppelbödigkeit von Heroisierungen.

Gedächtnispolitik »von unten«: Die Suchfelder Grenzüberschreitung, Einsatz und Vorbild

Menschen wie Frank Edwards wollten nicht unbedingt Helden sein (Abb. 5). Sie wollten aber auch nicht einfach sterben. Obwohl kein explizites Quellenmaterial dazu existiert, liegt es nahe, die ›football charges‹ in Anschluss an Ian Adams als eine Form der Gedächtnispolitik ›von unten‹ zu betrachten. Angesichts des Einsatzes des Lebens als ultimative Grenzüberschreitung spielte die Frage nach dem Sinn des eigenen Sterbens eine besondere Rolle. Die Inszenierung des Angriffs durch die kickenden Soldaten kann als selbstheroisierende Form des Schreibens ihrer eigenen Geschichte interpretiert werden – als Versuch der Sinngebung für Tod und Verwundung. Indem sie ihre eigene (Über-)Lebens- und Todeserfahrung in einem mythopoetischen Akt gestalteten, versuchten die Soldaten, mit Unsinn, Sinn in der Sinnlosigkeit zu stiften und in Erinnerung zu bleiben.

Mit seinem Schlachtruf »Play up, London Irish!« knüpfte Edwards – oder so taten es zumindest die Erzähler der Geschichte – an die Zeile »Play up! Play up! and play the game!« aus Henry Newboldts Gedicht *vitaï lampada* (1892) an. Als ein prägendes Sinnmuster von Sport, Krieg und selbstlosem heroischem Soldatentod stellte die im letzten Drittel des 19. Jahrhunderts geschaffene Verknüpfung eine jederzeit nutzbare mobilisierende Heroisierungsstrategie bereit, um den unsichtbaren Zwang zur Freiwilligkeit des Kriegsdienstes und zur Opferbereitschaft auszuüben.[9] Ein wei-

gotten for the time being. But I do not think for a second that the ball was brought for that purpose.[5]

Here, it is not the 'sporting warrior' who enters the stage and showcases 'sporting spirit' and 'fighting spirit'. Rather, the unspeakable briefly appears in MacGill's account, only to disappear again immediately: the helplessness and powerlessness of the soldiers in the face of the reality of industrial mass warfare. Kicking a football enabled soldiers to exchange the reality of the battlefield with an imagined playing field. This act, which created a feeling of self-empowerment and agency, could be helpful in fighting nervousness and fears, overcoming resistance and as a distraction from the horrors of war and the danger of death. Playing football enabled soldiers to continue to fight, less daunted by death, and provided them – by intention or not – with the symbolic material for heroization processes (Fig. 4).

Contemporary sources confirm that soldiers in many situations tried to understand the war landscapes, monstrous as they appeared in their unfamiliarity, through the popular and widespread logic of the playing field.[6] As a substitute for reality, sport permitted soldiers to temporarily swap reality and the atrocities of war for a slice of peace, thus enabling them to take a break from the conflict. This form of reality substitution occurred primarily after and in-between battles, but occasionally also during combat action itself.[7] An eyewitness testimony given by a participant in the Loos battle, printed in *Weekly Dispatch*, illustrates this inversion when it describes Edwards and his comrades playing "as if" they were on their home playing field in London.

The 'football charges' were thus an extreme form of escape from reality – a break from fighting while fighting. Given most humans' inhibition to kill, kicking the football also served to distract the soldiers not only from the danger of being killed but also from the thought of killing enemy soldiers. Football was a means of distancing oneself, an individual defence mechanism, and a sort of "waterproofing" against the brutality and cruelty of war. Within a military organisation that revolved around orders and obedience, playing football in a situation involving a high risk of death and injury offered a vestige of individual agency: selfdetermination, resistance, autonomy and civilian identity.[8] In this case, escapism and mobilising heroism were not mutually exclusive; rather, their interaction led to an independent, complex form of heroization of the soldier and civilian citizen who had been thrown into this situation. As a war volunteer or conscript, the soldier hero of mass warfare not only endured war but transformed powerlessness into agency. Their identity as a civilian human being remained intact during the horrors of war, bravely facing war and death in a playful way. Instead of using sport to make light of war by equating the one with the other, the soldiers used sport as a means with which to push war to the back of their minds, at least temporarily. This gesture contains elements of

Abb. 5: Die Namen von Pubs und Inns haben in Großbritannien oft einen historisch-lokalen Bezug. Seit 2012 ziert ein Bild von Frank Edwards das Pub-Schild des »Rifleman« in Twickenham, unweit von Edwards' Wohnort. Das Schild wurde im Beisein einer Delegation der *London Irish Rifles* – und des vermeintlichen Balls von Loos – von der Bürgermeisterin des Ortes enthüllt. Im Hintergrund der Darstellung sind Elemente aus dem Aquarell von »Lady Butler« zu sehen. Auf diese Weise wird nicht nur ein bekanntes Heldennarrativ fortgeschrieben, sondern auch die selbstermächtigende Geste des einfachen britischen Soldaten in den heutigen Alltag getragen.

Fig. 5: The names of pubs and inns in the UK often have a historical and local connection. Since 2012, a picture of Frank Edwards has adorned The Rifleman's pub sign in Twickenham, not far from where Edwards lived. The sign was unveiled by the town's mayor in the presence of a delegation from the London Irish Rifles – and the alleged Loos football. Elements from "Lady Butler's" watercolour can be seen in the background. This not only perpetuates a well-known heroic narrative, but also brings the self-empowering gesture of the ordinary British soldier into everyday life today.

terer Bezugspunkt ist ein zentraler Erinnerungsort der britischen Geschichte: die *Charge of the Light Brigade* (Abb. 6). Bei dieser Attacke ritten im Krimkrieg 1855 britische Kavalleristen aufgrund unzureichender Informationen und unklarer Befehle – kurz: Führungsversagen – einen äußerst verlustreichen und gleichzeitig erfolglosen Angriff. Einer der größten Fehlschläge der britischen Militärgeschichte wird über die Zeiten hinweg medial als Symbol für den Mut, Einsatz des Lebens und den Heroismus der Tat des britischen Soldat:innentums verklärt und ist tief in die Erinnerungskultur eingeschrieben. In einem berühmten Gedicht zur Schlacht von Lord Tennyson wird der Zusammenhang zwischen Angriff, heroischer Grenzüberschreitung und Erinnerung und generationsübergreifender Vorbildfunktion deutlich: »When can their glory fade? / O the wild charge they made!«

Die *Irish Rifles* knüpften mit ihrem wilden Angriff an zentrale Bezugspunkte der britischen Populärkultur und Militärgeschichte an. Das bereits seit der Antike etablierte und regelmäßig reaktivierte Motiv der ›lions led by donkeys‹, das den vorbildlichen Heldenmut, den Einsatz und die Opferbereitschaft der einfachen Soldaten und Offiziere dem mangelhaften Können und dem Versagen der höheren militärischen Führung gegenüberstellte, ließ sich problemlos auf die bevorstehende Situation des festgefahrenen Grabenkriegs übertragen. Allerdings hatten die Infanteristen von 1915 keine Pferde für einen Todesritt.[10] Auch hatten sie keine Flugzeuge,

a refusal to engage in war, and thereby highlights the double standard inherent in heroizations that becomes obvious in the oscillation between courage in the face of death and escapism.

Memory politics "from below": the search fields of boundary crossing, commitment and role models

People like Frank Edwards did not necessarily strive to become heroes but they did not want to die either (Fig. 5). Although no explicit source material on the subject exists, it seems reasonable to regard the 'football charges' as a form of memory politics 'from below', as argued by Ian Adams. Given that putting one's life at stake is the ultimate crossing of boundaries, the question of the meaning of one's own death is particularly relevant. The soldiers' football attack can be interpreted as a selfheroizing way of narrating their own story – as an attempt to make their death and injury meaningful. The soldiers used their playfulness to transform their experience of life and death into a mythopoetical act, so that their experience on the front would have meaning and be remembered.

With his battle cry of "Play up, London Irish!", Edwards – or at least the narrators of the story – took up the line "Play up! Play up! And play the game!", taken from Henry Newboldt's poem *Vitaï Lampada* (1892). The meaningful link between sport, war, and the selfless he-

Abb. 6: Geschichten, Gedichte und Bilder liefern einen gesellschaftlich und kulturell geprägten Kanon des Heroischen: das Rohmaterial, um auch sinnlosen und überwältigenden Situationen Sinn zu geben. Eine medial in der britischen Militärgeschichte tief verankerte heroische Erzählung ist die von der »Charge of the Light Brigade«. Die Nähe des militärischen Fiaskos auf der Krim von 1854 zu dem an der Somme von 1916 wird hier nicht nur durch den Maler – ebenfalls Richard Caton Woodville Jr., – sondern auch durch die Analogie des einfachen, heldenhaften britischen Soldaten angesichts einer verlustreichen Schlacht hergestellt.

Fig. 6: Stories, poems and images provide a socially and culturally shaped canon of the heroic, the raw material for giving meaning to senseless and overwhelming situations. One heroic narrative that is deeply rooted in British military history is that of the "Charge of the Light Brigade". The proximity of the military fiasco in the Crimea in 1854 to that of the Somme in 1916 is not only established by the painter – Richard Caton Woodville Jr., as well – but also by the analogy of the simple, heroic British soldier in the face of a battle full of losses.

um sich in ein ebenfalls von Sportanleihen durchzogenes Heldenepos des ritterlichen Luftkampfes einzuschreiben. Immerhin hatten sie Fußbälle, die zumindest für ein todesmutiges Spiel und die Aktualisierung und Aneignung etablierter Heldenerzählungen durch die Soldaten selbst taugten und sich hervorragend in die Muster der Berichterstattung einbinden ließen und Verbreitung fanden. Erfolge machen Heroisierungen leicht. Niederlagen gestalten sich schwierig. Das grenzüberschreitend Unerwartete wie das Kicken eines Fußballs hilft, als symbolische Kompensation heroische Geschichten erzählen zu können. Allein das ›Wie‹ der Tat ist dazu geeignet, das ›Was‹ – den Misserfolg – zu überblenden

Der Sinn der Sinnlosigkeit: Die Suchfelder Polarisierung und Publikum

Die Presseberichte der Schlacht von Loos griffen die ›football charge‹ auf und etablierten sie als Motiv und Vorbild. Das Konzept der ›football charge‹ fand dann einige Monate später während der Somme-Schlacht 1916 nach einer ähnlichen In-

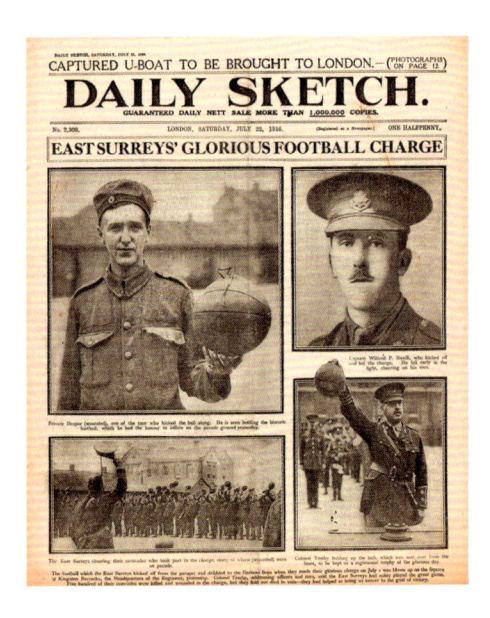

Abb. 7: Die »glorious football charge« der *East Surreys* an der Somme 1916 wurde breit rezipiert, wie hier im auflagenstarken *Daily Sketch*. Dass Captain William Neville während der Schlacht gefallen war, trug wohl zur Heroisierung bei. Ähnlich wie nach der »Charge of the Light Brigade« ließen sich durch heroische Erzählungen von kickenden Soldaten die hohen Verluste und das Scheitern der Offensive relativieren. Die angebliche Überlegenheit des britischen Charakters konnte so das kollektive Scheitern und die militärischen Fehlentscheidungen überlagern. Der Ball erscheint gleichsam als Reliquie und wird selbst zum Objekt der Heroisierung.

Fig. 7: The East Surrey's "glorious football charge" on the Somme in 1916 was widely publicised, as seen here in the well-circulated "Daily Sketch". The fact that Captain William Neville was killed during the battle probably contributed to the heroization. Similar to the aftermath of the Charge of the Light Brigade, heroic tales of soldiers playing football were used to relativise the heavy losses and failures on the offensive. The alleged superiority of the British character was thus able to overshadow collective failures and poor military decisions. The football appears as a relic, so to speak, and becomes an object of heroization itself.

roic death of a soldier – a link that emerged in the last third of the 19th century – provided a heroization strategy that could be used anytime to mobilise voluntary military service and encourage self-sacrifice.[9] Another point of reference is an event which has a central place in British history and memory: the *Charge of the Light Brigade* (Fig. 6). This attack occurred during the Crimean War in 1855, when insufficient information and unclear orders, i.e. failed leadership, caused British cavalrymen to launch an extremely high-casualty yet unsuccessful attack. Over time, one of the greatest blunders in British military history has been glorified in the media as a symbol of courage, of risking one's own life and of the heroism of British soldiers. It is now deeply entrenched in the country's culture of remembrance. The connection between attack, heroic boundary crossing, remembrance and a cross-generational role model function is conveyed in a famous poem about the battle by Lord Tennyson: "When can their glory fade? / O the wild charge they made!"

With their wild attack, the *Irish Rifles* drew on central points of reference in British popular culture and military history. The motif of the 'lions led by donkeys', which has existed since antiquity, has been reactivated frequently throughout history and juxtaposes the ordinary soldiers' and officers' exemplary bravery, commitment and willingness to make sacrifices with the higher military leadership's incompetence and failure. It is a motif which could easily be transferred to the situation of static trench warfare. The infantrymen of 1915 may not have had horses[10] or even aircraft with which to partake in a heroic attack, but they did have footballs – footballs they could use in a fearless game and to update and appropriate established heroic narratives, which made attractive stories for the media coverage of the war and were spread widely. Successes readily lend themselves to heroization. With defeats, it is more difficult. The unexpected crossing of boundaries, such as the kicking of a football on a battlefield, is a symbolic act of compensation that helps narrating heroic tales. The mere 'how' of the deed can outshine the 'what', i.e. the failure.

Sense in senselessness:
the search fields of polarisation and audience

Press reports about the battle of Loos picked up the 'football charge' and established it as motif and model. A few months later, the concept of the 'football charge' received broad media coverage again after a similar charge by Captain Neville and a company of the *East Surreys* occurred during the Battle of the Somme in 1916 (Fig. 7). Whereas the battle at Loos had been a failure, the battle of the Somme turned into an outright catastrophe. The first day alone claimed the lives of 19,240 British soldiers. Despite the enormous losses and the fact they had been defeated, the story of the 'football charge' of the *East Surreys* once again meant that the me-

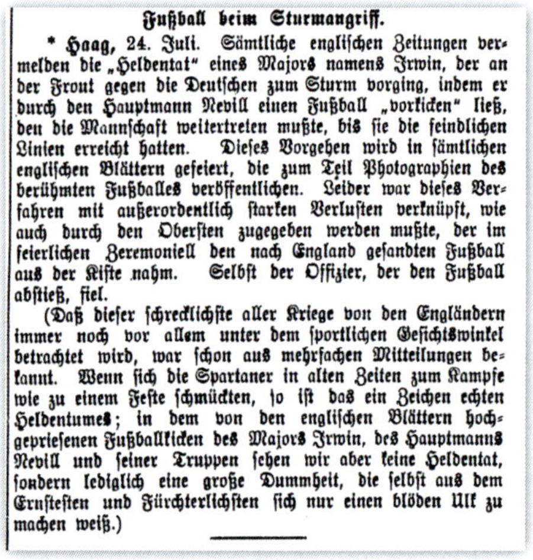

Fußball beim Sturmangriff.

* **Haag, 24. Juli.** Sämtliche englischen Zeitungen vermelden die „Heldentat" eines Majors namens Irwin, der an der Front gegen die Deutschen zum Sturm vorging, indem er durch den Hauptmann Nevill einen Fußball „vorkicken" ließ, den die Mannschaft weitertreten mußte, bis sie die feindlichen Linien erreicht hatten. Dieses Vorgehen wird in sämtlichen englischen Blättern gefeiert, die zum Teil Photographien des berühmten Fußballes veröffentlichen. Leider war dieses Verfahren mit außerordentlich starken Verlusten verknüpft, wie auch durch den Obersten zugegeben werden mußte, der im feierlichen Zeremoniell den nach England gesandten Fußball aus der Kiste nahm. Selbst der Offizier, der den Fußball abstieß, fiel.

(Daß dieser schrecklichste aller Kriege von den Engländern immer noch vor allem unter dem sportlichen Gesichtswinkel betrachtet wird, war schon aus mehrfachen Mitteilungen bekannt. Wenn sich die Spartaner in alten Zeiten zum Kampfe wie zu einem Feste schmückten, so ist das ein Zeichen echten Heldentumes; in dem von den englischen Blättern hochgepriesenen Fußballkicken des Majors Irwin, des Hauptmanns Nevill und seiner Truppen sehen wir aber keine Heldentat, sondern lediglich eine große Dummheit, die selbst aus dem Ernstesten und Fürchterlichsten sich nur einen blöden Ulk zu machen weiß.)

Abb. 8: Eine völlig andere Einordnung des Sturmangriffs mit Fußbällen zeigte sich in der deutschen Presse. Der Kommentator des *Wochenblatts für Zschopau und Umgegend* konnte in seiner Auswertung der britischen Berichte die dort behauptete Heldenhaftigkeit nicht nachvollziehen. Er betrachtete die »football charge« als »blöden Ulk«. Die britischen Soldaten – unter ihnen sogar ein Offizier – seien dem fürchterlichen Krieg mit zur Schau gestellter Sportlichkeit und großer Dummheit begegnet. Die in der britischen Öffentlichkeit hergestellte heroisierende Verbindung von Sport und Krieg war inkompatibel mit dem Repertoire der Heldennarrative der deutschen Seite.

Fig. 8: The German press had a completely different view of attacking with footballs. In his evaluation of the British reports, the commentator of the "Wochenblatt für Zschopau und Umgegend" (weekly newspaper for Zschopau and the area) could not comprehend the heroism claimed there. He regarded the football charge as a "stupid joke". The British soldiers – and an officer among them! – were going about this terrible war with flaunted sportsmanship and utter stupidity. The heroizing connection between sport and war created in British public opinion was incompatible with the repertoire of heroic narratives on the German side.

szenierung durch Captain Neville und eine Kompanie der *East Surreys* ein breites mediales Echo (Abb. 7). Während die Schlacht von Loos ein Fehlschlag war, entwickelte sich die Schlacht an der Somme zu einem Fiasko. Allein der erste Tag kostete 19.240 britische Soldaten das Leben. Trotz der ungeheuerlichen Verluste und dem ausbleibenden Sieg bot die Geschichte der ›football charge‹ der *East Surreys* erneut die Möglichkeit, vom Triumph des britischen Charakters, vom Kampfgeist und der Courage des englischen Soldaten und schließlich von der Leistungsfähigkeit der neuen Freiwilligenverbände zu berichten. Sie sollte den Soldaten an den Fronten und den Beobachter:innen in der Heimat Mut machen und Zuversicht verbreiten. Dass William »Billie« Neville in den ersten Minuten des Angriffs starb, unterstrich nochmals Opfermut und Opferbereitschaft. Die Betonung, dass die fußballspielenden Truppenteile in Loos und an der Somme – als einige der wenigen Einheiten überhaupt – die gesetzten Angriffsziele erreichten, unterstrich die Bedeutung von Sportsgeist, Angriffswillen und moralischer Überlegenheit des britischen Soldaten gegenüber seinen deutschen Gegnern.[11] Die Heroisierung der ›football charges‹ in der der Öffentlichkeit diente als Versuch, Sinnlosigkeit mit Sinn zu überschreiben. Die deutsche Presse, die auf die britische Berichterstattung reagierte, vermochte

dia could focus on the triumph of British character, on the British soldier's fighting spirit and courage, and, ultimately, on the achievement of the new all-volunteer corps of Kitchener's Army. It was intended to encourage and give hope to the soldiers at the front lines and the observers at home. The fact that William "Billie" Neville fell within the first minutes of the attack yet again underlined the victims' courage and willingness to make a sacrifice. The media emphasised the fact that it had been the football-kicking troops in Loos and at the Somme that actually achieved the objectives of their attack – as one of the few units to do so – as evidence for the relevance of their sporting spirit, their will to attack and the moral superiority of the British soldiers over their German opponents.[11] The public heroization of the 'football charges' was an attempt to infuse meaningless deaths with meaning. For the German press, however, the British newspapers' sporting analogies were merely proof of the eccentricity of the British opponent. What military officials thought about these heroized gestures remains unclear. However, following the break from the war at Christmas 1914, which saw the famous football games between the opponents in no man's land, it was forbidden to bring footballs into the frontlines (Fig. 8).[12]

In times when societies were trying to cope with the traumatic experiences of war, the 'football charges' offered a positive story. They were stories of small victories in times when great successes failed to materialise. These offbeat actions generated optimism and self-assurance and have persisted, as heroization, through the generations from wartime until the present. The image of the *Tommy* kicking a football about in a hail of bullets represented a kind of steadfastness and maintenance of the existing order in times of war. Recourse to the interpretation resources inscribed in the 'football charges' helped society to heal its wounds and restore a sense of national (especially male) identity. The 'football charges' thus enabled a conservative, retrospective way of dealing with the World War experience.

For a long time, Frank Edwards remained a nameless soldier – a sort of Everyman – in the heroization processes (Fig. 9). After all, it is not the individual but the idea and the deed that provide the source material for the heroization and a figure to identify with during industrial mass warfare. The game and the auratically charged ball embodied the heroic act of the ordinary soldier. Accordingly, footballs figured prominently in the regiments and in the opulent reenactments of World War I battles during the 1920s, thereby continuing the same heroization narratives. This continues to this day. An image of the (restored) ball that was allegedly kicked through no man's land by the London Irish decorated a Royal Mail stamp in 2015 that was part of a series to commemorate World War I (Fig. 10).

The prospect of becoming a hero was a central element in the mobilisation of society. The fact that the Allies won the war produced classic victor heroes. A look at the 'football charges' reveals not only the glorification of victory but also some

in den Sportanalogien allerdings nur den Beweis für die Verschrobenheit des britischen Gegners zu erkennen (Abb. 8). Wie die Militärbürokratie diese heroisierten Gesten bewertete, bleibt offen. Zumindest war nach den Auszeiten des Krieges an Weihnachten 1914 mit den Fußballspielen zwischen den Fronten die Mitnahme von Bällen in die vordersten Linien untersagt.[12]

In Zeiten, in denen Gesellschaften versuchten, mit den traumatischen Erfahrungen des Krieges umzugehen, lieferten die ›football charges‹ eine positive Geschichte. Sie waren Erzählungen von kleinen Siegen im Rahmen ausbleibender großer Erfolge. Die wahnwitzigen Aktionen generierten trotz allem Zuversicht und Selbstvergewisserung und setzten sich von der Kriegszeit bis heute als Heroisierung durch die Generationen fort. Das Bild des im Kugelhagel fußballspielenden *Tommy* stand für Unerschütterlichkeit und die Erhaltung bestehender Ordnungen inmitten des Krieges. Der Rekurs auf die in den ›football charges‹ eingelagerten Deutungsressourcen eignete sich zur Heilung der Wunden der Gesellschaft und zur Wiederherstellung nationaler (insbesondere männlicher) Identität – und damit für einen konservativen rückblickenden Umgang mit der Erfahrung des Weltkrieges.

Frank Edwards tauchte lange Zeit in den Heroisierungsprozessen als unbekannter Soldat – als eine Art Jedermann – auf (Abb. 9). Denn gerade nicht die Person, sondern die Idee und die Tat lieferten das Rohmaterial für die Heroisierung und Identifikationsmöglichkeiten im industrialisierten Massenkrieg. Das Spiel und hier der auratisch aufgeladene Ball verkörperten den heldischen Akt der einfachen Soldaten. In den Regimentern und opulenten Reenactments der Schlachten des Ersten Weltkriegs während der 1920er Jahren spielten dann auch die Fußbälle eine große Rolle und setzten die Heroisierungserzählungen fort. Das gilt bis heute. Der vermeintliche (restaurierte) Ball, den die *London Irish* durch das Niemandsland kickten, zierte 2015 eine Briefmarke der Royal Mail in einer Serie zum Gedenken an den Ersten Weltkrieg (Abb. 10).

Die Aussicht, ein Held zu werden, war wesentlicher Teil der Mobilisierung der Gesellschaft. Die Tatsache, dass die Alliierten den Krieg gewonnen haben, hat klassische Siegerhelden hervorgebracht. Blickt man auf die ›football charges‹, werden neben der Glorifizierung des Sieges zudem Paradoxien von Heroismus und Heroisierungen deutlich. Ob Eskapismus, Handlungsmacht oder die Deutung im Rahmen bestehender Heldenerzählungen, die ›football charges‹ zeigen, dass der Platz des Heroischen auch dort ist, wo die Sinnlosigkeit regiert. Wenn nahezu alle Möglichkeiten der Deutung erschöpft sind, um Handlungen und Ereignissen Sinn zu verleihen, wenn die Sinnhaftmachung an ihre Grenzen stößt, dann schlägt die Stunde des Heroischen. Das Sinnlose ist die Heimat vieler Held:innen – bis heute.

Abb. 9: Der »Footballer of Loos« wurde zum Sinnbild von Mut, Charakterstärke und heroischer Todesverachtung verklärt. Diese Silberstatue überreichten Offiziere der *Royal Irish Rifles* 1929 ihren Nachfolgern – einem Bataillon der *Royal Ulster Rifles*. Über die Heroisierung wird so eine Traditionslinie hergestellt, die von der Vergangenheit über die Gegenwart in die Zukunft verweist.

Fig. 9: The "Footballer of Loos" became a symbol of courage, strength of character and heroic contempt for death. In 1929, officers of the Royal Irish Rifles presented this silver statue to their successors – a battalion of the Royal Ulster Rifles. Heroization thus establishes a line of tradition that points from the past to the present and into the future.

London Irish Rifles' football from Loos

Abb. 10: Zum hundertsten Jahrestag gab die britische Royal Mail eine Briefmarkenserie zum Thema »The Great War 1915« heraus. Eines von sechs Motiven bildet der Ball aus der Schlacht von Loos. Als erinnerungskulturelle Ikone steht er – mehr als Porträts der Beteiligten es vermocht hätten – für das, was Brit:innen mit der Schlacht von Loos verbinden. Der Ball wird selbst zum Helden.

Fig. 10: To mark the centenary, the British Royal Mail issued a series of stamps commemorating "The Great War 1915". One of its six designs is the football from the Battle of Loos. As an icon of the culture of remembrance, it symbolises – more than portraits of the participants could ever do – what Britons associate with the Battle of Loos. The football itself becomes a hero.

paradoxes in the heroism and heroizations. Be it escapism, agency or the interpretation in the context of existing heroic narratives – the 'football charges' illustrate that the heroic also has its place in situations where meaninglessness reigns. When nearly all interpretative possibilities of making sense of the actions and events are exhausted, when the process of making sense of something has reached its limits – then the hour of the heroic has come. The senseless has been home to many heroes – and continues to be.

Anmerkungen

1 Zu den *football-charges* hat v. a. Ian Adams geforscht. Siehe exemplarisch und thesenreich Adams 2012. Ausgezeichnete Recherche und Material bietet auch Harris 2009. Hier auch die Angaben zu den Medienberichten über die Schlacht und der Rekonstruktion des Ereignisses.
2 Hierzu Donaldson 2021.
3 So Bröckling 2015, S. 102, mit Verweis auf Bowden 2013. Für eine erweiterte Fassung des Bröckling-Textes siehe Bröckling 2016.
4 Siehe Mason und Riedi 2010.
5 MacGill 1916, S. 253.
6 Vgl. Luedtke 2012, S. 107–113.
7 Vgl. Mason 2011, S. 46; Mason und Riedi 2010, S. 92.
8 Vgl. Adams 2015, S. 220.
9 Die Wehrpflicht wurde in Großbritannien erst 1916 eingeführt. Davor stellten Freiwillige einen Großteil der *British Expeditionary Force*.
10 Vgl. Adams 2012, S. 824.
11 Vgl. Donaldson 2021, S. 76–78.
12 Vgl. Adams 2012, S. 824.

Notes

1 Research into the 'football charges' has been done most notably by Ian Adams. For examples and many theses, see Adams 2012. Excellent investigation and material is also provided in Harris 2009. Also look here for information on the media reports about the battle and the reconstruction of the event.
2 Cf. Donaldson 2021.
3 According to Bröckling 2015, p. 102, with reference to Bowden 2013. For an extended version of the Bröckling text, see Bröckling 2016.
4 Cf. Mason and Riedi 2010.
5 MacGill 1916, p. 253.
6 Cf. Luedtke 2012, p. 107–113.
7 Cf. Mason 2011, p. 46; Mason and Riedi 2010, p. 92.
8 Cf. Adams 2015, p. 220.
9 Compulsory military service was introduced in Great Britain as late as 1916. Before that, volunteers accounted for the majority of the British Expeditionary Force.
10 Cf. Adams 2012, p. 824.
11 Cf. Donaldson 2021, p. 76–78.
12 Cf. Adams 2012, p. 824.

© 2024 Frank Reichherzer, Publikation: Wallstein Verlag; DOI https://doi.org/10.46500/83535581-012 | CC BY-NC-ND 4.0

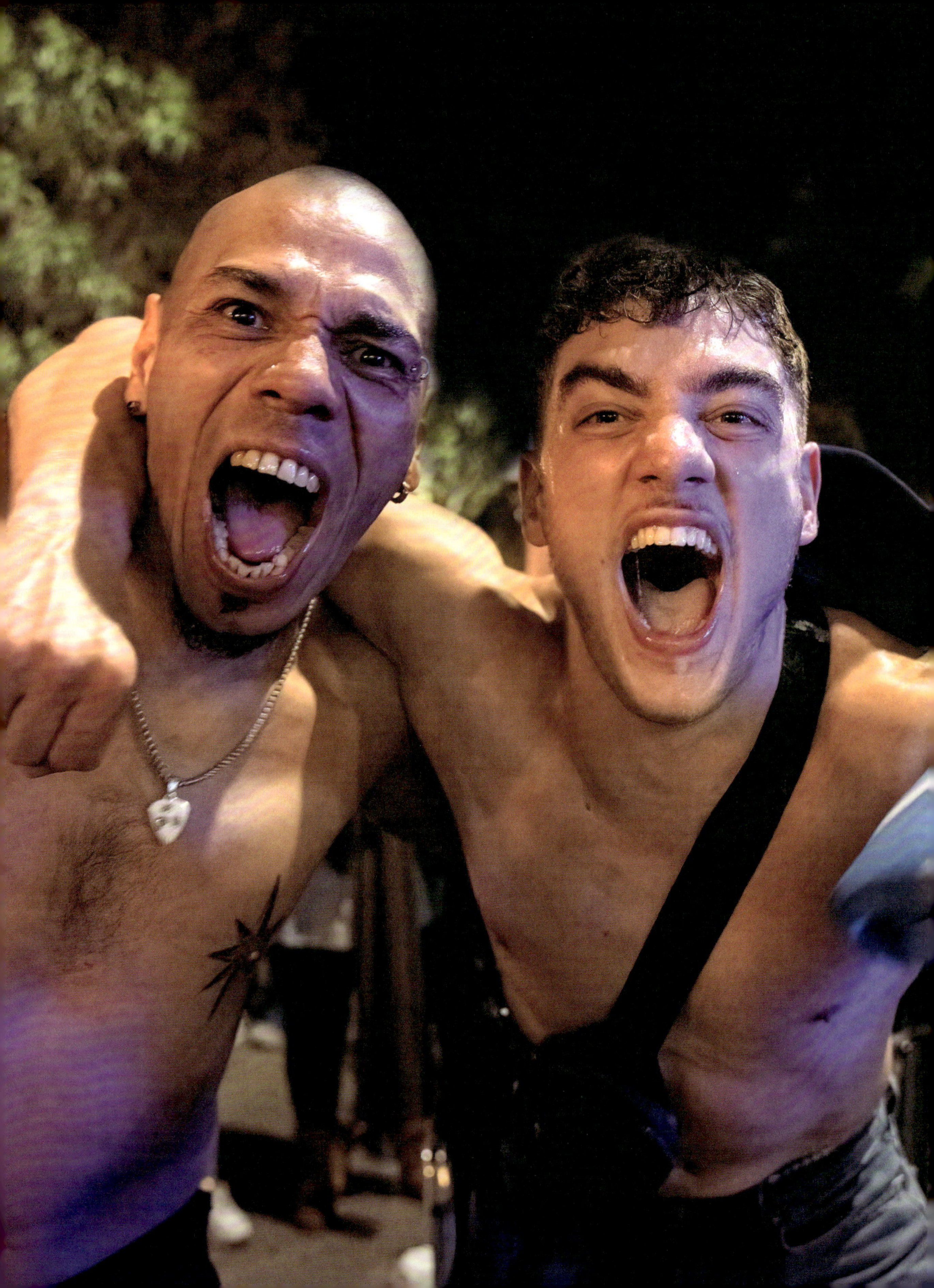

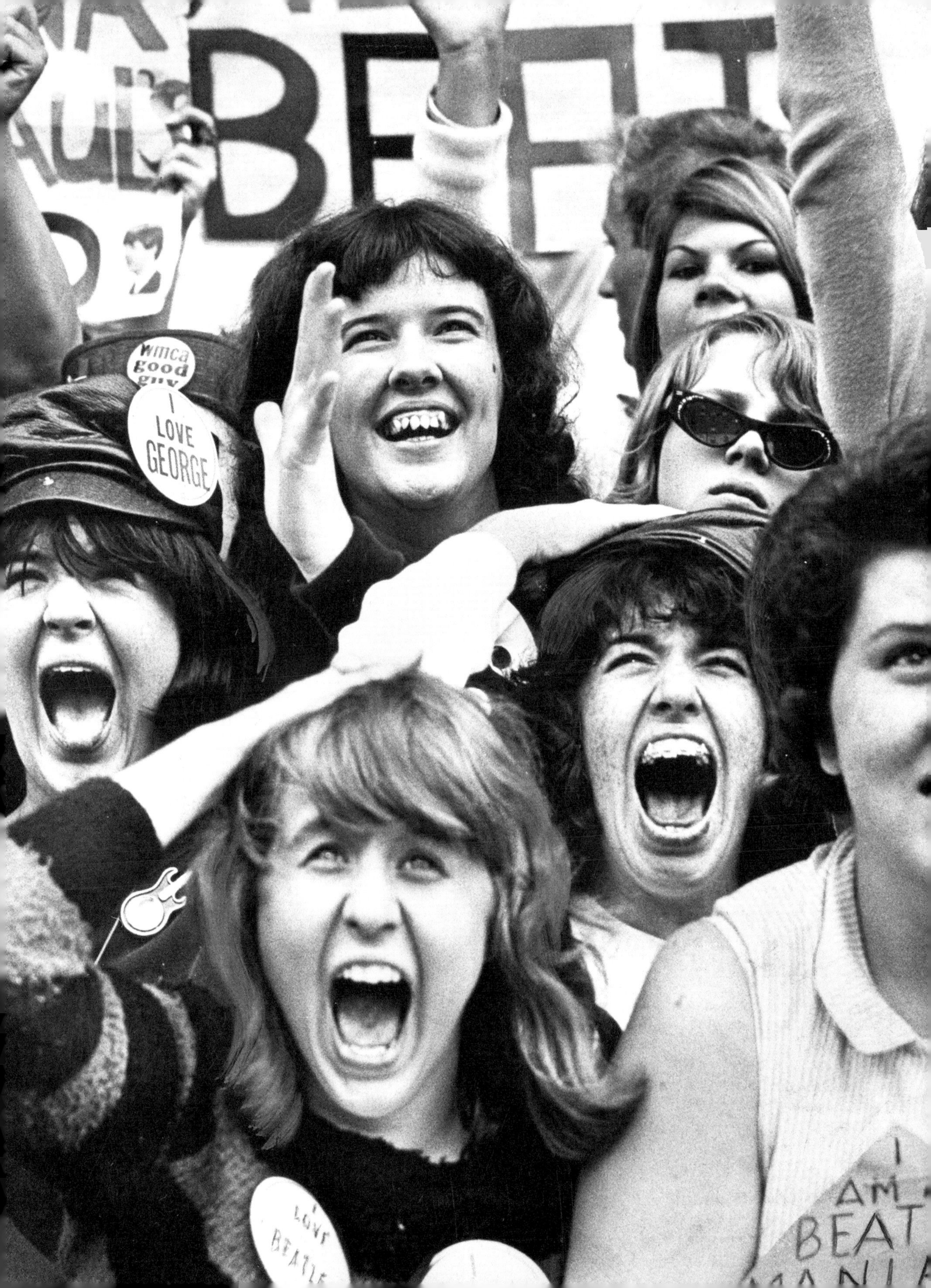
wmca good guy
I LOVE GEORGE
I LOVE BEATLE
I AM BEAT

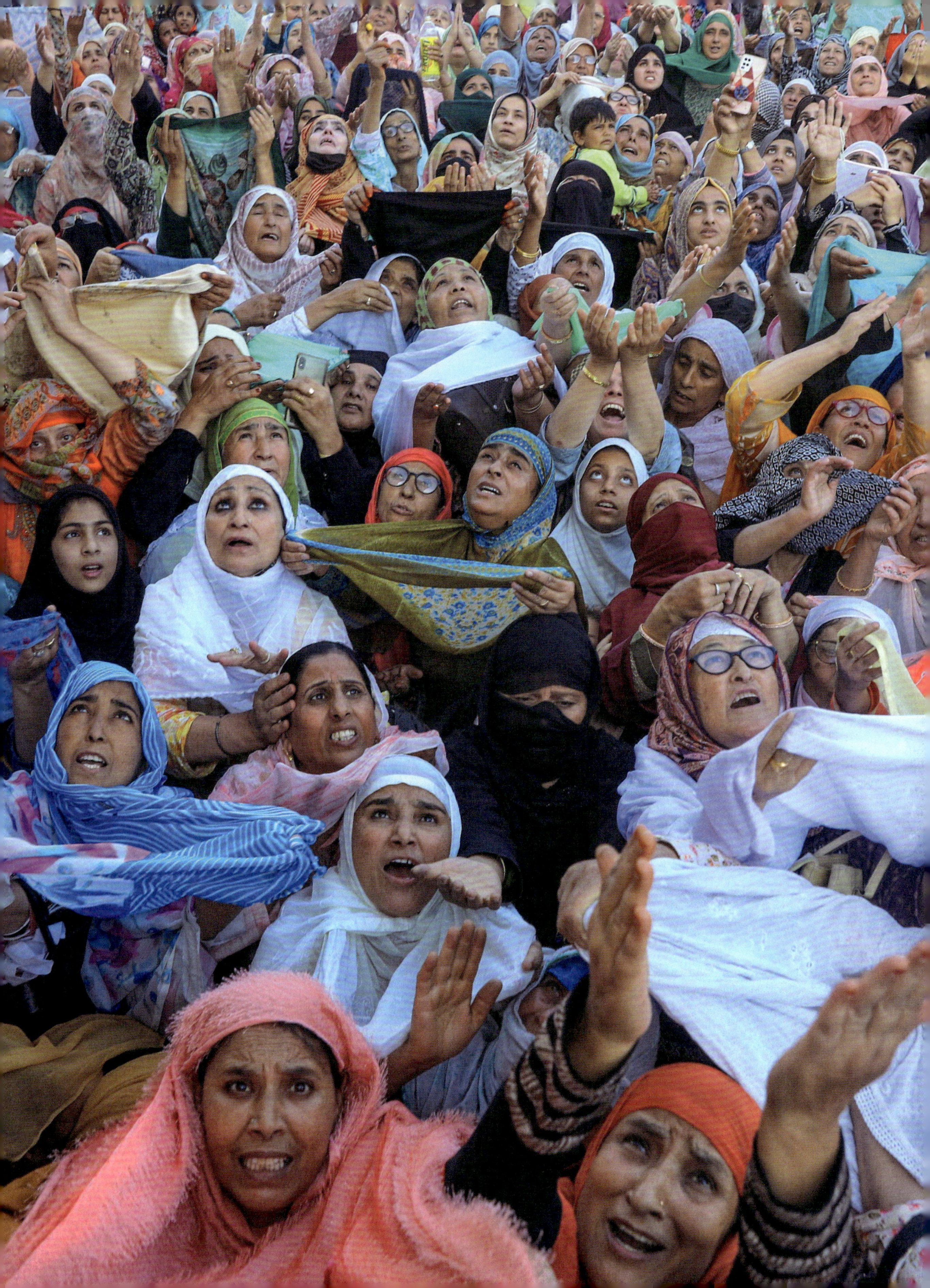

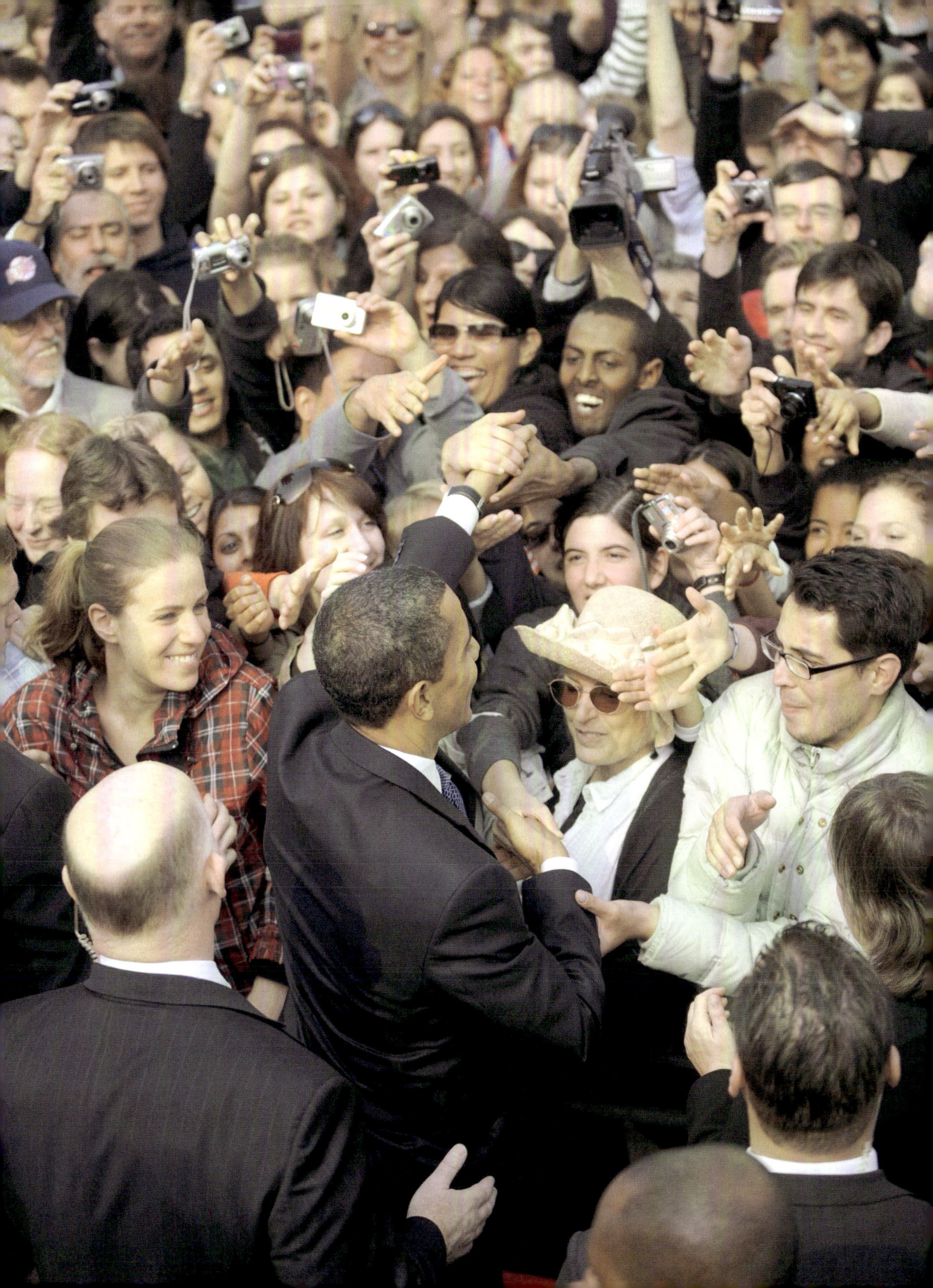

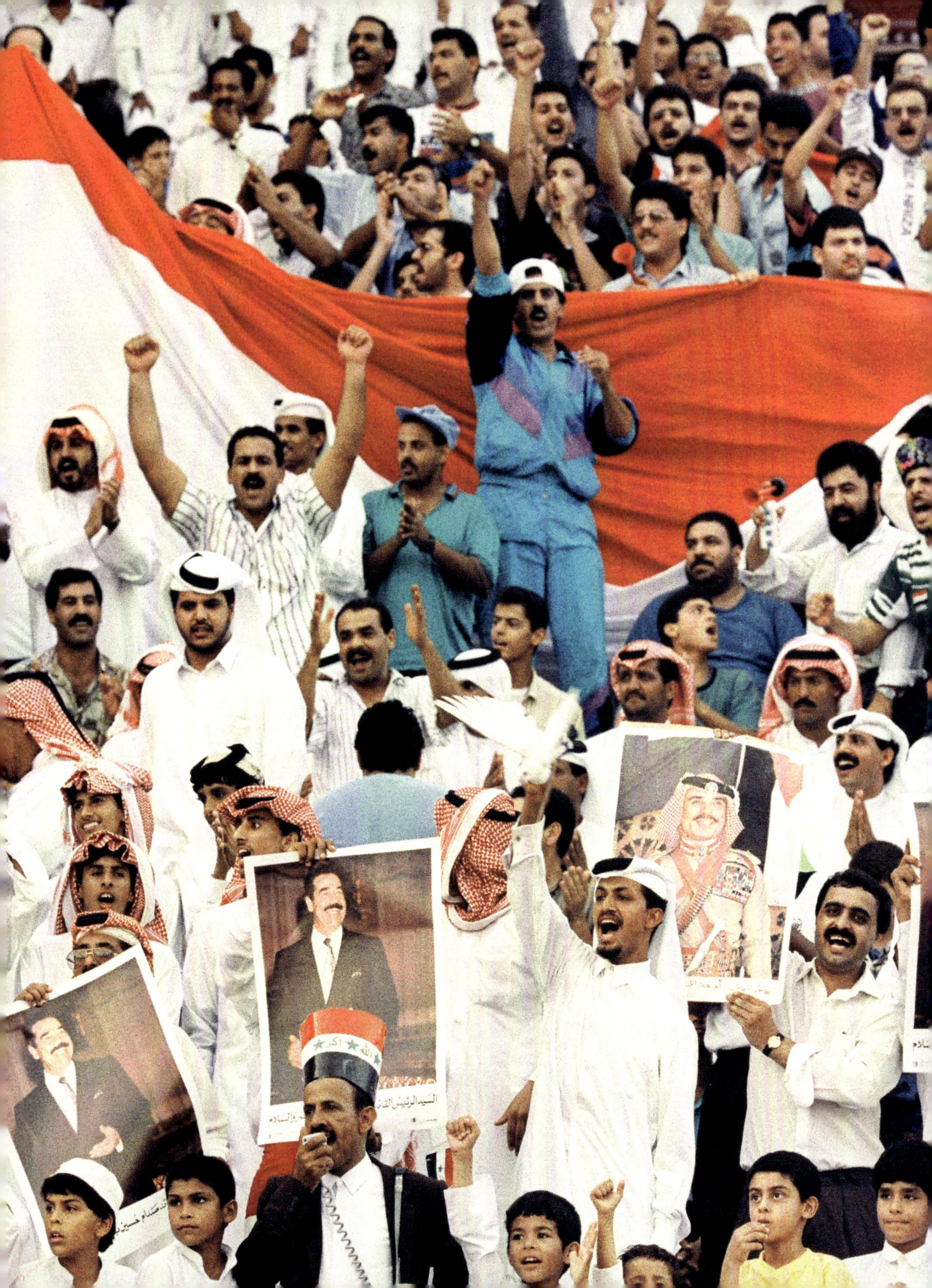

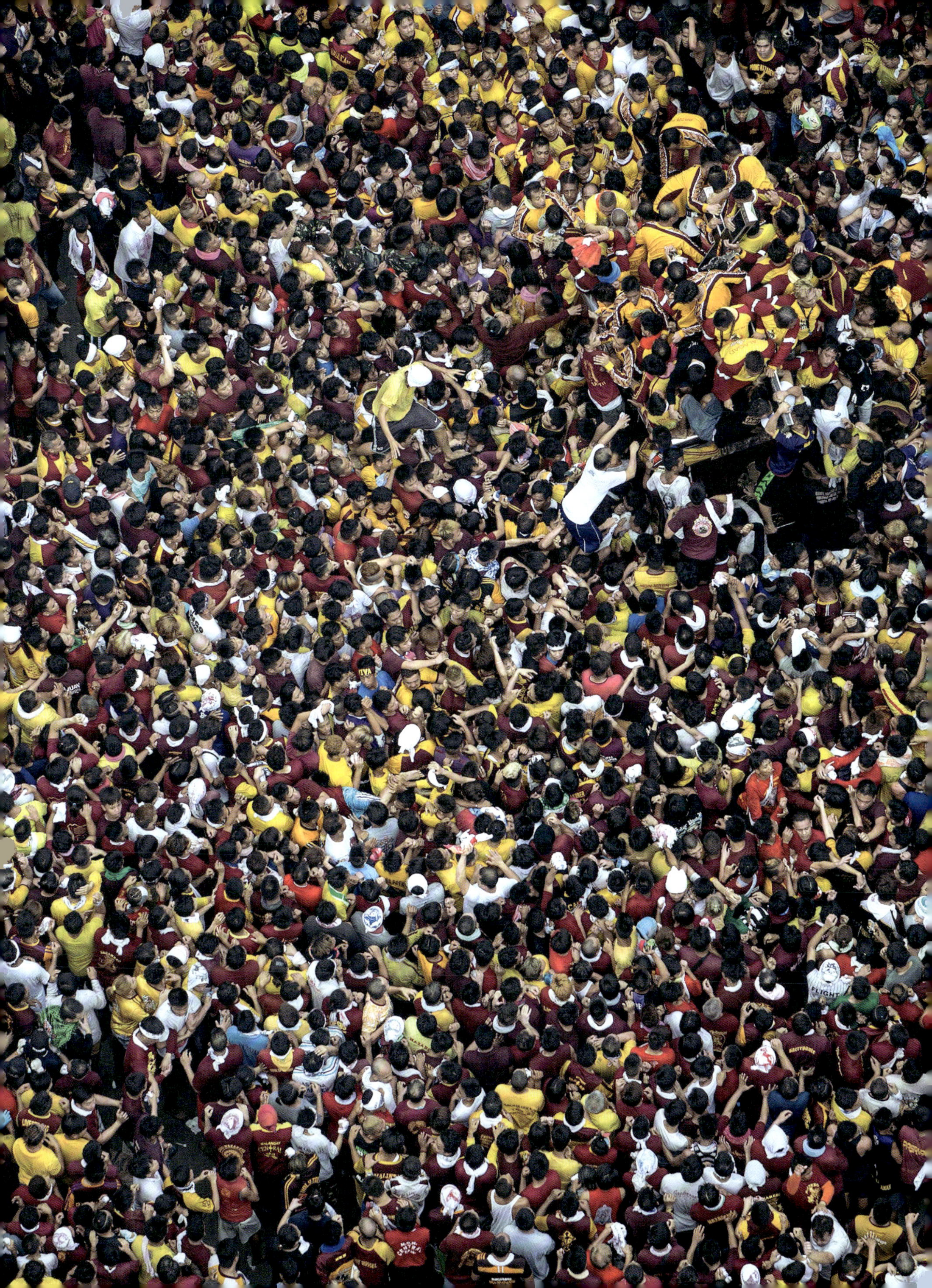

PRINZIP HELD*

von Helgard Haug und Daniel Wetzel (Rimini Protokoll)
und Dominik Steinmann (Büro unbekannt Berlin)

Ausstellung

Heroisches? Helden? Rumms! – auch Heldinnen oder Held:innen? Smash!! – daraus eine Ausstellung machen? Mit Wissenschaftler:innen der Uni Freiburg, die sich 12 Jahre mit dem Thema beschäftigt haben? Zischhhhh! Gemeinsam mit dem Militärhistorischen Museum der Bundeswehr? Wooooops? Boing. Oh wirklich?

Die Anfrage kam sehr unverhofft. Aber schnell wurden die Ausgangsfragen der Wissenschaftler:innen und des Kurator:innenteams auch zu unseren – und durch neue ergänzt: „Wieso brauchen wir Held:innen?" und „Wie werden sie gemacht?", „Welche Bilder kommen uns in den Sinn, wenn wir das Wort ‚Held' hören?", „Welcher Liedzeilen können wir uns nicht erwehren?", „In welche Posen verdrehen sich unsere Körper, beim Hören des Wortes ‚Heldin'?" „Wem würden wir – wenn überhaupt jemandem – den Held:innenstatus zugestehen?" und „Wo bleiben sie denn, die Held:innen, um uns zu ‚retten' und alles zu einem ‚Happy End' zu führen?" Seufz.

Wir steckten die Köpfe zusammen, begannen mit Plänen, diskutierten sie mit allen Beteiligten ausführlich, rieben uns auf, an dem Prinzip Held* Whaaaat!

Ort der Held*-Austragung ist der Hangar 5 auf dem Flugplatz Gatow. Auf dem Museumsgelände befindet sich auch allerlei Kriegsgerät, vom „Einmannbunker" über Kampfflieger bis zur Pershing – Zeugnisse verfehlter Heldenideologien? Wer kommt hier her, um sich was anzuschauen? Wir selbs hätten es wahrscheinlich nicht mitbekommen, dass hier etwas Interesse-Steigerndes, Irritierendes, Anregendes, Los-Tretendes, Überraschendes losgeht. Phump. Ta. Ta. Und das tut es: Wenn sich die Besucher:innen dem Hangar nähern, hören sie Klänge und entdecken ein amorphes Etwas, das ähnlich den Tentakeln eines unbekannten Wesens aus der Halle herauswächst, sich aufbläht und wieder verflacht.

Slaaaarp...!

Es rumpelt, schlürft und dröhnt. Was geht da drinnen vor sich?

Exhibition

Heroic? Heroes? Rumms! – Heroines too? Smash!! – make an exhibition out of it? With scientists from the University of Freiburg who have been working on the topic for 12 years? Zischhhhh! Together with the Military History Museum of the German Armed Forces? Wooooops? Boing. Oh really?

The enquiry came very unexpectedly. But the initial questions posed by the scientists and the curatorial team quickly became ours – and were supplemented with new ones: "Why do we need heroes?" and "How are they made?", "What images come to mind when we hear the word ‚hero'?", "Which song lines can we not resist?", "What poses do our bodies contort into when we hear the word ‚hero'?" "Who – if anyone – would we grant hero status to?" And "Where are they, the heroes, to 'save' us and bring everything to a 'happy ending'?" Sigh.

We put our heads together, came up with plans, discussed them at length with everyone involved, and worked ourselves up over the "Prinzip Held"Whaaaat!*

The location of the "Prinzip Held" event is Hangar 5 at the Gatow airfield. The museum site is also home to all kinds of war equipment, from "one-man bunkers" and fighter planes to the Pershing – evidence of misguided heroic ideologies? Who comes here to see what? We ourselves probably wouldn't have realised that something interesting, irritating, stimulating, unleashing, surprising was going on here. Phump. Ta. Ta. And that's what it does: As visitors approach the hangar, they hear sounds and discover an amorphous something that grows out of the hall like the tentacles of an unknown creature, inflates and then flattens out again.*

Slaaaarp...!

It rumbles, slurps and roars. What's going on in there?

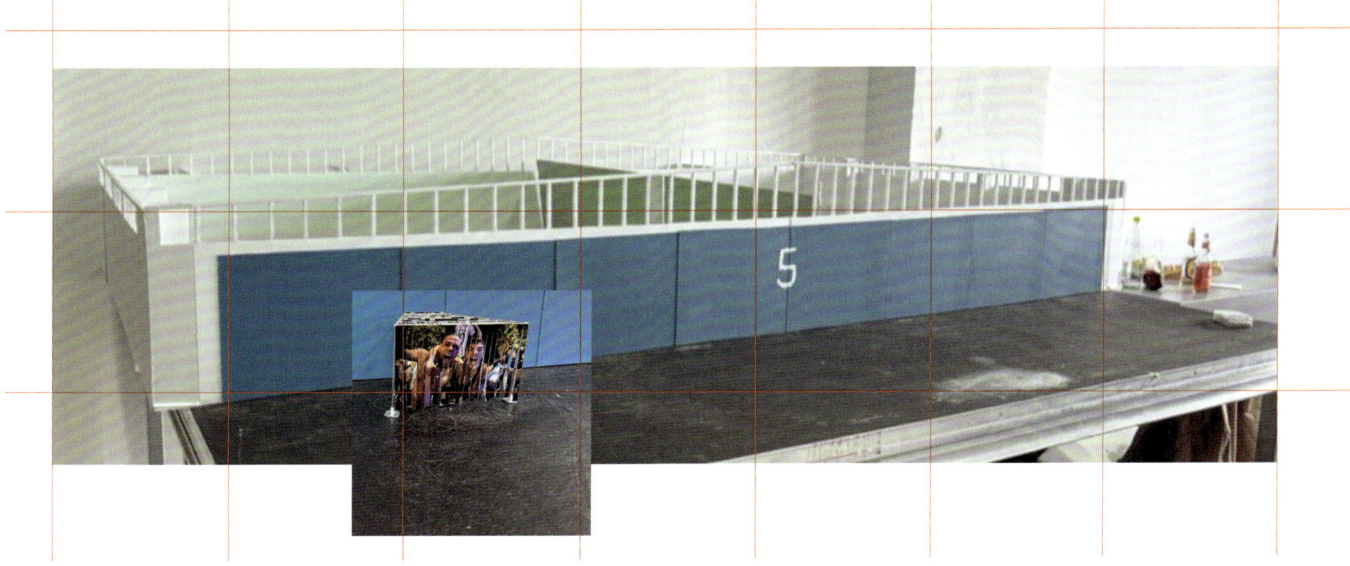

PUBLIKUM
AUDIENCE

Im Publikum. Gang durch eine Bilderschleuse. Ein Flatterbild aus Lamellen durchstreifen, Abstand gleich Null. Trichtersog. Menschenmassen-Sound von oben. Wann begeben sich Menschen in Massen und wie entsteht dann etwas „Gewaltiges"? In Versammlungen von Begeisterten, Überzeugten, Trauernden, Schaulustigen, Rekrutierten, Protestierenden, Mitgerissenen, Ausrastenden…?

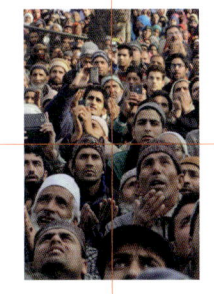

In the audience. Walk through a picture lock. Wander through a fluttering image of louvres, distance equal to zero. Crowd sound from above. When do people get into crowds and how does something "powerful" come about? In gatherings of the enthusiastic, the convinced, the mourners, the onlookers, the recruited, the protesters, the carried away, the rioters…?

Spiel, Feld, vollgestellt. 44 Installationen, aus ausrangierten Möbeln der Bundeswehr und Alltagsobjekten improvisiert, sind arrangiert für Manöver in Haltungen, Blickwinkeln und Sichtachsen.

Die Erstausstattung der Bundeswehr bis zur Olympiade 1972 war durchgehend „Eiche, hell", furniert. Seit 1990 gilt „Buche, dekor". Dazwischen war die Zeit der „Olympiamöbel": Spinde, Stockbetten, Tische, Aktenböcke, Stühle, Regale in Weiß, Dunkelgrün (Heer), Blau (Luftwaffe, Marine), Kress (heute Orange, Ausbildungsbereiche).

Die Farb-Skala der Oberbegriffe, die das Feld der Fallbeispiele strukturieren, greift sie auf und ergänzt sie.

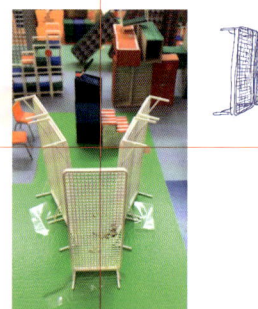

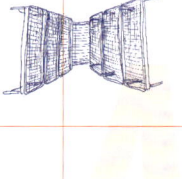

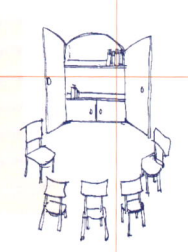

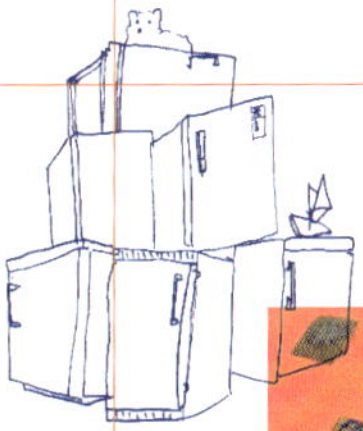

Game, field, crowded. 44 installations, improvised from discarded Bundeswehr furniture and everyday objects, are arranged for manoeuvres in postures, perspectives and points of view.

Until the 1972 Olympics, the Bundeswehr's original furnishings were all "oak, light-coloured", veneered. Since 1990, it has been "beech, decorative". In between was the time of the "Olympic furniture": lockers, bunk beds, tables, filing cabinets, chairs, shelves in white, dark green (army), blue (air force, navy), cress (today orange, training areas).

The colour scale of the generic terms that structure the field of case studies picks them up and supplements them.

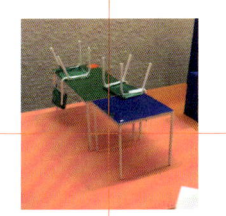

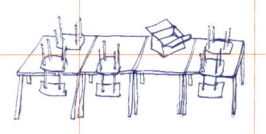

Heroisches Kollektiv mit Anführer – Ballhausschwur
Heroic Collective with a Leader – The Tennis Court Oath

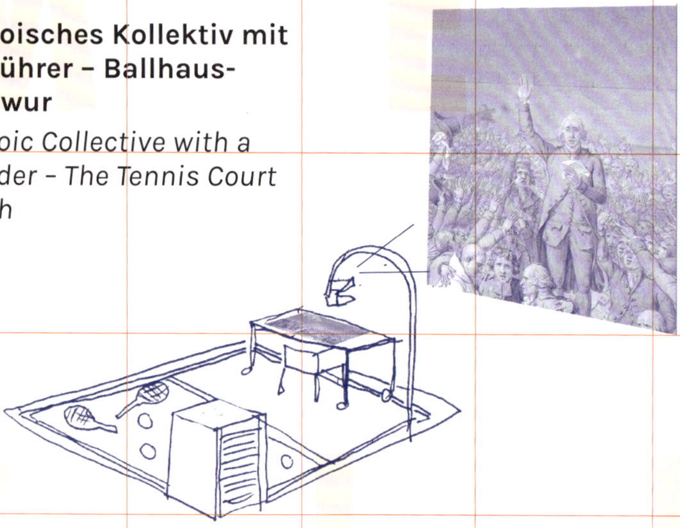

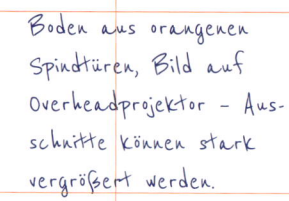

Boden aus orangenen Spindtüren, Bild auf Overheadprojektor – Ausschnitte können stark vergrößert werden.

MEDIALISIERUNG
MEDIALISATION

Stauffenberg
Stauffenberg

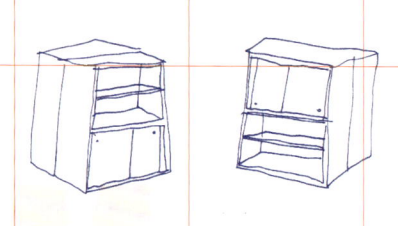

Zwei Büroschränke, einer auf den Kopf gestürzt. Beide Schränke zeigen Bild- und Text-Material.

Alltagsehrungen – Postman's Park
Everyday Honouring – Postman's Park

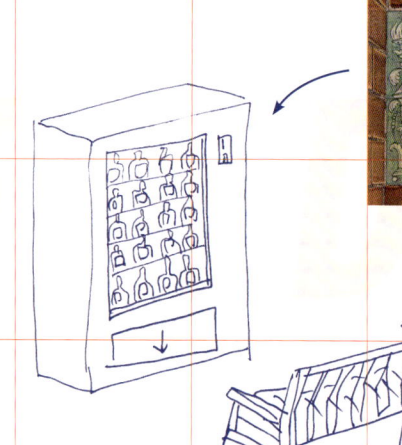

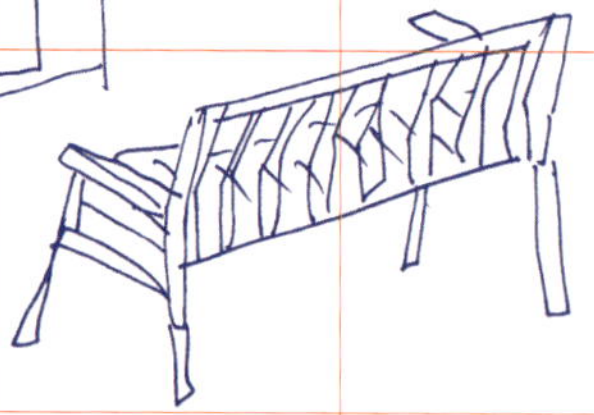

Snack-/Getränkeautomat. In den Fächern Reproduktionen der Tafeln. Polstermöbel der BW zur Pausen-Bank modifizieren.

Propagandakompanien der Wehrmacht
The Wehrmacht Propaganda Companies

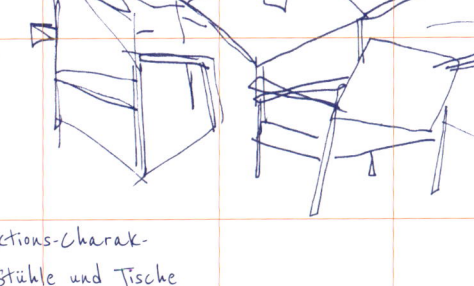

Redaktions-Charakter, Stühle und Tische schräg angeschnitten, alles unbequem, wackelig.

Neue Helden an alter Stelle – Stürze von Kolonialdenkmälern I
New Heroes in Previous Places – Toppling of Colonial Monuments I

Helden und Widersprüche – Stürze von Kolonialdenkmälern II
Heroes and Contradictions – Toppling of Colonial Monuments II

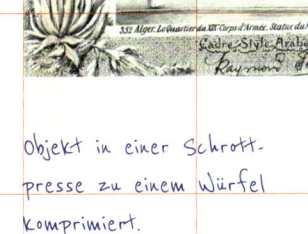

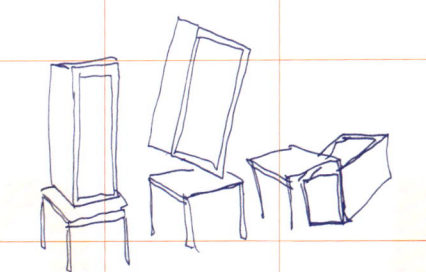

Objekt in einer Schrottpresse zu einem Würfel komprimiert.

Spind auf Tisch. 3 Standbilder des Kippmoments. Bilder aus beiden Kolonialismus-Cases als Postkarten in Drehstände.

Vorbild als Frage der Perspektive – Li Wenliang
Role Model as a Matter of Perspective – Li Wenliang

VORBILD
ROLE MODELS

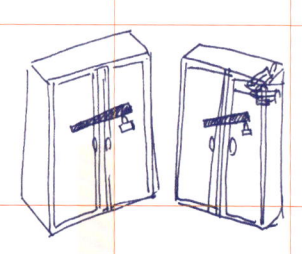

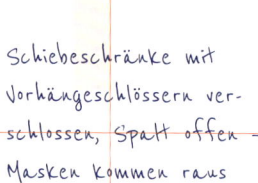

Schiebeschränke mit Vorhängeschlössern verschlossen, Spalt offen – Masken kommen raus

Kollektives Heldentum – Helden der Arbeit
Collective Heroism – Heroes of Labour

Nicht nachmachen – Sullenberger, Snowden, Daschner
Don't imitate – Sullenberger, Snowden, Daschner

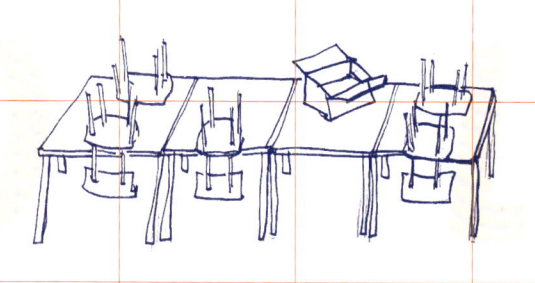

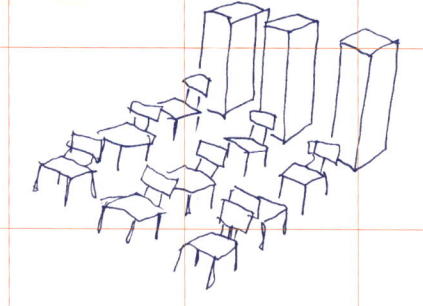

3 Spinde, 9 Stühle – 1 Stuhl tanzt aus der Reihe.

Tische zu einem großen Tisch vereint, hochgestellte Stühle ringsum (VEB-Arbeitsfläche)

Kein Held ohne Vorbilder – Stefan George

No Hero without Role Models – Stefan George

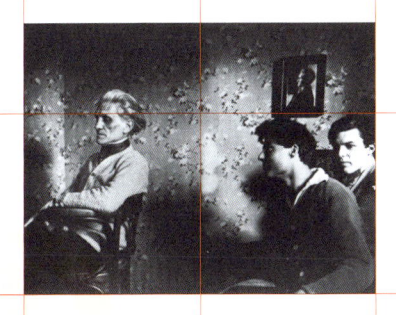

Fortschrittsheldin – Walentina Tereschkowa, Kosmonautin

Heroine of Progress – Cosmonaut Valentina Tereshkova

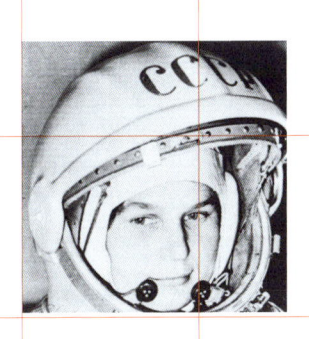

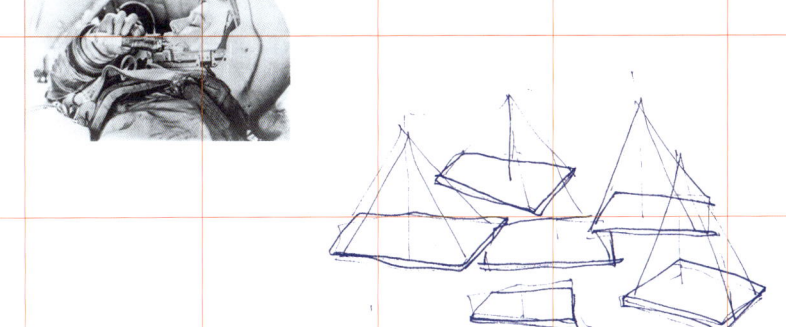

Liege-Sessel: der Blick geht nach oben. Alle Bilder hängen an der Decke.

geheimer Zirkel / Stuhlkreis - innen Schrift auf dem Boden. Schrank zu einem Altar umgearbeitet.

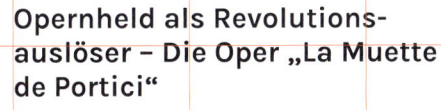

Opernheld als Revolutionsauslöser – Die Oper „La Muette de Portici"

Opera Hero triggers a Revolution – The Opera "La Muette de Portici"

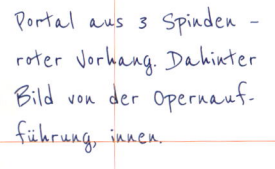

Portal aus 3 Spinden - roter Vorhang. Dahinter Bild von der Opernaufführung, innen.

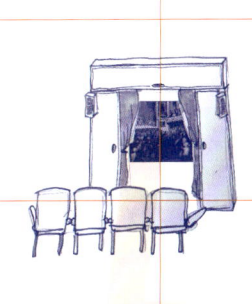

**Polarisieren und einen –
Klimaaktivist:innen**
*Polarise and Unify –
Climate Activists*

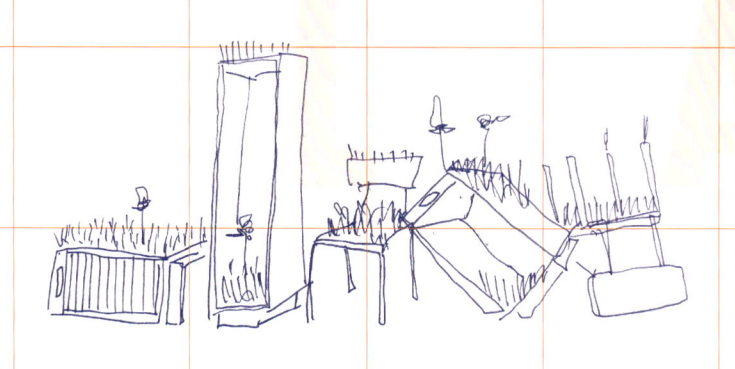

Straßenblockade aus Möbeln, Pro- und Contra-Sticker drauf. Bepflanzung.

POLARISIERUNG
POLARISATION

**Gefolgschaft als Selbstverzwergung
– Starke Männer**
Followership as Self-deprecation – Strongmen

Islamischer Staat (IS)
Islamic State (IS)

Readymade:
Einmannbunker

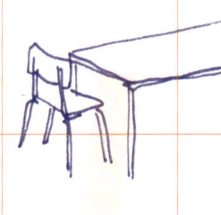

Zwischen Egalität und Elite – Das Eiserne Kreuz
Between Equality and Elite – the Iron Cross

4 Tische, Tischbeine aufgebogen, um das Kreuzsymbol genauer zu treffen, Bild- und Textmaterialien innen.

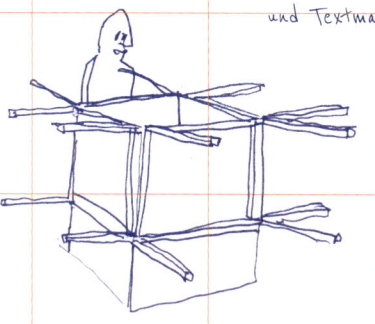

Wehrmacht und SS
Wehrmacht and SS

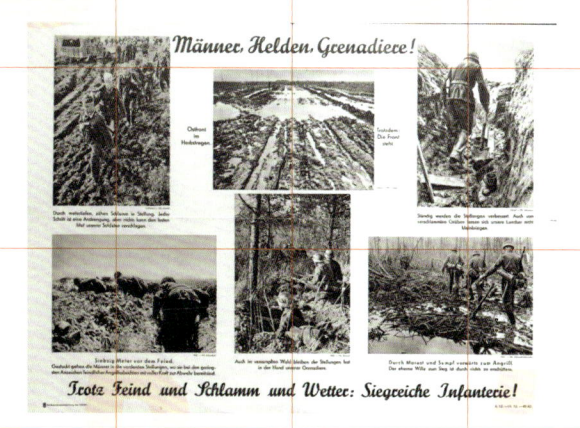

Spind, Stuhl, Tisch schwarz lackiert – wie Schatten

Ein Tisch so lang wie Putins Tafel, Beine angesägt, sodass er schräg abfällt, Hör- und Leseort jeweils an einem Ende. Eiweißzusatznahrung?

Tupfer und Skizzen statt Marmor und Leinwand. Keine klassischen Exponate, keine illustrative Deutbarkeit, sondern Anordnungen, Konstellationen aus Objekten und Reproduktionen, Texte, die einen gedankenspielerischen Tief- und Umgang anbieten.

Dabs and sketches instead of marble and canvas. No classic exhibits, no illustrative interpretability, but rather arrangements, constellations of objects and reproductions, texts that offer a thought-provoking depth and dialogue.

Heroischer Gesetzgeber
Heroic Legislator

Treppe aus Aktenböcken in den Hades + Klavier: geöffnet: ertönt die Musik.

Held der Entgrenzung – Orpheus
Hero of the Dissolution of Boundaries – Orpheus

Stuhlstapel in Anlehnung an Parlament nach hinten ansteigend Blickachse geht über Fallbeispiel Washington (Rednerpult) in Richtung Front der Gangway (Fallbeispiel Melli Beese.)

Alexander der Große
Alexander the Great

in alle Richtungen mit Möbeln: maximale Expansion

Erste sein – Melli Beese, Pilot
Being the First (Female) – Melli Beese, Pilot

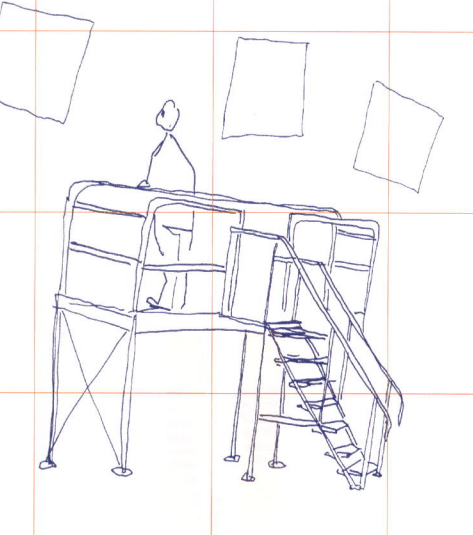

Gangway (Fluggasttreppe) zur Übersicht über die Ausstellungs-"Welt". Blick auf die Bildmaterialien: abwärts.

GRENZÜBERSCHREITUNG
CROSSING BOUNDARIES

Heldentod
Heroic Death

Zum frommen Andenken!
an unsern lieben, unvergeßlichen Sohn, unsern guten Bruder, Schwager, Onkel, Neffen und Vetter, Soldat

Albert Haßdenteufel

Unterwachtmeister der ᛋᛋ-Polizei der sein junges, hoffnungsvolles Leben am 15. Februar 1942 im Alter von 21 Jahren für Deutschlands Größe bei den Kämpfen im Osten hingegeben hat. Er folgte nach 14 Monaten seinem Bruder Werner, der den Fliegertod über England fand. Ihr einziger Wunsch war ein Wiedersehn in der Heimat.

In tiefer Trauer:
Frau Wwe. Peter Haßdenteufel geb. Schmidt, **Walter Haßdenteufel** (z. Zt. im Felde), **Fr Rosa Heblich** geb. Haßdenteufel mit Tochter **Christel**, **Ludwig Heblich** (z. Zt. im Felde), die **Großeltern**, alle **Anverwandten** und **Familie Fritz Müller**
Elversberg-Saar u. im Felde, im März 1942.

Spinde als Stelen. Soldatenfriedhof. Bilder und Bildlegenden in Spinden (Beleuchtung innen). Rückseitig über alle Rückwände aufgeteilt ein einziges Bild von einem Soldatenfriedhof.

Provokation als Empowerment
– Tom of Finland
Provocation as Empowerment – Tom of Finland

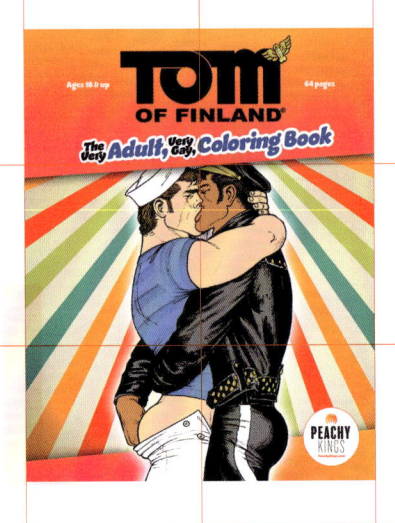

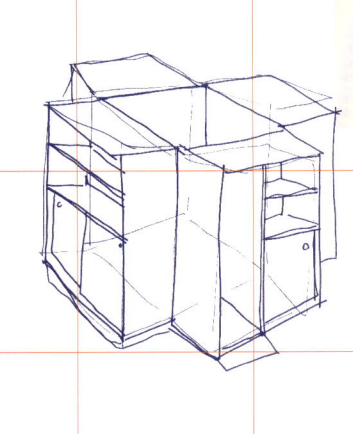

Spiegelkabinett mit Originalzitaten aus Sophokles – die immer wiederkehrende Heldin

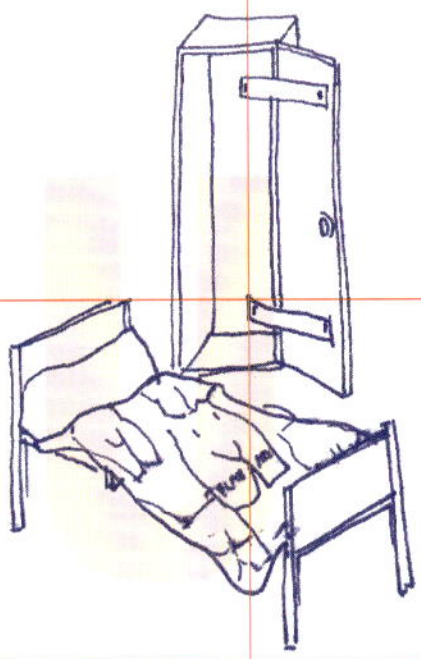

Aufbegehrende Frauen
– Antigone
Rebellious Women – Antigone

Schrank wird zum Sportgerät: mit Therabänder an den Türen – es läuft Queen

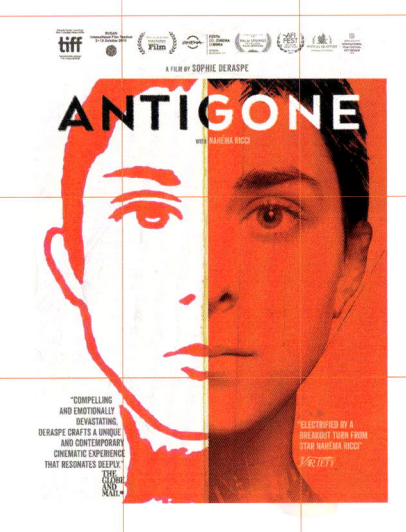

Heroische Gewalt
Heroic Violence

Gitterkasten mit zerbrochenen Spiegelstücken auf dem Boden

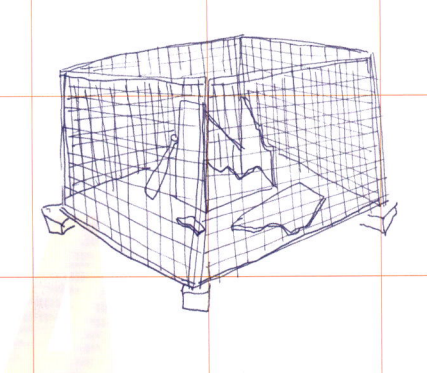

HANDLUNGSMACHT

AGENCY

Objekte, die heroisieren – Die Kalaschnikow
Objects that Heroise – The Kalashnikov

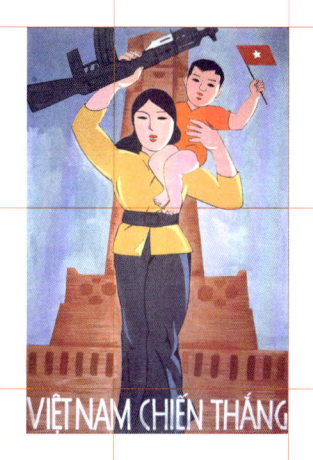

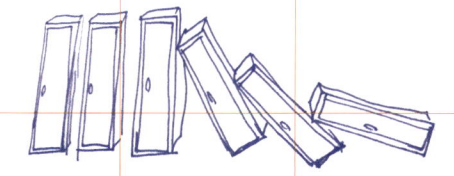

Ritterturnier mit Bürostühlen und Schwimmnudeln

Label „Ritter"
Label "Knight"

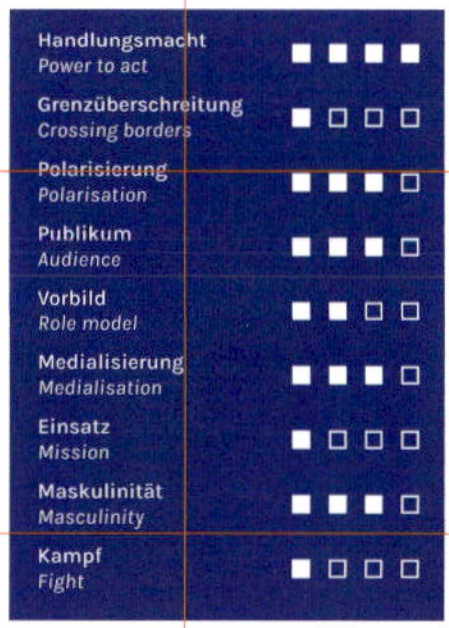

Spinde mit Fototapete beklebt – in verschiedenen Kipp-Positionen – wie beim Domino.

Hero*-Score: Wie viele Anteile eines jeden heroischen Oberbegriffs kommen wohl in jedem Fallbeispiel zur Wirkung? Und in welchem Verhältnis stehen sie zueinander?

Auch die Kernaussage zum jeweiligen Fallbeispiel ist offen an den Möbeln angebracht.

Hero*-Score: How much of each heroic component comes into play in each case study? And how do the results relate to each other?

The key statement for each case study is also openly displayed on the furniture.

**Wirtschaftskrieger –
Elon Musk und
Mark Zuckerberg**
*Economic Warriors –
Elon Musk and
Mark Zuckerberg*

**Empowerment – das Civil
Rights/Black Power
Movement**
*Empowerment – the Civil
Rights/Black Power Movement*

Exorbitant hohe Stühle, die
sinnbildlich für den Börsen-
kurs und Reichtum stehen

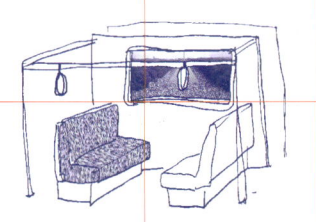

Situation in öffentlichen
Verkehrsmitteln, Alltagsras-
sismus, Anlehnung an Rosa
Parks

KAMPF

FIGHTING

**Heldentum und
Staatsbürger in Uniform
– Bundeswehr**
*Heroism and Citizen in
Uniform – Bundeswehr*

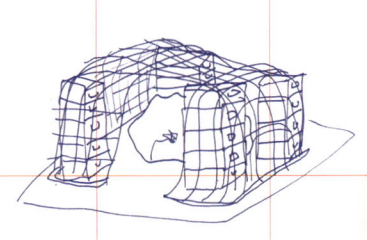

Transport der Gedenksteine.

Ritter als Saubermänner
The Knight as Goddy-two-shoes

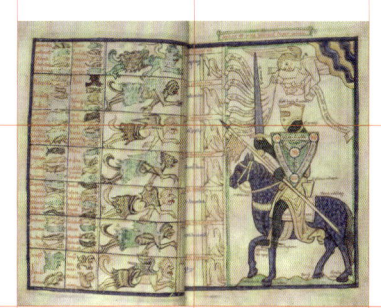

Nationalhelden
National Heroes

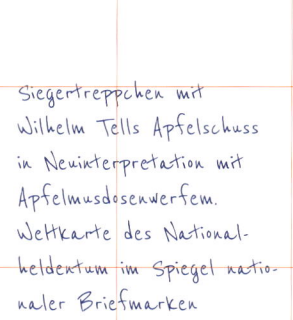

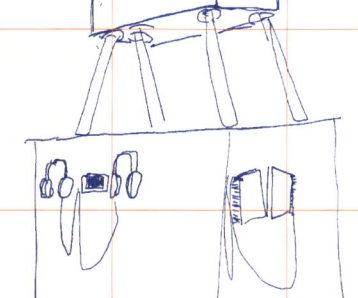

Siegertreppchen mit Wilhelm Tells Apfelschuss in Neuinterpretation mit Apfelmusdosenwerfern. Weltkarte des Nationalheldentum im Spiegel nationaler Briefmarken

Suworow-Orden
The Suvorov Order

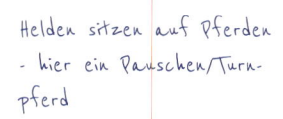

Helden sitzen auf Pferden – hier ein Pauschen/Turnpferd

Prinzip Held* ist eine Wissenschaftsausstellung und auch ein Hörstück mit mehr als 5 Stunden Länge. An jedem Ort eine Hörstation mit den Stimmen derer, die den jeweiligen Fall erforscht und beschrieben haben.

Prinzip Held is a science exhibition and also an audio play lasting more than 5 hours. At each location there is an audio station with the voices of those who have researched and described the respective case.*

Blaulichtfreiwillige
Emergency and Rescue Service Volunteers

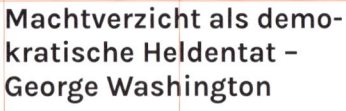

Machtverzicht als demokratische Heldentat – George Washington
Abdication of Power as a Democratic Heroic Act – George Washington

Rednerpult aus Rollschränken für Speech of Resignation. Gummistiefel daneben. Blick in die Parlamentsanordnung von Harrington.

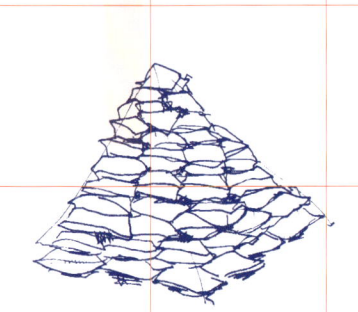

Denkmal aus Sandsäcken, Sanduhr auf Pyramide symbolisiert geopferte Zeit der Freiwilligen

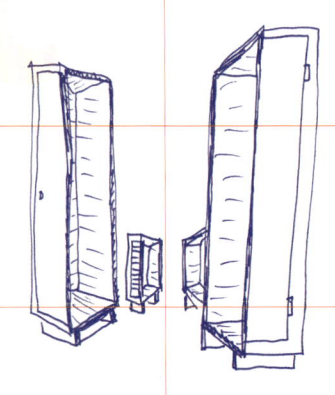

Kerbalaparadigma
The Karbala Paradigm

Möbel aufgeschnitten im Verhältnis 2:1 (schiitisch, nur diese schmallere Seite ausgestattet mit Bildmaterial).

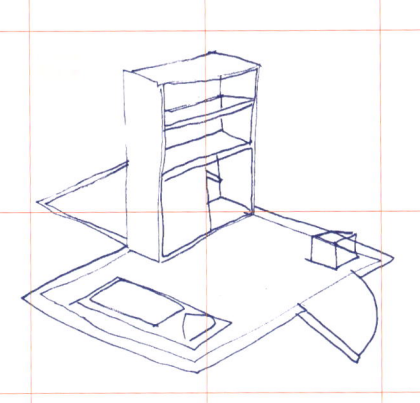

Gartenlaube mit Versteck als Schrank und aufgemaltem Grundriss

interaktive Familienaufstellung mit Babyspinden

Stille Helden
Silent Heroes

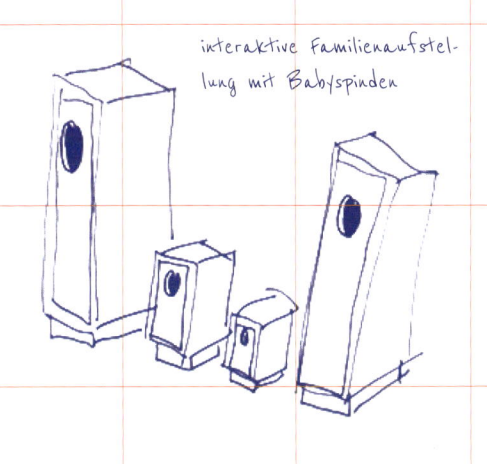

Eltern
Parents

EINSATZ
COMMITMENT

Desertieren
Desertion

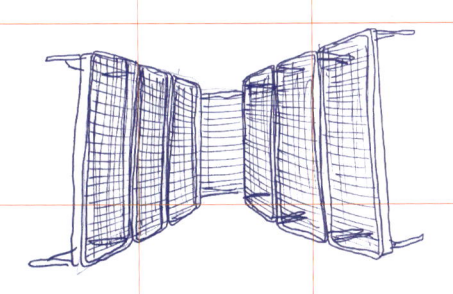

Sich verengende Wände aus Feldbetten, gefluchtet

Heroische Körperlichkeit – Hercules Farnese
Heroic Physique – The Farnese Hercules

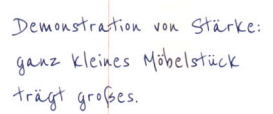

Katharina DER Große
Catherine the Great Emperor

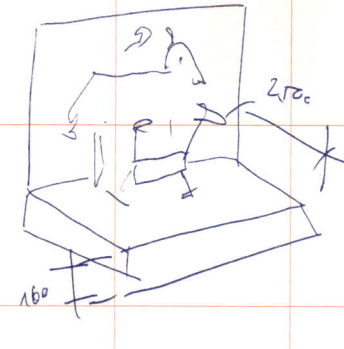

Demonstration von Stärke: ganz kleines Möbelstück trägt großes.

Kopie des Herrensitzes des Gemäldes auf Hometrainer, dazu heorischer Damenduft aus Flacon

Politik mit offenem Hemd
Politics with an Unbuttoned Shirt

MASKULINITÄT
MASCULINITY

Modifizierter Sessel als Anthropomorphismus männlicher Politiker in lässiger Sitzhaltung

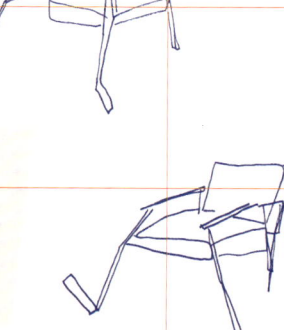

Polare Männlichkeiten
– Fridtjof Nansen

*Polar Masculinities
– Fridtjof Nansen*

Krieg als heroischer Bewährungsraum –
Kriegsfotografinnen

*War as a Heroic Realm –
Female War Photographers*

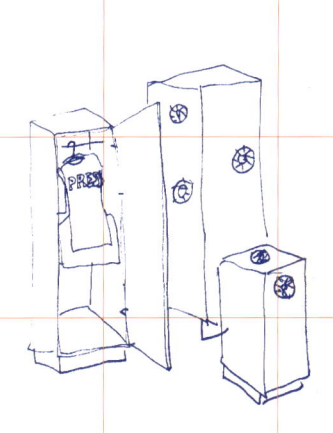

Blick durch die Linse (mechanische Irisblenden) ermöglicht Betrachtung von Fotografien

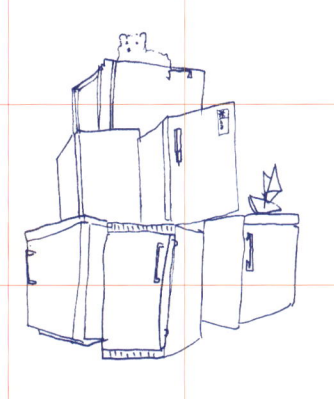

Alte Kühlschränke, gestapelt wie Eisberg, Bildmaterial als Magnete. Stapel Wolldecken (Bundeswehr)

Es gibt keine vorgedachte Reihenfolge, in der die Fallbeispiele besucht werden sollten. Jede gewählte Strecke durch das Labyrinth ohne Trennwände legt einen eigenen unsichtbaren „roten Faden".

There is no predetermined sequence in which the case studies should be visited. Each chosen route through the labyrinth without partitions creates its own invisible "red thread".

Held*maschine

Durch einen schmalen Gang betreten die Besucher:innen einen weiteren Bereich der Halle. Der Gang wird von zwei Zuschauertribünen gebildet. Hier befindet sich die Held*arena, in der nichts geschieht oder erklingt, wenn nicht gehandelt wird: Die Arena ist von einem Tresen umgeben. Dort sind 20 Hebel eingelassen. Durch jeden einzelnen Hebel können die Besucher:innen ein Teilstück einer großen Figur aktivieren. Wird ein Hebel betätigt, hat das eine direkte Auswirkung auf das Gebilde, auf den Sound, das Licht und auf die anderen Teilstücke.

Dieser Held* türmt sich unterschiedlich auf – je nach Reihenfolge der benutzten Mechanismen. Wenn andere Besucher:innen die Held*figur entstehen lassen, können wir auf einer der beiden Tribünen Platz nehmen. Dort vervollständigt sich das Bild der permanent im Werden und Vergehen befindlichen Figur durch Klänge und Licht bzw. Projektionen – immer dann, wenn zumindest jemand, wenn nicht bis zu zwanzig Leute diese Held*maschine „aufrecht erhalten".

Die künstlerische, interaktive Installation der in permanenter Veränderung befindlichen Held*maschine bildet ein zentrales Element der Ausstellung. Auswüchse davon sind schon außerhalb des Gebäudes bemerkbar. Verlassen die Besucher:innen den Hangar, kommen sie noch mal an dem Tentakel, dem Helden-Auswuchs, vorbei. Drinnen wird wohl gerade ein Held* gemacht! Smash! Rums!

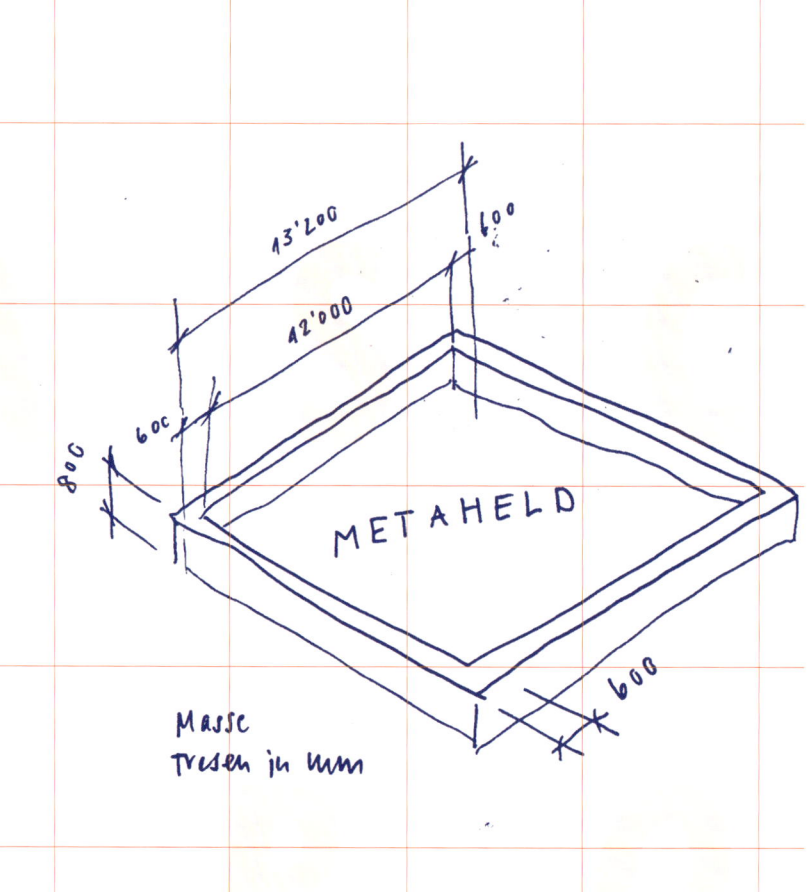

kabelkanal

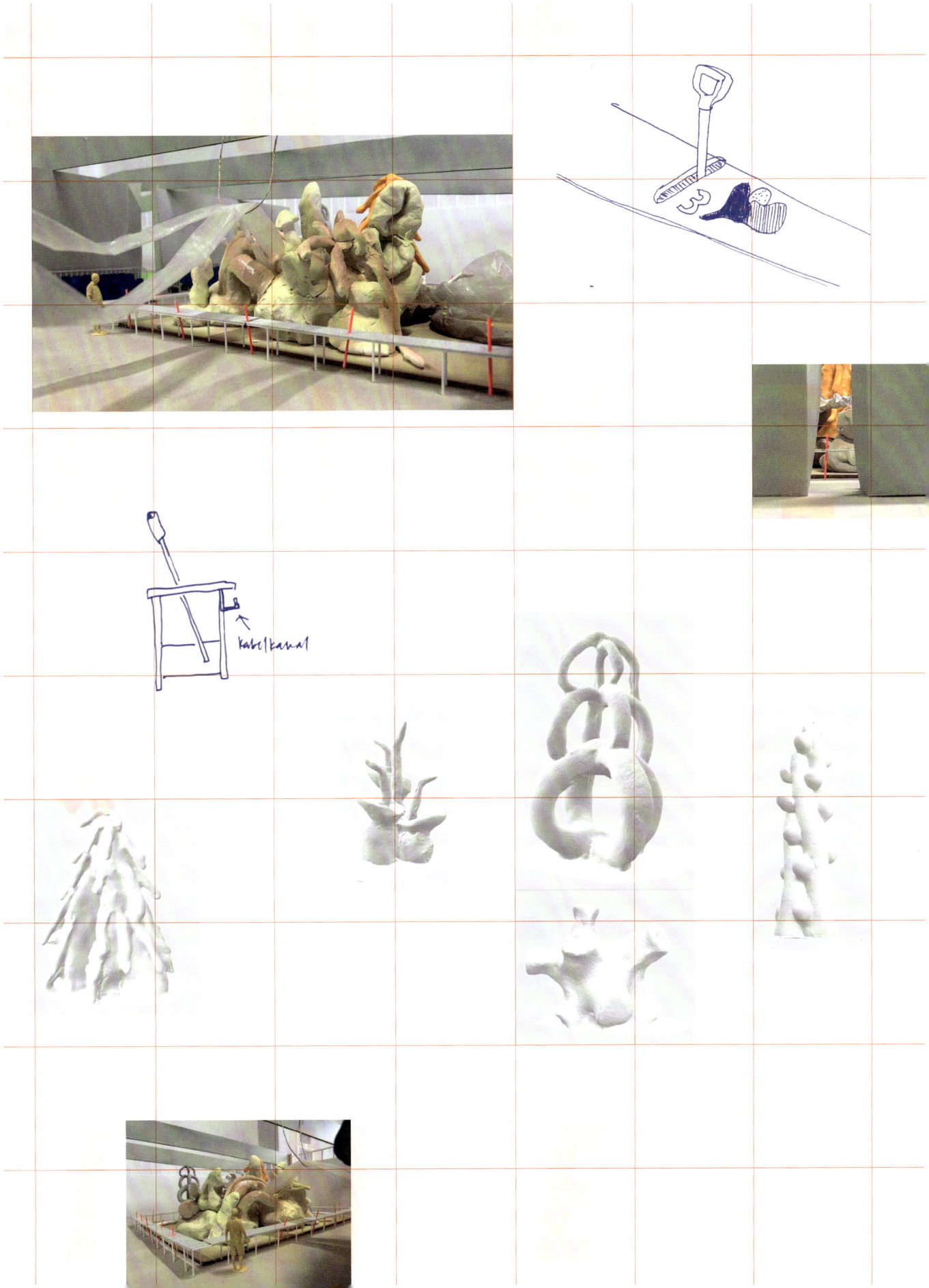

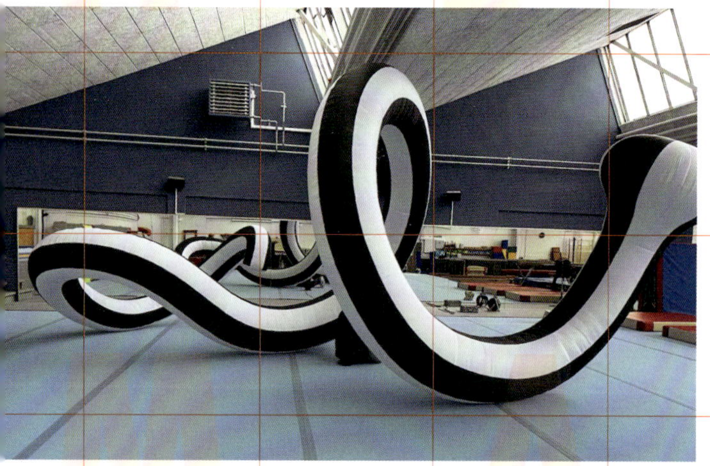
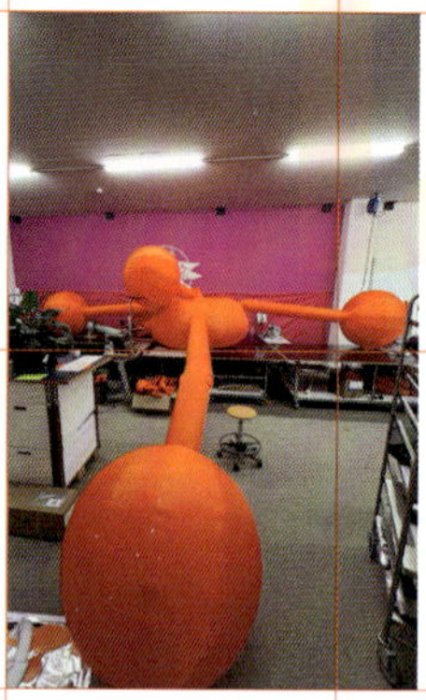
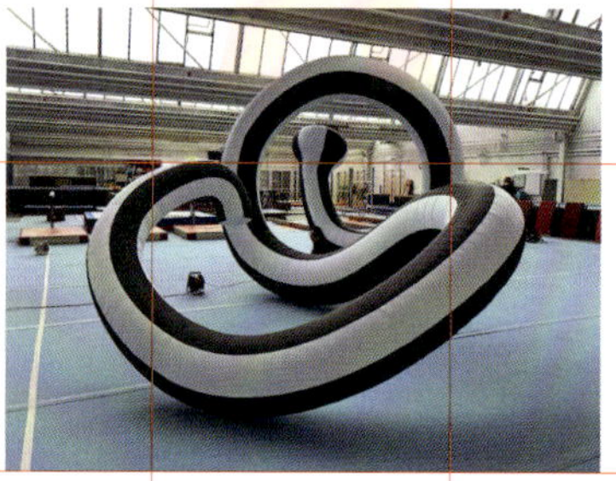
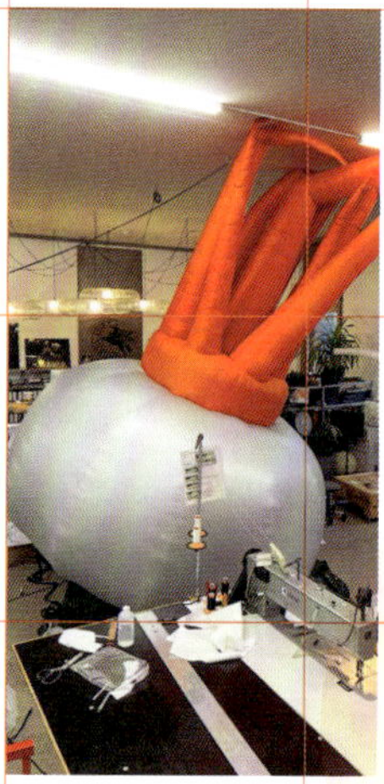
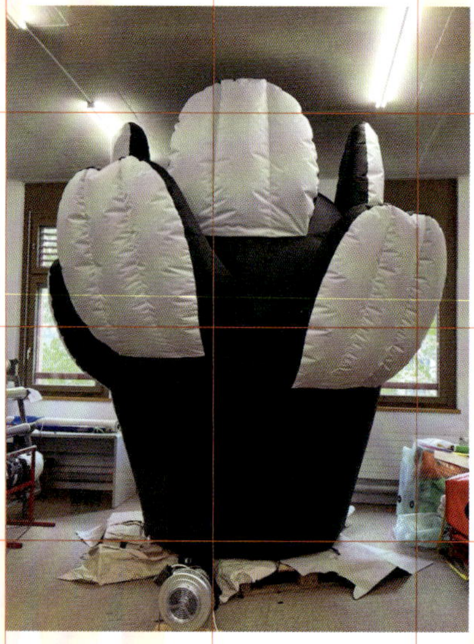
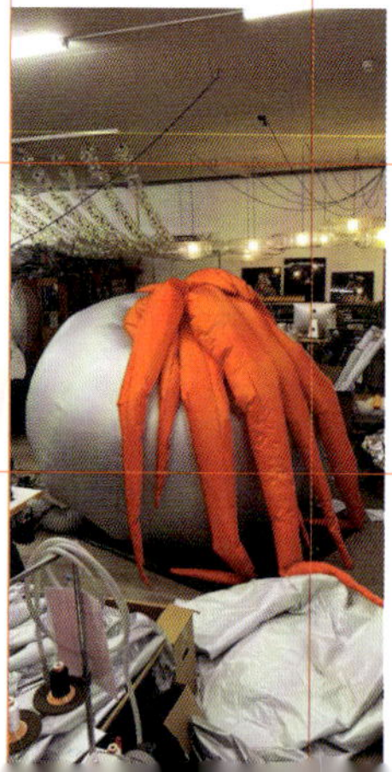

Hero*machine

Visitors enter another area of the hall through a narrow corridor. The corridor is formed by two spectator stands, where the Hero* Arena is located, in which nothing happens or sounds unless action is taken: The arena is surrounded by a counter. There are 20 levers set into it. Each individual lever allows the vistors to activate a section of a large figure. When a lever is activated, this has a direct effect on the structure, on the sound, light and on the other sections.

This hero* piles up differently – depending on the order and number of the 20 mechanisms used. When other visitors create the hero* figure, we can take a seat on one of the two grandstands. There, the image of the figure, which is permanently in the process of becoming and passing away, is completed by sounds and light or projections – whenever at least someone, if not up to twenty people, "maintain" this hero*machine.

The artistic, interactive installation of the hero*machine, which is constantly changing, forms a central element of the exhibition. Visitors leaving the hangar will pass the tentacle – the hero's outgrowth – once again. Inside, a hero* is probably being made! Smash! Smash!

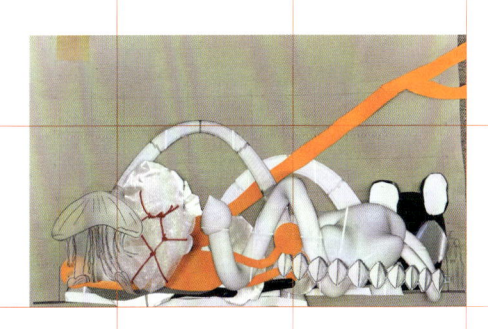

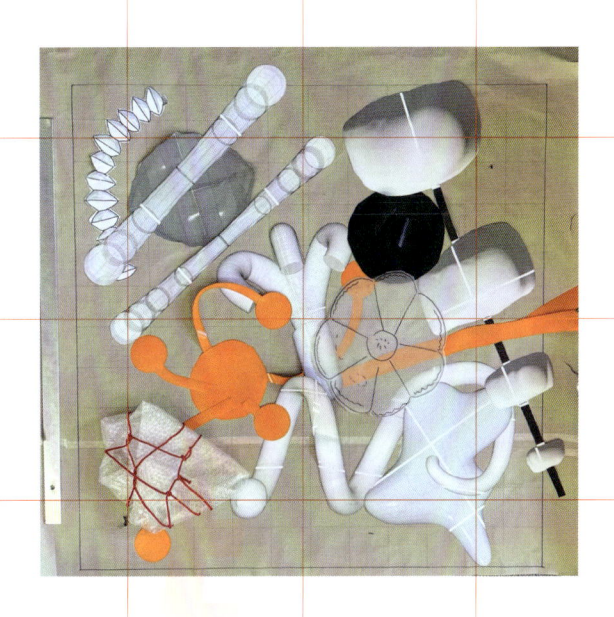

LITERATUR | WORKS CITED

Achilles, Achim. 2006. Maradona Celebrates 20th Anniversary of »Hand of God« Goal. In: *Der Spiegel*. 23. Juni 2006. www.spiegel.de/international/world-cup-blog-maradona-celebrates-20th-anniversary-of-hand-of-god-goal-a-423235.html (31. Mai 2023).

Adams, Ian. 2012. Over the Top, ›A Foul; a Blurry Foul!‹. In: *The International Journal of the History of Sport* 29, 813–831.

Adams, Ian. 2015. Football. A Counterpoint to the Procession of Pain on the Western Front, 1914–1918? In: *Soccer & Society* 16, 217–231.

Albertz, Anuschka. 2006. Exemplarisches Heldentum. *Die Rezeptionsgeschichte der Schlacht an den Thermopylen von der Antike bis zur Gegenwart*. München

Arend, Jan. 2023. Sehnsucht nach dem besseren Mann. In: *Frankfurter Allgemeine Zeitung*, 6. Juli 2023, 14.

Asch, Ronald G. und Michael Butter (Hg.). 2016a. *Bewunderer, Verehrer, Zuschauer. Die Helden und ihr Publikum*. Würzburg.

Asch, Ronald G. und Michael Butter. 2016b. Verehrergemeinschaften und Regisseure des Charisma. Heroische Figuren und ihr Publikum. In: *Bewunderer, Verehrer, Zuschauer: Die Helden und ihr Publikum*. Hg. von dens. Würzburg, 9–22.

Aurnhammer, Achim und Hanna Klessinger. 2018. Was macht Schillers Wilhelm Tell zum Helden? Eine deskriptive Heuristik heroischen Handelns. In: *Jahrbuch der Deutschen Schiller-Gesellschaft* 62, 127–149.

Aurnhammer, Achim u.a. 2024. Ästhetiken des Heroischen: Darstellung – Affizierung – Gesellschaft (Reflexionen des Heroischen). Göttingen.

Belting, Hans. 2005. Der photographische Zyklus der »Museumsbilder« von Thomas Struth. In: Hans Belting u.a. (Hg.). *Thomas Struth. Museum Photographs* (Ausstellungskatalog, Hamburger Kunsthalle, 1993–1994). München, 108–127.

Bexte, Peter. 2005. Sinne im Widerspruch – Diderots Schriften zur bildenden Kunst. In: *Denis Diderot. Schriften zur Kunst*. Hg. Peter Bexte. Berlin, 291–325.

Binhack, Axel. 1998. Über das Kämpfen. Zum Phänomen des Kampfes in Sport und Gesellschaft. Frankfurt am Main.

Blumenberg, Hans. 2014. *Präfiguration. Arbeit am politischen Mythos*. Hg. Angus Nicholls und Felix Heidenreich. Berlin.

Brecht, Bertolt. 1967. Fragen eines lesenden Arbeiters. In: *Bertolt Brecht. Gesammelte Werke*, Band 9. Frankfurt am Main, 656–657.

Borri, Francesca. 2017. The Maldives: Where Jihadists are Heroes. *Norwegian Refugee Council*. 14. März 2017. www.nrc.no/perspectives/2017/where-jihadists-are-heroes/ (29. Mai 2023).

Bowden, Mark. 2013. The Killing Machines. How to Think About Drones. In: *The Atlantic*. 15. September 2013. www.theatlantic.com/magazine/archive/2013/09/the-killing-machines-how-to-think-about-drones/309434/ (3. Oktober 2023).

Bröckling, Ulrich. 2015. Heldendämmerung? Der Drohnenkrieg und die Zukunft des militärischen Heroismus. In: *Behemoth. A Journal on Civilisation* 8.2, 97–107.

Bröckling, Ulrich. 2016. Drohnen und Helden. In: *Vom Weihegefäß zur Drohne. Kulturen des Heroischen und ihre Objekte*. Hg. Achim Aurnhammer und Ulrich Bröckling. Würzburg, 291–301.

Bröckling, Ulrich. 2019. Antiheld. *Compendium heroicum*. 28. Februar 2019. DOI: 10.6094/heroicum/ahd1.0.

Bröckling, Ulrich. 2020. *Postheroische Helden. Ein Zeitbild*. Frankfurt am Main.

Bundesministerium der Verteidigung. 2018. Die Tradition der Bundeswehr. Richtlinien zum Traditionsverständnis und zur Traditionspflege. www.bmvg.de/resource/blob/23234/6a93123be919584d48e16c45a5d52c10/20180328-die-tradition-der-bundeswehr-data.pdf (16. Mai 2023).

Busch, Werner. 2014. Das Pathos der Sinnlosigkeit. Moderne Geschichtserfahrung in Francisco Goyas »Erschießung der Aufständischen«. In: *Bilder machen Geschichte. Historische Ereignisse im Gedächtnis der Kunst*. Hg. Uwe Fleckner. Berlin, 221–233.

Butter, Michael. 2016. *Der »Washington-Code«: Zur Heroisierung amerikanischer Präsidenten, 1775–1865*. Göttingen.

Carlyle, Thomas. 1901. *Über Helden, Heldenverehrung und das Heldentümliche in der Geschichte*. Leipzig.

Conermann, Stephan. 2006. *Das Mogulreich*. München.

Connell, Raewyn. 2005. *Masculinities*. 2. Edition. Oxford.

Connell, Raewyn. 2015. *Der gemachte Mann. Konstruktion und Krise von Männlichkeiten*. Wiesbaden.

Donaldson, Peter. 2021. *Sport, War and the British. 1850 to the Present*. London.

Doyé, Werner M. 2001. Arminius. In: *Deutsche Erinnerungsorte*, Band 3. Hg. Étienne François und Hagen Schulze. München, 587–602.

Eckert, Georg, u.a. 2024. *Umbrüche und Umdeutungen: Heroisierungen in historischer Perspektive* (Reflexionen des Heroischen). Göttingen.

Eich, Peter, Ralf von den Hoff und Sitta von Reden. Freiheitsheld (Antike). *Compendium heroicum* 10. Februar 2023. DOI: 10.6094/heroicum/fhhd1.2.20230210.

Emirbayer, Mustafa und Anna Mische. 1998. What Is Agency? In: *American Journal of Sociology* 103.4, 962–1023.

Enwezor, Okwui. 2017. Bildermachen. Ein Gespräch mit Thomas Struth. In: *Thomas Struth*. Hg. Thomas Weski und Ulrich Wilmes. München, 298–311.

Fanon, Frantz. 1986. *The Wretched of the Earth. The Handbook for the Black Revolution that is Changing the Shape of the World*. New York.

Feitscher, Georg. 2019. Körperlichkeit. *Compendium heroicum*. 1. August 2019. DOI: 10.6094/heroicum/kd1.0.20190801.

Feitscher, Georg. 2021. Erinnerung und Gedächtnis. *Compendium heroicum*. 16. Juni 2021. DOI: 10.6094/heroicum/egd1.3.20210616.

Feitscher, Georg. 2022. Heroische Qualitäten. In: *Compendium heroicum*. 29. Dezember 2022. DOI: 10.6094/heroicum/hqd1.0.20221229.

Feitscher, Georg. 2023. *Schlüsselkonzepte des Heroischen*. Göttingen.

Feitscher, Georg und Olmo Gölz. 2023. Sacrifice. In: *Encyclopedia of Heroism Studies*. Hg. Scott Allison u.a. Cham, 1–7.

Fried, Michael. 2008. *Warum Photographie als Kunst so bedeutend ist wie nie zuvor*. Mosel.

Foucault, Michel. 1983. *Der Wille zum Wissen. Sexualität und Wahrheit 1*. Übers. Ulrich Raulff und Walter Seittrer. Frankfurt am Main.

Foucault, Michel. 1988 [1969]. Was ist ein Autor? In: *Schriften zur Literatur*. Hg. von dems. Frankfurt am Main, 7–31.

Gaehtgens, Thomas W. und Gregor Wedekind (Hg.). 2009. *Le culte des grands hommes 1750–1850*. Paris.

Gage, Brandon. 2023. »Take Away Grandpa's Facebook«: House Republican Blasted after Bizarre Late-term Abortion Rant. *Alternet*. 31. März 2023. www.alternet.org/take-away-grandpas-facebook/ (29. Mai 2023).

Gelz, Andreas u.a. 2015. Phänomene der Deheroisierung in Vormoderne und Moderne. In: *helden. heroes. héros. E-Journal zu Kulturen des Heroischen* 3.1, 135–149. DOI: 10.6094/helden.heroes.heros/2015/01/13.

Gibbs, Nancy. 2014. Person of the Year. The Choice. *Time Magazine*. 10. Dezember 2014. time.com/time-person-of-the-year-ebola-fighters-choice/ (31. März 2023).

Giesen, Bernhard. 2004. *Triumph and Trauma*. Boulder.

Gilmour, Colin. 2018 . Orden und Ehrenzeichen. *Compendium heroicum*. 24. August 2018. DOI: 10.6094/heroicum/orden.

Gölz, Olmo. 2019a. Helden und Viele – Typologische Überlegungen zum Sog des Heroischen. Implikationen aus der Analyse des revolutionären Iran. In: *helden. heroes. héros. E-Journal zu Kulturen des Heroischen*, Special Issue 7: Heroische Kollektive. Zwischen Norm und Exzeptionalität, 7–20. DOI: 10.6094/helden.heroes.heros./2019/HK/02.

Gölz, Olmo. 2019b. Martyrdom and Masculinity in Warring Iran: The Karbala Paradigm, the Heroic, and the Personal Dimensions of War. In: *Behemoth* 12.1, 35–51. DOI: 10.6094/behemoth.2019.12.1.1005.

Gölz, Olmo. 2022. Kollektive. *Compendium heroicum*. 5. September 2022. DOI: 10.6094/heroicum/kolld1.2.20220905.

Gölz, Olmo und Cornelia Brink. 2020. Das Heroische und die Gewalt. Überlegungen zur Heroisierung der Gewalttat, ihres Ertragens und ihrer Vermeidung. Einleitung. In: *Gewalt und Heldentum*. Hg. Olmo Gölz und Cornelia Brink. Baden-Baden, 9–29.

Gründler, Hana. 2019. *Die Dunkelheit der Episteme. Zur Kunst des aufmerksamen Sehens*. Berlin.

Halberstam, Judith. 1998. *Female Masculinity*. Durham.

Harper, Tobias. 2020. *From Servants of the Empire to Everyday Heroes. The British Honours System in the Twentieth Century*. Oxford.

Harris, Ed. 2009. *The Footballer of Loos*, New York.

Hegel, Georg Wilhelm Friedrich. 1986. *Vorlesungen über die Ästhetik*, Band 1. Frankfurt am Main.

Heinemann, Gustav. 1969. Eid und Entscheidung. Gedenkrede des Bundespräsidenten Gustav Heinemann am 19. Juli 1969 in der Gedenkstätte Plötzensee, Berlin. *Stiftung 20. Juli 1944*. www.stiftung-20-juli-1944.de/reden/eid-und-entscheidung-dr-dr-gustav-heinemann-19071969 (16. Mai 2023).

Hemkendreis, Anne. 2023. Isaac Juliens »True North«: Bewahrende, verweigerte und schmelzende Gesten der Heroisierung. In: *helden.heroes.héroes. E-Journal zu Kulturen des Heroischen*, Special Issue 9: Heroische Gesten. Formensprachen politischer Körperlichkeit, 31–40. DOI: 10.6094/helden.heroes.heros./2023/HG/04.

Herzner, Volker. 1980. Die »Judith« der Medici. In: *Zeitschrift für Kunstgeschichte* 43.2, 139–180.

Himmler, Heinrich. 1943. Rede des Reichsführers-SS bei der SS-Gruppenführertagung in Posen am 4. Oktober 1943 (Document 1919-PS). In: *Trial of the Major War Criminals Before the International Military Tribunal*, Band 29: Documents and Other Material in Evidence. Numbers 1850-PS to 2233-PS, Nürnberg 1948, 110–173.

Hochbruck, Wolfgang. 2019. Feuerwehrleute. *Compendium heroicum*. 19 August 2019. DOI: 10.6094/heroicum/fd1.0.20190819.

Hubert, Hans. 2013. Gestaltungen des Heroischen in den Florentiner David-Plastiken. In: *Heroen und Heroisierungen in der Renaissance*. Hg. Achim Aurnhammer und Manfred Pfister. Wiesbaden, 181–217.

Hughes, Heather. 2021. Memorializing RAF Bomber Command in the United Kingdom. In: *Journal of War & Culture Studies* 16.3, 1–23. DOI: 10.1080/17526272.2021.1938840.

ʿImāra, Sāmī. 2015. »Būtīn .. Baṭal min hāṭā z-zamān«. *al-Ahrām*. 8. Februar 2015. gate.ahram.org.eg/daily/News/51451/135/358826/%D9%85%D9%84%D9%81-%D8%AE%D8%A7%D8%B5/%D8%A8%D9%88%D8%AA%D9%8A%D9%86-%D8%A8%D8%B7%D9%84-%D9%85%D9%86-%D9%87%D8%B0%D8%A7-%D8%A7%D9%84%D8%B2%D9%85%D8%A7%D9%86.aspx (29. Mai 2023).

Kantarbaeva-Bill, Irina. 2017. Vasily V. Vereshchagin (1842–1904): *Vae victis* in Asia and in Europe. In: *Cultural History* 6.1, 21–36. DOI: 10.3366/cult.2017.0133.

Kaplonski, Christopher. 2004. *Truth, History and Politics in Mongolia. The Memory of Heroes*. London.

Kemp, Wolfgang. 1985. Death at Work. A Case Study on Constitutive Blanks in Nineteenth-Century Painting. In: *Representations* 10, 101–123.

Koch, Daniel. 2018. »Wir suchen keine Götter in Weiß. Wir suchen Helden in Grün.« Das Heldenkonzept der Bundeswehr. In: *helden. heroes. héros. E-Journal zu Kulturen des Heroischen* 6.1, 57–59. DOI: 10.6094/helden.heroes.heros./2018/01/05.

Khosrokhavar, Farhad. 2005. *Suicide Bombers: Allah's New Martyrs*. London.

Lindner, Martin und Nils Steffensen (Hg.). 2023. *Classical Heroes in the 21st Century. New Perspectives on Contemporary Cinematic Narratives of Antiquity*. Baden-Baden.

Lopenzina, Drew. 2021. Columbus Falls: Recovering Indigenous Presence in the Public Sphere. In: *Resources for American Literary Study* 43.1–2, 176–205.

Lotman, Jurij M. 1972. *Die Struktur literarischer Texte*. München.

Luedtke, Brandon. 2012. Playing Fields and Battlefields. The Football Pitch, England and the First World War. In: *Britain and the World* 5.1, 96–115.

Lugones, María. 2010. Toward a Decolonial Feminism. In: *Hypatia* 25.4, 742–759.

Luhmann, Niklas. 1995. Die Autopoiesis des Bewußtseins. In: *Soziologische Aufklärung 6. Die Soziologie und der Mensch*. Opladen, 55–112.

MacGill, Patrick. 1916. *The Great Push. An Episode of the Great War*, London.

Masr, Mada. 2014. Actress Says Egypt Needs a Hitler Figure. *Mada Masr*. 14. Februar 2014. www.madamasr.com/en/2014/02/04/news/u/actress-says-egypt-needs-a-hitler-figure/ (3. August 2023).

Maradona, Diego. 2007. *Diego Armando Maradona with Daniel Arcucci and Ernesto Cherquis Bialo. The Autobiography of Soccer's Greatest and Most Controversial Star*. New York.

Marstaller, Vera und Dorna Safaian. 2023. Heroische Gesten. Einleitung. In: *helden. heroes. héros. E-Journal zu Kulturen des Heroischen*, Special Issue 9: Heroische Gesten. Formensprachen politischer Körperlichkeit, 3–8. DOI: 10.6094/helden.heroes.heros./2023/HG/01.

Mason, Tony und Eliza Riedi. 2010. *Sport and the Military. The British Armed Forces 1880-1960*. Cambridge/New York.

Mason, Tony. 2011. The Military, Sport and Physical Training. In: *Routledge Handbook of Sports Development*. Hg. Barrie Houlihan und Mick Green. London, 42–50.

Meuser, Michael. 2002. ›Doing Masculinity‹. Zur Geschlechtslogik männlichen Gewalthandelns. In: *Gewalt-Verhältnisse. Feministische Perspektiven auf Geschlecht und Gewalt*. Hg. Regina-Maria Dackweiler und Reinhild Schäfer. Frankfurt am Main, 53–79.

Mommertz, Monika. 2015. Gender. In: Ralf von den Hoff u.a.: Das Heroische in der neuen kulturhistorischen Forschung. Ein kritischer Bericht. In: *H-Soz-Kult*. 28. Juli 2015. www.hsozkult.de/literaturereview/id/fdl-136846.

Müller, Claudia und Isabell Oberle. 2020. Durchhalten. *Compendium heroicum*. 12. Februar 2020. DOI: 10.6094/heroicum/dud1.1.20200212.

Pink, Johanna. 2018. Dekolonisation. *Compendium heroicum*. 26. April 2018. DOI: 10.6094/heroicum/dekolonisation.

Pink, Johanna. 2020. Nationalheld. *Compendium heroicum*. 18. Februar 2020. DOI: 10.6094/heroicum/nd1.1.20200218.

Rankin, Lindsay E. und Alice H. Eagly. 2008. Is His Heroism Hailed and Hers Hidden? Women, Men, and the Social Construction of Heroism. In: *Psychology of Women Quarterly* 32.4, 414–422. DOI: 10.1111/j.1471-6402.2008.00455.x.

Plackinger, Andreas u.a. 2024. *Männer, Helden und Held:innen. Effekte des Heroischen in Geschlechterordnungen* (Reflexionen des Heroischen). Göttingen.

Rousseau, Jean-Jacques. 2009. Über die Tugend des Helden (1751). In: *Zeitschrift für Kulturphilosophie* 3.1, 117–128.

Ruchatz, Jens. 2023. Bild-Schrift-Konstellationen. In: *Handbuch Zeitschriftenforschung*. Hg. Oliver Scheiding und Sabina Fazli. Bielefeld, 109–129.

Safaian, Dorna. 2022. Greta Thunberg und die Ambivalenz heroischer Vulnerabilität. In: *helden. heroes. héros. E-Journal zu Kulturen des Heroischen*, Special Issue 8: Climate Heroism, 21–32. DOI: 10.6094/helden.heroes.heros./2022/CH/03.

Safaian, Dorna u.a. 2024. *Held:innen: Personalisierung – Subjektivierung – Autorität (Reflexionen des Heroischen)*. Göttingen.

Schlechtriemen, Tobias. 2016. The Hero and a Thousand Actors. On the Constitution of Heroic Agency. In: *helden. heroes. héros. E-Journal zu Kulturen des Heroischen* 4.1, 17–32. DOI: 10.6094/helden.heroes.heros./2016/01/03.

Schlechtriemen, Tobias. 2018. Der Held als Effekt. *Boundary work* in Heroisierungsprozessen. In: *Berliner Debatte Initial* 29.1, 106–119.

Schlechtriemen, Tobias. 2019. Handlungsmacht. In: *Compendium heroicum*. 14. November 2019. DOI: 10.6094/heroicum/hd1.0.20191114.

Schlechtriemen, Tobias. 2021. Grenzüberschreitung. In: *Compendium heroicum*. 15. Juni 2021. DOI: 10.6094/heroicum/gd1.1.20210615.

Sicardi, Arabelle und Sarah Tanat-Jones. 2020. *Queer Heroes. 53 LGBTQ-Held*innen von Sappho bis Freddie Mercury und Ellen DeGeneres*. München.

Söntgen, Beate. 2007. Am Rande des Ereignisses. Das Nachleben des 19. Jahrhunderts in Andreas Gurskys Serie »F1 Boxenstopp«. In: Beate Söntgen u.a (Hg.). *Andreas Gursky (Ausstellungskatalog, Kunstmuseum Basel, 2007–2008)*. Ostfildern, 49–68.

Sonderforschungsbereich 948. 2019a. Attraktionskraft. In: *Compendium heroicum*. 4. Februar 2019. DOI: 10.6094/heroicum/atd1.0.

Sonderforschungsbereich 948: 2019b. Held. In: *Compendium heroicum*. 1. Februar 2019. DOI: 10.6094/heroicum/hdd1.0.

Sonderforschungsbereich 948. 2019c. Medialität. In: *Compendium heroicum*. 16. Juli 2019. DOI: 10.6094/heroicum/md1.0.20190716.

Sonderforschungsbereich 948. 2022a. Heroisierung. In: *Compendium heroicum*. 18. August 2022. DOI: 10.6094/heroicum/hed1.2.20220818.

Sonderforschungsbereich 948. 2022b. Bewunderung und Verehrung. In: *Compendium heroicum*. 13. September 2022. DOI: 10.6094/heroicum/buvd2.0.20220913.

Sonderforschungsbereich 948. 2022c. Präfiguration. In: *Compendium heroicum*. 9. September 2022. DOI: 10.6094/heroicum/pfd1.1.20220909.

Sophokles. 2013. *Antigone*. Übers. Kurt Steinmann. Stuttgart.

Tacke, Charlotte. 1995. *Denkmal im sozialen Raum. Nationale Symbole in Deutschland und Frankreich im 19. Jahrhundert*. Göttingen.

Tilg, Stefan. 2021. Amazone. *Compendium heroicum*. 16. Juni 2021. DOI: 10.6094/heroicum/ad1.0.20210616.

Tilg, Stefan und Ralf von den Hoff. 2018. Zweikampf. *Compendium heroicum*. 23. Januar 2018. DOI: 10.6094/heroicum/zweikampf.

von den Hoff, Ralf u.a. 2018. Imitatio heroica. In: *Compendium heroicum*. 9. Oktober 2018. DOI: 10.6094/heroicum/imhd1.0.

Weber, Max. 2013. *Gesamtausgabe Abt. Bd. 23. Wirtschaft und Gesellschaft. Soziologie. Unvollendet 1919-1920*. Hg. Edith Hanke und Wolfgang Schluchter. Tübingen.

Wedekind, Gregor. 2014. Schiffbruch des Zuschauers. Théodore Géricaults »Floß der Medusa« als Dekonstruktion des Historienbildes. In: *Bilder machen Geschichte. Historische Ereignisse im Gedächtnis der Kunst.* Hg. Uwe Fleckner. Berlin, 235–253.

Weski, Thomas. 2017. Über das Bild hinaus. In: *Thomas Struth.* Hg. Thomas Weski und Ulrich Wilmes. München, 11–17.

Zwierlein, Cornel. 2020. Der Mörder als Held? Jacques Clément als ligistischer Staatsgründungs-Held und Märtyrer-Heroe des Papsttums, 1589. In: *Gewalt und Heldentum.* Hg. Olmo Gölz und Cornelia Brink. Baden-Baden, 47–66.

ABBILDUNGSNACHWEISE | IMAGE CREDITS

Anne Hemkendreis
HELD:INNEN UND IHR PUBLIKUM.
Zur Wahrnehmung und Bildwerdung wirkmächtiger Figuren

Abb. 1 / S. 26: Thomas Struth, »Audience 7, Florenz 2004«, Chromogenic print, 179,5 × 288,3 cm, Florenz 2004 (© Thomas Struth)

Abb. 2 / S. 27: Donatello, »David«, Bronzestatue, Florenz um 1440 (bpk / Scala – courtesy of the Ministero Beni e Att. Culturali)

Abb. 3 / S. 29: Detail aus Abb. 1 / S. 20 (© Thomas Struth)

Abb. 4 / S. 32: Kurt Raab in »Satansbraten« (Regie: Rainer Werner Fassbinder), BRD 1976 (IMAGO / Everett Collection)

Abb. 5 / S. 34: Vor dem Fahrradgeschäft von Herrn Pierre Cloarec hat sich eine Menschenmenge versammelt. Der Ladenbesitzer nimmt an der Tour de France teil. Pleybon, Frankreich, Juli 1939 (Robert Cappa © international center of photography / Magnum Photos)

Abb. 6 / S. 35: Installationsansicht von Thomas Struths »Art Institute of Chicago 1, Chicago 1990« (links) in der Ausstellung »Making Time« im Prado, Madrid (Foto: Atelier Thomas Struth, 2007)

Abb. 7 / S. 37: Thomas Struth, »Louvre 4, Paris 1989«, Chromogenic print, 187,0 × 211,0 cm, Paris 1989 (© Thomas Struth)

Abb. 8 / S. 38: Jean-Léon Gérôme, »The Execution of Marshal Ney«, Öl auf Leinwand, 65,2 × 104,2 cm, 1855–65 (Sheffield Museums Trust / Bridgeman Images)

Abb. 9 / S. 40: Barnett Newman, »Vir Heroicus Sublimis«, Öl auf Leinwand, 242,2 × 541,7 cm, 1950–51 (Peter Barritt / SuperStock / Bridgeman Images © Barnett Newman Foundation / VG Bild-Kunst, Bonn 2024)

Abb. 10 / S. 41: Andreas Gursky, »Rückblick«, Tintenstrahldruck, 2015 (© Andreas Gursky / Courtesy Sprüth Magers / VG Bild-Kunst, Bonn 2024)

Vera Marstaller
MEDIALISIERUNG

Abb. 1 / S. 48: Santiago Barbeito, Deckenmalerei mit Lionel Messi und Diego Maradona nach Michelangelos Fresko »Die Erschaffung Adams«, anlässlich der Fußball-WM gefertigt im April 2018, Buenos Aires, 13.6.2018 (Amilcar Orfali / Getty Images)

Abb. 2 / S. 49: Jacques-Louis David, »Der Schwur im Ballhaus am 20. Juni 1789«, Federzeichnung / Tusche, 66 × 101,2 cm, Paris 1791 (bpk / RMN – Grand Palais / Gérard Blot)

Abb. 3 / S. 52: Seite aus der Sonderausgabe »Frankreichs Zusammenbruch« der Zeitschrift »Die Wehrmacht«, 6.7.1940, S. 24 (MHM, BAAZ0215)

Abb. 4 / S. 53: »Memorial to Heroic Self-Sacrifice« (Denkmal für heroische Selbstaufopferung), City of London, 11.8.2017 (mauritius images / Chris Dorney / Alamy / Alamy Stock Photos)

Abb. 5 / S. 54: Frida-Kahlo-Lookalikes während des Versuchs, den Guinness-Weltrekord für die größte Versammlung von Menschen, die als Frida Kahlo verkleidet sind, zu brechen, Dallas Museum of Art, 6.7.2017 (picture alliance/AP Photo | Tailyr Irvine)

Abb. 6 / S. 55: Lediesis, »SuperFrida«, Neapel 2020 (SuperFrida – Lediesis)

Abb. 7 / S. 56: Fußballtraining unter dem Deckengemälde (vgl. Abb. 1 / S. 42), Buenos Aires, 24.4.2018 JUAN MABROMATA / AFP / Getty Images)

Abb. 8 / S. 57: Michelangelo Buonarroti, »Die Erschaffung Adams«, Fresco, 280 × 570 cm, Vatikan 1511/1512 (akg-images)

Abb. 9 / S. 61: Feierstunde im Ehrenhof des Bendlerblocks zum Gedenken an den Widerstand gegen den Nationalsozialismus, Berlin, 20.7.2006 (© 2006 Bundeswehr | Mandt)

Johanna Pink
POLARISIERUNG

Abb. 1 / S. 65: Souvenirladen mit Objekten, die Bilder des syrischen Präsidenten al-Assad, des russischen Präsidenten Putin und des Hisbollah-Führers Nasrallah zeigen, Damaskus, 27.2.2022. (LOUAI BESHARA / AFP / Getty Images)

Abb. 2 / S. 66: Mitglieder der Klimaprotestgruppe »Extinction Rebellion« während einer Blockade der verkehrsreichsten Straßen im Stadtzentrum von Manchester, 31.8.2019 (mauritius images / Alamy Stock Photos / Dave Ellison)

Abb. 3 / S. 67: Verächtliches Meme gegen Greta Thunberg, Instagram-Post, Dezember 2019 (published by bojkottagreta, Instagram)

Abb. 4 / S. 68: Martin Erl, Karikatur zum Tag der Menschenrechte, 10.12.2019 (picture alliance / dieKLEINERT.de / Martin Erl | Martin Erl)

Abb. 5 / S. 70: Wassilij Wassiljewitsch Wereschtschagin, »Die Apotheose des Krieges«, Öl auf Leinwand, 127 × 197 cm, o. O. 1871 (akg-images)

Abb. 6 / S. 71: Ehrenwache vor dem Regierungspalast in Ulaanbaatar, Mongolei, 16.5.2024 (mauritius images / Andrey Shevchenko / Alamy / Alamy Stock Photos)

Abb. 7 / S. 73: Amerikanische Aktivist:innen reißen die Statue von Christoph Kolumbus auf dem Gelände des State Capitol nieder, St. Paul, Minnesota, USA, 10.6.2020 (picture alliance / ZUMAPRESS.com | Chris Juhn)

Abb. 8 / S. 74 l.: Queen Mum enthüllt ein Denkmal für »Bomber Harris«, London, 31.5.2024 (picture-alliance / dpa | PA John Stillwell)

Abb. 9 / S. 74 r.: Denkmal für »Bomber Harris« nach einer Farbattacke, London, 29.10.1992 (»Bomber« Harris monument, 1992 CC BY-SA/2.0 – © Christopher Hilton - geograph.org.uk/p/3333572)

Abb. 10 / S. 76: Mahnwache im Andenken an den Freiheitskämpfer Bhagat Singh anlässlich seines 83. Todestags in Lahore, Pakistan, 23.3.2014 (mauritius images / Pacific Press Media Production Corp. / Alamy / Alamy Stock Photos)

Abb. 11 / S. 77: Die ugandische Klimaaktivistin Vanessa Nakate, die Friedensnobelpreisträgerin Malala Yousafzai und die schwedische Aktivistin Greta Thunberg bei ihrer Teilnahme an einem »Fridays For Future«-Protest vor dem schwedischen Parlament in Stockholm, 10.6.2022 (picture alliance / REUTERS | Reuters Staff)

Stefan Tilg
KAMPF / FIGHTING

Abb. 1 / S. 81: Klimaaktivist:innen der »Letzten Generation« werden von einem Verkehrsteilnehmer mit Wasser überschüttet, Autobahn A100, 25.5.2023 (picture alliance / dpa | Paul Zinken)

Abb. 2 / S. 83: Gerard Butler als König Leonidas im Film »300« (Regie: Zack Snyder), USA/Kanada 2006 (picture-alliance / Mary Evans Picture Library)

IMAGE CREDITS

Abb. 3 / S. 84:	Banner an einem Haus an der Rheinuferpromenade mit der Aufschrift »Danke an alle Helden des Alltags. Gemeinsam gegen Corona«, Düsseldorf, 5.4.2020 (picture alliance / dpa | David Young)
Abb. 4 / S. 86:	Deckengemälde in der Kirche in Woldendorp bei Groningen, 5.5.2018 (Hardscarf, https://commons.wikimedia.org/wiki/File:Westerwijtwerd_-_Friese_kampvechters.jpg, https://creativecommons.org/licenses/by-sa/4.0/legalcode)
Abb. 5 / S. 87:	Ukrainische Briefmarke »Russisches Kriegsschiff, f*ck dich …!«, Ukraine, 12.4.2022, (Boris Groh, https://commons.wikimedia.org/wiki/File:Stamp_of_Ukraine_s1985.jpg, »Stamp of Ukraine s1985«, als gemeinfrei gekennzeichnet)
Abb. 6 / S. 89:	St. Georg tötet weiblichen Drachen, aus einem Stundenbuch des Sarumer Usus, Frankreich 1440–1450 (Oxford, Bodleian Library MS. Auct. D. inf. 2. 11, fol 44v)
Abb. 7 / S. 90:	100-Meter-Sprintrennen bei den Invictus Games 2014, London, 11.9.2014 (Ben Hoskins / Getty Images for Invictus Games)
Abb. 8 / S. 92:	Moritz von Schwind, »Der Sängerkrieg auf der Wartburg«, Aquarell und Bleistift auf Papier, 47,8 × 75,1 cm, o. O., 1837 (Staatliche Kunsthalle Karlsruhe, VIII 2467, CC0)
Abb. 9 / S. 95:	Paul Zeaiter, »Elon Musk gegen Mark Zuckerberg« (Paul ›ZEET‹ Zeaiter (Instagram, TikTok – @OGZEET))

Tobias Schlechtriemen
GRENZÜBERSCHREITUNG

Abb. 1 / S. 96:	Münze mit Kopf Alexanders des Großen mit Binde des Gottes Dionysos, Elefantenskalp und Widderhorn, Gold, 3.-4. Jh. n. Chr. (mauritius images / PRISMA ARCHIVO / Alamy / Alamy Stock Photos)
Abb. 2 / S. 97:	Melli-Beese-Lounge im Flughafen Berlin-Tempelhof, 9.5.2010 (Steffen Sauder, Melli Beese Lounge, https://www.flickr.com/photos/feffef/4592648707/, CC BY-NC-SA 2.0 DEED)
Abb. 3 / S. 98:	Skulptur von Rosa Parks im National Civil Rights Museum, Memphis, Tennessee, USA, 7.5.2020 (mauritius images / Martin Thomas Photography / Alamy / Alamy Stock Photos)
Abb. 4 / S. 101:	Greta Thunberg im Dokumentarfilm »I Am Greta« (Regie: Nathan Grossman), Deutschland/Schweden 2020 (mauritius images / Cinema-Legacy-Collection / Hulu /THA)

Abb. 5 / S. 103:   Titelseite der »Daily News« zur Notlandung des US-Airways-Flug 1549 im Hudson River, New York, 16.1.2009 (New York Daily News Archive / Getty Images)

Abb. 6 / S. 104:   Keyvisual von »Unterwelt – Partizipative App-Oper auf Grundlage des Orpheus-Mythos«, Uraufführung am 29. Juni 2019 in der Staatsoper Hannover (Niedersächsische Staatstheater Hannover GmbH)

Abb. 7 / S. 106:   Antoine-Félix Bouré, Statue des Lykurg im 1883 eingeweihten Justizpalast in Brüssel, 22.6.2012 (mauritius images / Jozef sedmak / Alamy / Alamy Stock Photos)

Abb. 8 / S. 107:   Sébastien Norblin, »Antigone donnant la sépulture à Polynice«, Öl auf Leinwand, 114 × 146 cm, 1825 (bpk / RMN - Grand Palais)

Abb. 9 / S. 110, 111:   Mayur Shelke rettet ein Kind aus einem Gleisbett vor einem herannahenden Zug, Aufnahmen einer Überwachungskamera, Vagani, Indien, 17.4.2021 (INDIA MINISTRY OF RAILWAYS / AFP)

Dorna Safaian
HANDLUNGSMACHT

Abb. 1 / S. 114:   Szene aus »Spider-Man 2« (Regie: Sam Raimi), USA 2004 (IMAGO / Allstar)

Abb. 2 / S. 117:   Carola Rackete verlässt das Seenotrettungsschiff Sea-Watch 3, Lampedusa, Italien, 29.6.2019 (picture alliance / REUTERS | GUGLIELMO MANGIAPANE)

Abb. 3 / S. 118:   Das 1901 eingeweihte Louis-Pasteur-Denkmal in Arbois, Frankreich (Horace Daillon, Bildhauer und Georges Debrie, Architekt), 2016 (mauritius images / Jason Knott / Alamy / Alamy Stock Photos)

Abb. 4 / S. 119:   Screenshot aus dem Bundeswehrvideo »Unsichtbare Helden: Kampfschwimmer befreien Geiseln«, 2024 (© Bundeswehr)

Abb. 5 / S. 121:   Szene aus »1917« (Regie: Sam Mendes), USA/UK 2019 (ddp / Capital Pictures)

Abb. 6 / S. 124:   Tom of Finland (Touko Laaksonen), ohne Titel, Graphit auf Papier, 1973 (© Tom of Finland Foundation / VG Bild-Kunst, Bonn 2024)

Abb. 7 / S. 125:   Nordvietnamesisches Propagandaplakat mit bewaffneter Frau, Vietnam 1977 (IMAGO / Gemini Collection)

Olmo Gölz

EINSATZ. Der Einsatz als bestimmendes Element des Heroischen

Abb. 1 / S. 128: Jacobus de Teramo, »Litigatio Christi cum Belial«, Buchseite, o. O. 1461 (© Bayerische Staatsbibliothek / Cgm 48)

Abb. 2 / S. 131 l.: Abraham Storck, »Walfang im Polarmeer«, Öl auf Leinwand, 50,5 × 66,5 cm, 1654–1708 (Rijksmuseum, SK-A-4102, CC0 1.0 DEED)

Abb. 3 / S. 131 r.: Greenpeace-Aktivist:innen versuchen, das Verladen eines Wals auf das Walfang-Fabrikschiff Nisshin Maru zu verhindern, Südlicher Ozean, 11. 1. 2006 (picture-alliance / dpa / dpaweb | Jeremy_Sutton-Hibbert / Handout)

Abb. 4 / S. 134: Thomas Krejtschi, Buchcover für »John Maynard« von Theodor Fontane, 2008 (Kindermann Verlag)

Abb. 5 / S. 135: Abbas al-Musawi, »Die Schlacht von Kerbela«, Öl auf Leinwand, 175,4 × 341,6 cm, spätes 19. / frühes 20. Jahrhundert (Photo © Brooklyn Museum / Gift of K. Thomas Elghanayan in honor of Nourollah Elghanayan / Bridgeman Images)

Abb. 6 / S. 136: Franz Dorrenbach, Kriegerdenkmal auf dem ehemaligen Neuen Garnisonfriedhof (heute Friedhof Columbiadamm) in Berlin, 1925, 27. 6. 2014 (picture alliance / dpa | Wolfgang Kumm)

Abb. 7 / S. 138: Gedenktafel für verfolgte Kriegsdienstverweigerer, Karlsruhe 18. 2. 2022, (Jensbuko, https://commons.wikimedia.org/wiki/File:Karlsaue_6.jpg, https://creativecommons.org/licenses/by-sa/4.0/legalcode)

Abb. 8 / S. 139: John Eckstein, George-Washington-Statue mit der Inschrift »First In War / First In Peace / And / First In The Hearts Of / His Country«, Philadelphia, ca. 1806 (© 1806 The Society of the Cincinnati)

Abb. 9 / S. 143: GSG 9 Situationstraining, o. O. / o. D. (Bundespolizei)

Georg Eckert

VORBILD

Abb. 1 / S. 145: Rouwhorst + Van Roon, »Gandhi, King, Mandela: We Have A Dream«. Plakat zur Ausstellung in der Nieuwe Kerk, Amsterdam 2017–2018 (Graphic Design: Rouwhorst + Van Roon, Amsterdam)

Abb. 2 / S. 146: Plakat zum Kinofilm »Alexander« (Regie: Oliver Stone), USA 2004 (IMAGO / United Archives)

Abb. 3 / S. 148:   Celtic- und Rangers-Fans während eines Fußballspiels, Celtic Park, Glasgow, 10. 9. 2016 (Steve Welsh / Getty Images)

Abb. 4 / S. 149:   Porträtskulpturen des Dichters Stefan George und von Angehörigen des George-Kreises (Foto: Chris Korner/DLA Marbach)

Abb. 5 / S. 151:   Württemberg‹sches Turnfest in Reutlingen, 1845, Postkarte (Landesarchiv Baden-Württemberg, Hauptstaatsarchiv Stuttgart, E 146 Bü 8468)

Abb. 6 / S. 152:   César-Auguste Hébert (Graveur) nach Henri Hendrick (Maler), »Beginn der belgischen Revolution in Brüssel am 25. August 1830« (© Look and Learn / Bridgeman Images)

Abb. 7 / S. 153:   »Ruhm und Ehre unseren Aktivisten. Tag der Aktivisten – 13. Oktober 1951«, Bild-Text-Plakat, 85 × 59 cm, DDR 1951 (akg-images)

Abb. 8 / S. 154:   Walter Gropius vor dem Wettbewerbsentwurf des Chicago Tribune-Gebäudes, Berlin, 15. 5. 1933 (picture alliance / AP | anonymous)

Abb. 9 / S. 155:   Königin Elisabeth II. mit Angehörigen der Victoria Cross und der George Cross Association, London, 16. 5. 2018 (IMAGO / i Images)

Abb. 10 / S. 156:   Frank Nowlan, »James Hill Jones, VC, Attacking the Enemy«, Öl auf Leinwand, 54 × 83,2 cm, o. O. 1893, (Llyfrgell Genedlaethol Cymru / The National Library of Wales, Accession number PZ05054)

Abb. 11 / S. 158:   Claus Schenk Graf von Stauffenberg in der »Wolfsschanze« mit Adolf Hitler, der den General der Flieger Karl Bodenschatz begrüßt. Rechts daneben steht Generalfeldmarschall Wilhelm Keitel. Kr. Rastenburg/Ostpreußen, 15. 7. 1944 (akg-images)

Abb. 12 / S. 159:   John Everett Millais, »The Black Brunswicker«, Öl auf Leinwand, 104 × 68,5 cm, 1860 (akg-images / WHA / World History Archive)

Abb. 13 / S. 163:   Gedenkstein von der Marwitz, nach 1781, Dorfkirche Friedersdorf (Gemeinde Vierlinden, Ldkr. Märkisch-Oderland), um 2020 (Familienarchiv von der Marwitz)

Abb. 14 / S. 164:   Donatello, »Judith und Holofernes«, Bronzeguss, Florenz 1453–1457 (Raffaello Bencini / Bridgeman Images)

Joachim Grage
MASKULINITÄT

Abb. 1 / S. 170:   Walhalla – Viktoria und Büsten an der Ostwand, Donaustauf, 19. 5. 2016 (© Bayerische Schlösserverwaltung, Rainer Herrmann, München)

Abb. 2 / S. 171:   Ein Kadett der Suworow-Militärschule steht während der Abschlussfeier an der Moskauer Militärkadettenschule vor dem Porträt Suworows, 12.6.2004 (DENIS SINYAKOV / AFP / Getty Images)

Abb. 3 / S. 174:   Hans Bohrdt, »Der letzte Mann«, 1914 (akg-images)

Abb. 4 / S. 175:   Ausstellungsansicht aus der documenta 6 mit Ulrike Rosenbachs »Herakles – Herkules – King Kong. Die Vorbilder der Mannsbilder«, Kassel 1977 (© documenta archiv / Foto: Dieter Schwerdtle © Ulrike Rosenbach, VG Bild-Kunst, Bonn 2024)

Abb. 5 / S. 177:   Tätowierter Seemann und sein Vogel, der auf einem Modell eines Schiffes sitzt, 24.4.1940 (Mitchell Library, State Library of New South Wales and Courtesy ACP Magazines Ltd)

Abb. 6 / S. 178:   Vladimir Putin reitet im Urlaub auf einem Pferd, Russland, 4.8.2009 (IMAGO / ZUMA Press)

Abb. 7 / S. 179:   Emmanuel Macron im offenen Hemd, 17.4.2022, © Foto: Soazig de la Moissonnière (Offizielle Fotografin von Emmanuel Macron / Instagram - https://www.instagram.com/p/Ccc0oBLLTVP)

Abb. 8 / S. 180:   Begeisterte Frauen strecken ihre Hände nach Adolf Hitler aus, o.O. 1940 (SZ Photo/Süddeutsche Zeitung Photo)

Abb. 9 / S. 183:   John Charles Dollman, »A Very Gallant Gentleman«, Öl auf Leinwand, 1913 (Bridgeman Images)

Abb. 10 / S. 184:   Melli Beese beim Unterricht in ihrer Flugschule, Berlin, 1.4.1912 (ullstein bild - Berliner Illustrations Gesellschaft)

Abb. 11 / S. 185:   Eine Widmung mit der Aufschrift »Mensch, Mann, Held« liegt neben Blumen am Urnengrab des getöteten Malte C. am Waldfriedhof Lauheide, 4.10.2022 (picture alliance / dpa | Bernd Thissen)

Frank Reichherzer
MIT DEM FUßBALL DURCHS NIEMANDSLAND. Suchfelder des Heroischen in der Sinnlosigkeit des Massenkrieges. Ereignis: »The best kicked goal in history«

Abb. 1 / S. 190:   Harry Tyers, »LOOS. Hi Ref.! blow up! he's off-side«, 1915 (The Tyers' Family und The London Irish Rifles Regimental Association)

Abb. 2 / S. 191:   Elizabeth Southerden Thompson, Lady Butler, »A London Irish at Loos«, 1916 (mauritius images / The Picture Art Collection / Alamy / Alamy Stock Photos)

Abb. 3 / S. 193:   Britische Soldaten beim Fußballspielen, Thessaloniki/Griechenland, 25.12.1915 (Universal History Archive/UIG / Bridgeman Images)

Abb. 4 / S. 195:   Richard Caton Woodville Jr., »The Surreys Play the Game«, Zeitungsgrafik in »The Illustrated London News«, Londo,n 29.7.1916 (picture alliance / Mary Evans Picture Library)

Abb. 5 / S. 198:   Wirtshausschild des »Rifleman Pub«, Twickenham, England, 13.10.2015, (mauritius images / Mick Sinclair / Alamy / Alamy Stock Photos)

Abb. 6 / S. 199:   Richard Caton Woodville, »The Charge of the Light Brigade«, Heliogravüre, London 1895 (© National Army Museum / Bridgeman Images)

Abb. 7 / S. 200:   Titelseite der Zeitung »Daily Sketch«, London, 22.7.1916 (mauritius images / John Frost Newspapers / Alamy / Alamy Stock Photos)

Abb. 8 / S. 202:   Artikel »Fußball bei Sturmangriff« im »Wochenblatt für Zschopau und Umgegend«, Zschopauer Tageblatt u. Anzeiger, Zschopau, 29.7.1916 (SLUB Dresden, http://digital.slub-dresden.de/id512512809-1916072901)

Abb. 9 / S. 205 o.:   Statue »Footballer of Loos« (The London Irish Rifles Regimental Association)

Abb. 10 / S. 205 u.:   Briefmarke der Royal Mail mit dem Ball aus der Schlacht von Loos, 2015 (Mit freundlicher Genehmigung der The London Irish Rifles Regimental Association, Briefmarken-Design © Royal Mail Group Limited 2015)

PRINZIP HELD*. Eine Ausstellung

akg-images / Album / Prisma, S. 226 r. o.

akg-images / Interfoto S. 222 r.

akg-images / Universal Images Group / Underwood Archive S. 230 r. o.

akg-images S. 223 l., 231 r. o.

Alpha Stock / Alamy Stock Photo S. 232 l.

Archiv Volksbund Deutsche Kriegsgräberfürsorge e. V. S. 227 l.

© Axel Springer SE S. 221 l. o.

BArch, Bild 183-1983-0617-302 S. 227 r.

Bayerische Staatsbibliothek München, 2 Belg. 84 f-2, S. 293, urn:nbn:de:bvb:12-bsb11455618-1 S. 223 r. u.

bpk / Hamburger Kunsthalle / Christoph Irrgang S. 217 r. u. r.

bpk / Kunstbibliothek, SMB, Photothek Willy Römer / Willy Römer S. 216 l. u.

bpk / RMN - Grand Palais / Agence Bulloz S. 234 l. u.

Bundeswehr / Thomas Bierbaum S. 230 l. u.

Bundeswehr / Torsten Kraatz S. 230 r. u.

buttinette Textil-Versandhaus GmbH, Industriestr. 22, 86637 Wertingen, Tel. 08272/9966-6, E-Mail: service@buttinette.de, www.buttinette-fasching.com S. 229 r. u.

Carl T. Gossett / NYT / Redux / laif S. 209, 217 m.

Cinema Libre Studio S. 228 r.

EPA-EFE / FAROOQ KHAN S. 210, 216 l. o.

Familie Rosenthal S. 233 l.

Freiwillige Feuerwehr Denzlingen S. 232 r.

From the British Library archive / Bridgeman Images S. 231 l. u.

Heritage Images / Fine Art Images / akg-images S. 234 r.

IMAGO / Everett Collection S. 223 m. o., 223 m. u.

IMAGO / Gemini Collection S. 229 l. o.

IMAGO / Pond5 Images S. 229 r. o.

IMAGO / ZUMA Press S. 218 l. o., S. 224 r.

© Look and Learn / Bridgeman Images S. 217 r. u. l.

Mario Tama / Getty Images S. 222 l. u.

mauritius images / Gonzales Photo / Alamy Stock Photos S. 217 l. o.

mauritius images / Shawshots / Alamy / Alamy Stock Photos S. 217 l. u.

mauritius images / Steve Tulley / Alamy / Alamy Stock Photos S. 220 r.

MHM Berlin-Gatow, W. Heldenmaier S. 224 l. u.

MHM, BBAN6189 S. 225 r.

Nasjonalbiblioteket / National Library of Norway, 3c113, public domain S. 235 l. u.

Nasjonalbiblioteket / National Library of Norway, 3c119, public domain S. 235 l. o.

Noam Galai / Getty Images S. 230 l. o.

NOEL CELIS / AFP / Getty Images S. 213, 216 r. m. u.

PEACHY KINGS © Tom of Finland Foundation / VG Bild-Kunst, Bonn 2024 S. 228 l.

Photo © Brooklyn Museum / Gift of K. Thomas Elghanayan in honor of Nourollah Elghanayan / Bridgeman Images S. 232 u.

Photo © CCI / Bridgeman Images S. 223 r. o.

Photo © Fine Art Images / Bridgeman Images S. 231 l. o.

Photo © Photo Josse / Bridgeman Images S. 226 l. o.

picture alliance / AA / Anadolu Agency S. 217 m. u.

picture alliance / AP Photo | Rich Pedroncelli S. 216 r. m. o.

picture alliance / ASSOCIATED PRESS | Uncredited S. 233 u.

picture alliance / dpa | Anja Niedringhaus S. 235 r.

picture alliance / dpa / MAXPPP | Vallauri Nicolas S. 216 r. u.

picture alliance / Heritage Images | The Print Collector S. 217 l. m.

picture alliance / REUTERS | Shamil Zhumatov S. 231 r. u.

picture alliance / ZUMAPRESS.com | Dr. Li Wenliang S. 222 l. o.

picture alliance / ZUMAPRESS.com | Ximena Borrazas S. 208, 217 o.

picture-alliance S. 220 l. u.

picture-alliance / dpa | epa Thew S. 211, 216 l. m.

picture-alliance / dpa | Roland Scheidemann S. 234 l. o.

Printerado e. K. S. 233 r.

Privatbesitz S. 221 r.

Public domain (CC0), Rijksmuseum, RP-P-OB-81.802 S. 226 l. u.

Rimini Protokoll S. 214–215, 216 m. o., 216 r. o., 218–219, 225 r., 226 r. u., 231 r. m., 236–239

The Asahi Shimbun / Getty Images S. 212, 216 m. u.

Toto @ Matinino, https://www.flickr.com/photos/matinino/49924892831/, CC BY 2.0 DEED S. 221 l. u.

IMPRESSUM | IMPRINT

Ausstellung

Prinzip Held*
Von Heroisierungen und Heroismen
vom 21.06. bis 03.11.2024

Projektleitung MHMBw	Dr. Doris Müller-Toovey (MHMBw)
Produktionsleitung MHMBw	Stefan Kontra M.A. (MHMBw)
Projektleitung Teilprojekt T SFB 948	Prof. Dr. Ralf von den Hoff (SFB)
	Dr. Gorch Pieken (ZMSBw)
Leitung wiss. Kuratierung und Konzeption	Dr. Gorch Pieken (ZMSBw)
Wiss. Kuratierung, Textredaktion und Lektorat	Katja Widmann M.A. (SFB)
Wiss. Kuratierung und Curator on Site	Andreas Geißler M.A. (MHMBw)
Museumsberatung	Oberstleutnant Dr. Heiner Bröckermann (ZMSBw)
Ausstellungstexte	Katja Widmann M.A. (SFB), Dr. Gorch Pieken (ZMSBw), Andreas Geißler M.A. (MHMBw)
Bildrecherche	Steffen Jungmann M.A. (MHMBw)
Lizenzierung	Steffen Jungmann M.A., Daniel Schmiedke M.A. (MHMBw)
Bildrecherche und Textarbeiten	Mag. Ansgar Snethlage (MHMBw)
Wiss./stud. Hilfskraft	Alina Casanova M.A. (SFB)
	Justus Widmann (SFB)
	Jacob Hovde (SFB)
	Michelle Kollmann (SFB)
	Emelie Mayer (SFB)
	Charlotte Kleinert (SFB)
	Camilla Körner M.A. (SFB)
Praktikantin	Ina Derboven (ZMSBw)
Kommunikation, Marketing, Presse- und Öffentlichkeitsarbeit	Jan Kindler M.A., Dipl.-Germ. Gerrit Reichert, Neele Dinges M.A., Hauptmann Ann-Kathrin Nicolai (MHMBw), Alexandra Lauck (Rimini Protokoll)
Unterstützung Kommunikation durch SRH Fernhochschule	Prof. Dr. Thomas Bippes, Johannes Ebner, Aileen Hufschmidt, Hans-Christian Tetzner
Bildung und Vermittlung	Karin Grimme M.A. (MHMBw)

Handreichungen für Lehrende an Schulen (SFB 948, Teilprojekt Ö)	StR Mathias Jehle, Kristina Seefeldt M.A., Prof. Dr. Wolfgang Hochbruck, Jan Bahr B.A., Jessica Pape M.Ed., Dipl-Pol. Daniel Kirchner, StR Nina Kurus, Claire Steffen B.A., Tijen Kara, Jacob Hovde B.A., Greta Engerer B.A.
Führungsmanagement	Bereich Museumspädagogik MHMBw Berlin-Gatow
Übersetzungen	Bundessprachenamt
Unterstützung engl. Lektorat	guiskard studio Editorial Services
Grafische Bearbeitung Booklets, Werbemedien	Christian Nimpsch, Alexander Nickel (MHMBw)
Grafikproduktion	Kommando Strategische Aufklärung, Abt. J2 QS/Produktionsunterstützung
Technik und Schnitt Interviews/Ausstellungsmedien	Berlin: Volkan T error (Noizdamar) Freiburg: Jacob Hovde, Charlotte Kleinert, Michelle Kollmann, Emelie A. Mayer Karlsruhe: Benjamin Breitkopf Dipl. Medienpäd., Dipl. Sozpäd. Wolfgang Krause, Medienzentrum der Universitätsbibliothek Freiburg
Traversensystem Planung/Betreuung	kursiv	text – objekt – raum GmbH, Thomas Bache
Traversensystem Planung/Montage	STRAIGHT Technical Solutions, Jens Graube
Bereitstellung von Traversenteilen der Ausstellung »Gewalt und Geschlecht«	Sven Birke M.A. (MHMBw)
Elektrik	Rimini Protokoll, Marcel Kempe (MHMBw)
Beschaffungsmanagement MHMBw Berlin-Gatow	Hauptfeldwebel Ronny Altrichter (MHMBw)
Infrastrukturbetreuung MHMBw Berlin-Gatow	Hauptmann Alexander Hering (MHMBw)
Geschäftsführung SFB/Schnittstelle zwischen operativer Steuerung und Budgetierung	Dr. Sebastian Meurer, Paula Schulze M.A. (SFB)
Schnittstelle Rechnungs- und Kassenwesen SFB	Maria Villalobos (SFB)
Leihgaben und Schenkungen für die Szenographie	Luftumschlagzug LTG 62 THW Landesverband Berlin, Brandenburg, Sachsen-Anhalt; Ortsverband Herzberg
Bereitstellung Bw-Mobiliar für Szenographie	Bereich Restaurierung MHM Berlin-Gatow, Hauptfeldwebel Jessica Fleischmann, Hauptmann Alexander Hering (MHMBw)

Rimini Protokoll – Gestaltung

Künstlerische Leitung	Helgard Haug und Daniel Wetzel
Konzept & Gestaltung	Helgard Haug, Daniel Wetzel, Dominik Steinmann

Szenografie	Dominik Steinmann
Mitarbeit Szenografie	Anna Knöller
Grafik Konzept & Design	Ilona Marti
Gestaltung Inflatables in Zusammenarbeit mit	Urs Meier, Luft & Laune
Interaction & Interface Design, Programmierung & Elektronik Inflatables	Georg Werner
Audios/Interviews	Helgard Haug, Daniel Wetzel
Licht Design, Layout LED-Wand	Robert Läßig
Sound Design	Rozenn Lièvre
Video Design	Stefan Korsinsky
Mitarbeit Recherche & Koordination	Grit Lieder
Werkplanung technische Umsetzung, Bauüberwachung	Thomas Bache, kursiv | text – objekt – raum GmbH
Produktion Inflatables	Urs Meier, Luft & Laune
Produktionsleitung	Juliane Männel
Mitarbeit Produktion	Ksenia Lukina
Ausstellungsproduktion und -aufbau	MHMBw Berlin-Gatow, Bereich Ausstellung und Restaurierung Rimini Protokoll Produktionsteam (u.a. Vladimir Bondarenko, Lisa Eßwein, Kristian Könner, Julian Lück, Felix Leopold Noe, Klaudiusz Schimanowski, Hendrik Voigt, Georg Werner) Dominik Steinmann, Anna Knöller
Keyvisual	Ilona Marti
Werbemedien	Ilona Marti mit Unterstützung von Alexander Nickel, Christian Nimpsch (MHMBw)
Ausstellungsgrafik	Ilona Marti mit Unterstützung von Alexander Nickel, Christian Nimpsch (MHMBw)
Praktikant	Lewin Ott (kursiv | text – objekt – raum GmbH)
Besonderer Dank an	Emma Clarke und PJ Stanley, Claudia Ludwig und die Technik der Volksbühne am Rosa-Luxemburg-Platz, Dr. Christian Russenberger (Universität Rostock), René Rosette – BRAL Reststoff-Bearbeitungs GmbH

Autor:innen/Pat:innen der Fallbeispiele

Kein Held ohne Vorbilder – Stefan George	Prof. Dr. Achim Aurnhammer
Erste sein – Melli Beese, Pilot	Prof. Dr. Cornelia Brink

Desertieren	Prof. Dr. Ulrich Bröckling
Stauffenberg	PD Dr. Georg Eckert
Machtverzicht als demokratische Heldentat – George Washington	PD Dr. Georg Eckert
Nationalhelden	PD Dr. Georg Eckert
Zwischen Egalität und Elite: Das Eiserne Kreuz	PD Dr. Georg Eckert
Kerbalaparadigma	Dr. Olmo Gölz
Empowerment – Das Civil Rights/ Black Power Movement	Dr. Olmo Gölz
Gewalt und Heldentum	Dr. Olmo Gölz
Gefolgschaft als Selbstverzwergung – Starke Männer	Dr. Olmo Gölz
Polare Männlichkeiten – Fridtjof Nansen	Prof. Dr. Joachim Grage
Held der Entgrenzung – Orpheus	Morten Grage M.A.
Opernheld als Revolutionsauslöser – Die Oper »La Muette de Portici«	Morten Grage M.A.
Polarisieren und einen – Klimaaktivist:innen	Dr. Anne Hemkendreis, Dr. Dorna Safaian, PD Dr. Tobias Schlechtriemen
Provokation als Empowerment – Tom of Finland	Mag.a phil. Rebecca Heinrich, BA und Dr. Vera Marstaller
Heldentum und Staatsbürger in Uniform – Bundeswehr	Prof. Dr. Wolfgang Hochbruck
Blaulichtfreiwillige	Prof. Dr. Wolfgang Hochbruck
Heroisches Kollektiv mit Anführer – Ballhausschwur	Prof. Dr. Ralf von den Hoff, PD Dr. Tobias Schlechtriemen
Heroische Körperlichkeit – Hercules Farnese	Prof. Dr. Ralf von den Hoff, Prof. Dr. Anna Schreurs-Morét
Wehrmacht und SS	Dr. Vera Marstaller
Propagandakompanien der Wehrmacht	Dr. Vera Marstaller
Aufbegehrende Frauen – Antigone	Dr. Vera Marstaller
Krieg als heroischer Bewährungsraum – Kriegsfotografinnen	Dr. Vera Marstaller, Prof. Dr. Cornelia Brink, Antonia Wind, BA
Heroischer Gesetzgeber	Dr. Sebastian Meurer
Kollektives Heldentum – Helden der Arbeit	Prof. Dr. Dietmar Neutatz
Suworow-Orden	Prof. Dr. Dietmar Neutatz
Fortschrittsheldin – Walentina Tereschkowa, Kosmonautin	Prof. Dr. Dietmar Neutatz
Objekte, die heroisieren – Die Kalaschnikow	Prof. Dr. Johanna Pink
Islamischer Staat (IS)	Prof. Dr. Johanna Pink

Stürze von Kolonialdenkmälern I – Neue Helden an alter Stelle	Prof. Dr. Johanna Pink
Katharina DER Große	Dr. Andreas Plackinger
Politik mit offenem Hemd – Marat und Macron	Dr. Andreas Plackinger
Alexander der Große	Prof. Dr. Sitta von Reden
Heldentod	Kay Schmücking M.A.
Stürze von Kolonialdenkmälern II – Helden und Widersprüche	Prof. Dr. Berny Sèbe
Eltern	Kristina Seefeldt M.A., Jan Bahr
Alltagsehrungen – Postman's Park	Dr. Ulrike Zimmermann

Ausstellungsbegleitende Publikation

Prinzip Held*
Von Heroisierungen und Heroismen

Herausgeber	Ralf von den Hoff und Gorch Pieken im Auftrag des Zentrums für Militärgeschichte und Sozialwissenschaften der Bundeswehr und des Sonderforschungsbereichs 948 der Universität Freiburg
Leiter Fachbereich Publikationen am ZMSBw	Dr. Christian Adam (ZMSBw)
Wiss. Redaktion	Philipp Multhaupt M.A. und Dr. Ulrike Zimmermann (SFB)
Textredaktion und Lektorat	Katja Widmann M.A. (SFB)
Bildredaktion	Mag. Ansgar Snethlage und Steffen Jungmann M.A. (MHMBw)
Lizenzierung	Steffen Jungmann M.A. (MHMBw) und Esther Geiger (ZMSBw)
Stud. Hilfskraft	Justus Widmann (SFB)
Übersetzungen	Bundessprachenamt
Engl. Lektorat	Ella Norman, Jordan Reid, Philipp Multhaupt M.A. (SFB)
Übersetzungen komm. Bildunterschriften	guiskard studio Editorial Services
Rimini Protokoll	
Gestaltungskonzept	Helgard Haug, Daniel Wetzel, Ilona Marti
Gestaltung Cover & Ausstellungsteil/Styleguide	Ilona Marti
Gestaltung und Satz Essays, Lithografien	Wallstein Verlag
Druck und Verarbeitung	Westermann, Zwickau

Online-Portal/heroicum.net

Das zentrale Online-Portal heroicum.net macht die Ergebnisse und Publikationen aus der wissenschaftlichen Arbeit aller drei Phasen des Sonderforschungsbereichs 948 zugänglich und nachhaltig nutzbar. Es gibt Interessierten die Möglichkeit, auf Veröffentlichungen des SFB zuzugreifen und sich vertieft mit ausgewählten Themen aus der Forschungsarbeit des SFB zu beschäftigen.

Teilprojektleitung INF –
Universitätsbibliothek Freiburg
Dr. Antje Kellersohn
Prof. Dr. Franz Leithold
Dipl. Forstw. Oliver Rau

Projektbeschäftigte
Dipl.-Ing. Rainer Rombach
Paula Schulze M.A.
Laure Kervyn M.A.
Elena Wiener B.A.
Elke Möller M.A.

Dieses Werk ist im Open Access unter der Creative-Commons-Lizenz CC BY-NC-ND 4.0 lizenziert.

Die Bestimmungen der Creative-Commons-Lizenz beziehen sich nur auf das Originalmaterial der Open-Access-Publikation, nicht aber auf die Weiterverwendung von Fremdmaterialien (z. B. Abbildungen, Schaubildern oder auch Textauszügen, jeweils gekennzeichnet durch Quellenangaben). Diese erfordert ggf. das Einverständnis der jeweiligen Rechteinhaberinnen und Rechteinhaber.

Bibliografische Information der Deutschen Nationalbibliothek: Die Deutsche Nationalbibliothek verzeichnet diese Publikation in der Deutschen Nationalbibliografie; detaillierte bibliografische Daten sind im Internet über http://dnb.d-nb.de abrufbar.

© Autorinnen und Autoren 2024
Publikation: Wallstein Verlag GmbH, Göttingen 2024
www.wallstein-verlag.de
ISBN (Print) 978-3-8353-5581-1
ISBN (Open Access) 978-3-8353-8076-9
DOI https://doi.org/10.46500/83535581